SLAVERY AND REFORM IN WEST AFRICA

Western African Studies

Slavery and Reform in West Africa

Toward Emancipation in Nineteenth-Century Senegal and the Gold Coast

TREVOR R. GETZ

Ohio University Press
ATHENS

James Currey
OXFORD

Ohio University Press
Scott Quadrangle
Athens, Ohio 45701

James Currey Ltd
73 Botley Road
Oxford OX2 0BS

© 2004 by Trevor R. Getz
First published 2004

12 11 10 09 08 07 06 05 04   5 4 3 2 1

Published in the United States of America
by Ohio University Press, Athens, Ohio 45701

Cover photograph, "Un rue de Guet Nidas. Jeune Saint-Louisiennes et tente de
Mauses," c. 1900, by Edmond Fortier appears courtesy of the Centre Edmond Fortier,
online at http://home.planet.nl/~kreke003

Library of Congress Cataloging-in-Publication Data
Getz, Trevor R.
Slavery and reform in West Africa : toward emancipation in nineteenth-century
    Senegal and the Gold Coast / Trevor R. Getz.
    p. cm. — (Western African studies)
Includes bibliographical references and index.
ISBN 0-8214-1520-4 (alk. paper) — ISBN 0-8214-1521-2 (pbk. : alk. paper)
    1. Slavery—Senegal—History—19th century. 2. Slavery—Ghana—History—
    19th century. 3. Slaves—Emancipation—Senegal. 4. Slaves—Emancipation—
    Ghana. I. Title. II. Series.
HT1399.S4 G48 2004
306.3'62'0966309034—dc22

                                                                2003018106

British Cataloging in Publication Data is available upon request.
ISBN 0-85255-449-4 (James Currey cloth)
ISBN 0-85255-444-3 (James Currey paper)

Contents

Maps

Tables

Acknowledgments

I AM INDEBTED TO MY COLLEAGUES in many ways for their assistance over the past six years; without them it would have been difficult, if not impossible, to complete this manuscript. First and foremost is my friend and mentor, Richard Rathbone, whose intellectual guidance, friendly encouragement, and diverse contacts facilitated my research and writing every step of the way. I am also very grateful to John Parker for his continual assistance and for questioning the minutiae in many of my more difficult chapters, and to Wayne Dooling and Ian Brown for their support. Several other scholars have pointed me toward and helped me understand themes in this dissertation. I must especially thank Suzanne Miers, Michel Dortmund, Martin Klein, and Robert Addo-Fening. Esperanza Brizuela-Garcia and Chloe Campbell provided encouragement, ideas, and support. Finally, the comments of Gareth Austin and Tom McCaskie forced me to reevaluate my arguments and reapply myself to my details. In some cases, the most critical readings have been the most helpful.

My gratitude also extends to the staff of numerous archives that I have consulted over the past three years. The imperturbable Mr. Sowah and his reading room staff at the National Archives of Ghana deserve special recognition for their willingness to run up and down stairs for the numerous files I ordered each day. The chief records officer, Augustine Mensah, went far beyond the call of duty in finding files and illustrations for my consideration. Similarly, Saliou Mbaye's staff at the Archives Nationales du Sénégal were extremely helpful. Pères Joseph Carrard and Paul Coulon kindly assisted me during my brief stint at the Archives de la Congregation de Saint-Esprit. I would also like to recognize the archivists at the School of Oriental and African Studies, Public Records Office, British Library; and the Archives Nationales–France and the Centre des Archives d'Outre-Mer. A number of documents from the Basel Mission Archives were provided by Veit Arlt, to whom I am deeply indebted. Other documents were available as abstracts produced by Paul Jenkins. Some funding for my first trip to West Africa was generously provided by the University of London Irwin Trust and the School of Oriental and African Studies Award for Fieldwork; a summer research grant from the University of New Orleans enabled me to return to Ghana in the summer of 2000. I am further beholden to colleagues in the departments of history at the University of New Orleans and San Francisco State University who continued to support my research with scholarly and friendly advice.

Nor would it be possible to ignore the moral support of my friends and relatives. During two trips to Accra I spent several wonderful months in the home of Emily Asiedu, and there met many friends, including Serwa, the Afedu brothers, Pietro Deandrea, and Malika Kraamer. In Dakar, Abdou Aziz Ndiaye was indispensable in organizing trips, explaining Wolof culture, and entertaining me in his family's home. Finally, Edward Orrell's assistance in both research and writing, and his companionship while in Ghana, are greatly appreciated. By far my most enduring supporters have been my parents, Wayne and Jennifer Getz, who, for the past twenty-five years, have guided my efforts to become an academic. To them, and to my sister Stacey and brother-in-law Robert, I owe an immense debt. My uncle and first historian role model, Michael Pincus, also helped encourage me along the way. My final word of thanks, however, must be reserved for my wife and traveling companion, Jessica, who endured malaria, *aggresseurs,* and the cold of English winter to see this book successfully written.

Introduction

THIS IS A BOOK ABOUT the gradual transformation, reform, and attempted abolition of slavery in the nineteenth century in two zones of European-African interaction: French Senegal and the British Gold Coast. It focuses upon a comparison of the opportunities, agency, and actions of European and African actors in two geographically and socioculturally disparate regions. Comparative studies such as this one are, by definition, studies in opposition. In some respects, this makes it difficult for the author to achieve the specificity of a purely local study. However, the tension inherent in the contrast of places and times can also reveal overarching themes; and this, in turn, can aid in the interpretation of evidence of continuity and change at the local level.

In his influential 1983 synthesis, *Transformations in Slavery,* Paul Lovejoy pointed out that the discourse on slavery in Africa has been particularly lacking in such studies, suggesting that this topic "has suffered from the opposite problem to that of over-synthesis. . . . There are some brilliant local studies, which have their own implications in terms of the study of slavery in general, but these . . . suffer from a failure to place the particular case in the context of Africa as a whole, or even specific regions within Africa."[1] Lovejoy was writing at the crest of a renewed academic interest in African slavery. Historians of African descent, such as Walter Rodney, had begun to investigate the evolution of slavery in several regions of West Africa in the late 1960s,[2] and during the next decade, monograph-length studies had been produced on servitude in areas as diverse as Zanzibar and Sierra Leone.[3] The Wolof and Sereer polities of Senegal north of the Gambia River were no exception. The French priest and missionary François Renault compiled a framework study of the origins and impact of French policies on slavery in Senegal in the early 1970s, and historians at Dakar's Institut Fondamental d'Afrique Noire also investigated issues surrounding emancipation. Most notable among these historians is M'Baye Guèye, who published the seminal scholarly article on emancipation in St. Louis and Gorée.[4] Attention was similarly drawn to slavery by Ray Kea's superb study of seventeenth-century society in the Gold Coast, including the sociopolitical and economic roles of slaves.[5]

Paul Lovejoy thus had a variety of materials from which to draw when writing *Transformations in Slavery*. In addition to a number of regional studies, the Africanist community's interpretation of slavery had been advanced by comparative anthropological studies such as Orlando Patterson's *Slavery and Social Death,* and by Igor Kopytoff and Suzanne Mier's anthology of anthropological and historical studies, *Slavery in Africa*.[6] Lovejoy was thus able to identify a number of core issues in the study of slavery and emancipation in Africa. Among these were themes in domestic and trade slavery, the impact of transformations wrought by Islam, the Atlantic slave trade and its abolition, and manumission and emancipation.

The modern study of emancipation, of which this book forms a part, arose out of this dynamic discourse on slavery both in Africa and outside it, and this book draws somewhat on a number of monographs, articles, and anthologies on emancipation from the 1970s and 1980s. Important works from this period span a thematically diverse range, from analyses of imperial policy and colonial rule to ethnographic works relating to slave agency. More recent works have emphasized the agency of slave owners and studies of postemancipation transformations in social hierarchies and labor practices.

The Gold Coast region has been the subject of one of the more fully developed regional discourses on emancipation in Africa. For his chapter "The Abolitionist Impulse" in *Transformations in Slavery,* for example, Lovejoy drew heavily upon a somewhat revisionist article on emancipation on the Gold Coast by Gerald McSheffrey. In this article, "Slavery, Indentured Servitude, Legitimate Trade, and the Impact of Abolition in the Gold Coast, 1874–1910," McSheffrey for the first time located slaves at the center of an emancipation equation, arguing that slaves in Akan polities were the most important agents in emancipation.[7] McSheffrey's contribution was part of a growing discourse on emancipation in the Gold Coast led by Raymond Dumett, who was engaged in analyzing the formation of antislavery ordinances from the perspective of the British colonial apparatus, and Marion Johnson, who focused on the supply of slaves to and from what would become the Northern Territories.[8] These two historians collaborated to produce a chapter in a 1988 anthology engaging McSheffrey's arguments and outlining further research questions that could contribute to our understanding of emancipation in the Gold Coast and other regions of modern Ghana.[9]

The anthology in which Dumett and Johnson's chapter appeared was *The End of Slavery in Africa*.[10] Edited by Suzanne Miers and Richard Roberts, this volume was promoted as a sequel to *Slavery in Africa* and included studies encompassing diverse regions of Africa. Perhaps most importantly, it proposed a theoretical and comparative framework for exploring a number of themes, such as the role of the colonial state, modes of liberation, the "ambiguities" of freedom, and the impact of emancipation on indigenous societies.[11]

Interest in emancipation on the Gold Coast has grown over the last few years. Much of the new research has been carried out by a Ghanaian scholar, Kwabena Opare Akurang-Parry, who has written intensive articles dealing with both colonial policy and slave agency in the postemancipation Gold Coast.[12] Akurang-Parry's work provided new perspectives and has raised interesting questions as to the interpretation of the actions of both Europeans and indigenous peoples. Emancipation also forms an important component of the recent work of Peter Haenger, whose excellent study of slavery and reform deals largely with the impact of the Basel Mission on slaveholding but also illuminates a number of other issues surrounding the end of legalized slavery on the Gold Coast.[13]

The study of emancipation in Senegal has similarly crossed something of a threshold during the past few years, marked first by the publication of Martin Klein's 1998 monograph on emancipation in French West Africa, including Senegal, entitled *Slavery and Colonial Rule in French West Africa.*[14] Klein had already published several important articles on slavery in Senegal and the West African interior and contributed a chapter on slave agency and emancipation in coastal Guinea to *The End of Slavery in Africa.*[15] He further solidified his position at the forefront of the study of slavery in French West Africa when, in 1993, he produced the seminal Anglophone article on emancipation throughout French colonial West Africa.[16] His work did draw on that of Guèye and Renault, but it also added new dimensions both by exploring African initiatives and by expanding the field geographically to encompass the French protectorates as well as Senegal Colony. *Slavery and Colonial Rule in French West Africa,* published five years later, built on the foundation of this article and was influenced by important studies of emancipation in West Africa such as Lovejoy and Hogendorn's work on northern Nigeria and Ibrahim Sundiata's exploration of postemancipation Fernando Po and the Bight of Biafra.[17] Klein's work is in many ways a model for addressing the juxtaposition of colonial imposition of reforms to slavery and the initiatives of slaves. Nevertheless, its generous scope, although it achieved a necessary synthesis, forced Klein to concentrate on certain major regional transformations, allowing those of us who follow to pinpoint local trends.

Although Klein's *Slavery and Colonial Rule* informed this work from the very beginning, the publication of James F. Searing's *"God Alone Is King"* in 2002 forced a late reconceptualization of my approach to Senegalese history.[18] A sort of sequel to Searing's earlier insightful research into the Senegal River Valley political-economic complex, *"God Alone is King"* attempts to situate emancipation as a transformative process within a contemporary Wolof perspective, placing it at one corner of a triangle whose other points were formed by the expansion of Murid Sufism and peasant groundnut cultivation.[19] The publication of this book, which I quote extensively in late chapters, enabled me to build a truly comparative model in which local trends and relationships are perceived as being as important as imperial policies in formulating the actions of both slaves and slave owners. In an equally successful study, Alice Conklin has placed postfederation emancipation within the perspective of French imperial and colonial discourse by arguing that in the early twentieth century, the eradication of slavery became a central theme of the *mission civilisatrice.*[20] Several collected works have also recently appeared that bridge not just regions but continents.[21]

CONCEPTUAL FRAMEWORK

This work is intended to address perceived gaps in understanding the central role of Africans—slaves and slave owners—in the process of reform and emancipation. While not primarily an ethnographic study of indigenous societies, it is an attempt to place Africans as agents both in the implementation of colonial policy toward slavery and in the success and failure of reforms culminating in emancipation. It therefore incorporates an appraisal of the conditions under which reform, abolition, and emancipation could occur and places this within the framework of emancipation developed in the narrative. The positions and strategies of slaves, slave owners, and Europeans are discussed against the backdrop of a changing local environment and the conflicting demands of European metropoles for both stable, profitable African colonies and the abolition of indigenous slavery. By locating Africans within this model, this study illuminates the role of slave owners in shaping reform, as well as the agency of slaves in formulating modes of liberation and desertion, negotiating settlements, and developing postemancipation means of existence.

The most important feature of this study, and its greatest innovation, is that it undertakes a comparison between two geographically and ethnically distinct African regions that nevertheless underwent comparable transformational processes resulting in both divergent and similar results. By comparing the experiences of French/Senegalese and British/Gold Coast situations, this book makes significant advances in addressing two issues central to the discourse on emancipation: whether European-initiated emancipation generally represented continuity or transformation, and the relative importance of internal (African) agency and external (European) pressures.

For much of the nineteenth century, these two regions received disproportionate attention, as compared to neighboring areas, from European colonial powers. In the mid-1800s, the production of groundnuts joined the trade in gum in Senegal, and palm-oil cultivation took off in certain portions of the Gold Coast. These commodities helped to transform local concepts of slavery and at the same time increased the European commitment in these two areas. Thus, underpinning the events described in this book are the metropole's experiments in imperialism and colonialism, which were, as Frederick Cooper rightly points out, not so much "a coherent set of practices and discourses . . . as a set of hegemonic projects."[22]

The eradication of slavery, as a colonial project, was a theme of growing importance in the early nineteenth century and would form a cornerstone of liberal and progressive rationalizations for the occupation of Africa by the end of the century. Abolitionism can be found alongside the eradication of ritual murder in validations of the French Republic's colonial ventures, and next to the conversion of pagans in Britain's popular imperialist dogma. However, little action was actually taken to end slavery before pacification was nearly complete, and thus abolition within the African colonies was, with a few exceptions, a twentieth-century project. For much of Senegal and the Gold Coast, by contrast, early and significant involvement in local affairs by Europeans led to the first strong European initiatives against indigenous slavery in West Africa—the 1848 act of emancipation in colonial Senegal and the proclamation of emancipation in 1874 on the Gold Coast. These initiatives, based on nineteenth-century perceptions and events, shared characteristics that provide an interesting contrast with the more prevalent twentieth-century antislavery initiatives carried out in other parts of West Africa. In fact, one could argue that these two regions served as laboratories and models for subsequent efforts to deal with slave trading and holding in other African colonies.

A key experience for colonial agents in Senegal and on the Gold Coast, and one from which important conclusions were drawn, was the relative success of local resistance strategies against antislavery initiatives. The long history of European interaction had led to the establishment of strong Euro-African trading communities protective of their rights to own slaves. Additionally, the nineteenth century was a period in which chiefly officeholders and Islamic bodies were key to shaping and delimiting the expansion of European political authority. The groups generally resisted unilateral attempts to reform slavery. The strength of the proslavery lobbies in both regions led directly to the establishment by both Britain and France of forms of indirect rule that would leave postemancipation settlements largely in the hands of slaves and their owners.

The specific results of emancipation in Senegal and the Gold Coast reflect both the differences and the similarities between the two regions. This book undertakes to analyze the causes and results of emancipation both within the two regions generally and within diverse sociopolitical segments specifically. In the first chapter, the basis of comparison is established, and important historical themes and actors are introduced. Following chapters deal with the interacting processes of the expansion of European authority, initiatives to reform slavery and the internal slave trade, and the agency of both slaves and slave owners on both the societal and individual levels.

Within this comparative structure, this volume advances the scholarship on emancipation in several ways. It presents a new understanding of how local factors—the attitudes of European administrators, intercontinental economics, and, most importantly, significant indigenous resistance—placed Africans centrally in the resolution of slave reforms, generally resulting in the failure of the implementation of reforms. The volume contributes to our comprehension of the circumstances in which these measures could be—and sometimes were—transformative, especially through the initiative of slaves. It investigates the mechanisms of slave desertion and emancipation. Finally, this book is intended to add to the reader's knowledge of the integrated slave routes that fed slaves into the coastal regions and the extent to which they were extinguished in the nineteenth century.

A NOTE ABOUT ORTHOGRAPHY

One unfortunate legacy of the haphazard attitude toward African culture and society that characterized nineteenth-century European intervention is a marked confusion over the spelling of indigenous personal and place names. Administrators and missionaries tended to impose their own preferred names for people and regions, and one place in which this is most obvious is the judicial record, in which, as I show, the interior origins of many slaves left magistrates baffled as to their ethnic affiliations.

In the postcolonial period, Africans have attempted to reclaim their own lo-cales and histories, and I support that by endeavoring, where possible, to use either the modern appellations designated by African governments or, failing that, the spellings preferred by African academics of note. As a result, I have largely adhered to the orthography of the Senegalese historian Boubacar Barry and the Ghanaian scholars Robert Addo-Fening, Francis Agbodeka, and Akosua Perbi.

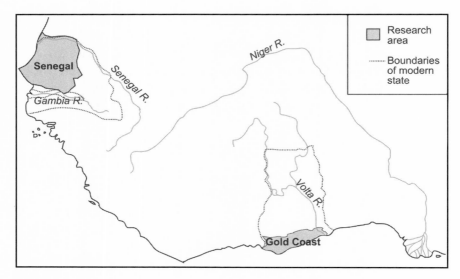

MAP 0.1
Study Areas: The Wolof and Sereer States of Senegal and the Gold Coast Region

CHAPTER I

The Era of the
Atlantic Slave Trade

FOR THE PURPOSES OF THIS STUDY, the period following the criminalization of the Atlantic slave trade in the early nineteenth century is the narrative present. This period is characterized by several major transformations, but these nineteenth-century manifestations were shaped, constrained, and guided by African societies and individuals who exhibited a remarkable connection with their past. Moreover, the societies and states of both regions had emerged from a complex history of settlement, migration, social and political development, and cultural exchange with neighboring peoples. Both the Gold Coast and Senegal had been on the periphery of the great empires of the Niger bend, had received waves of settlers from the West African interior, and were connected by trading networks to other parts of the macroregion and even to each other. Senegal, in addition, was on the frontier of the Saharan zone. These African connections would not disappear after the sixteenth century, despite the growing importance of the Atlantic trade.

Nevertheless, the transatlantic slave trade must be recognized as central to the increasing significance of slavery in West African societies and economies, and in this trade, the Gold Coast and Senegal were among the earliest participants. The experiences of the slave trade have been the subject of numerous monographs and countless articles. In West African history, they are sometimes portrayed as *the* defining feature of the precolonial period, leading to radical social and economic changes. This notion is highly politicized and for the regions

1

under consideration here must be qualified somewhat. While the transatlantic slave trade was a catalyst for sociocultural change within the small seaboard "frontier" areas of Euro-African interaction, its effect became more diffuse the farther one traveled from the coastal zone.

This chapter is not intended as either a comprehensive ethnography or a study of the Atlantic slave trade. Its purpose is threefold: to ascertain the borders of this study in space and time, to establish its comparative structure, and, finally, to examine aspects of the dynamic African societies that formed the setting of this struggle over the issue of slavery.

BOUNDARIES

Since the subject of this study is the interaction between specific groups of colonial and African actors, its limits are more defined by human geography than ecology. Thus the regions included in this study can be said to be the Wolof and Sereer states of Senegal and the Akan and Ga-Adangme societies of the Gold Coast. To a greater or lesser degree, the populations of these regions shared a common experience of European intervention in the nineteenth century that exceeded that of regions farther in the interior. This intervention was concentrated on the coast and gradually diminished inland. Coastal towns such as St. Louis, Dakar, Cape Coast, and Accra were centers of Euro-African interaction, whereas large interior states such as Akyem Abuakwa and Jolof maintained a more indirect association with events on the coast until late in the century. States farther removed from the coast and European influence—especially Asante and Fuuta Tooro—had long-established and dynamic relationships with coastal states, but had distinct experiences during the nineteenth century and are not included in this study.

These boundaries are not rigid. During the period in focus, frontiers of colonial expansion and borders between African states shifted. Moreover, ethnicity and state do not necessarily equate, and both subjugated and semiautonomous ethnic minorities existed within the territories claimed by organized states. Finally, the balance of power between competing European powers did not completely resolve itself until late in the nineteenth century.

Ecologically, both regions were affected by the distinct ecological banding that characterizes the environment of West Africa. By 1850 the Senegal River delta was firmly within the arid Sahelian zone. The southern bank of the river during this period constituted the northern boundary of the Wolof state of

Waalo. Cultivation, mostly of sorghum and millet, was largely limited to the river's banks, as the preceding centuries had seen the advance of the Sahara and the transition of the area surrounding the lower Senegal to pastoral rather than agricultural use.[1] South of the river, the territory of the Wolof-led states of Kaajor, Baol, and to a lesser extent the interior state of Jolof transitioned gradually to a more fertile landscape until, in the far south, the population of the Sereer states of Siin and Saalum inhabited a wetter complex of river deltas and forests. From west to east there was also an ecological transition. The westernmost point of Senegal was the collection of Wolof-speaking Lebu fishing and farming villages of the Câp Vert Peninsula, while in the east there lay the dry basin of the Ferlo, which is outside the boundaries of this study.

In contrast, the Gold Coast is a hilly and fertile region falling well within the band of forest stretching across the south of the West African bulge. Both the fertile coastal plain and the hills of the Akuapem-Togo Range supported extensive yam and plantain cultivation. An especially wide coastal plain in the eastern third of the region was thick with Ga-Adangme settlements, but aside from the Ewe people of the Voltaic basin, the region was dominated by Akan-speaking polities.

PRECOLONIAL POLITICAL ELITES IN WESTERN SENEGAL

Within both the Senegalese and Gold Coast populations, ethnic and lineage identification were separate from citizenship in a state. This differentiation was more marked, however, in Senegal. In the two large Sereer polities, the state was controlled by dominant Mandinka lineages, the *gelowar,* who had arrived as outriders of the Mali Empire in the twelfth and thirteenth centuries.[2] The aristocracy of the states to the north were Wolof, like the majority of their inhabitants. In both regions, however, a significant amount of power lay with the lineage patriarchs, or *jambur.* The jambur wielded considerable power with the commoners through their position in the kinship system, their control over land, and their ability to recruit soldiers from among their lineage. In Siin and Saalum, at least, their rights were even enshrined in state constitutions. While aristocratic families consistently attempted to attract the jambur as clients, the power of the jambur was in fact augmented by the arrival of Islam, which by the nineteenth century had won converts throughout the Wolof region. Muslims tended to occupy their own villages led by *sëriñ-làmb,* or titled marabouts — religious officials whose political position roughly equaled that of the jambur.[3] The result, by the nineteenth

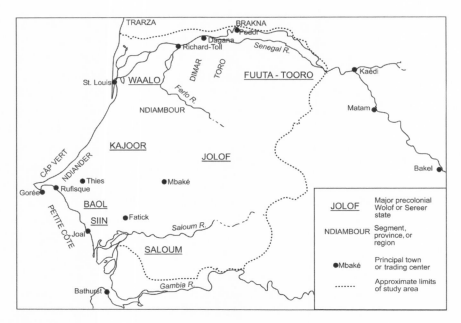

MAP 1.1
The Wolof and Sereer States of Senegal, c. 1800

century, was a patchwork of territory under the control of various groups — semi-autonomous Muslim communities, ethnic minorities, and aristocratic lineages.

The power of the aristocracies was largely military. They provided security to the agricultural and pastoralist villages in return for taxes. Aristocratic families succeeded to the throne through a system of patronage, and such patronage was costly. At the top of the aristocracy were the *garmi* and *lingeer,* members of aristocratic lineages eligible to provide rulers.[4] However, raiding protected villages was self-defeating, since it alienated the jambur. As a result, the military aristocracies augmented their wealth through external raids and wars, the result of which was not only looting, but also capturing and enslaving individuals.[5]

For Waalo this process of class stratification was even further complicated by the spread, in the seventeenth and eighteenth centuries, of Hassani Arab populations down to the northern bank of the Senegal River. These groups, particularly the Trarza emiral family, were structured much like the Wolof aristocracy in that their means of survival was exacting tribute or pillaging local communities. The climax of the Hassani expansion came in a 1775 offensive that left many north-bank Wolof villages under Trarza control, while raids across the river produced large numbers of slaves both for Trarza slave villages and for export across the Sahara.[6]

PRECOLONIAL POLITICAL ELITES IN THE GOLD COAST

The Akan migration was a pivotal event in the history of the Gold Coast.[7] The immigrants absorbed a number of preexisting groups while only a few, such as the Ga-Adangme of the Accra coastal plain and mountains of Krobo, remained independent. Within the numerous Akan polities that emerged from this process, two notable sets of sociopolitical institutions emerged. The first were *mmusuatow* (sing. *abusua*)—matrilineal kin groups—which were the principal organizing units for trade, ritual, and labor. These lineage affiliations were central to organizing the labor needed to clear the dense brush of the interior, and they controlled inheritance, land tenure, and succession. The second was the development of *obirempon* or *oblempon* stools, or thrones, often linked to entrepreneurs who settled new areas with the aid of clients and slaves or to merchants made wealthy through the expanding coastal trade.[8] Members of a few elite abusua lineages, together with the *obirempon,* made up the *ohene* (chiefly) class. However, commoners could gain authority through positions in the patrilineal, populist *asafo* militia and fraternal companies that began to appear in the Akan states in the seventeenth century.

The normative political model for the Akan polities was one of paramount chieftains supported by a council of chiefly officeholders representing important

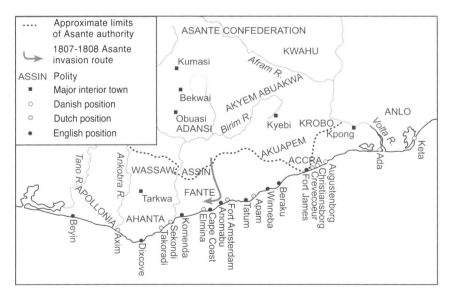

MAP 1.2

Political Divisions of the Gold Coast, Showing Asante and European Positions, c. 1807

lineages, as well as division heads with territorial and ritual responsibilities.[9] Nevertheless, eighteenth- and nineteenth-century sources suggest that this description disguises a wide diversity of institutions and techniques. Henry Meredith, for example, noted that "the government along the coast partakes of various forms. At Apollonia it is monarchical and absolute. In the Ahanta country it is a kind of aristocracy. In the Fantee country, and as far as Accra, it is composed of a strange number of forms; in some places it is vested in particular persons, and in other places lodged in the hands of the community."[10]

Often, paramount stools could be contested by a broad category of claimants, with several eligible lineages, both matrilineal and in rare cases patrilineal, competing for power.[11] Moreover, the limits and authority of governments were constantly evolving as states expanded. Autochthonous populations such as the Guan-speaking villages of the Akuapem Hills were slowly being brought under state control, necessitating political flexibility in that state.[12] Similarly, in the eighteenth century, several states in the interior—Akwamu, Denkyira, Wassa, Akyem Abuakwa, and Asante, especially—underwent a process of bureaucratic development to deal with their expanding borders. By contrast, most coastal polities such as the several paramountcies of the Fante remained quite small and based on a single urban center.[13] The Ga-Adangme populations of the coast adhered to a similar model which, however, followed a generally patrilineal system for determining succession, and which in the mid-eighteenth century came under the flag of an expansionist Asante state.

Throughout the nineteenth century, Asante expansionism was also a political reality for all the peoples of the Gold Coast. Assin was an early acquisition of the Asante, and states of the western interior—including Wassaw, Assin, and Aowin—had been occupied in the mid-eighteenth century, although Wassaw opportunistically joined anti-Asante coalitions in the 1730s and again in 1765. In the east, Asante had defeated an Akyem army and subjugated Accra in 1742. Despite continuing trouble with the *okyemfo* (peoples of Akyem), the road to Accra became Asante's primary outlet to the sea, at the expense of the Dutch settlement of Elmina, which still lay beyond the sometimes-hostile territory of the myriad of Fante city-states, which, in their attempt to carve out a middleman position in various goods between the Europeans and Asante and points farther north through their markets at Foso and Manso, tended to be antagonistic to Asante aims.[14] In 1807 Asante armies chasing rebels from Assin— including the recalcitrant Assin Attendansu leader Apute—occupied Fante. Asante administrators would remain in Fante until the early 1820s, although never very comfortably.[15]

Traditions of Slavery

The differences in the political structures of Senegal and the Gold Coast obscure one basic commonality—in both regions, the power of the state was based largely on the control of people, rather than land. As a result, both state and lineage heads relied for their power on a complex system of patronage in which they were supported by a variety of dependent clients. This system was especially important because of the fragmented nature of both Senegalese and Gold Coast political systems. For rulers, dependents decreased their reliance upon rival lineages eligible for the stool or throne. They also served to counteract the power of competing nonaristocratic elites such as the jambur and sëriş in Senegal.[16] In the Gold Coast, similarly, dependents' ownership of enslaved dependents may have been a decisive factor in the evolution of the obirempon stools, and they served to insulate the aristocracy from the leadership of the asafo companies. As it was found to be preferable in both regions to exert the strongest possible hold over clients, both regions were characterized by slavery as a political tool.

While it is evident that the institution of slavery in these regions was marked by some diversity, it is also clear that the institutions of slavery in the Gold Coast and Senegal prior to the Atlantic slave trade shared certain characteristics.[17] Among them was the dominance in both regions of a "domestic" mode of production based upon the lineage and client systems over a slave mode of production. Ray Kea's work suggests that production in the Gold Coast was centered upon peasants in agrarian hamlets, while some highly organized polities maintained a tributary mode of production based on labor contributions or rent-in-kind.[18] Similarly, in Senegal there is an absence of evidence for organized slave labor in sorghum and millet cultivation, despite investigation of the problem by Boubacar Barry, although admittedly this may have been less true in the Trarza borderlands of the far north.[19]

In both regions this reliance upon free labor can be explained to some extent by the dominance in slave owning of aristocrats and chiefly officeholders who perceived slaves as political tools.[20] While a dramatic increase in the use of slavery for domestic and agricultural purposes would occur in the nineteenth century, slavery in both regions evolved largely, though not exclusively, as a function of the kinship form of organization central to political and social institutions among these regions' populations. Within such systems, slavery generally took on a highly assimilative form as slaves adopted their masters' cultures over time. The Akan, for example, had a complex slave hierarchy, in which *odonko,* or purchased slaves, and *domum,* or war captives, were gradually assimilated into domestic slaves who could in some cases marry, amass property, and even seek legal redress.[21] Martin Klein and James Searing have identified a similar assimilative structure in Senegal, especially in the Sereer states of Siin and Saalum.[22] In both regions, however, assimilation was neither uniform nor guaranteed, and this assimilative structure would be further weakened in the eighteenth and nineteenth centuries.

However, at least one major difference between Senegal and the Gold Coast must be pointed out. Whereas the Gold Coast was a consumer of slaves, it was not a major producer prior to the era of the Atlantic slave trade. Northern Senegal, on the other hand, supported a thriving trans-Saharan slaves-for-horses trade. Portuguese slave traders, alighting on the Waalo coast in the fifteenth century found themselves competing with an established network of "Moorish" traders from across the desert.

FROM PERIPHERY TO FRONTIER—THE ATLANTIC SLAVE TRADE

The Atlantic slave trade as a worldwide or even African phenomenon is somewhat outside the scope of this study, but it is interesting to note that the experiences of the Gold Coast and Senegal were similar to each other and contrasted significantly with those of their West African neighbors. Both regions were integrated into the world economy earlier than were their neighbors: Northern Senegal attracted Portuguese seeking slaves and other goods in the 1440s,[23] and the Gold Coast's gold production brought Europeans into that region as slave suppliers, rather than consumers, in the 1470s.[24]

In the third decade of the seventeenth century, Dutch ascendancy at sea and a desire to control the slave trade to Brazil led to the Dutch capture of two Portuguese posts: Gorée Island off the coast of Senegal (1639) and El Mina on the Gold Coast (1637). French acquisition of Caribbean islands for the production of sugar resulted in the formation of the Compagnie des Indes Occidentales in 1664; its directors almost immediately secured Senegalese slaves to work its plantations, operating from the post of St. Louis on an island in the Senegal River Delta claimed by France in 1659. In 1677 the French Crown acquired Gorée. British merchants also began to obtain positions in Africa in the seventeenth century. In 1672 the Royal African Company was formed to trade with the Gold Coast, and consequently forts were built at "Dixcove, Secondee, Commendah, Anamaboe, Winnebah, and Accra, [as well as] Cape Coast Castle."[25]

The trade in slaves from Senegal and the Gold Coast experienced similar cycles of expansion in the early eighteenth century and then decline as the trade shifted to the Bight of Benin, Biafra, and the Congo. In the 1700s the value of slaves exported from the Gold Coast exceeded that of gold.[26] Throughout the early eighteenth century, competition among the Akan states of the interior, especially Akwamu and the Akyem states (before 1730) and more latterly Asante expansion at the expense of these and other states, provided a consistent supply of slaves to coastal middlemen.[27] Asante expansion to the northeast also meant a diversion of the gold trade toward the interior to North African trade routes, reinforcing the importance of the trade in slaves on the coast.[28] However, the reign of Asantehene (paramount chief) Osei Kwadwo between 1764 and 1777 was marked by stability and relative peace, and European wars in the late eighteenth century and early nineteenth century deflected shipping away from West Africa.[29] Trade on the Gold Coast picked up again to approximately seventy-four thousand captives exported per year in the 1790s,[30] but the relative importance of the Gold Coast continued to diminish; the region provided only about 7 to 8 percent of African slave exports at the turn of the century.[31]

Senegal experienced a somewhat similar cycle. Although an early producer of slaves for the Atlantic market, slave exports from Senegal, following the French acquisition of Gorée in 1679, stayed below an average of three thousand a year for the entire Senegambia region, and many of these slaves came from the British Gambia and Casamance regions, outside Senegal proper.[32] French and British shipping data show that slave purchases largely declined after 1730, excepting brief flurries following regional upheavals, as in 1775 when approximately eight thousand were shipped from St. Louis.[33] Most of the slaves initially came from the interior, either the Galaam region or deep in the western Sudan,[34] and coastal Senegalese states tended to retain slaves deemed desirable, especially males, for their own purposes.[35] By the time the Atlantic slave trade was outlawed by the British in 1807, then by the Americans in 1808 and the French in 1819,[36] Senegal, like the Gold Coast, had ceased to be a major supplier of slaves to the Atlantic market,[37] contributing only about 3 percent of slave exports to the Atlantic world around the turn of the century.[38]

BEYOND THE NUMBERS GAME: WAR, DEPOPULATION, AND STAGNATION

The importance of placing the slave trade within a work on postabolition Africa lies in understanding the impact of this trade on the African societies involved. Only in a limited sense can this impact be expressed statistically. More important are questions of social, political, and economic transformation and the despoiling effects of this trade. However, the magnitude of these changes is not entirely clear, and they have been at the center of a wide-ranging discourse based largely on quantitative data.

The debate surrounding slave exports from Senegambia—comprising Senegal, the Casamance, Guinea, and Guinea-Bissau—is an excellent example of the dynamics of this quantitative debate. The seminal work on this topic is Philip Curtin's *Economic Change in Precolonial Africa.* In this work, Curtin presented what even his critics admit is a highly detailed study on export numbers, suggesting a total export estimate from this region of 304,330 slaves from 1681 to 1810.[39] Paul Lovejoy, in his important 1983 work, *Transformations in Slavery,* largely accepted Curtin's pre-1750 figures, adding only a statistically insignificant 3,200 slaves.[40]

However, Curtin's statistics have come under an attack mounted mostly by African scholars, and at the fore are Charles Becker and Boubacar Barry. Their challenge is significant not just in debating abstract figures, but for understanding the concrete significance of the slave trade to Africa. Curtin's statistics had been used to support an argument that the importance of the Atlantic slave trade to Africa had been exaggerated.[41] He imputed that the value to Africa of the slave trade was less than that of the internal trade and that the resultant social changes were, to some extent, changes that would have occurred anyway because of the integration of the region into the Atlantic trading complex. In short, the effect of the Atlantic slave trade was limited.[42]

Becker and Barry attacked this attempt to "minimise the importance of the Trans-Atlantic slave trade"—Becker, in a response published a year after Curtin's work, and Barry, as recently as 1998.[43] They asserted that Curtin omitted important sources, including data on smugglers, and that he advanced arbitrary figures without adjusting for missing data.[44] Becker and Barry advanced the theory that the Atlantic slave trade was much more important as a transforming force in West Africa than Curtin allows, indeed, that it irreversibly retarded the development of West African states. "Contrary to Curtin," Becker stated, "we estimate that the evolution of Senegambia cannot be understood except in the precise context of the Atlantic trade."[45]

Complicating this issue further, James Webb has shown significant evidence that the more enduring trans-Saharan and internal trades in slaves probably had a more abiding impact on northern Senegal, including Waalo, than did the shorter Atlantic slave trade. Webb's theory is based largely on a horses-for-slaves exchange that, he argues, ushered in a military revolution based

largely on cavalry. According to his figures, in northern Senegal the volume of
the Atlantic slave trade exceeded that of the trans-Saharan trade only for the
period 1710 to 1759, although he admits that his statistics are "problematic
and . . . speculative."[46] Webb's work thus raises questions about theories put
forward, chiefly by Barry, that suggested Waalo's decline was primarily a result
of the exactions of the Atlantic trade. However, Webb's theory has in turn been
attacked by James Searing, who argues that evidence of extensive royal cavalry
forces during this period is questionable. Searing suggests instead that increased importation of firearms into Baol and Kaajor was a more significant factor in the eighteenth-century military revolution in Senegal.[47]

THE POLITICAL IMPACT OF THE ATLANTIC SLAVE TRADE

It appears likely that the Atlantic slave trade prompted a significant adjustment
within many West African societies. Admittedly, the evidence is problematic.
Some assertions made in support of this argument are unproven, and some may
be discounted. However, the mass of evidence suggests that socioeconomic, military, and possibly demographic changes occurred within the region between the
mid-sixteenth and the beginning of the nineteenth centuries, and that the slave
trade contributed to these changes.

For example, it has been argued that the slave trade was a catalyst, in both
Senegal and the Gold Coast, for a cycle of wars in the eighteenth century.
Conflict wracked the Senegalese regions of Waalo,[48] Kaajor, Baol,[49] Siin, and
Saalum for several decades.[50] Similarly, clashes between the Akan states of
Akyem, Akwamu, and Akuapem, and the subsequent Asante expansion at their
expense, stretched across much of the eighteenth century.[51] However, it is not
as clear as might be desirable that these wars were the direct result of the Atlantic slave trade. These conflicts may have occurred without the impetus of the
slave trade, as a natural expression of state-building, the acquisition of slaves
being simply a bonus for the victors. This view was promoted by Asantehene
Osei Bonsu of the Asante, who told the trader Joseph Dupuis that the ongoing
conflicts in the region were motivated by political and status concerns, rather
than by greed: "I cannot make war to catch slaves in a bush, like a thief. . . . But
if I fight a king, and kill him when he is insolent, then certainly . . . his gold,
and his slaves, and the people are mine too. . . . I did not make war for slaves,
but because Dinkera (the King) sent me an arrogant message and killed my
people."[52]

Other sources, however, support the argument that the Atlantic slave trade transformed the dominant model of conflict in West Africa from one that was basically political in nature to one motivated by economic gain through the capture of and trade in slave captives.[53] British observers on the Gold Coast certainly thought so, and leading figures testified before Parliament that "the pretexts [for wars] are various; the real cause [is] . . . the desire for plunder" and that "slaves formed the principal part" of that plunder.[54]

Furthermore, the growth in scale and ferocity of conflict among Akan states seems to have originated in the mid-1700s, concurrent with the expansion of the slave trade, by which time states such as Akyem Abuakwa maintained highly organized mechanisms for exporting slaves to coastal entrepôts.[55] Control over gold fields, rather than slaves, appears to have been the motivating factor behind the Akyem-Akwamu conflict. Nevertheless, Robert Addo-Fening suggests that prior to its 1730 defeat of Akwamu, Akyem Abuakwa had not been a major participant in the slave trade, but that that event had "placed numerous prisoners in the hands of Akyem" and transformed the state into a major slave exporter.[56] Similarly, the 1744–45 and 1746–47 Asante victories over Gonja and Gyaman both precede and follow periods of increased slave exports from the Gold Coast, suggesting that conflict in the interior not only increased the supply of exported slaves, but was also a response to increased demand for slaves on the coast.[57]

Despite the fact that it is unclear to what extent the demand for slaves directly affected the number and size of conflicts, it has been postulated that the importation of guns and horses in exchange for slaves may have indirectly led to an expansion in wars and raids across West Africa. Muskets, which became desirable trade items in the seventeenth century, were required both for defense and conquest, and it is claimed that elites dealt in slaves in order to purchase weapons, in turn using the weapons to acquire more slaves.[58] When one state or party thus established regional superiority, its neighbors were also forced to arm and, in order to do so, were forced to acquire slaves to sell to European slave traders on the coast in exchange for arms.

As noted above, this gun-slave cycle was especially clear in Senegal, where the Atlantic slave trade appears to have intensified the development in the seventeenth century of a dedicated slave-soldier caste emerging in Kaajor and later spreading to other Wolof and Sereer monarchies and garmi lineages.[59] These are the groups identified in the colonial record as the *ceddo,* warriors—often of slave origin—equipped with firearms and horses and easily adapted to slave raiding.[60] Particularly at risk from such raids were the Sereer minorities within the Wolof monarchies of Baol and Kaajor. The ruling dynasties raided these and other outlying populations in order to exact tribute, punish rebellious villages, and acquire captives, most of whom were retained as slaves.[61] In part, this growing militarization of the Sereer and Wolof states can be explained by the aristocracy's need to plunder external populations to support their many dependent clients.[62] However, the increasing references to ceddo in the historical record during this period may be indicative of a more fundamental power struggle. Wolof sources suggest that the term *ceddo* applies not solely to the warrior-slave caste, but to the party of the aristocracy as a whole. By the nineteenth century, the central ideological and military conflict in Kaajor and Baol was being fought between the ceddo (aristocratic or traditionalist party) and the sëriş (Muslim party).[63]

On the Gold Coast, large numbers of flintlock muskets were imported in the 1680s and 1690s and used to arm the recently developed missile-oriented *levée* armies in the interior states of Akwamu and Denkyira.[64] As noted above, this period immediately preceded the expansion of Akwamu and its annexation of Akuapem. These conflicts in turn led to increased slave exports and an increase in the number of slaves co-opted into the military retinues of aristocrats and kings. Slave raids by the Akwamu may have forced the smaller, autochthonous Adangme populations of Krobo, Shai, and Osudoku to seek shelter in the difficult mountainous terrain behind the Akuapem Hills.

Nevertheless, the argument that the Atlantic slave trade alone directly caused a massive expansion of war is not as compelling as it may initially appear. Not only were many seemingly economically motivated conflicts probably at least partly driven by political motivations, but John Thornton has suggested that the idea of going to war to acquire slaves probably originated in West Africa long before European intervention. Since slaves were the primary sources of personal wealth in African regions like the Gold Coast and Senegal, where land was not privately owned, the accumulation of slaves—rather than the acquisition of territory—had traditionally been the objective of wars (107). Although Thornton's evidence is based largely on Benin and Kongo, this argument compels us to reevaluate whether European intervention and the Atlantic slave trade were responsible for vastly elevated levels of warfare.

Evidence for both the Gold Coast and Senegal, for example, suggests that European guns and horses were not as central as previously believed to the expansion of warfare in these regions, bringing the gun-slave cycle into question. The shift in warfare on the Gold Coast was largely brought about by socioeconomic changes in the interior states of Akwamu and Denkyira, rather than on the coast, and preceded the introduction of firearms (161–64). Horses, moreover, were useless in the forested zones of this region. Similarly, the horses that were so useful to the ceddo of the Senegalese *sahel* largely came from Sudanese breeders, not European traders, and were acquired through the long-standing trade with the Trarza and other Moorish groups. Likewise, early models of the musket — time-consuming to load, inaccurate, and difficult to use on horseback — were thus probably not as useful as previously thought.[65]

Nevertheless, the Atlantic slave trade at least accelerated the process of pillaging and destruction in some areas. Waalo, for example, not only served as a raiding ground for Trarza Moors supplying slaves to the Saharan trade, the Portuguese, and the French after the sixteenth century, but was subject to the depredations of its own ceddo. In this border region, the Atlantic slave trade exacerbated conflicts between Muslim villages and the ceddo who oppressed them, between rival aristocrats dependent upon the redistribution of loot to keep the loyalty of their clients, and between the Wolof and Trarza leaderships.[66] Thus, by 1819 large parts of this Senegal River Delta state had been rendered "entirely sterile."[67] We must similarly consider the experiences of the Adangme, above, and the independent Sereer populations outside the borders of Siin and Saalum, who were forced to seek refuge in defensible terrain and were stifled by the raids of the expansive Akwamu and the predatory Wolof regimes of Kaajor and Baol, respectively.

There is also evidence that the economic realignment resulting from the Atlantic slave trade encouraged the instability of the larger Senegalese states themselves. In the sixteenth and seventeenth centuries, the Jolof Confederation broke apart as its coastal provinces gained power from their status as middlemen in the slave trade, Kaajor seceding first, followed by Waalo and Baol. The Jolof core in the interior was isolated from the Atlantic trade and quickly lost its regional ascendancy.[68] The new coastal states quickly fell to squabbling over contested regions and for regional ascendency (86). Thus the Atlantic slave trade tended to encourage small armed states as the dominant system of organization in Senegal. Within these polities, however, older principles of state administration rooted in lineage relationships gave way to the dominance of warlord aristocracies supported by slave armies (80). As a result, Barry and Becker argue, development stagnated, locking these states into subsistence economies (31).

The Gold Coast shows similar signs of suffering long-term economic injury from slave raiding.[69] The destruction of the centralized Ga-Adangme kingdom of Ayawaso (greater Accra) by Akwamu raids between 1677 and 1681, for example, may have been devastating enough that much of the cultivated area of the coastal plain reverted temporarily to wilderness.[70] Events culminating in the subsequent defeat of Akwamu by an allied army led by Akyem in 1730 appear to have similarly depopulated the Nyanoase region of Akwamu, reflected in figures that show a decline in the number of men this area could muster from several thousand in 1695 to "a few hundred" in 1735.[71]

Using such evidence, proponents of the theory that the Atlantic slave trade retarded economic development in West Africa argue that regional depopulation —both directly through export as slaves and indirectly through warfare, migration, and famine—held Africa back from a demographic breakthrough. For example, sources from the 1820s indicate that French plantations in Waalo failed partly because of decreased populations leading to labor shortages.[72] Barry attributes this to the Atlantic slave trade, although a contributing factor was the expansion of the Trarza Moors to the north, financed largely through profits from gum production and sale, rather than the slave trade.[73] Klein similarly argues that the slave trade "probably limited the development of other forms of trade and productive activity both because it involved the export of labor," and because ceddo slave raiding and sectional conflict expanded.[74]

Depopulation certainly appears to be a logical result of slave trade. Unfortunately, quantitative evidence has been difficult to produce, except for a few coastal microregions. Patrick Manning attempted to overcome this in a 1985 study in which he extrapolated the effect of the slave trade from West African population censuses for 1931. His results appear to show that from the early eighteenth century onward, population growth slowed significantly, a result he confirms in his 1990 work *Slavery and African Life*.[75] Manning, however, has based his argument on a controversial assumption: his calculations of the probable populations of African regions prior to the Atlantic slave trade.[76] Manning's statistics for pre–slave trade populations are "estimated by backward projection from colonial-period population figures,"[77] an undertaking made difficult by the fact that, as Manning admits, the slave trade had a "seriously negative and distorting impact" on the African population.[78] Similarly, Manning is unable to show that West Africa, which bore the brunt of the effects of the slave trade, traveled a statistically different demographic path from regions of Africa unaffected by this trade.

More recently, David Eltis has suggested that the Atlantic slave trade was too diffuse over time and place to have had a major effect on West African populations.[79] Eltis and fellow historian David Richardson have based their recent findings on statistical analyses that use an increasingly integrated database of

slave-trading voyages based at the W. E. B. DuBois Institute, containing records
of slave voyages by European and American slavers from 1595 to 1845 that
suggest that demographic shifts may have occurred, but only in small regions.[80]
Data for the Gold Coast, for example, indicate that about 90 percent of all exported slaves embarked from just three ports—Accra, Anomabu, and Cape
Coast Castle—while trade in Senegal focused on Gorée and St. Louis.[81] Periodic population declines did occur in specific regions, such as greater Accra and
Waalo, but only following disruptive and infrequent events such as conquest or
civil war. In general, there is little evidence of drastic population shifts. While
we cannot exclude the possibility that these may have occurred, and while statistical data is increasingly available, evidence of long-term depopulation
trends within Gold Coast and Senegalese societies remains elusive. Such evidence we do have suggests that the question of the impact of the Atlantic slave
trade should be further addressed on a microregional level, acknowledging local
variations.

THE EVOLUTION OF COASTAL SOCIETY

If slave-supplying African societies were clearly victims of the Atlantic slave
trade, then the societies that raided them were active participants in the profitable slave trade. However, those who benefited the most were the slave-selling
societies on or with access to the coast. In the Gold Coast, the state of Akwamu
and the Fante-speaking polities expanded their power by monopolizing exports
to the Dutch and some British coastal factories; Elminans were especially active
participants.[82] Following the allied victory over Akwamu in 1730, traders in
Elmina encouraged the asantehene to send them slaves.[83] Whereas the interior
Adangme states were largely victims of Akwamu slave raids in the early eighteenth century, the coastal Adangme towns such as Ningo, Ada, and Prampram
sold slaves to Europeans along with other goods, and Ga merchants in Accra
flourished as exporters of people captured by the Akwamu in their wars.[84] After
1742 Accra became especially active in exporting large numbers of victims of
the Asante wars of expansion. Likewise, following the breakup of the Jolof Confederation, coastal successor states such as Baol and Kaajor halted the export of
their own productive slave population, instead dealing in slaves from the interior and turning their own slaves to producing supplies for the slave caravans as
well as spinning and weaving cotton cloth.[85] In the slave-supplying societies of
both the Gold Coast and Senegal, it was the chiefs, aristocrats, paramounts, and

kings who conducted much of the trade, using armies augmented by slave re-tainers such as the ceddo and *ahenfo* and sanctioning raids and wars for the ac-quisition of trade slaves.[86]

However, it was the development of distinct Euro-African middlemen com-munities around European posts, rather than the transformation of traditional African polities, that was the primary factor leading to the reconception of de-pendency relationships on new terms. By 1702 there were twenty-six British, Danish, and Dutch forts on the Gold Coast, from Beyin by the Tano River to Prampram near the Volta.[87] European merchants, especially the factors of char-tered trading companies, conducted a factory trade from such posts along the entire coast, but only a few forts developed large settled middleman communi-ties. Among the most important by 1700 were the Dutch commercial establish-ment at Elmina; the British headquarters only kilometers away at Cape Coast Castle; and the Ga-Adangme polity of Accra, which hosted Dutch, Danish, and British forts.[88] Similarly, despite the construction of inland factories along the Senegal River, urbanized Euro-African communities in eighteenth-century Senegal were largely confined to the island entrepôts of St. Louis and Gorée. Within these towns, the simple "floating trade" in slaves and other commodities was replaced by a more complicated and centralized commercial system. For slave vendors and buyers, this system represented a major advance as slaves could be securely "stored" in the forts or in stronghouses until a trading ship arrived. However, for St. Louis at least, it was not slaves, but gum, that most stimulated the growth of commerce, especially approaching the nineteenth century.[89]

These municipalities were frontier zones, areas of interaction and fusion be-tween African and European peoples. Gorée and St. Louis were populated mostly by an African and Euro-African trading class of *habitants* and petty *traitants,* along with their slaves, and a smaller number of *noires libres* (free blacks) and European administrative and merchant personnel. In St. Louis the Euro-Africans were not only commercial middlemen but also the key purchasers of Trarza gum during the last decades of the eighteenth century, and they were constantly striving to expand their trading networks along the Senegal River.[90] The habitant commu-nity developed during the eighteenth century as a class of petty bourgeoisie who played a central role in the two large towns both as political actors and as profes-sional middlemen in several trades, the gum trade being the most prestigious.[91] In Gorée the habitant class included a significant body of *signares,* initially the wives and concubines of Europeans who had amassed their own economic and political power. Euro-African society adopted elements of European culture and dress, and many families adopted or inherited French or Portuguese names—

among them were Laports, Franciers, Pécarres, and Baudins.[92] Habitant families were not only related to indigenous elites, but made political and economic alliances with them through marriage and contract.[93] The result of these various relationships was divisions within the habitant community "between rich and poor, Christian and Muslim."[94] Nevertheless, the community remained unified partly by their ongoing struggle against the monopoly of the royally chartered commercial companies, such as the Compagnie commerciale d'Afrique, which monopolized the transatlantic leg of the slave and gum trades.[95] In 1789 they expressed their perceived identity as a bourgeois trading class by sending *cahiers de doléance* to the Estates Generales demanding an end to the company's monopoly.[96]

Similar but distinct merchant societies arose in coastal polities of the Gold Coast in the seventeenth and eighteenth centuries.[97] These communities were also a cultural *mélange*—indigenous Africans commingled with the descendents of company servants brought from other parts of Africa, slaves, and Euro-African families with names such as Bannerman, Cleland, Hesse, Barnes, and Swanzy. The resulting communities adopted many of the attributes of local cultures. Politically, this meant that the stools of Cape Coast and Elmina were generally passed down through their matriline, whereas leadership of the divisions in predominantly Ga Accra remained largely inherited through the patriline, despite both the growth of the Euro-African community and a period of occupation by the matrilineal Asante.[98] Whereas Euro-Africans tended to dominate middleman positions between European merchants and African traders and adopted an identity somewhat removed from neighboring African communities, the line between the two populations was highly permeable.[99] Moreover, Euro-Africans carefully maintained important economic and consanguineous links with the indigenous community and in practice often filled important economic and political positions. Their positions as cultural and economic brokers helped maintain a certain fluidity of identity within these zones of interaction.

Within and around these societies, slavery was gradually transformed from a largely cultural and political institution into a largely economic one. The selling of slaves was the foundation of the process by which this occurred. By the beginning of the nineteenth century, the coastal forts and posts sold most slaves from these regions into the Atlantic trade.[100] Many of the slave vendors were chiefly officeholders or merchants, but small traders selling one or two slaves can also be found in the historical record.[101] The practice of diverting captives from export to use within the community developed relatively swiftly. The European powers each maintained a force of slaves as workers and artisans, and even sent them as traders into the interior. In Elmina there were about 184 company slaves in 1645.[102] Reports from 1725 show 367 slaves in Cape Coast serving as carpenters, gold takers, coopers, gunners, cooks, brick makers, blacksmiths, chapel servants, canoemen, doctors' servants, goldsmiths, armorers, and common servants.[103] By the turn of the nineteenth century large numbers of slaves were in the hands of individual merchants in both locations—some of whom owned up to several hundred individuals. Evidence indicates they were used as porters, domestic servants, and trading agents, and in cultivation.[104]

The rise in slaveholding both within Euro-African society and in surrounding coastal communities was directly linked to the private accumulation of merchant capital that was much more common in these areas than in the interior. The accumulation of wealth by some merchants led to the concentration and acquisition of labor power as well as land and goods.[105] Ray Kea has pointed out that, in the seventeenth century, communities of slaves held near coastal towns not only produced foodstuffs, but also generated currency for their masters by selling agricultural goods in town markets and by mining gold (200). It is unclear how complete this transformation was and exactly when it took place. Certainly, early in the seventeenth century the evidence indicates that the goods sold in market towns and along the coast had been more often "the surplus production of peasant family households rather than that of slave family households" (16). However, there is some evidence from the 1630s and 1640s that wealthy indigenous merchants established farming villages near Cape Coast, which may have been worked by slaves.[106] Thus, Kea suggests that in some Akan regions at least, by the eighteenth century "slaves and bonded freemen . . . became the principal sources of subsistence for nonfarming urban dwellers and of social wealth for the dominant classes" (16, 165). John Parker has shown a similar transformation occurring among the Ga, characterized by the mid-eighteenth-century rise of oblempon stools. The occupants of these stools were distinguished for their wealth and their "control over large retinues of retainers or slaves," in contrast with the traditional chiefly officeholders whose authority was based on their relationship with their free subjects.[107]

Urban Senegalese slavery in St. Louis and Gorée evolved around French needs. The French administration did not generally keep its own slaves. Instead, a system was developed in which slaves were acquired by the habitant community and sometimes by large merchant houses and rented to the French government, resident merchants, and ships' captains. Slaves were employed as *laptots* (canoemen), skilled workmen, millet grinders, cleaning women, laundry workers, and even musicians.[108] The defense of the two islands also partially depended on slaves who were mobilized by their masters when conflict threatened.[109] The relationship between slaves and masters that evolved in St. Louis and Gorée provides a firm contrast to that of traditional Wolof and Sereer societies. Male slaves, especially the many laptots of St. Louis who were engaged in the riverine trade into the interior, received a wage consisting of a portion of the money paid to their master for their services, and could acquire considerable property.[110] This fusion society thereby created a class of slaves whose role was entirely economic, supplementing the domestic and trade slaves in the community. These slaves even appear to have enjoyed a certain type of economic—if not social—mobility, using their wages to purchase boats and hire their own laborers.[111] However, this mobility did not extend to liberation—it was rare for slaves, however wealthy, to be able to purchase their own freedom.

In addition to using slaves as laborers, habitant society recognized slaves as status symbols. For example, female slave parasol bearers accompanied the signares on their promenades along N'dar Tout or around town and signified the signares' elite status.[112]

THE EXPANSION OF SLAVERY

In 1853 Brodie Cruickshank suggested that "there is reason to believe that, during some period of their history, the slave was protected by a more humane code of laws."[113] However, he was forced to admit that indigenous slavery in the nineteenth century was not as benign an institution as was depicted by colonial and company sources. Indeed, evidence suggests that over the preceding four hundred years the slave trade had acted as the catalyst for a transformation in both the numbers and the positions of domestic slaves. The growth of slavery within Africa was most marked in the previously discussed coastal societies in which the export trade was most important. However, by the early nineteenth century, the ratio of slaves to free people within the Gold Coast appears to have risen even away from the coast, prompting Cruickshank to remark that "here [on the Gold Coast], domestic slavery is the root and foundation of the whole social system."[114] Slave populations in the Senegalese kingdoms of Siin, Saalum, Kaajor, and Waalo appear to have grown as well, both through the forced conversion of peasant village populations to slavery and through the diversion of slaves from the export trade to meet labor needs.[115]

This expansion of slavery within indigenous society, while gradual, was evident in both the Gold Coast and Senegal. As slaves became more valuable as trade commodities, slave owners developed new methods of acquisition, a phenomenon of which the growth of warfare is only one indication. Punishment was another method of procurement. Meredith noted that "during the slave trade, [the laws] all agreed in their ultimate tendency, that of slavery: for a trifling offence a man lost his liberty."[116] Enslavement also appears to have replaced fining as the most common punishment in the Sereer states.[117] Other Europeans noted a growing trend toward slavery as the result of famine and insolvency. There appears to have been an upsurge in the incidence of parents' selling their children, or even themselves, into slavery to avoid starvation. It also became more difficult to effect liberation. In Senegal, the manumission of children born to slave mothers and free fathers appears to have become virtually unknown,[118] and Captain Maclean, longtime administrator of the Gold Coast, reported that by the nineteenth century slaves were "seldom manumitted by their masters."[119]

It was not only methods of slave acquisition and retention that were affected by the adjustments wrought by the needs of the Atlantic slave trade. As intercontinental trade grew, slaves were to some extent sucked into the production of trade goods and foodstuffs. Much has been made of this "transformation of slavery," proposed by Paul Lovejoy in his book of the same name: "The pull of the market had the effect of pushing indigenous forms of slavery further away from a social framework in which slavery was another form of dependency in societies based on kinship relationships to a system in which slaves played an increasing role in the economy."[120]

One of the cornerstones of Lovejoy's hypothesis is the logical assumption that the slave trade must have stimulated the production and sale of foodstuffs to feed nonproductive slaves designated for export overseas. It is clear that millions of slaves were moving from the interior to the coast, where they were housed, sometimes for long periods of time, until a slave ship appeared to carry them away. These slaves therefore needed to be fed at three stages—in caravans, in the barracoons, and on the ships themselves. Add to this the evidence that large numbers of slaves were being retained by coastal West African societies and that urban populations who were not themselves agriculturally productive were increasing, and it seems logical that slaves would have been increasingly diverted into agricultural production.

Unfortunately, the evidence that a slave mode of production was emerging in either region during this era is unclear. Much is made of reports that Cape Coast merchants employed slaves in "plantations" by 1822.[121] But we know that the word "plantation" was often loosely applied to the cultivation of crops for local consumption. Still, it is not too far a stretch to believe that slaves belonging to merchants here may have been engaged in farming crops for sale in the towns and forts; and certainly chiefly officeholders, merchants, and resident Europeans of urban Gold Coast settlements fed themselves with produce from slave-worked farms.[122] That a market economy existed is clear—by the seventeenth century peasants in coastal societies were beginning to pay land "rent" in the form of gold, which they acquired by selling a portion of their goods at urban markets.[123] However, the introduction of slaves to this market economy appears to have been limited to farms surrounding urban coastal enclaves, and the growth of slave-worked farms in the early nineteenth century may have been more a result of the abolition of the slave trade than of the trade itself.[124]

States in the interior, such as Akwamu and Akuapem, may have emphasized the promotion of commerce rather than the expansion of cultivation and viewed slaves as products for export rather than as labor for the production of food-stuffs.[125] One exception was the clearing of bush for agricultural production in forested regions of Adanse and Amanse, which Ivor Wilks argues became a task for unfree labor as early as the fifteenth and sixteenth century.[126] Here, as on the coast, the upsurge in slavery was related to the accumulation of merchant capital created by a rise in the mining and trading of gold in these regions—the profit from this industry being used by merchant families to purchase land and slaves.

For Senegal, the evidence for a slave mode of production is only slightly more compelling. Slaves heading toward St. Louis were conveyed a great distance, as many of them came from Gaajaga and even farther inland. Searing has suggested that during this period the provisioning of such caravans was linked to a form of slavery "associated with both an extension in the size of agricultural units and an intensification of the labor process."[127] Indeed, French sources indicate that many Wolof slaves worked their masters' land for several days a week during this period.[128] However, peasant subsistence production remained dominant. French plantation administrators as late as the early nineteenth century, for example, found that Waalo—neighboring St. Louis—could still only provide free labor for plantations, and that slave labor for the purpose of cultivation was not readily available.[129] It appears that although the transformation of slavery to a more obviously economic arrangement began to spread to African societies during the Atlantic trade, it was still a very limited transformation.

THE TRANSFORMATION OF PAWNING ON THE GOLD COAST

The institution of pawning, on the other hand, was radically reinvented during the Atlantic slave trade. It appears probable that indigenous institutions of pawning, or debt bondage, originated as a method by which a husband's abusua could acquire rights to his wife's labor and children in a matrilineal society.[130] In the era of the slave trade, however, pawning underwent a transition from a negotiated transfer of authority between lineage groups to a fundamentally commercial transaction. The demand for slaves led to the clandestine selling of contractually acquired pawns into slavery, often for export. By the nineteenth century, Gold Coast societies were allowing the sale of pawns outright to a purchaser, ignoring the traditional protections of pawn status.[131] The line between pawns and slaves was thus blurred.

As pawns became vulnerable to the export trade, and as the demand for labor to replace individuals lost from slave-producing societies and to grow food for coastal communities continued to rise, elites developed strategies to enlarge their potential supply of pawns. Among the most significant methods by which they accomplished this appear to have been the development of punishment pawning and the growth in debt-producing customs. Throughout the eighteenth century, the size of fines given as punishment climbed precipitously. Indigenous chiefs levied increasingly enormous fines as punishment in cases of dispute. Not only those found guilty, but even occasionally the victors in litigation, ran up such enormous costs in bribes and legal fees that they became insolvent and were pawned to the very chiefs who heard their cases.[132] John Adams, a ship's captain who made a number of voyages to the region in the last years of the eighteenth century, wrote of cases he observed in Anomabu that "[the litigant] whose purse holds out the longest, saves perhaps his liberty, while his less wealthy antagonist and family are often doomed to slavery and exile."[133] Heavy damages were levied in cases such as adultery, which had not previously been punishable by financial penalty, and many false cases were brought before chiefs for the specific purpose of gaining pawns.[134]

Interest rates for contractual debts similarly surged. Before the Atlantic slave trade, there is no evidence that interest was laid on pawns,[135] but during the eighteenth century, interest of 50 to 100 percent became common both in pawning cases and for the borrowing of money in the coastal states.[136] Moreover, greedy creditors used nonpayment as a justification for enslaving not only the pawn or debtor, but members of the debtor's abusua as well. When this did not satisfy their demands, it became common for creditors to kidnap and sell "any person or persons belonging to the said family, or even to the same country, state, or town, with the debtor."[137] This type of kidnapping, known as *panyarring*, was closely related to the increased demand for slaves and pawns created by the redirection of enslaved individuals into the Atlantic slave trade. The 1842 Parliamentary Select Committee, which generally accepted pawning as "voluntarily entered into" and "not abstractly unjust or unreasonable," nevertheless argued that by that date the spread of the practice of panyarring had made the institution of pawning "liable to much abuse, and much resembling slavery" and argued that thus "it should be the object of our policy to get rid of [pawning], even among the natives."[138]

Evidence of panyarring becomes especially prevalent with the introduction of missionaries in the 1850s and 1860s (see chapter 3), but some sources make it clear that it occurred in the late eighteenth century and the early 1800s as well.[139] It seems evident that it was the voracious demand of the Atlantic slave trade that distorted the traditional custom of pawning. African elites took the initiative to find new supplies of people for export, and the institution of pawning was convenient for their needs. There is evidence that the panyarring of individuals found "on pathways, in forests, and on plantations" had become an accepted part of both interstate and interdivisional conflicts, and that individuals captured in this manner were sold to slave dealers on the coast.[140]

Not only was panyarring an efficient method of recruiting slaves for export, but, due to the kinship-based roots of the institution, the children of female pawns (the majority of pawns were still female because of the nature of traditional pawning) belonged to creditors, lending them additional value as retained slaves. Given the new high interest rates, pawns were unlikely to be redeemed, and if they were, creditors still stood to make a great profit. The combination of high interest rates, panyarring, and the clandestine export of pawned individuals for export combined to make pawning an important tool for slave merchants.

In this environment, changing cultural traditions contributed to the rise in pawning. Funeral and initiation rites reached a destructive level of extravagance in the eighteenth century as families put themselves in debt to pay for vastly inflated ceremonies and rituals.[141] Records of colonial tribunals do not stretch back this far, but governmental reports speak of "ruinously expensive fetish ceremonies" and the economic embarrassment of "the expenses attending the celebration of all the principal events of life" greatly expanding the practice of pawning.[142] By the nineteenth century, the widespread institutions of panyarring and pawning bore little resemblance to the lineage-based model from which they had developed.

THE ATLANTIC SLAVE TRADE AND GENDER

Social transformation in the wake of the Atlantic slave trade was not confined to the institution of pawning. The role of gender in Senegalese and Gold Coast societies was distorted by the demands of the trade and, more importantly, the accompanying demands on labor by coastal societies servicing the slave trade. In order to understand this phenomenon, we have to return to statistics briefly.

Women, we know, had traditionally formed a significant proportion of slaves in West Africa. Because of local cultural paradigms, women in both Senegambia and on the Gold Coast were important workers in agricultural and marketing contexts, whose tasks tended to become the province of slaves in coastal societies during the era of the slave trade.[143] Women were also valuable for their reproductive capacity. In bridewealth societies, which characterized the populations of both the Gold Coast and Senegal, marrying a woman required a large outlay of resources.[144] In addition, in the dominant matrilineal societies of both regions, women and their offspring still belonged to their matrilineage after marriage. Reproducing with slaves was a strategy that outflanked both of these constrictions, as masters avoided expensive bride-price payments and retained ownership of the offspring. Unions with female slaves were probably not preferable for first marriages, as they conferred no status, but certainly slaves were useful as additional wives and concubines, increasing as they did a man's reproductive and production potential.[145]

Statistics indicate that the Atlantic slave trade reinforced this equation. Plantation owners in the New World paid higher prices for slaves they perceived to be the best workers—young men—and these therefore formed the majority of the Atlantic trade.[146] This phenomenon has been quantified by a series of historians. A survey of slaves imported into Jamaica from the Gold Coast for the period 1764–1788, for example, included 11,176 men and 5,565 women.[147] French shipping statistics from Senegambia indicate a ratio of 175 men for every 100 women withdrawn from the coast,[148] whereas another study suggests a statistic of four to one for the Senegal River region alone.[149] Together, records of pre-abolition Atlantic slave traders indicate that their shipments included approximately 60 percent men and 40 percent women—leaving perhaps three million extra women in coastal markets towns and along the slave route.[150]

Although these statistics show that consumers in the New World favored male slaves, the matter was not simply a question of demand. African slave vendors probably preferred to retain female slaves both for their own domestic needs and because they brought a higher price in the Saharan trade.[151] The demand for men and women was therefore somewhat balanced, if serving several markets. Consequently, the rise of female slavery in coastal societies was largely a question of choice. Local slave owners preferred to retain female slaves and export a greater percentage of males. Coastal communities during this period tended to experience a marked rise in polygamy and to have a high proportion of enslaved females.[152] Much of the evidence of this dates from slightly later than the Atlantic slave trade period, but is still illustrative in showing the effects of this transition. The slave population of French Senegal (the vast majority in Gorée and St. Louis) in 1845, for example, was 4,248 males and 5,865 females.[153] Similarly, the Methodist Missionary Society indicates a high proportion of slave wives among their congregants at Cape Coast in the 1830s,[154] and Claire Robertson argues that a majority of nineteenth-century slaves in Accra were female.[155] As we will see in later chapters, British colonial records indicate similar trends after the inception of organized judicial records some fifty years after the end of the Atlantic slave trade. It is not too bold to argue from these various sources that by the nineteenth century women formed the majority of slaves in coastal regions, especially as traditionally female tasks such as market vending and domestic work made up the majority of slave tasks in towns such as Cape Coast, Accra, Gorée, and St. Louis.

West African society cannot be said to have been immediately and radically transformed by the Atlantic slave trade. Instead, its limited effects were just the beginning of a long period of transformation in which regional variation would continue to be an important factor. The export trade initiated a longer period of new economic development, integration into the Atlantic world, and transformation of indigenous social and political institutions. Much of this change would occur only after the "abolition" of the export trade across the Atlantic in the nineteenth century.

Still, for Senegal and the Gold Coast, indications of the changes to come were becoming evident on the coast and littoral by 1800. Europeans and their partners on the African coast were the beneficiaries of a realignment of trade routes and power toward the Atlantic Ocean. These evolving coastal communities incorporated African culture and combined it with European ideas such as mercantilism. It was here, and in a limited number of nearby polities, that social and economic paradigms regarding slavery shifted first, spreading slowly to neighboring societies and then inland to the larger states of the interior. A slave mode of production did not become the norm, but slaves began to grow crops to sell in town markets and to provision the convoys of export slaves. The number and proportion of locally held female slaves grew, and larger numbers of slaves were retained by the trading powers and by individuals. On the Gold

Coast, pawning underwent a systematic change, becoming harsher and losing its connection to the lineage system from which it developed. In both regions, new elites rose to exploit the commoditization of slaves and the commercial opportunities created by the Atlantic trading network. Both these new groups and older, established orders were forced to define their relationship to the European representatives.

Thus, as the populations of Senegal and the Gold Coast entered the nineteenth century, they were societies in varying degrees of flux. At this critical juncture, European powers unilaterally ended the Atlantic slave trade, disregarding the input of the various indigenous groups. This would establish a pattern for metropolitan-African relations in the nineteenth century. Unable to influence the decision itself, merchants, chiefly officeholders, slave owners, and slaves would all struggle to impress their desires on the application of the law in an attempt to define the shape slavery would take in the period following abolition.

CHAPTER 2

The Crisis of Abolition, Legitimate Trade, and the Adaptation of Slavery

THE CRIMINALIZATION OF THE ATLANTIC slave trade did not produce a reversion to precontact traditions of slavery in West Africa. Rather, its termination induced a wide and sociologically significant set of new transformations of dominance relationships. For slaves, slave owners, and administrators, abolition was a prototype crisis, a practice round for emancipation. During this period slave-owning elites developed the strategies of negotiation, evasion, and opposition that they would put to effective use in subsequent periods. Similarly, European administrators learned to balance metropolitan demands for increased commercial productivity, potential threats to the political and economic integrity of the colonies from African opposition to antislavery legislation, and the stringent demands of the abolitionist lobby. The administrative structures and policies that emerged from this potent mix in the coastal enclaves of this period would form the models for later colonial states.

Slavery itself changed in response to the crisis of abolition. The roles of slaves in cultivating trade goods and serving as laborers and soldiers expanded, even as fluctuating slave prices and increased demand for agricultural labor expanded slave ownership to individuals outside the traditionally powerful and affluent slave-owning classes. The trend toward a slave mode of production, begun by the Atlantic slave trade, was exacerbated by the expanding production of legitimate goods in this era as a trade in raw materials gradually re-placed the traffic of people.

ABOLITION DE JURE

The abolition of the Atlantic slave trade was largely a nineteenth-century story. The first significant calls for the institution's demise began in the 1780s in the Protestant northern European states. On March 16, 1792, Denmark became the first European power to forbid the slave trade to its citizens.[1] Only a small number of slaves were carried annually on Danish-flagged ships, however, and the decree did not take effect until 1803. Even after this date British and German plantation owners in the Danish Caribbean continued to import slaves legally. More importantly, abolitionism firmly took root in Britain during this period. Although there were distinct philosophical roots to British abolitionism, the near-legendary historian of abolition, Roger Antsey, has argued that "it was mainly religious conviction, insight and zeal which made it possible for antislavery feeling to be subsumed in a crusade against the slave trade and slavery."[2] In England, evangelical and missionary ideals took hold among a class beginning to accumulate capital. Beginning in the 1780s, educated English and Scotsmen such as Sir Samuel Romilly, Thomas Clarkson, and Thomas Walker — men who had links both to capitalist institutions and to nonconformist churches — began to lead petition drives meant to influence Parliament to pass abolitionist legislation. Because of the credentials of the movement's leaders, these efforts quickly gained the support of "cities and towns, churches and vestries, and a wide range of private and public organizations."[3] By 1793 lower-class radicals had emerged as a major force in the abolitionist movement, which was also driven by an environment of "intellectual and theological change."[4]

The abolitionist movement was closely related to the mature state of capitalism within England. The mobilization of a massive system for exporting slaves during the previous centuries, accompanied as it was by conflict, the plundering of agricultural villages, and the reduction of production potential, interfered with the gathering and export of raw materials that British companies needed from Africa.[5] The industrial revolution's demand for these materials drove the abolitionist process among mercantilists.[6] There is some debate as to which factor — ideological or commercial — was more significant in contributing to abolitionism in Britain. The general consensus of historians is that "industrialisation created social classes and political groups which, lacking any strong vested interest in

Atlantic slavery and jockeying for power with older mercantile forces which did, allied with those who opposed the dealings in human beings on theological and humanitarian grounds."[7] For our purposes, however, this issue is tangential. The involvement of merchants in the abolitionist movement, for whatever reason, was vital to its success, and contributed to the government's decision to abolish the slave trade in 1807.[8] The subsequent act of Parliament banning the export of slaves from Africa was no half measure, and the prescribed punishment included the forfeiture of any ship involved in the slave trade and a £100 fine for each slave confiscated—a substantial amount for the time.[9] The law was further amended in 1811 to include punishment by transportation to a penal colony for the arrested officers of slave ships.[10]

The French embraced abolition somewhat less enthusiastically. Prerevolutionary French society did not foster an environment in which abolitionism could flourish. The revolutionary government's prohibition of slavery in 1794 was therefore something of a shock, and the decree was not enforced in either the Caribbean colonies or Africa. It was ultimately revoked by Napoleon Bonaparte in 1802.[11] Napoleon did, for political reasons, issue an imperial decree forbidding the slave trade to French shipping during the Hundred Days' rule of 1815, but the Restoration monarchy chose to ignore it.[12] Subsequently, abolition was imposed upon France by the alliance (chiefly Britain) formed against it through the second Treaty of Paris in 1815. The abolition clause, perceived by the French populace as an attempt by maritime Britain to further its ambition to control the seas, was also largely ignored. When, in January 1817, a royal ordinance reprised Napoleon's 1815 decree forbidding the slave trade, and, on April 15, 1818, it was finally promulgated, a cruiser squadron was almost immediately dispatched to West Africa—not in hopes of catching slavers, but in order to challenge British supremacy over the region.[13] As a result, French enforcement of laws intended to eradicate the export trade in slaves was extremely weak.

ENFORCEMENT AND EVASION: THE ILLEGAL SLAVE TRADE

The abolition of the export of slaves from Africa was decreed by the European metropoles, which intended that much of the responsibility for its enforcement would lie with officials dispatched from Europe—specifically, the commanders of cruiser squadrons. In fact, however, officers of the Company of Merchants Trading to Africa and colonial officials based in coastal posts and towns played a large role in the struggle against the illegal trade. Simultaneously, African and Euro-African slave traders and their maritime trading partners attempted to elude patrols and evade abolition laws. Thus, contrary to the expectations of the French Ministry of the Navy and the British Admiralty, the success of the anti-slave-trade squadrons was, in effect, reliant on the actions of onshore actors.

The strong British naval presence off the Gold Coast caused an immediate decline in the scale of the export slave trade, from approximately eight thousand slaves per year in 1800 to about a quarter of that in 1815.[14] The two other European powers represented on the coast played only a small role in the abolition of this trade. The Danish had already promulgated abolition, and the Dutch followed suit in 1813—although they continued to recognize the export of unfree "apprentices," however, neither acted resolutely to interdict slavers.[15] An 1819 treaty that gave British cruisers the right to search Dutch vessels—subsequently extended to the Spanish, Portuguese, and other European and American vessels—was more decisive.[16] As a result of this treaty, the export of slaves from traditionally active ports such as Accra, Elmina, and Komenda declined quite drastically in the second decade of the nineteenth century. To slave smugglers, the major drawback of all these ports was their direct exposure to the ocean. More effective smuggling positions in Guinea and Nigeria were hidden behind mazes of creeks, but from Apollonia to the Volta River, the Gold Coast seaboard was relatively open.

The effect of abolition on the slave-trading establishment of the Gold Coast was therefore almost immediate. T. Edward Bowdich and other travelers of this period report evidence of abandoned slave-trading factories near the coast. Large slave markets such as Mansu were found in ruins.[17] As late as 1821, Hutton visited Komenda, Apollonia, "Tatum," and "Succondee," and noted that they had been abandoned by the servants and officials of the Company of Merchants because of lack of trade.[18] The Dutch settlements were similarly crippled by abolition, especially after 1818.[19] The British Company of Merchants was so impoverished that the Crown assumed possession of their assets in 1822.[20]

Concurrent with abolition, however, 1807 was also the year that Asante defeated an alliance of Akan states and captured the Fante polities, taking significant numbers of captives.[21] With the collapse of the Atlantic trade—Asante's largest market for war captives—the asantehene cast about for other possible solutions. No doubt a portion could still be sold in coastal states, but this market was already glutted; prices in the coastal regions had declined from more than nine ounces of gold in 1803[22] to around seven ounces in 1807.[23] Moreover, by this point the savanna was a provider, rather than a consumer, of slaves.[24] Thus, the asantehene begged the British authorities to reinstitute the trade until at least 1820, but they were unsuccessful.[25] Following this refusal, Asante merchants began increasingly to redirect trade east to the Volta River. The Anlo-Ewe populations of this region were outside British authority, and its terrain was also characterized by a series of convoluted creeks perfect for hiding both canoes and oceangoing vessels.[26] It appears probable that many Akan slaves were diverted down this Voltaic route or eastward from Accra into this region and subsequently exported from slave coast ports.[27] Much of this illegal trade was run by merchants from Accra, Ada, and other eastern communities with a significant European presence. Euro-Africans, especially, figure prominently. Sam Kanto Brew was an Anglo-Irish-Fante merchant who acted as a middleman in the illegal trade, acquiring the asantehene's friendship and exchanging Spanish guns for Asante slaves.[28] Euro-African traders from Dutch Accra were so deeply involved in the trade that the British resorted to bombarding the town in an effort to disrupt their activities.[29] Despite the risks and British interference, the potential profits were more than enough to appeal to coastal merchants. In 1817 a company officer wrote to his superiors in despair: "The people of the Coast are the brokers of those of the interior who supply the slaves. . . . This trade is . . . beyond all comparison so indolent and lucrative, that even were there any appeal to their feelings, it would not influence it in competition with such inordinate gain."[30]

Although strict British law deterred most British shipowners from the trade, it could not limit the availability of slaves, and merchants of other European powers were eager to take the place of the British. From 1815 onward, Spanish, Portuguese, and Brazilian vessels began to appear off the western Gold Coast, often crewed by Americans and Cubans and largely geared toward the voracious market for plantation labor in Brazil and Cuba.[31] As antislavery squadrons became more effective and slave suppliers shifted eastward to the safer Volta creeks, these slave ships did so as well. Quite early, records show that European slave vessels had ceased to appear along the sandy, well-populated coast between Cape Coast Castle and Accra. As late as 1858, however, Spanish ships were being captured east of Accra.[32] In 1860, slave marts were still supplying these vessels from Keta and along the Volta.[33] It was not until 1873 that an administrator, Governor Harley, was able to report that "no slaves have been exported from this settlement within the last three years."[34] The export trade, far from being easily abolished, had lingered for more than half a century, with slave commerce simply being diverted from the Gold Coast proper to new areas.[35] An alliance of flexible indigenous elites and mercenary European merchants had adapted the trade to exploit geographic holes in the enforcement of abolition.

The stretch of coastline between the Senegal River and the Siin-Saloum Delta also experienced an appreciable initial decline in slave exports following the promulgation of abolition.[36] The British occupation of St. Louis and Gorée at the beginning of the century and its blockading of continental Europe led to a temporary cessation of all export trade from Senegal, including slaves. However, as slaves began to accumulate on both islands, the habitant community began to exert pressure to restart the trade, and when they failed to sway the British administration, they began to smuggle slaves through villages on the Waalo Coast.[37] Upon their reacquisition of St. Louis in 1816, the returning French were faced with an established smuggling network that avoided St. Louis entirely. Admittedly, the illegal trade from Senegal was minor compared to that of the Gambia and Southern Rivers region, since the sandy beaches off northern Senegal were easily patrolled. However, slavers off the Senegalese coast openly flouted the abolition act, and French authorities were initially powerless to stop them. In June 1818, the brig La Dorado hove to at Gorée, then at St. Louis, and evaded a rather pitiful attempt to board her before taking on human cargo at the Wolof village of Portudal on the Petite Côte. The distraught commandant of St. Louis excused himself on the basis of a lack of manpower, complaining, "I cannot . . . discharge my responsibility with such feeble resources."[38]

In June 1818, French warships were finally dispatched to West Africa. However, the cruisers, manned by apathetic crews and initially directionless, did not capture their first slave ship for twenty months.[39] In the absence of a real naval commitment, coastal authorities were forced to take up the slack, taking three ships in 1818 alone.[40] In 1819 the French Crown finally dispatched an envoy, Baron Mackam, to investigate accusations made by the governor of Sierra Leone of slave trading during Baron Julien Schmaltz's term of office as administrator of Senegal.[41] Mackam returned with a strongly worded report condemning both naval and civil authorities. However, the case went no further. Schmaltz's hastily written explanations had been accepted by the minister of the navy, who put an end to Mackam's "odious imputations."[42] Perhaps the minister's stance was influenced by his own vulnerability to these accusations as the direct superior of both the colonial and naval officials stationed in Senegal. Nor was there any serious official support for a more stringent approach outside the naval ministry. As late as 1826, the ordained punishment for slave trading was simply that ship and cargo be confiscated, and that the ship's captain suffer interdiction from the king's vessels for life.[43]

This situation, however, was transformed over the next year. A groundswell of support for abolition had emerged among influential businesspeople in the mid-1820s, and in 1826 three hundred shipowners petitioned against the trade.[44] This lobby could not be ignored as previous, more radical abolitionist groups had been, and in response the Crown promulgated the Loi rèlative à la répression de la traite des noirs on April 25, 1827.[45] The act increased punishment for indicted slave traders, including banishment for captains and up to five years' imprisonment for the crews of slavers. Indicative of the complete reversal of the Crown's attitude toward slavery, application of the new law was swift, and the captain of the Deux fréres, captured in October 1827, was banished, his backers fined Fr 17,080.[46] A portion of the fine went as prize money to the crew of the cruiser that captured the slave ship—as provided for by an 1825 ordinance.[47] If the declining numbers of French slave ships sighted by British squadrons in the following years are any indication, the new laws were effective. By the 1830s the energy of French naval crews now operating largely against Iberian- and Brazilian-flagged vessels and with the added incentive of prize money was conspicuously greater than previously. Within the decade, French patrols had proven themselves, and smuggling from Senegal to the Americas ceased to be significant.

SLAVE OWNERS AND THE "CRISIS OF ABOLITION"

The abolition of the overseas commerce in slaves represented a defining crisis for slave traders in Senegal and the Gold Coast, including the numerically small but powerful community of Africans and Euro-Africans, participating aristocrats, and chiefly officeholders. As the overseas slave market disappeared and no other commodity emerged to take its place, segments of both groups began to experience a marked decline in export earnings.

For northern Senegal, the abolition of the export slave trade coincided with a decline in gum production.[48] Despite the continuing overland slave trade into the region, the period directly following British abolition saw a decrease in the island's population for the first time in a century as the economic situation took a sharp downturn and habitants sold off their slaves and released their free servants.[49] But abolition posed the greatest threat not to merchant elites but to the aristocracy. The overland slave trade in Senegal, as we have seen, was mainly the prerogative of traditional rulers and their ceddo armies, who used the profits to secure their power in the form of guns and men, resources that gave them the ability to procure more slaves and conduct them safely to the coast. The end of the Atlantic slave trade threatened this monopoly, "depriv[ing] the aristocrats of their main source of income and power."[50] The habitant community no longer demanded slaves, since local needs were satisfied and the export trade was in gradual decline.[51] As a result, the resources of Wolof and Sereer slave-trading aristocracies began to wane.[52]

Merchants and chiefly elites (often one and the same) within such Gold Coast polities as the Fante city-states and Accra similarly saw their positions threatened by the decline of the Atlantic slave trade. The chiefly officeholders of these two regions were probably the segment of the local populace most vulnerable to a "crisis of adaptation" following abolition. Whereas, as we will see, the newer obirempon stools and the merchant class generally adapted reasonably well to the new reality, it has been posited that for these two coastal regions, abolition was the first step in the gradual decline of the less flexible class of chiefs.[53]

The slave-trading elites of Senegal and the Gold Coast initially reacted to this crisis through the strategy of evasion, clandestinely supplying transatlantic smugglers with slave cargos. The drawback of this option was that it entailed great risk. In areas such as the Bight of Benin and southern Senegambia, slave exports did not show a marked decrease, but Senegal and the Gold Coast did witness a massive decline in slave exports, indicating that smuggling was not the preferred option.[54] Again, this was due largely to the open nature of the coastline of both regions, which was largely devoid of the maze of creeks characterizing more successful smuggling environments. It soon became clear that the limited smuggling options could not handle the continuing supply of slaves to the coast, and significant numbers of slaves began to be retained in coastal towns and around former slave-trading posts.[55]

Theoretically, slave owners could have ceased to trade and own slaves entirely. However, this was not realistic. Slaves continued to be important assets for both Senegalese and Gold Coast elites. Thus, administration reports from as late as the 1830s and 1840s indicate that in neither area did slave imports to the coast decline. By 1836 around ten thousand slaves lived in St. Louis and Gorée, and importation into the colony from as far away as Galaam was still common.[56] Colonial Office sources for the Gold Coast similarly reported "a large body of persons held in slavery in the African forts" in 1841, as well as in the surrounding coastal polities.[57] However, in certain regions this excess became a valuable resource as slaves were reconverted from "product" to "producer" of raw materials as the abolition of the Atlantic slave trade nudged along an already existing commerce in "legitimate goods." Production of these goods had, to some extent, been retarded by the slave trade, since their production was generally regarded as less profitable than the trade in people. However, as Atlantic slave merchants began to turn away from slave trading or to avoid West Africa because of the high risk of capture by cruiser squadrons, the price of slaves dropped on the coast. This had the dual effect of diminishing the profits of slave trading and of making slaves more cheaply available to those needing labor to produce legitimate goods. The result was a growing diversion of slaves into an internal servility controlled by African and Euro-African entrepreneurs, in which the slaves became laborers in the production of export goods.

THE EUROPEAN PLAN TO RESOLVE THE CRISIS OF ABOLITION

Abolition was an act of the metropole, imposed from above on administrators, company officials, and Africans alike. Conversely, the wishes of the metropole had remarkably little impact on the day-to-day running of the African possessions. Not only was it recognized that administrators in Africa had more experience and knowledge than those in Europe, but the logistics of communication meant that the responsibility for carrying out initiatives and responding to challenges resided in officials in Africa. In the absence of telegraphs and telephones, and depending on the availability of passing ships and the vagaries of wind, it often took several months for inquiries to reach the metropole and be acted upon, and for replies to return to administrators.[58]

Both the French Ministry of the Navy and Colonies, which directly administered the St. Louis and its dependencies, and the Company of Merchants Trading to Africa, which exercised the queen's authority in the Gold Coast forts and up to a cannon shot away, were interested in promoting trade and cultivation.[59] In 1822 the French minister of the navy and colonies wrote to Baron Jacques-François Roger, the first French commander and administrator of Senegal, of "the firm intention of the government to encourage the development of cultivation . . . in Senegal."[60] Similarly, the Company of Merchants instructed Governor (Colonel) G. Torrane to instruct chiefs to "turn their thoughts to *Agriculture* and *Commerce* as the only means of obtaining [European goods]."[61] Thereafter, however, they gave their respective administrators great leeway to carry out their orders. However much the home offices were in favor of increased legitimate trading, and however much they wished they could meddle, the ball was obviously in the court of the administrators.[62]

On the Gold Coast, those officials were initially officers of the Company of Merchants.[63] For the most part, the company officials were merchants themselves, had themselves owned and dealt in slaves before the 1807 abolition, and had suffered in the decline following abolition.[64] They therefore had a vested interest in reinvigorating trade, and based on economic assumptions prevalent among the merchant classes of Europe at the time, the mechanism they chose for this regeneration was the plantation.

Most of the raw materials bound for England from the Americas came from plantations, but plantation cultivation had never really been successfully carried out on a large scale in western Africa, and the results of several experiments on the Gold Coast were far from inspiring. In 1778 the Danish entrepreneur and scientist Dr. Paul Isert had contracted for slave labor for an attempted coffee plantation on the Accra plains, but the plantation had failed after his death in 1789.[65] In the early nineteenth century, the Danish made further attempts to cultivate sugar, cotton, and tobacco, but failed because of damage done by Asante invaders and the kidnapping of slave laborers from the plantations.[66] The Dutch—who were more sympathetic to the Asante and might have avoided their aggressions—failed to make a concerted effort to reinvigorate trade at their posts during the abolition crisis. The Company of Merchants, however, was not dissuaded. Attempting to learn from the Danish failures, the officers of the Company of Merchants planned to promote coffee cultivation in midsized, independent plantations around each of the coastal forts, where they would be well protected. It was believed that the local populace would soon see the profitability of this venture. "Let the people dependent on our Forts employ their free time clearing small spots of Ground for Coffee Plantations, for their own sole emolument. The Free Natives will soon . . . follow the example," argued the company's board of directors in London.[67]

During the same period, the French government was also searching for a marketable commodity to replace the slave trade as a money earner for the colony. The gum trade revived somewhat after abolition, to the delight of the habitants, but, alone, it could not justify the continuing expense of the colony to the French government. Baron Jacques François Roger, in his 1821 official memoirs, retrospectively noted that "during the abolition . . . gum . . . nearly exclusively . . . commanded the attention of commerce."[68] The minuscule French settlements—St. Louis, Gorée, and a few small factories along various waterways—comprised very little arable land, and Roger believed that only cash-crop cultivation could save the colony. Therefore, at the beginning of Roger's term in 1819, attempts were made to buy land from Waalo aristocrats, and the minister of the navy accepted a plan based upon the establishment of privately leased plantations outside the colony, to be worked by wage laborers.[69] Thus, the conclusion reached by both European administrations—French and British—was that cultivation by plantation was the key to economic success for their colonies.

PALM OIL AND SLAVE LABOR ON THE GOLD COAST

In the event, cash-crop production did intensify in the Gold Coast, but not in the manner in which the Company of Merchants had conceived. The failure of coffee-plantation schemes became apparent quite quickly, as Akan and Ga-Adangme producers judged that demand did not justify having small coffee plantations protected by British cannons. Instead, farmers in the eastern interior quickly seized on a commodity in high demand in industrial Britain—the viscous fats produced by the oil palm. As the demand for palm oil rose, farmers began to convert significant portions of the forest to plantations, a task that required significant labor. Although lineage-based production probably continued to dominate both this bush-clearing process and palm-oil processing, large numbers of slaves were also diverted into these jobs.

Slave prices on the Gold Coast had continued to fall after 1807; in some accounts purchasers were paying as little as three ounces of gold for an adult slave—less than a third of the 1803 price.[70] This phenomenon made slave owning affordable for the first time for farmers and traders outside the urban merchant class and the chiefly elite, although it was still out of reach for most peasants. Prices stayed low for about a decade before recovering around 1820 as internal demand grew.[71] Measurable agricultural exports, stagnant until late in the second decade of the 1800s, began to rise as oil-palm plantations were being brought on line, and the recovery of slave prices is one indication of the gradual expansion of palm-oil farms in the interior Adangme state of Krobo and to a lesser extent in the Akan state of Akuapem.

Palm oil had been imported from West Africa to Britain for decades. The orange pulp extracted from the seed of certain African palms was useful in making soap and other household products. But the sudden increase in demand was attributable to another of its qualities. Palm oil, both from the fruit and the kernel, is a superb machine lubricant, and in the nineteenth century, Britain was rapidly industrializing. In 1818, the first year in which export figures are clear, Great Britain imported 29,310 cwt. (hundredweight), or 1,641 tons, of treated palm oil. By 1821, imports had reached 102,490 cwt. (5,739 tons) and seemed destined to continue to rise.[72] These bright prospects attracted to the Gold Coast middlemen and farmers, who saw the boom in palm oil coming long before locally based European merchants began to pick up on it.

However, the regions of Krobo and Akuapem that first capitalized on this trend, and hence had most of the newly planted oil palms, were located in an area of the interior that was especially susceptible to Asante attacks. Asante-British relations had deteriorated in the decade following Asante's 1807 occupation of the Fante polities, during which British administrators may have clandestinely supported Fante rebels from British headquarters at Cape Coast. Despite an 1817 treaty aimed at reconciling the two powers, tensions rose following the failure of the ambassador to the asantehene's court, Joseph Dupuis, to bring an acceptable treaty back to London. Opposition from the Company of Merchants Trading to Africa, which held the charter for the settlements until 1821, effectively killed the treaty in Parliament.[73] Thus, between 1821 and 1830, British Crown officials, and later the Committee of Merchants, saw the first fruits of this fledgling economic recovery disappearing in the face of Asante raids.[74] In exasperation, the committee installed a new governor, Captain George Maclean, in 1830 with a mandate to restore commerce by any means possible. Maclean offered the asantehene, Osei Yaw, a truce, promising to safeguard his commercial access to the Atlantic through the coastal states, thereby satisfying his most important demand.[75] Also signatory were a number of rulers of polities "allied" with Britain—eight of the Fante paramounts, now firmly in the British camp, as well as the rulers of Denkyira, Wassaw, Assin, Twifo, and Amanahia. A similar treaty was signed between the Asante and the Danish in the next year.[76] Thus, 1831 ushered in an unprecedented peace, allowing palm-oil production to flourish in the interior.

By the late 1830s, the maturing palm-oil plantations began to require even more slave labor. Palm-oil production was labor-intensive, especially as the oil had to be expressed and treated prior to export.[77] Because even extended families could not supply all the labor necessary on export-oriented farms, slaves were incorporated into the process. Despite the fact that slave purchase prices rose with demand in the 1820s and 1830s, slave labor was still cheaper than wage labor and land was largely available to free members of the community. Some scholars have argued that palm oil cultivation "took place within the framework of traditional agriculture," but it is clear that slaves had, in fact, begun to play an important role in the production of this commodity.[78] Cruickshank, for example, personally observed that slaves sold in Krobo and Akuapem by Asante traders were used by the palm-oil industry,[79] and more recently Inez Sutton has shown that there was an ownership connection between slave laborers on plantations in Akuapem and their owners based in Accra.[80] However, it is from Basel Mission sources in Krobo that the most compelling evidence comes.

Some of this information deals with Ologo Patu, the *konor,* or paramount chief, of the Yilo Krobo state. In 1851 Patu was fined one thousand *kabes* by a magistrate for not appearing in a court case.[81] It was known, of course, that the konor possessed a massive number of slaves, but his ability to produce palm oil in order to pay off the fine surprised even the local Basel Mission agents, who discovered that his wives processed palm oil "all year round" on a central farm.[82] The oil was cultivated on an extensive series of oil-palm plantations surrounding this central site, throughout which were spread *crooms,* or hamlets, for his "slaves and children."[83]

By the mid-1860s the evidence for slave labor on oil-palm plantations is even more compelling. During the middle third of the nineteenth century, Krobo merchants had developed a system of *huzas,* rectangular-strip oil-palm plantations, somewhat distant from the Krobo heartland.[84] Slaves worked on these new farms to clear the bush, planting young oil palms alongside food crops. While these oil palms developed over a period of three to five years, foodstuffs grown between and in the shade of the palms not only fed the cultivators but also were transported into the towns and sold in markets. These young plantations were cleared and at least initially worked mainly by slaves who "produce[d] a rich harvest for themselves and their heads of family."[85] After the palms matured, their produce provided a further profit for the slaves' masters. A missionary Roes noted that the slaves lived in meager huts and worked "mostly naked" in the fields, and that free laborers worked among them.[86] Joseph Mohr noted that by the mid-1850s families in Akuapem were "retaining their slaves in order to make a lot of palm oil" as well.[87] Moreover, as both Krobo and Akuapem lacked the navigable rivers that made transportation of palm oil in some West African regions relatively cheap, and since pack animals were not available in the forest zone, human porterage was the only alternative for carrying treated oil and nuts to the coast. These porters probably included a significant proportion of slaves. Ologo Patu is known to have been able to send as many as two hundred "people" to the coast at a time.[88]

Nor was a transformation in slaveholding limited to these eastern oil-producing states. In Accra, as well, small-scale slaveholding appears to have grown as "even small farmers, fishermen, and women petty traders often [owned] one or two slaves."[89] Similarly, John Parker points to the rise during this period of Euro-African merchants, *owula,* whose political prominence owed something to their ownership of large bodies of slaves working plantations outside Accra.[90] Several plantations were actually oriented toward the production of coffee, promoted by the British and Danish administrations and succored by Basel missionaries who arrived in the Gold Coast in 1828, having been invited by the Danish administrator of Accra in 1826.[91] The mostly German Basel missionaries' ideals were "shaped by the doctrines of Württemburg pietism, which stressed the ideal of self-contained rural communities of 'scholar farmers,'" and hence, John Parker has argued, they "distrusted what [they] considered to be the morally corrupting urban milieu of Accra." Failing to establish a significant congregation in Accra, they quickly spread into the eastern interior, especially the oil-producing regions of Akuapem and Krobo, and later Akyem Abuakwa.[92]

In 1840 the society began to cultivate coffee on a model farm in Domonasi in support of the continuing British initiative to promote coffee and fruit cultivation among indigenous planters.[93] This operation took on a distinctly evangelical air under the influence of the Basel missionaries. At Domonasi, autochthonous leaders were invited to observe the entire coffee preparation operation, and were encouraged to take seeds, equipment, and knowledge back to their communities.[94] But, ironically, the few coffee plantations, mostly on the plains of Accra, that did arise from this effort used the very labor that abolition was intended to end. The largest plantations, owned by Euro-African merchants Swanzy, Lutterodt, and others, appear to have been worked mainly by gangs of slaves.[95]

Admittedly, Krobo, Accra, and to a lesser extent Akuapem represent extreme examples of economic transformation and the introduction of a slave mode of production on the Gold Coast. For much of the rest of the region, "legitimate commerce" for overseas export remained a distant prospect and slave owning an economically marginal activity. However, such evidence as that for Ologo Patu must be contrasted with the arguments of historians such as Edward Reynolds, who has argued for a gradualist interpretation of the impact of abolition. Reynolds argues that "African societies in the [Gold Coast] had traditional institutions which were inimical to easy integration with the international exchange economy," and that initial experiments at transformation served only to slowly create the conditions necessary for large-scale cash-crop cultivation in the 1890s and beyond.[96]

Instead, the half-century following British abolition of the slave trade should be viewed as having had a significant impact on the use of slaves and the production of cash crops for at least the eastern third of the Gold Coast. The internal sale of slaves, previously directed toward domestic and stool slavery, easily expanded to incorporate the dealing of slaves for agricultural use after 1807. Maclean's peace of 1831 further facilitated the commercialization of agriculture, to which slave and pawn labor was directed.[97] Abolition, rather than ending slavery, facilitated its replacement by an indigenous market that furthered the integration of servile labor into the capitalist production system. The next few decades would see a continuation of this shift.

THE FAILURE OF PLANTATIONS IN SENEGAL

There are certain parallels between the situation of the merchants and aristocrats of the Wolof and Sereer states, along with their compatriots in St. Louis and Gorée, and those of their counterparts along the Gold Coast, following the abolition of the export trade in slaves. As for the Gold Coast, in Senegal there was also a similar potential savior in the form of an oil crop—in this case peanuts — although admittedly somewhat later. It was not until 1829 that the first shipments of peanuts from British Gambia were reported, and it was around the same period that French merchants became interested in these "oily nuts."[98] In December 1828 a group of merchants urged Governor Jean Quillaume Jubelu in St. Louis to purchase a peanut oil press for the colony, although there was still little interest among peasant cultivators.[99] The level of interest rose, however, as habitants searched for a replacement for the gum trade that was again in decline, and by 1840 the administration had begun to grant groundnut concessions to habitants.[100] This expansion was matched by a growing acceptance of peanut oil in French commerce and industry, evidenced by demands from Parisian *commerçants* for a reduction in the peanut-oil tariff in 1843.[101] For the period prior to the 1850s, I have been able to uncover little evidence of a role for slaves in this agricultural revolution, which was dominated mainly by an increasingly Muslim class of peasant producers.

In fact, it seems that after 1818 the coastal towns of Senegal, in contrast to the Gold Coast, did not see the stockpiling of large numbers of slaves in the early nineteenth century. There are three reasons for this. As suggested in chapter 1, this northern portion of Senegambia had become even more marginal in the Atlantic slave trade by the early nineteenth century than the Gold Coast had, probably contributing only several hundred slaves annually. Additionally, most of the captives shipped to the coast came from far in the interior and could be easily diverted down the Gambia River, rather than the Senegal River.[102] Most importantly, however, the trans-Saharan route remained open to the shipment of slaves, and James Webb has suggested that slaves earmarked for the coast were probably sidetracked to this still-important route.[103] For many French merchant houses, however, abolition was still something of a crisis, and the Ministry of the Navy hit upon a plan for salvation similar to that proposed for the Gold Coast, and at the center of this plan were the habitants.

The habitant communities of St. Louis and Gorée had used the confusion of the revolution and the Napoleonic wars to make significant inroads into the power of the French companies. Before 1789 trade from the Senegalese coast had been controlled by French companies who had received a royal mandate to trade in slaves and gum. The last of these was the Compagnie commercial d'Afrique, which was given an exclusive patent in 1774.[104] The habitants chafed under the heavy hand of this monopoly, which kept them from freely selling their slaves, gum, and millet to transatlantic merchants. In 1789, as the Estates Generales were considering their cahier, the St. Louisian habitants terminated their contracts to provide slaves for the company. Within the year, the Estates Generales had granted the community a modicum of self-government, with popular suffrage for all landowners, under the authority of a mayor (*maire*), who replaced the company-appointed municipal magistrate.[105]

As a form of civil administration, the office of mayor came to assume an important role, both in St. Louis and later in Gorée as well. By the end of the 1820s the two mayors were largely responsible for hygiene and petty justice. They were important intermediaries with the surrounding populations and were given a monopoly on recruiting labor, interpreters, and clerks for the French authorities.[106] In 1824 their power was expanded still further to include policing the town and exercising judicial authority over slaves and unpropertied Africans, and their position as middlemen with neighboring states was formalized.[107] In 1829 Governor Jubelu informed the minister that the mayor of St. Louis had been charged with ensuring that unregistered slaves were not illegally brought onto the island.[108] In 1819 the Euro-African trader Michel Pellegrin represented France in peace negotiations with the Trarza Moors.[109]

It is no surprise, therefore, that Baron Julien Schmaltz, the administrator and commander charged with making Senegal profitable again, should turn to the habitants for assistance in identifying a location in which to promote his scheme of developing cash-crop plantations. The desired elements for the target location were cheap labor, available land, and easy transportation. Schmaltz first considered the vast expanse of Fuuta Tooro, where he planned that land would be rented by the administration and turned over to habitants and French entrepreneurs who would purchase laborers from local chiefs.[110] However, the rulers of the Fuuta perceived the proposal as a cover for French expansion, and the plan fell through.[111] Schmaltz therefore transferred his attention to Waalo, which was both proximate to St. Louis and relatively fertile, and asked the mayor to negotiate a treaty with the *brak* (king) of Waalo in 1819.[112] By the provisions of this treaty, the French agreed to pay an annual fee in return for land suitable for cultivation and the brak's aid in recruiting labor.

The brak agreed to the treaty largely because he saw the French as an ally against the Trarza Moors who persisted in raiding Waalo for slaves and booty.[113]

However, although the treaty stipulated that the chiefs of Waalo would provide laborers and replace runaways, the brak felt no real need to enforce this stipulation in an already tight labor market, and the French were forced to turn to the habitants to provide laborers.[114] The habitant community, however, refused to divert their slaves from high-paying commercial labor to low-paying cultivation work.[115] The administration thus found itself in a quandary, forbidden by royal decree from owning slaves and unable to find free labor.[116] Searching for a solution, Schmaltz was faced with a second problem. As the antislavery squadron came into operation, captives freed from slave ships were beginning to accumulate in the two coastal cities. In 1818 a fortunate event provided the possibility of solving both problems.

This catalytic event was the seizure of the slave brig *De Postillion* in early 1818.[117] The ship was carrying a number of captives, of whom at least twenty-six appear to have survived, and the administration was loathe to pay for their support. Thus they were placed in the hands of the mayor for employment "on works of public utility," mostly in the St. Louis hospital.[118] However, as the labor shortage in Waalo became more apparent, they were redeployed to the agricultural projects. By 1823 eight of them were working on the colony's plantations at Richard-Tol and at the *habitation royale* (royal plantation), effectively transforming them into field laborers.[119]

The act to formalize this forced labor of ostensibly freed *recaptives* was written by Governor Roger, who had replaced Schmaltz in 1822 and was prompted by the metropole's growing concern for Senegal's commercial future. The Ministry of the Navy had approved the use of freed slaves in January 1822, provided they were treated as free laborers and definitively manumitted after fourteen years of labor for the government.[120] This system of indenture, in which the laborers were known as *engagés à temps,* was sanctioned by an 1823 ordinance. Engagés were to be appropriated from among captives confiscated from slave ships or brought illegally into the colony for the government's use as laborers. They were to be engaged for fourteen years or until the age of twenty-one if minors. However, this act contained a flaw with unforeseen consequences: article 4 did not limit indenture to the government but permitted its extension to private individuals in some cases.[121]

By 1825, in addition to Crown holdings, there were thirty-four private plantations in Waalo. Many of the owners were French, but a considerable number appear to have been St. Louisian habitants.[122] With considerably more than six hundred hectares under cultivation, these establishments were of significant size. The administration's plantations added approximately 230 hectares. The number of engagés working the private plantations is unknown, but approxima-tions can be teased out from the records. In January 1823 the government had thirty-six engagés working its four plantations; by the end of 1824 that number was up to seventy-two.[123] During the next four years the total number of gov-ernment engagés hovered around one hundred, but it is uncertain how many of those worked in the fields.[124] A number were deployed by the administration in boat crews and as construction workers. Similarly, between 1823 and 1839 there were 213 individuals engaged to private subjects in Gorée.[125] In total throughout the colony there were 2,930 indentures between 1818 and 1842.[126] A proportion of the government indentures were for purposes other than culti-vation, and some engagés acquired by private individuals were used as domestic servants, but clearly a large number of engagés were used as field hands. It is unfortunate that the names of purchasers are missing from the St. Louis records, as these could reveal a link between plantation owners and indentures. How-ever, from the Gorée documents it is clear that the family of Jean Pierre, who owned a twenty-one-hectare plantation at Lampsar, acquired twenty-nine en-gagés in 1835, the majority of whom were young males suitable for cultivation labor.[127] Nevertheless, even the influx of laborers brought by the engagé system was never enough for the plantations, despite Roger's 1826 claims of success.[128] By 1827 most of the privately held plantations had failed,[129] and in 1831 the gov-ernment's plantations were abandoned.[130] In 1837 the last private cultivators gave up.[131]

   The failure of the plantation scheme was the result of an alliance of elites who opposed the plantations. As early as September 1819 the Trarzas had re-voked their treaty with the French and begun raiding Waalo villages.[132] In the following decade, several peace agreements were reached, but none held for long. In addition, the aristocracy of Waalo was not firmly behind the French. Part of the explanation for this lay in mistranslations in the 1819 treaty. The French believed they had purchased arable land. The Wolof understanding, however, was that the land had only been leased, and several landowners dis-puted French claims so strongly that in 1827 a gunboat had to be placed on the Senegal River.[133] In addition, the peasantry of Waalo was increasingly coming under the influence of Muslim leaders from the east and north. In 1830 the mara-bout Diile Faatim Tyam Kumba declared a holy war and invaded Waalo. The invasion was quickly defeated, but added greatly to the confusion in the re-gion.[134] Without the habitant's laborers and slave-soldiers, the French could not hang on to the region, and the majority of the habitants proved unwilling to help the administration. It is possible that leaders among the habitants, including the mayor, saw the plantations as threatening peace in the region and as potentially alienating the Trarza. This would have cut off the gum trade, which was a much surer source of income than the French agricultural experiments.[135]

The great majority of the region's gum arabic was cultivated in Mauritania, significantly upriver from St. Louis. The workforce was composed at least partly of unfree gangs of laborers.[136] In fact, it seems probable that at least a portion of the surplus of captives created by the abolition of the oceanic slave trade had been redirected to feed the growing demand for laborers in these orchards.[137] The habitants, already denied their lucrative position in the Atlantic slave trade, now depended on this flourishing gum trade, and they accordingly failed to assist the French, instead carefully tending their relationships with the Trarzas.[138] The French were therefore forced to abandon plantations, but they did so relatively unscathed. Waalo, on the other hand, was left with a civil conflict involving aristocratic ceddo, a rising Islamic force supported by peasants, and Trarza invaders. After 1840, and with the advent of groundnut cultivation, the effects of this destabilization would become more pronounced, widespread, and significant.

A PREVIEW OF EMANCIPATION: THE *RÉGIME DES ENGAGÉS*

The *régime des engagés* (engagé system) was originally conceived as a system of employing captives, seized from illegal slave traders, in agricultural production for fourteen years of indenture to be followed by a definitive manumission. This institutionalized "liberation," while gradual, must have seemed almost honorable, even to abolitionists. However, the 1823 ordinance that institutionalized *engagement* in practice allowed engagés to fall into the hands of private individuals.[139] This, together with the labor and military demands of colony and empire, was to expropriate the system over the next twenty years, transforming the régime des engagés into a form of institutional slavery open to abuses by both the administration and elites. Conversely, the regulations governing engagement also provided a loophole for some slaves to seek their freedom. This grand experiment presaged the struggles of the postemancipation period as the metropole's intentions were subsumed by the practical needs of the administration, the manipulation of the habitants defending their dominant position, and the limited agency of slaves.

French abolitionism was at its height in the 1820s, and the régime des engagés was apparently perceived as an acceptable alternative to slavery by abolitionists. French activists even went so far as to suggest that the system be adapted to replace domestic and agricultural slavery: "It seems to me . . . that the city of St. Louis, which is the seat of your administration, would have a great interest in not employing or possessing slaves, and substituting *engagés* for service with families, in small cultivation, and in commerce."[140]

The commonly held sentiment that the régime des engagés represented an "egalitarian, honourable, and useful" alternative to the slave trade lent a moral dimension to the plan and facilitated two major permutations.[141] First, the idea that the habitants could be induced to replace slavery with engagement led to article 4 of the 1823 ordinance allowing private ownership of engagés. Equally importantly, this concept facilitated a shift in the mode of acquisition of engagés by the government from confiscation to purchase.

The French administration appears to have purchased its first slave under this system in April 1818, when an eighteen-year-old male slave named Amadu was acquired in a deal with a slave owner in St. Louis.[142] However, the majority of engagés continued to be acquired through confiscation until the system was opened to private owners in 1822 (see table 2.1), following which alternative sources were explored.[143] Between 1825 and 1829 the administration hired the Compagnie de Galam to purchase at least 433 slaves, mostly Bambaras, from the interior, representing 14 percent or more of all engagés during this period.[144] In the 1830s the government also attempted to purchase outright privately owned slaves who performed well while under contract to the administration. There are several cases of slaves who were rented by the government to work in the hospital, for example, who were subsequently purchased from their masters in 1837 and 1838 and converted into engagés.[145]

Engagés were used by the government not only as labor on plantations, but also as boat, construction, and especially hospital workers.[146] By 1840 the régime des engagés was so central to labor recruitment in Senegal that the administrative body of Senegal Colony, the *conseil d'administration* (administrative council), agreed unanimously that it could not be ended without threatening both the commerce and the defense of the colony.[147]

Defense was an important issue for the French administration, especially since European soldiers easily succumbed to African diseases. Therefore, in 1819 Schmaltz suggested that liberated slaves be used first as workers for engineer platoons and then as enlisted soldiers.[148] In order to induce recruits to join, a signing bonus was promised. Yet, in practice, as the government failed to recruit free Africans, this money often simply represented the fee to masters who turned their slaves over to French authorities.

TABLE 2.1

Engagés Registered in Senegal Colony, 1818–1846

Year	Patron	Number of engagés	Source
1818	Government (all)	25	a
1819	Government (all)	0	a
1820	Government (all)	1	a
1821	Government (all)	40	a
1822	All	145	a
1823	All	175	a
1824	All	170	a
1825	All	183	a
1826	All	219	a
1827	All	183	a
1828	All	207	a
1829	All	104	a
1830	All	105	a
1831	All	126	a
1832	All	48	a
1833	All	93	a
1834	All	151	a
1835	All	172	a
1836	All	145	a
1837	All	54	a
1838	All	99	a
1839	All	160	a
1840	All	98	a
1841	All	120	a
1842	All	107	a
1843	Government	44	b
1844	Gorée (private)	27	c
1844	St. Louis (all)	185	d/e
1845–46	All	39	f
TOTAL		3,225	

Sources:

a: ANSOM Sénégal XIV/21, Relevé des nombre des Rachats suivis d'affranchissement conditionnel, Decarrett, May 31, 1843, St. Louis.

b: ANSOM Sénégal XIV/20, Bouet à Ministre, February 23, 1843, St. Louis.

c: ANSOM Sénégal XIV/21, Matricule des engagés à temps de Gorée, January 2, 1844.

d: ANSOM Sénégal XIV/21, Affranchissements Conditionnels par le Gouvernment pendant l'année 1844, Decarret, St. Louis.

e: ANSOM Sénégal XIV/21, Affranchissements Conditionnels par diverse de St. Louis pendant l'année 1844, Decarret, St. Louis.

f: ANSOM Sénégal XIV/21, Matricule des engagés, l'année 1846, St. Louis.

The practicality of this arrangement later helped "convince" authorities in the metropole of the moral righteousness of this policy of *rachats* (repurchases) when in 1827 the policy of rachats was taken a step further.[149] The abolition of slavery had led to a labor shortage throughout the French Empire. Consequently, in April that year, the minister ordered Governor Gerbidon to investigate the formation of a battalion of six hundred men, not only for domestic service, but also for use overseas in Madagascar and French Guyana. He left the mode of recruitment open to the governor's discretion.[150] Gerbidon chose to purchase slaves for the usual indenture of fourteen years, train them, and put them on ships without disclosing their destination.[151] The parallels to the slave trade were evident to contemporary abolitionists. In 1828 a letter was published in the liberal antislavery merchant paper *Journal de Commerce* that charged that the "slave trade is recommencing in Senegal . . . and the government itself is conducting this trade."[152] The government's response, in the royalist *Messenger des Chambres,* was to argue that the engagement, for a limited period, was a vast improvement for recruits who had formerly been slaves, and that the soldiers would help enforce the abolition of slavery in Madagascar.[153]

The blandishments of the abolitionist press had little effect on the recruiting system. Between 1828 and 1848, rachats remained the primary recruiting tool for French Senegal. In 1828 the blueprint for a military contingent called the *compagnie des noirs* was developed. It was conceived that this entirely African unit would take on much of the responsibility for the security of St. Louis. In 1832 King Louis-Phillipe approved Fr 65,681 to pay for the enlistment, armament, and training of the company, although the unit did not become fully independent until 1836.[154] There were to be two types of recruits: volunteers enrolled for seven years and slaves "ransomed" by the government from the interior and indentured for fourteen years.[155] As it turned out, no volunteers enrolled, and the 119 members of the unit in 1845 were all engagés.[156] Furthermore, they had all been acquired under an exclusive contract in which the Compagnie de Galam undertook to recruit Bambaras at Bakel.[157] This forced movement of unfree individuals from the interior to St. Louis is strikingly similar to the forced migration, along the same path, that occurred during the Atlantic slave trade. In seeking to replace the system that provided labor during the Atlantic slave trade, the French response was essentially to emulate it.

The commercial elite of Senegal Colony, the habitants, also managed to profit from the crisis that initially threatened to destroy their power. Habitants were initially opposed to the engagés, whom they feared would threaten the rental market for slave artisans.[158] From 1820, however, they had begun to acquire engagés for themselves. Post-1824 registers, especially, reveal a pattern of acquisition of individual engagés by private Africans and Euro-Africans, whereas important habitant families and European companies such as Maurel & Prom often owned as many as forty.[159] Although acquired legally as engagés, these individuals were often treated as slaves. Unable to command their own labor or seek their freedom, engagés were often reported as deceased and reintroduced into the slave market when prices rose.[160] Most of the others were retained past their fourteen-year term. A comparison of the number of definitive manumissions after fourteen years, in table 2.2, with the number of engagés initially registered, in table 2.1, gives some idea of the disparity between the figures.

TABLE 2.2

Liberations after Fourteen Years, 1831–1841

Year	Definitive liberations
1831	50
1832	4
1833	2
1834	4
1835	8
1836	12
1837	4
1838	6
1839	4
1840	3
1841	5
TOTAL	102

Source: ANSOM Sénégal XIV/21, Relevé des nombre des Rachats suivis d'affranchissement conditionnel, Decarrett, May 31, 1843, St. Louis.

Although death and desertion undoubtedly claimed many engagés, table 2.2 shows that in the first eleven years, only 7 percent of the engagés reported in table 2.1 appear to have been definitively liberated fourteen years later, a suspiciously low number. This abuse drew the notice of abolitionists and some administration officials, although condemnation was strongest in the metropole.[161] In 1827 Roger introduced an ordinance requiring patrons to account for engagés, instituting punishment for missing engagés, and requiring that new engagés be informed of their rights, but enforcement appears to have been lax.[162]

In response to pressure from the metropole to address this problem, Governor Louis-Edouard Bouët-Willaumez overlooked his own opposition and that of the conseil d'administration[163] and reluctantly drafted an ordinance forbidding the introduction of engagés into the colony as of March 1, 1844, excepting military recruits.[164] The ordinance, like so many before it, was never properly implemented, and debate continued. Opponents argued that ending the regime would lead to a revival of slavery, despite the fact that it had never significantly decreased.[165] This argument nevertheless ensured that the system continued until 1846, when a new law was passed to replace the 1844 ordinance, and the régime des engagés was finally ended.[166]

I have argued that engagés ended up being, in many ways, de facto slaves. Their situation was similar to the slaves' in that they had no control over their own labor and no freedom to leave employment, at least for fourteen years. Thus, they had few options. Engagés could simply attempt to serve their fourteen years, hoping for freedom, but we know that many were never liberated. If they worked for the government they could attempt to gain an early release for "good behavior," although examples of this parole are thinly spread in the historical record.[167] Engagés could, and did, run away—a common strategy for slaves as well. There is evidence of desertion as early as 1818, but exact numbers are not known.[168] Certainly it was difficult for those recruited by the Compagnie de Galam from the interior to return home through high-risk areas in which they were likely simply to be captured and reenslaved.

What is even more interesting is that the system of engagés provided an opportunity for slaves. Slaves and engagés worked alongside one another, and just as masters converted engagés into slaves, slaves often pretended to be engagés and claimed their freedom from authorities.[169] It is unclear exactly how this worked, but it appears that slaves would pretend to be an engagé who had previously been owned by their own masters, who had been sold, had deserted, or had died. In the era before photography validated identity papers, this subterfuge could have succeeded. By 1844 there was a significant number of such cases, but administrators usually decided against the alleged slave-turned-engagé.[170] The exact number of cases cannot be determined, as there are no quantitative legal records for this period. Additionally, the usually pro-habitant officials may have perceived as cases of impersonation some cases in which masters attempted to retain engagés fraudulently by alleging that the engagés were slaves.

The impact of abolition was distributed unevenly in West Africa. For the chiefly officeholders of the Gold Coast and the aristocracy and ceddo of Senegal, the effect was quite pronounced, threatening their profitable control over slave exports. For the European companies that interacted with them, abolition similarly threatened profitability, and the European presence on the coast was consequently initially reduced.

It has been proposed for both regions that the result of abolition was the diminishment of the power of these "traditional" elites at the expense of merchant classes who were more flexible. The long-term response of these merchants and trading communities was to replace the slave trade with a commerce in "legitimate" goods, which it was fortunate was becoming feasible just as abolition was being implemented. The British and French governments encouraged this activity. However, their schemes for putting these plans into action invariably consisted of encouraging the establishment of plantations near the coastal forts to grow export crops. In both the Gold Coast and Senegal, administration officials reckoned without the agency and abilities of indigenous elites. Initially, chiefs and merchants organized an illegal slave trade and diverted slave caravans to areas in which abolition was not enforced. For Senegal, with its Sahelian frontier, this was a somewhat effective strategy, but not so for the Gold Coast. There, merchants moved quickly to exploit the British demand for palm oil by sponsoring organized production in Akuapem and Krobo, while failing to join in the scheme to grow coffee along the coast. The habitants' role in sabotaging the Waalo plantations that threatened their expanding interests in the gum trade can be seen as a similar promotion of their own interests.

Politically, one result was the growing involvement of the British and French governments in these two regions. The British Crown assumed control of the possessions on the Gold Coast from 1822 to 1828 and again, definitively, in 1843. They also began to meddle in local politics by negotiating treaties with Asante. The French government similarly invested heavily in Waalo. The growing peanut industry, although its crops were not usually worked by slaves, would exacerbate this trend in the 1850s. Through these moves, the great powers were drawn toward expansive colonialism in both regions.

The crisis of abolition certainly never threatened to end slavery within these sections of Africa. Abolition and the subsequent rise in legitimate commerce, rather than replacing slavery with wage labor, showed that institutions of captivity were resilient enough to survive and thrive.

Prohibitions on the official use of slaves also meant that the colonial state began to experience labor shortages. The French system of engagés à temps was initially intended to replace slave labor with freed captives who were conditionally liberated under a fourteen-year indenture. However, the manpower requirements of the French government and the active involvement of habitants led to its transformation into a regime under which more than three thousand individuals were placed in a servile relationship, and only a small proportion were eventually liberated. Although some slaves exhibited agency in attempting to use the system to gain their liberation, the system of engagés remained a relationship of dependency that was slavery in all but name. This type of interaction between slaves, slave owners, colonial officials, and the metropole, allowing the institution of slavery to stave off externally generated challenges, presaged later resolutions of continuing attempts by European capitals to reform slavery from without.

CHAPTER 3
Rules and Reality
Anteproclamation Slavery and Society on the Gold Coast

AT FIRST GLANCE, it could be argued that in the period following the abolition of the Atlantic slave trade, the policies of the administration of the Gold Coast gradually paved the way for full emancipation. In this teleological view, anteproclamation policies represented a deliberate attempt to reduce the central role of slavery within society in preparation for the introduction of capitalism and wage labor. In fact, however, the several reforms of the period 1807–1874 formed not a series of methodical and planned steps, but instead a series of experiments that—despite a string of external edicts and the interference of an enlarged missionary community—failed to transform dependency relationships for the majority of slaves and slave owners.

This argument is not intended to imply that the events of this period were marginal to the process of emancipation. During these crucial years, various modes of liberation were explored by members of servile classes. Organizations of traditional and educated elites that would be crucial in organizing postproclamation resistance coalesced, and the attitudes and strategies that would be applied by government and missionary agents in the postproclamation period were formulated and discussed. On a regional level, British influence increased at the expense of other European powers, eventually paving the way for British hegemony on the coast. Similarly, the continuing ambitions of Asante to establish a secure presence on the coast clearly marked them as Britain's nemesis in a conflict that would play itself out in the last quarter of the century. Thus the interior and coastal states of the Gold Coast were actors in a cycle of conflict and détente that would in 1874 culminate in the imposition of increased British military and civil power, and consequently lead to the imposition of antislavery laws.

However, although important social and economic factors coalesced during this period, slavery was not really any closer to its end in 1873 than it was in 1807, and even on the latter date, the chief justice of the still-diminutive Gold Coast Colony would defend the policy of turning away refugee slaves in recognition of the rights of slave owners in neighboring territories.[1] Nor, during this period, was it clear that indigenous elites would simply accept the potential imposition of British laws restricting slavery. It would take the shock of the 1873 Sangreti (Anglo-Asante) War, and the attention it focused on the region, to cause a radical departure from previous policy and thereby genuinely usher in emancipation.

RESTRICTING SLAVE OWNERSHIP IN THE WAKE OF THE 1834 EMANCIPATION

Slavery lost its legal recognition in most parts of the British Empire when the 1833 Act for the Abolition of Slavery in the British Colonies, which provided for the abolition of slavery by August 1, 1834, was introduced.[2] All slaves in regions under British suzerainty henceforth were "absolutely and forever manumitted."[3] In the confusion surrounding the promulgation of this act, Governor George Maclean, acting for the Committee of Merchants, wrote to the Colonial Office for clarification as to how the 1833 act applied to the Gold Coast.[4] The response, embodied by a royal order in council, was that it did not. The great "philanthropic" act applied only to Crown colonies—Antigua, Bermuda, Bahamas, St. Christopher, Dominica, Grenada, St. Lucia, Trinidad, Mauritius, and the Cape Colony.[5] Consequently, Maclean was allowed great leeway in dealing with slavery. Other than requiring the chief's signatory to the treaty of 1831 to restrict panyarring, Maclean himself declined entirely to interfere with slave owning among the settlements' allies and neighbors.[6]

The officials of the Committee of Merchants initially tried to ignore the 1833 act, just as they had ignored abolitionist pressure, exerted as early as 1807, to forbid Europeans from owning slaves. Even within the forts, company officers continued to hold and use slaves.[7] After the committee, responding to abolitionist pressure, forced this practice underground in the late 1830s, officers simply purchased debt contracts from African merchants and became the "patrons," and de facto masters, of large numbers of pawns.[8] Although Maclean's administration was largely absolved of responsibility for this state of affairs by the Parliamentary Committee on West Africa in 1842,[9] such abuses were one reason that the Colonial Office, sensitive to the abolitionist lobby, brought the possessions back under Crown control in 1843.[10]

The Act for the More Effectual Suppression of the Slave Trade of that year was also a response to the state of affairs both in the Gold Coast and other West African possessions. The act "extend[ed] and appl[ied] to British subjects wheresoever residing" provisions of previous acts, including those regarding dealing in slaves, importing slaves, and holding slaves and pawns.[11] Although the act applied only to Europeans, Maclean's successor, Governor R. M. Worsley Hill (RN),[12] was immediately faced with a number of Fante and Ga-Adangme chiefs who were laboring under the impression that their slaves were to be confiscated.[13] The apprehensive Hill quickly reassured them that their slave-owning rights had never been at issue. He further informed them that "the slave-trade was all that we prohibited," a patent untruth.[14]

The administration did not again attempt to extend the prohibition against slave owning until 1851, when another governor — Major Stephen Hill — issued a proclamation on the advice of his executive committee withdrawing legal recognition of the institution of slaveholding for "educated natives" of the Cape Coast, Accra, and Anomabu. This act had an economic, rather than moral, motivation. The British merchants represented on the committee simply felt these Euro-African and African traders held an unfair advantage over their European competitors through their access to slave labor. However, both Hill and the committee members were stunned by the indigenous response to the act. The paramount chief of the Cape Coast immediately recalled laborers he had undertaken to provide for civil construction projects, and the proclamation was ripped from town walls.[15] More significantly, a coalition of urban leaders opposed to the act quickly emerged, led by such important traders as Joseph Smith, William de Graft, and James Thompson. These activists and their supporters pursued several strategies — defending "domestic servitude" as essentially benign, disputing the legality of the law, and demanding compensation for their potential losses.[16] This proved too much for the governor. Recognizing that his position was legally tenuous and that political and military support of the Euro-African elite was essential, Hill declined to enforce the act.[17]

POLITICAL AND ECONOMIC REALITIES IN THE AFTERMATH OF ABOLITION

If the administration had no mandate and no will to end slave owning among the largely Euro-African urban elite who professed loyalty to the Crown, it is perhaps no wonder that the British had even less interest in moderating slave owning outside this group. British authority outside the coastal "possessions" was extremely limited. The sway of the Committee of Merchants had reached no farther than the towns abutting their forts until the end of the 1830s when some authority was reasserted by Maclean[18] on the basis of his personal reputation and the 1831 treaty establishing peaceful relations between the coastal powers and the asantehene.[19] Although this treaty guaranteed the role of Asante as a major power in the region, it also extended the administration's commitment as guarantor for the coastal states. Following the reassertion of a Crown administration in 1843, the Colonial Office and its appointees were largely content to maintain this status quo.[20]

As is also clear from the incident that concludes the preceding section, it was politically and economically expedient for administrators to support or at least overlook institutions of slavery. The production of legitimate goods suddenly expanded during this period, in the wake of the 1831 treaty, which made long-distance trade safe for the first time in decades.[21] Palm-oil export values climbed to £42,745 in 1841, and guinea-grain (melagueta pepper) and coffee production also rose, while internal trade increased commensurately.[22] Since the production and transportation of both coffee and palm oil used slave labor, the interests of administrators were firmly intertwined with those of slave owners by the 1830s.[23]

Political concerns also contributed to making emancipation an unattractive option for the administration. Just as the colonial administration's reliance on indigenous urban slave owners enabled them to resist challenges to their slave-owning rights successfully, British policy toward refugee slaves was bound by consideration of the Asante to the north. A renewal of conflict with the Asante would have threatened the economic development of the region, and during this period the administration consequently carefully avoided alienating the Asante authorities. This was a policy made more difficult by the 1843 Act for the More Effectual Suppression of the Slave Trade promulgated from the metropole, which prohibited British officers from assisting in the "carrying away of [individuals] to be dealt with as slaves."[24] Committee of Merchants' authorities had habitually returned slaves who sought refuge in their posts during the previous decade, a policy that allowed Asante traders the freedom to use slave carriers to transport goods to the coast. The 1843 act threatened this informal convention, and the British administration reacted (or failed to react) by ignoring this clause for as long as possible.[25]

When the abolitionist press in 1855 finally drew attention to their inactivity, Acting Governor Henry Connor suggested, not that further resources be given to aid enforcement of the act, but that a royal dispensation be given to exclude the Gold Coast from these provisions, since the colony could not survive an Asante onslaught.[26] Realpolitik continued to triumph into 1858, when (Acting Governor) Major Henry Bird not only continued not to enforce the 1843 runaway slave provisions, but threatened to fine or imprison any British subjects harboring or protecting runaway Asante slaves.[27] Throughout this entire period, British magistrates continued to return runaways, "well knowing that if sent back, [many] would be beheaded instantly on their return."[28] In hindsight, the British were correct in considering this issue an important keystone in their relationship with the Asante. The decision to reverse this policy in 1863 would cause a break in Anglo-Asante relations, causing the asantehene to send an army to menace the allied coastal polities.[29]

Nor were most slaves highly active in promoting emancipation, as they typically preferred a more pragmatic strategy. When, in the 1840s, Dr. Richard Madden, the Irish abolitionist who had been charged by Parliament to report on slavery in West Africa, instructed a number of slaves that they were free, they refused to take up their liberations unless "the Queen intended to give them something to eat, [otherwise] they would prefer to serve their masters who supplied their wants."[30]

If governors could not, before 1863, bring themselves to accept the letter of a law restricting the return of slaves to an outside power and could not count on significant slave agency, they were even more reluctant to promote any proposed scheme of emancipation. The mass liberation of slaves would have endangered their own economic projects and threatened to alienate the powerful political and economic elites within the Gold Coast. However, at the same time that they faced these domestic realities, colonial officials had to respond to abolitionists in the metropole. The result was the development of colonial propaganda that insisted that slavery on the Gold Coast was relatively benign. Perhaps Governor Benjamin Pine best explained the view expounded by his contemporaries: "The universal prevalence of Domestic Slavery throughout the Gold Coast is admitted by the stereotyped phrase of its apologists that it is 'interwoven into the whole framework of society there.' . . . [I]t has been represented as a mild form of slavery scarcely deserving of the name, but rather to be regarded as a patriarchal system of government whereby the mass of the people is kept in subjugation and provided for. It has been compared to the rule exercised by Chiefs over their clansmen or to the authority of Lords over their Vassals."[31] This notion proved an effective tool for rationalizing the colonial administration's continued recognition of domestic slavery, and it was soon put through its paces. Starting in the 1850s, officials were forced to defend their stance on slavery in the face of pressure not so much from distant metropolitan concerns, but from a new nongovernmental group within the region: the missionaries.

SLAVERY, MISSIONARIES, AND POLICY: 1833–1870

The Committee of Merchants had no real policy toward slavery beyond ensuring that nothing interfered with the increasing production of and commerce in legitimate goods. The committee, a purely commercial venture, was even more vulnerable to economic considerations than a Crown administration, and thus although their agents undertook various schemes to promote agriculture, they exhibited little interest in indigenous slavery beyond attempting to use it for their own ends.

Governor Maclean, however, was the exception to this rule and was responsible not only for establishing a détente with the Asante and reopening trade routes, but also for initiating the first experiments in reforming the colony's domestic servitude policy. In this task, Maclean espoused moderation. He was not tempted to emancipate domestic slaves or end human pawning. In fact, he regarded pawning as generally no worse than the English apprenticeship system and argued that in England and the colonies "to relieve a debtor of his obligations and to accept his services in lieu of the debt, is not uncommon."[32] Maclean further pled inability, arguing that he lacked the power to "release [pawns] from their pecuniary engagements."[33] However, he did act in a few incidents to mitigate harsh examples of pawning that were brought to his attention, forcing several merchants to allow their pawns to work off the principal of their debt.[34] Similarly, Maclean allowed the gradual manumission of some long-serving slaves when their masters died, "class[ing] them as debtors to the estate . . . on condition of their serving [either the estate or individuals who lent them money to pay off their debt] at low wages until they should come ask to repay the money advanced."[35] As governor he also exercised his right to free a small number of domestic slaves who could prove abuse, although he did not otherwise interfere with the institution.[36] In each of these cases, Maclean's actions represent less a policy than a series of reactions to specific situations.

Maclean's successors, the first governors of the settlements on the Gold Coast following the reversion to Crown rule in 1843, did not diverge from his policies of manumitting only slaves who were abused or could disprove the validity of their enslavement.[37] Like their merchant-administrator predecessors, these colonial officials had no real policy regarding domestic slavery. It was only with the

appointment of Benjamin Pine in 1857 that this changed. Pine was the first administrator to acknowledge that the actions of the colonial government in exercising jurisdiction over much of the coast amounted to official recognition of
domestic slavery, although he realized that mass emancipation could not be effected with the colony's resources at hand.[38] Furthermore, Pine felt that, since just
as British influence protected the people of the coast from the threat of invasion,
human sacrifices, and the oppression of chiefs, so also "although our jurisdiction
necessarily involves some recognition of slavery . . . this is scarcely to be regarded
as an evil, since it enables us to prevent its abuses."[39] As an initial measure, he
therefore issued a memorandum that in many ways presaged emancipation thir-
teen years later. Under Pine's policy, magistrates were forbidden from compelling
a slave or pawn to return to his or her master, although only in cases of abuse or
ownership by a British subject were magistrates ordered to emancipate the slave,
nonintervention otherwise being the watchword. Pawns seized because of a debt
owed by a relative or countryman were also to be freed by officers.[40]

The result was more a whimper than a bang. Pine was replaced by (Acting
Governor) Bird less than a year later, and courts largely persisted in actively returning slaves to masters. Few "illegally" panyarred pawns appear to have come
forward, partly because there was little advertisement of the proclamation.[41]
Still, by introducing into Gold Coast law the idea of nonrecognition of slave
relationships, rather than active emancipation, Pine pioneered a model strategy
in mediating between British abolitionism and Gold Coast political realism.

Other schemes were to emerge from another source—the activities of Protestant missionaries. Missionaries had been inconsistently active on the Gold
Coast since 1482. Portuguese Augustinians were first, followed by French Ca-
puchins at Assini in the 1630s, the English Society for the Propagation of the
Gospel at Cape Coast in the latter part of the seventeenth century, and the Dutch
Moravians at the beginning of the eighteenth.[42] However, these missionaries had
largely been interested in the spiritual well-being of the European community
and had generally confined their activities to the larger coastal trading posts.

After 1834, however, as the struggle against slavery shifted from the colonies in the New World to Africa itself, Protestant missionaries began to express
a new interest in combating slavery at the source—in Africa. As Susan Thorne
describes it, "The rationale for foreign missions shifted accordingly from atone-
ment for European guilt to a mechanism through which Africans might be lured
into alternative forms of trade." Thus Christianity and commerce were firmly
linked with the eradication of slavery in the language of Protestant evangelical
missionaries.[43]

The earliest of these new missions to reach the Gold Coast, the Basel Mission Society, settled its first mission "communities" in 1828 in the Danish zone of influence—including not only Accra but, for the first time, the interior regions of Akuapem and Krobo.[44] The European missionaries were assisted by a group of Jamaican families who had been brought over to form the nuclei of the Basel Mission congregations. These evangelicals were then dispersed into the interior, teaching the catechism, preaching the gospel, and opening mission schools for training teachers, clerks, skilled laborers, and catechists.[45]

The Basel Mission Society was joined by the Wesleyan Methodist Missionary Society in 1836. The Wesleyan Methodists were equally evangelical, but although the congregation sent agents as far as Asante, most of its effort initially focused on the Cape Coast area.[46]

Both of these societies reviled the institution of slavery, Wesley himself having had much to say on the subject, and both could have played a central role in promoting abolitionism in the Gold Coast, at least by acting as a watchdog over the administration.[47] Unfortunately, pragmatism intruded upon idealism as the realities of operating among local populations rapidly made themselves clear to the missions' officers. Missionary personnel were dispatched to remote locales and were charged with building churches, chapels, schools, and houses for themselves. They soon found that free labor was not readily available, especially where indigenous regimes were unsympathetic, and missionaries often had to employ pawns and slaves. The Wesleyans tried to palliate this operation by purchasing the contracts of pawns and deducting a portion of their wages until the purchase sum was cleared.[48] From the late 1850s through the early 1870s the Basel Mission Society also instituted a policy of purchasing slaves and allowing them to work off their "debt" to the mission under a policy similar to the French rachats.[49] However, they were also often forced to rely on the hired labor of slaves.[50] There was a fine line between liberating slaves by purchase and purchasing slaves for labor, and the missionary groups were clearly sometimes forced to operate on the "wrong" side. This situation was somewhat embarrassing for the missions, and colonial officials used such practices to deflect criticism of administration policy, especially from Wesleyan Methodist sources, at one point intimating that a leading Methodist, the Reverend Thomas Birch Freeman, was one of the largest purchasers of pawn contracts in the entire region.[51]

The congregations themselves initially attracted alienated or peripheral members of the community, such as slaves,[52] but Euro-African merchants, eager to associate themselves with their European identities, formed the most influential faction within the Wesleyan community.[53] The presence of this key slave-owning constituency, although welcome, further complicated the role of missionaries on this important subject, as clergy could not freely agitate against an institution supported by important members of their flock. The local Wesleyan committee consequently decided not to agitate directly against slavery, but rather to promote a capitalist mode of labor in order to "assist in creating a market-force economy to free slaves."[54] Working from the theory that cash cropping would stimulate wage labor, they carried out several schemes to promote the growth of cotton and other goods at a model farm at "Domonassi," aided by a grant from the Society for the Extinction of the Slave Trade.[55] The farm failed, but the missionaries clamored for further resources for a second attempt.[56] The Wesleyans at one point even attempted to recruit American ex-slaves to return and lead the project, but this effort was also unsuccessful.[57] These experiments in using capital to promote wage over slave labor proved only that the Gold Coast was not ready for the wage labor revolution.

The Basel Mission Society's experiment with emancipation was somewhat more extensive, and in fact was almost adopted as colonial policy. The Basel Mission Society, operating largely in the interior and drawing less of its congregation from among elites, ironically had more freedom to pursue antislavery policies. Slavery had been an issue discussed by missionaries in the field for some time, and in the early 1860s the debate came to a head, culminating in a dispute between the evangelist leadership in Basel and a number of lay agents in Africa. The Basel committee, supported by David Eisenschmid in Kyebi and several other field agents, argued that slavery was not only evil in and of itself, but was also the root of many other social and economic problems in indigenous society, and they therefore pushed for a rigorous approach.[58] The majority of the missionaries in the Gold Coast, however, opposed drastic measures. In the end, the strict abolitionists emerged victorious, and in 1863 the Basel Mission banned slaveholding among its members. Rather than alienating or expelling their slave-owning congregants, however, the Basel Mission forged a compromise whereby the slaves were declared debtors for a sum equivalent to their purchase price. Their masters paid the slaves a monthly wage for their labors, keeping a portion to recover the purchase price of the slaves. A significant number of these slaves also received the right to work a piece of land for themselves.[59] In one example, Jonathan Palmer freed three slaves on the "understanding that they would work for their former master for a small wage or for one or other of the missionaries."[60] The Basel Mission also began to reject important potential converts who were not willing to liberate their slaves.[61]

Although this scheme for gradual liberation drew inspiration from Maclean's efforts thirty years earlier, its scope was somewhat greater, as the Basel Mission congregation had several thousand members;[62] its effect was heightened when in 1865 the plan was presented in Parliament and its results evaluated, bringing the matter to the attention of the Crown.[63] Thus, the idea of transforming slaves into bonded workers had a precedent when, ten years later, administrators met to decide what form emancipation would take.

SLAVES TO THE STATE?: COLONIAL RECRUITING

Before the 1870s British policy on the Gold Coast was generally antiexpansionist, a reflection of the success of the policies of "informal empire" that stemmed not only from the lack of colonial fervor among the British population and a belief in free trade, but also from a desire to keep costs low.[64] The result was both a limiting of the extent of British jurisdiction and the undertaking of efforts to keep the number of relatively highly paid European officers low.[65] Both for these budgetary reasons and because European soldiers were susceptible to tropical disease, the colonial administration quickly adopted a policy of recruiting African troops.[66] The idea of using Africans as soldiers was not a novel one. In earlier periods, European merchant companies had often relied on town militias (asafo) as auxiliaries. In other parts of West Africa, the recruitment of Africans had a long history. The British had begun recruiting indigenous troops in Gorée in 1808, soon after capturing the Senegalese island.[67] There, they had encountered a wall of apathy in attempting to enlist volunteers and turned to slaves, whom they felt "would be happy to change their state" and could be purchased "for the consideration of about eighty to a hundred dollars each."[68] The same administration had also incorporated slaves confiscated under the 1807 anti–slave trading act into its military forces.[69]

The officer in charge of this effort in Senegal, Administrator Charles William Maxwell, was raised several years later to the position of governor of Sierra Leone (the senior government official in West Africa). In that role he promoted the recruitment of Africans to serve in British forts throughout the region, and communicated to the Committee of Merchants on the Gold Coast the possibility of inducing Fantes to join such a force.[70] The Committee of Merchants, unsure that they could find voluntary recruits, turned to slaves "emancipated" by the British cruiser squadron, requesting the conscription of about two hundred men to serve at Gold Coast forts.[71]

The number of exslaves recruited in this manner is unclear but could never have been very large, as the Committee of Merchants did not maintain a significant military force. The Crown administration inherited from the Committee of Merchants only 191 soldiers of the Gold Coast Corps and the militia.[72] This small force was subsequently augmented with the 1st West Indian Regiment, brought over to form the garrisons of the major forts.[73] Governor Hill, sensing the need for a larger force and unable to form a large body from volunteers, filled out the militia by "borrowing" slaves from local slave owners. Membership in the militia carried a monthly wage, and Hill found it convenient to simply pay a portion of that wage to the slaves' masters, continuing a long tradition of "wink[ing] at" such arrangements.[74]

Indeed, people of slave origin continued to form the bulk of the Gold Coast Corps throughout the 1840s and 1850s. A majority of voluntary recruits were runaway slaves—as many as 90 percent according to one colonial source.[75] Military officers tended to accept these runaways out of a desperate need for recruits, but the complaints of chiefs and slave owners led to a restructuring of the recruiting process in 1858 to a method whereby chiefs of the coastal towns were required to produce a quota of free recruits each year.[76]

Although the administration faced opposition from slave owners to their policy of recruiting runaway slaves, the indenture and "rental" of slaves were also soon forbidden by an 1852 decision by Secretary of State for the Colonies Henry Pelham-Clinton, Duke of Newcastle, that "the plan of purchasing men . . . even if in reality likely to tend to their ultimate freedom . . . could scarcely be understood in Africa except as implying a recognition by Her Majesty's Government of the principle of Slavery."[77] The subsequent decline in the muster of the Gold Coast Corps and the 1st West Indian Regiment (increasingly constituted of indigenous replacements for fallen or retired Caribbean soldiers) continued until 1862, whereupon the threat of war with the Asante forced the military commander of the region, Major Cochrane, to review this policy. Desperate for troops, Cochrane concluded that Governor Pine's 1857 order that administration officials should not "compel or order a slave or pawn to return to his master"[78] implied that "every British officer . . . might refuse to view any person as a [slave or] pawn" and thus allow for their enlistment as a free individual, a policy he ordered military recruiters to adopt.[79] When Governor Pine detailed this strategy to the Colonial Office, Secretary of State Newcastle firmly reiterated that "the enlistment of Slaves or Pawns to serve in Her Majesty's Forces is not to be practiced."[80] Following this order and complaints from several slave owners,[81] Pine thereafter and in no uncertain terms instructed the military establishment to cease recruiting slaves and pawns.[82] Despite appeals, the Colonial Office upheld the decision ending the recruitment of unfree individuals and runaway slaves in December 1863.[83]

The upshot was the continuation of recruiting problems for the military, which sought any potential solution that would raise the number of enlisted personnel. The first possibility, raised in the wake of the 1863 war, was to authorize a paid native levy in times of conflict, but the limitations of this untrained force were clear—it was simply no substitute for regular units.[84] As the demand for police and garrison troops increased following the acquisition of the Dutch forts in 1871, a decision was made to recruit troops outside the region at Lagos, a significant departure from previous policy.[85] The success of this experiment would have serious ramifications for labor opportunities for liberated slaves and freemen alike in the next quarter century.[86]

THE WAXING OF INDIGENOUS COASTAL ELITES: 1861–1873

The difficulties of recruiting African troops, along with the inadequate resources provided by the metropole, weakened the ability of the administration to exercise much influence prior to 1873. British authority and prestige east of the Cape Coast had declined in the 1830s and failed to recover even following the 1850 acquisition of the Danish territories in the east—the forts of Accra (Christiansborg), Prampram, Ningo, Keta, and Ada—and treaty authority over the rich regions of Krobo and Akuapem.[87] The administration attempted to rectify this situation by ordering a direct poll tax in the protected territories to raise revenue for infrastructure projects and personnel in 1852,[88] but the tax was extremely unpopular, and by 1854 a revolt was spreading from the former Danish regions west into Fanteland.[89] Opposition crystallized around the theme that the money was being misspent as the British administration failed to improve the infrastructure or place significant garrisons.[90] By 1857 Governor Pine was recommending a retreat from responsibilities outside the forts and settlements that comprised the colony.[91] The 1863 Asante raids further aggravated the situation, and the disgruntled Colonial Office refused to release funds to deal with the resulting turmoil in districts affected by the Asante incursions.[92]

The environment of resistance engendered by the Poll Tax Revolts carried into the late 1860s, as coalitions of aristocrats and educated merchants acted to control their own political destinies.[93] Among the Fante, this spirit of empowerment found further expression in resistance to a proposed exchange of territory between the British and the Dutch. The 1867 exchange, intended to normalize the European powers' respective coastlines, would have transferred to the Dutch authority over roads leading to Fante from Wassaw and Chama, thus placing a number of Britain's "allied" polities under Dutch authority.[94] The political leadership of the Fante refused to allow the expansion of Dutch authority to their Ahanta neighbors and the Fante polity of Komenda, who also rejected Dutch authority, instead maintaining "their resolution . . . whether accepted or not to maintain their true allegiance to the British flag under all circumstances and adversities."[95] As the Fante asafo spontaneously laid siege to the Dutch headquarters at Elmina, a council of Fante leaders met in the ancestral town of Mankessim. Although the immediate issue was the proposed exchange, the poll tax debacle and British failure to pay promised stipends led a convention of these officeholders to choose to form an independent confederation.[96] The government chosen by this convention proceeded swiftly to create a national militia and began to collect taxes.

The history of the Fante Confederation deserves a more nuanced and complex treatment than it can be given here, but the evolution of the confederation's leadership has some bearing on later developments. Although the move toward the Fante Confederation was initiated by kings and chiefs,[97] the bureaucracy was soon transferred into the hands of missionary- and colony-educated Euro-African merchant families, who began to exercise executive control.[98] As chiefly officeholders became disaffected with their declining political power, they turned back to the British, and in 1872 important chiefs began to disavow the confederation, seeing in British jurisdiction a way of regaining their authority from the urban, educated elite.[99] As a result, not only did the confederation fail, but a significant wedge was driven between the British officials and chiefs on the one hand and the merchant elite on the other.[100]

Nor was the Fante Confederation the only attempt at establishing an indigenous independent coastal federation. In the east, the expanding political and economic influence of Ga chiefs and Euro-Ga traders over neighboring and interior regions in the late 1860s transformed into a political movement. Resistance to British judicial and military authority in Accra spread to the towns of Ningo and Prampram, and even into the eastern interior. The culmination of this movement was the formation of the Accra Native Confederation modeled at least partly on the Fante Confederation in 1869.[101] Here again an internal conflict developed, as the Accra Confederation's leadership was formed of important urban merchants who essentially undermined the *mantsemei* (mantse stoolholders collectively) and claimed the leadership of the self-determination movement.[102]

The decline of British authority, made evident by the rise of these two confederations, was mirrored by an inability on the part of the administration to influence indigenous slavery in any manner. This was evidenced, in the late 1860s, by the chiefs' withdrawal of support for colonial courts, the only bodies willing to interfere with slaveholding in any way.[103] Admittedly, magistrates did, when approached, effect the release of some individuals, especially children, placed in bondage for debts contracted by persons other than themselves or their parents.[104] However, although relatives of pawns sometimes used the courts in this manner, the dramatic decline in colonial court cases during this period reflects both the reluctance of Africans to use British courts and the limited extent of British authority.[105]

━━

Largely as a result of resistance to the 1867 Anglo-Dutch exchange, on April 6, 1873, the king of Holland gave up his forts on the Gold Coast to the British in what would prove to be a watershed event for the Gold Coast region.[106] The succeeding two years would see Asante power on the coast broken, British hegemony established over the independence-minded coastal powers and even the interior states, and slavery banned.

On the eve of these events, however, none of this was foreseeable. Specifically, there was no established plan and no impetus for ending slavery. The preceding half century had been an era, at best, of experimentation with various small-scale schemes to end servile relationships, the most significant of which were not even initiated by the administration. Lacking the resources to enact such policies, even had they been found desirable, governors largely allowed Africans to decide the fate of slaves, a strategy that culminated in Benjamin Pine's noninterference policy. At no point during this period was the 1834 Emancipation Act promulgated in any part of the Gold Coast, outside the few physical structures that comprised the British forts, and even there runaway slaves were usually returned, until 1863, after which they were not returned but were still not encouraged to seek refuge.

Nevertheless, the experiments of the anteproclamation period were crucial to defining the postproclamation settlement. The failure of military officials to obtain sanction for slave-recruiting policies would have significant ramifications for exslave labor and enlistment. Pine's noninterference strategy would form the basis of the adoption of the model of emancipation eventually chosen by Governor George Strahan in 1874. The alienation of educated urban elites from the administration in the wake of the Fante and Accra confederations would have a great effect on these elites' power to resist the ordinances of emancipation, while the reconciliation of many chiefs would lend them the authority to negotiate their own solutions. Lastly, the firm establishment of missionaries would help push the development of wage labor and the rehabilitation of slaves in the next quarter century.

CHAPTER 4

The Grand Experiment

Emancipation in Senegal Colony

IN THE FIRST HALF OF THE nineteenth century, the free inhabitants of St. Louis and Gorée, like their counterparts in the trading entrepôts of the Gold Coast, appear to have been largely satisfied with the established conditions of slavery in the diminutive colony of Senegal. Nor were the locally posted agents of the French Ministry of the Navy any more motivated than their British counterparts to push for any real reform. Most of these officials were military officers, posted for short periods and with little real understanding of the local situation. Their primary motivation was to maintain the profitability of the colony and thus achieve quick promotion and posting elsewhere. This they were forced to do with the slim resources provided by the Ministry of the Navy and a relatively small force of European officials. Thus the administrators relied heavily upon the local habitant community and the long-serving *négotiants*—agents of the French trading companies—for both advice and commercial stability.[1] Neither of these groups saw abolition as serving its interests in any way.

Thus, here, as in the Gold Coast, there was little reason to expect any drastic change in official policy toward the institution of slavery. Events in Europe, however, were to introduce a challenge to this status quo briefly in 1848. The principles behind the revolution of that year in France itself were expressed in a drastic reversal of policy and a revival of humanitarianism and abolitionism, culminating in an emancipation decree promulgated throughout the empire. The administration's view of slavery in the fledgling colonies had always been linked to politics in the metropole, and the impact of this decree in Senegal Colony was potentially the transformation of the lives of the colony's six thousand slaves. In the event, however, an accommodation was reached between administrators and slave owners that would serve as a prototype for a pattern that would continue until the end of the century.

These events have been discussed to some extent by Martin Klein, who devotes half of a chapter to the 1848 emancipation and its immediate impact, and another half to longer-term effects that manifested themselves during and after Governor Louis Faidherbe's expansion between 1854 and 1865.[2] Klein's treatment of the subject does form a framework for understanding the events surrounding emancipation, but this chapter is an attempt to approach several topics outside Klein's scope. The first section covers attempts to reform slavery and debates on emancipation prior to 1848. These precedents illuminate the motivations and strategies of administrators in the metropole and in Senegal as well as slave-owning elites, and assist us in understanding the crisis of the sudden shift to emancipation. Much of this chapter is also concerned with the days surrounding the emancipation, in which we can see the specific social and economic characteristics of slavery in St. Louis and Gorée that led to a unique outcome for emancipation. Using this information, I am able in the last sections to engage with Klein, Mohamed Mbodj, and other historians, as well as Louis Faidherbe himself to discuss the de facto impact of emancipation.

FORMULATING EMANCIPATION?: MANUMISSIONS AND DEBATES, 1832–1848

Following the failure of the Waalo plantations in 1827, the French monarchy turned its attention to domestic concerns, and Senegal was somewhat neglected. A series of particularly inexperienced governors was imposed upon St. Louis, one for each of the twenty-one years between Roger's disgrace in 1827 and emancipation in 1848.[3] None of these administrators lasted long enough to formulate and carry out their own policies, and as a result most of the procedural regulations of this period were directly imposed by the Ministry of the Navy.[4] The various governors were solely responsible for the implementation of these regulations and the running of day-to-day affairs, reporting the results back to the minister. This, of course, was a particularly inflexible procedure since messages were passed between capital and colony via ship.

The official manumission policy was a case in point. The administration had a policy of *affranchisements définitives* (final liberations) for engagés who managed to survive their fourteen-year indenture. However, when the French government began to come under increased pressure from abolitionists following the revolution of July 1830, the Ministry of the Navy began to investigate the possibility of implementing the policy of rachats for all slaves within the two island towns. Consequently, they solicited the opinions of the various colonial governors.[5]

In St. Louis, Governor Thomas Renault de Saint-Germain (1831–1833) approached this issue with trepidation, aware of strong opposition to proposed reforms among the elite of the two towns. The constant changeover of administrators had vested the habitant community with an inordinate amount of power, and Saint-Germain was frustrated by their rejection of any system that would allow their skilled and valuable slaves to buy themselves free. Unlike in the Caribbean colonies, many of the slaves of the islands of St. Louis and Gorée, possessing a share of the wages their labor earned, could conceivably have purchased their freedom en masse under an institutionalized system of rachats.[6] Adopting the arguments of the urban slave owners wholesale, Saint-Germain therefore drew a picture for the Ministry of the Navy of a unique and benign system of slavery, in which slaves were able to earn wages and live well, suddenly torn apart by a mass exodus. He in turn appealed to the ministry's inherent thriftiness and predilection for public order, suggesting that the introduction of rachats would create a class of vagabonds and drains on the public purse, and implored them not to commit political suicide by alienating the habitants and signares upon whose support the administration relied.

A realist, Saint-Germain knew that these entreaties alone would be insufficient. Abolitionism was growing in popularity in France, and the government placed greater weight on the political capital it stood to gain in the metropole by appearing reformist. Furthermore, it was clearly disingenuous to argue on the one hand that slaves were a mainstay of commerce and in any case were paid wages, and on the other hand that emancipated slaves would automatically become penniless vagabonds. Therefore, he concentrated on making a complex argument that the habitant class, completely relying on their slaves for income, would be irreparably ruined by the loss of their skilled slaves. Reminding the naval minister that habitants and their slave laborers were the basis of the region's economy, Saint-Germain suggested as a compromise that if rachats had to be allowed, slaves in Senegal should be required to purchase their freedom by "replac[ing themselves] with another slave of the same value."[7]

This suggestion, of course, ran directly counter to the ministry's main objective of pacifying abolitionist critics and was largely ignored. Instead, in 1832 a royal ordinance was passed allowing slaves to purchase their freedom. The act required slaves to submit "through the mediation of either their master or the *procureur du roi* (royal attorney), a demand to be definitively recognized as free" after a six-month waiting period.[8] The act made clear that these manumissions could occur only with the agreement of the slaves' owners, to whom the slaves were presumably required to pay a certain amount. The ordinance deliberately left unclear the mechanisms under which these rachats would occur, which perhaps explains why it has been ignored by many historians of emancipation even though available records do indicate a small number of slave manumissions prior to 1848.[9] Analysis of the documents is made even more difficult by the unfortunate blending of rachat records with those of other forms of manumission, including the definitive emancipations of engagés. However, that specific cases of rachats did occur can be concluded from marginalia and details in tables. A scrawled notation in one notebook, for example, indicates that the freedom of a four-year-old girl named Fara was purchased by Tiaye M'Baye, a carpenter, for Fr 500,[10] and similar records of what appear to have been repurchase prices in other documents seem similarly to indicate occurrences of rachats.[11]

Along with the records of rachats there is evidence of a small number of individuals freed by the administration. Among these, the singular record of Aminata stands out. Aminata was a young female slave manumitted by the magistrates of St. Louis because of what one assumes was extraordinary abuse at the hands of her master.[12] This appears to have been a unique occurrence, as was the case of an unregistered engagé named Foutoura, freed by the courts because she had been introduced into the colony illegally, although it is not clear how or why.[13] However, like all slaves manumitted by these executive judgments, by the mechanism of rachats, or after fourteen years of service as engagés, Aminata and Foutoura became freedwomen but did not acquire the rights of citizens of the colony until three years after their manumission or, if minors, until three years after they had reached the age of majority.[14]

It is unclear how many slaves purchased or were granted their freedom between 1832 and 1848. Records held in the French archives in Provence and in Dakar do not agree on this issue, and it is often unclear whether the individuals discussed in the documents in either location were freed engagés or manumitted slaves.[15] Records from Dakar tell us that only 261 slaves purchased their freedom between the years 1830 and 1841, about twelve a year, and this suggests that rachats were periodic occurrences rather than a major phenomenon.[16] For the ministry, the "failure" of the rachats policy was an embarrassment. However, the blame must be placed firmly on the administration, which, either by oversight caused by the excessive gubernatorial turnover rate or by design, failed to pass even an ordinance officially confirming the royal act until 1840.[17] The administration's reluctant compliance with the *regime des rachats* was symptomatic of if its self-acknowledged inadequacy. The colony was so diminutive — French sovereignty still encompassing only the two principal islands and a small number of posts along the river — that antislavery laws should have been eminently enforceable.[18] But with no effectual leadership within the colony, and with France more than a month away by ship, no real policy against slavery was formulated.

Yet although perception and policy toward slavery remained essentially stagnant in Senegal, attitudes continued to change in the metropole. As the abolitionist movement began to flex its muscles in France, Senegalese colonial officials became more strident in dismissing proposed reforms. Even as they accepted that the metropole controlled both budgets and advancement, administrators realized that the Ministry of the Navy measured their success more on the stability and profitability of the colony than on their imposition of "moral" policies. Nevertheless, they felt the need to defend their continued sanction of slavery within the colony. In their dispatches to their superiors they attempted to deflect the increasing abolitionist pressure by suggesting that emancipation would carry its own humanitarian dangers. They implied that the welfare of slaves—especially the aged or infirm—would actually suffer if masters were released from their responsibilities. They repeated Saint-Germain's argument that emancipation would create a class of voluntarily unemployed. Both arguments may have had some sort of perverse validity. The skilled, wage-earning slaves of St. Louis, especially, relied on their masters for housing, which was not otherwise easily obtainable except on the nearby mainland. Similarly, unlike the policy of rachats, which would have had implications only for slaves held within the colony, full-scale emancipation had the potential of attracting unskilled refugee slaves from the hinterland who would find themselves without jobs or shelter, but unable to leave the limited space of the colonies without risking recapture.

Artfully, Acting Governor Louis Guillet further appealed against any reforms on the political and budgetary grounds most likely to concern ministerial officials, suggesting that neighboring peoples would withdraw from their commerce with the colony, that it would become necessary to mount expensive police operations in the interior, and that local customary law would break down and foment anarchy.[19] Recognizing the inevitability of some form of emancipation, Guillet proposed that the *émancipés* (freed slaves) be indentured to their masters for fourteen years, at the end of which an indemnity would be given, thus both softening the blow and compensating local slave owners.[20] This would at least mitigate the impact on the habitants, upon whom the weak governors relied for stability.

Although convinced by such arguments and therefore unwilling to effect the local enforcement of antislavery policies, the Ministry of the Navy continued to feel pressure from abolitionist sources, and in 1840 the emancipation debate reached a new level, culminating in the appointment of a special commission to

study the question of slavery in the colonies. This committee identified three potential modes of emancipation:

- Emancipation of children at birth, with the adult generation of slaves remaining
  with their masters.
- The purchase of all slaves from private owners by the state, which would then
  collect a portion of each slave's wages until the purchase price was fully paid.
- Conversion of slaves into apprentices for a period of time, following which they
  were to be definitively emancipated.[21]

All these solutions entailed a gradual transition from domestic slavery to
emancipation, the central variant being the state's role. Remarkably, however,
these suggestions were rejected as too gradualist not by abolitionists but by the
normally *esclavagiste* (proslavery) commander of Gorée. The commander dismissed
the idea of state regulation of gradual liberations, correctly perceiving that the administration, with its limited resources, could not competently regulate the work
of slaves. On the other hand, he recognized that the slaves of Senegal Colony, generally richer and more skilled than their Caribbean counterparts, would not accept
apprenticeship. "It is necessary," he wrote, "for their liberation to be both instan-
taneous and definitive."[22] Under such a formula, slaves, he believed, would stay at
their jobs and would cause a minimal disruption to commerce and society. However, the commander further argued, if this were to occur, an indemnity must simultaneously be paid to habitant slave owners. Thus, these arguments do not
really reflect a surprising reversal of opinion, but instead display a continuing
streak of pragmatism. Faced with the increasing possibility that French abolitionists would force through some sort of emancipation deal, the commander simply
chose to channel his resources into getting slave owners the best possible deal.

The next few years witnessed intense debate on the question of the elimination
of domestic slavery. In May 1842 a colonial commission was finally appointed in
Paris by the ever-reluctant Ministry of the Navy, which invited comments from all
the colonies on the possible consequences of emancipation and on the best mode
of liberation to adopt.[23] Unsurprisingly, the arguments of Senegalese officials
against any dramatic reform, supported by evidence assembled from hearings in St.
Louis and Gorée, were well received by the sympathetic commissioners.

The records of the hearings held in the colony are instructive, if predictable.
The *noires libres* (free blacks) and Europeans were divided on the subject of emancipation, but both signares and habitants almost uniformly declared themselves
opposed to any such plan, despite the offer of a cash indemnity. Nor was there
any division among the witnesses from the slave population, who unanimously

supported emancipation although astutely suggested that they would probably be happy to remain in residence with their owners and thus not threaten the economic status quo.[24] Nevertheless, the slaves could not have hoped that their testimony would receive equal weight with that of their masters. The statements of the habitants in particular were very convincing. In eloquent and convincing French (in a striking contrast to their slaves' patois), the habitants recognized the moral appeal of emancipation. However, they argued, slaves in the colony were not only more secure and had a higher standard of living than many noires libres but were also instrumental in conducting commerce and in feeding the colony.[25]

It is unsurprising, therefore, that the Paris commission publicly recognized the "differences" between Senegalese and Caribbean slavery. They agreed that there were differences between the two not only in the roles slaves played in the economy, but also in the fact that, in Senegal, unlike in the Caribbean, most masters were non-European and both masters and slaves were Muslims. The commissioners also pointed out the unique position of the colony, surrounded as it was by slave-owning societies.[26] Thus, the Paris commission yielded to pressure from an alliance of habitants and the colonial administration, declining to apply to Senegal the law of July 18, 1845, that established conditions for gradual emancipation in the Caribbean colonies.[27]

The limited compromise of 1848 did not satisfy the French abolitionist community. On April 24, 1847, a petition was presented to the Assemblée Nationale containing eleven thousand signatures, among them those of "3 bishops, 19 *vicaires généraux,* 858 priests . . . 7 members of the institute, 151 elected counsellors, 213 magistrates," and more than nine thousand property owners and merchants.[28] Among other issues, the abolitionists remonstrated the lack of any emancipation plan for Senegal.

Chastised by public opinion, the naval ministry prepared a draft of a gradual emancipation ordinance for the colony in 1847. The act was to set up a system enabling slaves to request their emancipation, with each case to be considered by the governor on an individual basis. The administration was to be given the power to force masters to accept a "reasonable" rachat price.[29] This further attempt to reach a compromise between metropolitan abolitionist pressure and colonial concerns implied that full emancipation would still be a long time in coming.

EMANCIPATION

In fact the 1847 royal ordinance was never passed, and in 1848 everything changed. In February of that year Parisians took to the streets and ministers on the left seized power, evicting the royal family and proclaiming a republic in early May. The republic's leaders were reformers and had close ties to the abolitionist movement, and it took only four days for the new government to name a commission, led by the legendary abolitionist Victor Schoelcher,[30] charged with "preparing an immediate act of emancipation in all the colonies of the Republic."[31]

The decree ultimately adopted was not the compromise of 1847 but an intellectual heir to the *déclaration des droits de l'homme.* The young, optimistic Republican government did not feel bound by local considerations of politics and economics. For Schoelcher and his colleagues, emancipation was about "human dignity" and slavery was castigated for "destroying the liberty of man" and "suppressing the natural principle of rights and needs."[32] As a result, the operative clauses of the decree were powerful and straightforward. Slavery was "entirely abolished," as was the regime des engagés. Furthermore, it became illegal for any French citizen to "possess, own, buy, or sell slaves" anywhere in the world. Since the inhabitants of Senegal had been granted representation in the Assemblée Nationale, this interdiction was extended to Senegalese habitants and signares. For contravention of this order, the provisional government decreed the worst imaginable sanction—the loss of French citizenship.[33] Thus, the provisions of the 1848 decree provided the framework for an envisioned post-emancipation settlement—a definitive end to domestic slavery in a society tightly integrated with France and peopled by citizens for whom the threat of losing citizenship was enough to ensure compliance. The provisional government's single concession to the slave owners was the promise of an indemnity to mitigate the loss of the income provided by the rental of their slaves.

For the military administrators of Senegal, the most controversial clause in the document was article 7, which declared that "the principle that 'the soil of France emancipates the slave who touches it' be applied to all colonies and possessions of the Republic."[34] The principle that touching French soil immediately conveys freedom, or *sol affranchis,* of course threatened the colony's economic and political ties with neighboring slave-owning societies. For thirty years, French policy had been engineered specifically to avoid conflict over this issue, which, it was anticipated, would alienate indigenous rulers and merchants. The operative clauses of the 1848 decree, so different from those suggested by the carefully crafted 1847 draft of the royal ordinance, threatened to crash into the unprepared colony like a cue ball, sending habitants, slaves, administrative officers, and neighboring Wolof and Sereer chiefs into their corners and then back in a collision of interests. Nevertheless, the provisional government made it clear to Governor Auguste Baudin that this time, at least, there was to be no

exemption from any part of the decree for Senegal. On May 7, the newly appointed naval minister, François Arago, sent a letter to ensure that the instructions contained in the decree were clear. Anticipating that resistance from the
administration in Senegal would center on article 7, Arago wrote, "According to
Article 7, the establishments on the west coast of Africa all become French
territory . . . therefore all slaves who touch the soil receive the right of freedom.
The situation of these establishments, in close proximity of countries where slavery exists, without doubt gives to this measure . . . a particular [difficulty]. But
this cannot be sufficient reason to place Senegal outside this essential national
principle."[35]

Arago's instructions on this and other matters clearly stated that the law had
to be implemented in Senegal with only a two-month warning before execution
and without exception.[36] However, in addition to an indemnity (which, to Baudin's relief, Arago continued to promise), the government made one concession
to prudence. Although in principle forbidding engagés as well as slaves, Arago
agreed that the government could keep under indenture soldiers who garrisoned
the inhospitable interior trading posts, effectively creating a loophole in an otherwise solid decree.[37] On June 23, 1848, Acting Governor Léandre Berlin Du
Château promulgated the royal decree for Senegal Colony, setting a definitive
emancipation date of August 23.[38]

EMANCIPATION: JULY AND AUGUST 1848

In the months leading up to August 23, 1848, St. Louis and Gorée seethed with
anticipation. The slaves of the colony, including skilled craftsmen and entrepreneurs as well as wage-earning laptots and *pileuses* (pounders of grain), formed a
politicized and somewhat mobile class.[39] As a group, they felt secure that demand for their services would remain high following liberation. As a result, they
were overjoyed by the promulgation of the emancipation decree, and in St.
Louis there were reports of slaves prematurely refusing to obey their masters.[40]
Similarly, the commandant of Gorée reported in July that a number of slaves had
expressed the intention of leaving their masters as soon as possible.[41] Meanwhile, slave owners, led by influential habitant families such as the Franciers
(who owned thirty slaves) and the Pécarres (who owned sixty-nine), signares in
Gorée, and the influential mayor of St. Louis began to implement strategies to
survive emancipation. Before 1848 threats by habitants to leave the colony in
order to conserve their slaves had been instrumental in keeping antislavery

legislation at bay, but these were shown to be a bluff.[42] Thus, following the April decree, slave owners largely accepted de jure emancipation and began to pursue a new set of strategies aimed at protecting their economic positions from potential ruin.

The provisional government expected that the promised indemnity would convince the habitant and signare communities to cooperate with emancipation. However, the amount of the indemnity was the subject of great debate in the Assemblée Nationale, and neither Baudin nor Du Château received instructions on the subject during the prepromulgation period.[43] The vague promise from Paris did little to reassure slave owners. As a result, some habitants tried to limit their losses. As early as April, some of the older signares, anxious about the possibility of losing such an enormous portion of their wealth in their old age, moved their slaves to the upriver trading entrepôts, *les escales,* prepared to sell them to the Trarza and Wolof markets if the indemnity proved too low. As emancipation jitters grew, other slave owners began to move slaves to villages in Kaajor and Waalo. Many of these slaves were smuggled out of the city even after the implementation of the August 23 emancipation and then sold.[44] Since habitants had strong links with the local communities and often owned mainland plantations that provisioned the colony, some also converted their urban slaves into farm laborers, but this was a strategy of last resort, as masters who did so lost most of the income of their skilled wage-earning slaves.[45]

The majority of masters did hang onto their slaves until the August 1848 emancipation, at which time they were given a further promise of an indemnity. In September, they were promised Fr 220 per slave, but the indemnity was not actually delivered until June 1852.[46] In the intervening period, while signares in Gorée begged the government for payment of compensation to replace their "sole means of existence," many others were forced to sell their indemnities to speculators such as the Maurel and Prom company for a small percentage of their face value.[47] In the end, the indemnity was reset to Fr 330 per slave, and the speculators walked off with enormous profits.[48]

Whereas some habitants and signares sold their slaves or hid them outside the colony, the vast majority grudgingly accepted the government's offer of an indemnity in exchange for their acceptance of emancipation. To a certain extent, this was because their slaves resisted attempts to deprive them of their liberation. In order to offset any potential rising by the habitants, Du Château had sponsored "Emancipation Clubs," which organized approximately five hundred slaves to oppose antiemancipation agitation by masters.[49] The clubs organized by Du Château kept slaves informed and organized to great effect. Their power climaxed in the weeks leading up to the date of emancipation. During this already tense period, a habitant was arrested in St. Louis for beating a slave. The ensuing trial brought about a protest by a group of slave owners opposed to the conviction of the slave owner. To their surprise, the protesters found themselves confronting approximately four hundred slaves, members of the emancipation clubs, who forced their masters to stand down.[50] For the first time in the history of slavery in Senegal Colony, slave owners confronted not just the administration but the opposition of their own slaves, and this factor made all the difference. The politicized slaves had much more at stake in the emancipation process than did the administration, and they refused to compromise. Their owners appeared defeated.

THE IMPACT OF EMANCIPATION: MASTERS AND SLAVES

Much of the historical commentary on the 1848 emancipation has concluded that this event signaled the beginning of the demise of the habitant slave-owning class. Francophone historians such as M'Baye Guèye and Roger Pasquier have concluded that habitants "were . . . the victims of that apparent *égalité*."[51] In 1967 Pasquier calculated that the level of the indemnity could never have equaled the income masters had previously generated from their slaves, in addition to which many impoverished slave owners were forced to sell their indemnities for a fraction of their value to European merchant houses. Even James Searing agrees that emancipation "undermined [the] social power" of the habitant class.[52]

The events of Emancipation Day, August 23, 1848, seem to bear out these contentions to some extent. In St. Louis, the governor posted the emancipation order at eight in the morning. By eleven "a vast quantity of men rehabilitated by France reformed in the *place* . . . [with] flags and signs of joy and liberty floating above the sea of human heads."[53] The joyful crowd, having cleansed itself of the dirt of bondage with the waters of the Atlantic Ocean, cried "a thousand times" "Vive la France, vive la liberté!" (Long live France, long live freedom) and banged on drums, exulting in its freedom. Gorée was the sight of somewhat less exuberant celebrations.[54] Surely, the power of the slave-owning classes, and specifically the habitants, was broken?

But after the demonstrations died down, and despite the free status of the former slaves, little had really changed. In Gorée the administration had desperately prepared to temporarily house and feed the hordes expected to leave their masters and throw themselves upon the charity of the administration.[55] In the event, almost all the newly freed men and women chose to remain with their masters, and there were initially no requests at all from former slaves for housing and food aid.[56] Even in St. Louis, only two hundred former slaves from a population of several thousand chose to seek shelter in the tents erected by the governor on the rocky, windswept Pointe du Nord.[57]

Why did slaves choose to remain with their masters? Governor Louis Faidherbe, who was appointed to lead the colony in 1854, noted that some signares had been so impoverished by the 1848 emancipation that their former slaves voluntarily continued to share their wages with them.[58] Faidherbe's view was somewhat facile. What was really happening was not a case of rich exslaves pitying their former masters. In fact, as Mohamed Mbodj suggested in his 1993 criticism of Pasquier and Guèye, the habitants and signares continued to dominate their former slaves by controlling the supply of labor and housing.[59] St. Louis and Gorée were both islands, and both had limited available land. However, both were also the exclusive centers of wage employment in their regions. Former slaves, especially on Gorée, thus found it difficult to leave and use their skills to earn wages on the mainland. As Klein points out, they were also unable to purchase any of the expensive and scarce land in the two towns.[60] Freed slaves therefore found themselves with no option but to remain with their former masters. As a result, in both Gorée and in St. Louis, a situation arose in which former masters were transformed into landlords, merely receiving rent instead of a share of the wages of their former slaves. The habitants retained power not only through their control of residences, but also by their ownership of the majority of the colony's boats and construction equipment and their position as providers of wage employment. As a result, relatively little social change occurred, in view of which one is perhaps justified in declaring that "emancipation did not change anything great in the social order."[61]

ARTICLE 7: THE PREDICTABLE REACTION OF INDIGENOUS STATES

Despite the grand experiment of emancipation and the particularities of slave-master relations within the colony, Senegal's administrators were as limited in the geographic and social scope of their power as were their British counterparts on the Gold Coast. Essentially, the two towns that made up the bulk of the colony were still surrounded by independent Wolof and Sereer states, all to some extent Islamicized and all to some extent controlled by semiautocratic traditional aristocracies, many of which were hostile to any perceived expansion of French authority.[62] Even the few armed posts along the Senegal River were feebly implanted.[63] The colony, moreover, continued to rely heavily upon their neighbors as trading partners.

The rise of the peanut industry in the 1830s, and particularly the 1840s, exacerbated French dependence upon Waalo and Kaajor especially. Although the first peanut concessions were granted within cannon shot of St. Louis, the colony simply didn't have the land necessary to meet France's growing demand for peanut oil, a demand that resulted in part from the British decision to concentrate on palm oil.[64] As a result, cultivation of the groundnut soared in the polities neighboring the French ports. By 1849 three million kilograms of peanuts were shipped annually from Kaajor, the center of cultivation, and peanut cultivation stretched from the Senegal River to the Saalum Delta.[65] Although some slaves may have been diverted into peanut production, and there were calls to conscript freed slaves from Gorée as farm laborers, few if any large-scale plantations emerged, and the preponderance of peanut cultivation was in the hands of peasants.[66] This peanut revolution, by increasing the colony's economic dependence upon the interior states, increased its vulnerability to boycotts by these very states. French officials were especially concerned that Siin and Saalum not divert their produce to the British positions along the Gambia River. The 1848 emancipation gave credence to these fears. However, because the 1848 decree emancipated slaves only in the colony, it was hoped that the rulers of Senegalese states would not object. Conversely, the principle embodied by the text of the degree—that "the soil of France frees the slave who touches it"—did threaten to alienate the colony's neighbors. The habitants, recognizing that their personal fortunes were tied to commerce with the interior, tried to convince the metropolitan government of this in a petition of February 15, 1849, calling for the revocation of the "soil liberates" policy.[67] As these notables feared, a number of slaves from Waalo, Kaajor, the Sereer states, and particularly the Lebu republics of Câp Vert fled to Gorée and St. Louis in the period following emancipation. Governor Baudin was personally sympathetic to the plight of indigenous slave owners, but told the Lebu chief of Dakar that his actions were constrained by orders from the metropole and he could only advise that masters living in the vicinity of the colony guard their slaves carefully.[68]

Although many of the individuals seeking freedom were actually the very slaves whom habitants had sold to the mainland in order to escape the effects of emancipation,[69] many more were slaves who transported from the interior the trade and food products upon which the colony relied.[70] As a result, indigenous traders began to refuse to bring their goods into Gorée and St. Louis,[71] although they relied on commerce with the colony as much as the habitants relied on commerce with them. Furthermore, the traders exerted political pressure upon their own rulers.[72] In February 1849 the situation came to a head with an argument over the slave of a Waalo trader who had sought refuge in St. Louis. Baudin, although engaged in negotiations with his own government over the policy, refused to return the individual. Consequently, the brak withheld cattle destined for the colony and the *damel* (king) of Kaajor embargoed shipments of peanuts;[73] as the conflict widened, the Trarzas initiated a gum embargo.[74] The fears of administrators and habitants had been confirmed, and indigenous responses to emancipation threatened the existence of Senegal Colony.

TWO STEPS BACK: EXPULSION OF RUNAWAYS AND *CONSEILS DES TUTELLES*

The 1848 emancipation decree was definitively worded and clearly supported by colonial officials in France. There could be no confusion as to its purpose. But within a year of its execution, authorities in France relinquished their abolitionist role and allowed the emasculation of two of the decree's most important clauses.

Article 7, which stated that "soil liberated," was the first to go. On the very day that saw the commencement of the joint embargo of goods to the colony, February 12, 1849, Governor Baudin, under siege by angry neighbors and worried habitants, wrote to Minister Arago, "I agree that the principle which declares all slaves who touch French soil are free is just, but in certain local conditions and needs, like those found in place in Senegal, the rigorous application is difficult and appears *contrary to human rights*."[75]

Baudin pleaded for a face-saving solution to his quandary. He argued that the colony would starve without food grown on the mainland, and painted a picture of thousands of refugee slaves overrunning the two islands. He was aware, however, that metropolitan officials had to satisfy their own abolitionist constituencies and could not backtrack. The mayor of St. Louis provided the solution, suggesting that refugee slaves be expelled through the application of an 1835 civil ordinance that gave the governor the power to eject "vagabonds"[76] who threatened public health and safety. By arguing that unemployed refugee slaves threatened the safety of the colony, Baudin could authorize civil authorities to return runaway slaves. Minister Arago consequently found himself confronted by a situation engineered entirely by Africans. Externally, indigenous powers threatened the economic future and provisioning of the colony. At the same time, the relatively high number of slaves fleeing to the two towns was overwhelming their resources.[77] Arago, aware that he would be unable to convince his colleagues to rescind article 7, seized on the compromise. On April 18 he wrote to Baudin agreeing to the plan, which had already been effectively implemented without his sanction. "In proclaiming the principle of liberation by [French] soil," Arago explained, "the Government of the Republic . . . never thought to do damage to the safety which is a right of French citizens living in our overseas possessions."[78]

The habitants and their allies had won a signal victory and showed that their power was undiminished. Not only had they retained the services and some of the income of their former slaves, but they had also achieved the de facto repeal of article 7. The administration soon made a further concession. Unable to care for emancipated juvenile slaves, Baudin acceded to suggestions from local leaders and allowed *patrons* (guardians) to take the children on as apprentices, to be compensated for housing and food costs by the child's labor.[79] It was clear that the *patrons* would generally be the children's former masters and that the system would be essentially a return to slavery, but the so-named *conseils des tutelles* (wardship councils), created to administer the placement of emancipated juveniles, were nevertheless approved by the ministry on November 13, 1849.[80] Between 1849 and 1874 a total of 213 children were subjected to the authority of the conseils. Many were child slaves returned to their masters in 1849. Others were simply orphans from the colony, from the posts along the Senegal River or Petite Côte, or even from Gabon. Most of the patrons were habitants, although some were French officials or, in very rare cases, relatives of the children. Even notorious slave owners such as Marie Labouré were allowed to act as patrons. Such a state of affairs appeared reasonable to the decision-making conseils, which were generally composed of several influential and formerly slave-owning habitants and an approximately equal number of French commercants and administrators.[81] Governor Faidherbe did attempt to reform the system in 1857 by ensuring that all minors were freed upon reaching the age of eighteen, but children continued to be bound into this condition of near-slavery until 1862.[82]

Like previous metropolitan policies aimed at limiting the institution of slavery, the emancipation of 1848 did not go as planned. Admittedly, the provisional government was successful in some respects; most importantly, around six thousand slaves in St. Louis and Gorée received their de facto freedom. However, many former slaves simply continued to be dependents, clients, and tenants of their former masters. Since they had enjoyed certain advantages—including wages—prior to emancipation, their position was relatively unimproved, even in terms of mobility. Certainly they could now leave their masters if they wished, but only to find another similar patron within the colony or to brave the dangerous paths of Waalo and Kaajor, attempting to evade the slave traders long enough to reach home. Most chose to stay with their masters. After 1854 the army also became an option, although not a desirable one.

The slaves of the colony of Senegal were "liberated" in 1848, except for those under eighteen, who were returned to their masters as apprentices under essentially the same conditions they had previously endured. However, after February 1849 slaves from outside the colony seeking refuge were ejected from the islands as "vagabonds" and dumped on the shores of the mainland where their masters picked them up and reenslaved them. The golden glow of France's paternalism was already tarnished by these events when, in 1854, a new governor took up his post in St. Louis and began plotting to expand French influence into the previously independent states of Senegal and beyond.

CHAPTER 5
Pragmatic Policies in Periods of Expansion

BY THE MIDDLE OF THE nineteenth century, slavery had become integral to the economies and societies of both the Senegal and Gold Coast regions to an unprecedented degree. The cumulative effects of four centuries of the Atlantic slave and "legitimate" trades far outweighed four decades of half-heartedly-implemented European policies aimed at controlling the use and transport of slaves and raising their status and condition. The 1848 emancipation in Senegal Colony had been limited both in scope—two diminutive island towns—and in effect. Similarly, the British had implemented few procedures affecting slavery, outside restricting European possession of slaves in the few forts and settlements they controlled.

The century midpoint, however, ushered in an unheralded increase in European involvement in both these regions that necessitated significant adjustments in the colonial policy toward slavery. During earlier episodes, the extent of both French and British sovereignty had been limited to coastal entrepôts and "factories" or "posts" along major trading routes. In the Gold Coast, de facto authority had been temporarily extended by Governor Maclean in the 1830s, but actual British jurisdiction was still limited to a small number of coastal positions. In Senegal, French authority beyond the two islands of St. Louis and Gorée was limited to the posts of Merinaghen in Waalo and Dagana, Bakel, and Senoudébon on the Senegal River.[1] The expansion of European authority outside these positions in the 1850s and 1860s provided the basis for a *potential* watershed for the institution of slavery in both regions, as European ideals of abolition were brought into play for greatly enlarged geographic regions and populations. This chapter introduces the framework of official policy within which the effect of European hegemony, the resistance of slave owners, and the agency of slaves will be discussed in the following chapters.

HARNESSING SLAVERY TO EXPANSION: SENEGAL

French power and authority were surprisingly limited in Senegal, despite several decades of commercial experiments and political interference in neighboring indigenous states. More worrying to the Ministry of the Navy at the time was that the colony's trading partners were showing signs of increasing destabilization. St. Louis's neighbor, Waalo, was the greatest concern. The failure of plantations had further weakened a state already disrupted by the depredations of the slave trade. With abolition, the ceddo-supported aristocracy had lost its primary source of income and was reduced to bickering over the "rents" and customs duties paid by the administration and habitant traders, respectively.[2] The aristocracy's authority was further reduced by the increasing Islamisization of the peasant population inspired by the jihad of Shayk Umar Tal upriver in Gaajaga and Fuuta Tooro.[3] The trading community of St. Louis was more alarmed by the Trarza Moors' increasing interference in the internal affairs of Waalo. The turmoil in Waalo was the perfect opportunity for the Trarzas to increase their control of the trade in gum arabic, a possibility that discomfited the *négotiant* representatives of French trading houses.[4] The complacent administration was finally awakened to this last threat by several influential merchants who demanded a military solution to the problem.[5] Governors and officials in Senegal were easily won over to their side by persuasive economic and political arguments. "The time has come," Governor Louis Pujol wrote the naval ministry as early as 1834, "when Waalo must pass under the domination of the French or that of the Maures."[6] Successive governors were, however, unable to take the initiative to bring Waalo firmly under French influence.

At this crucial juncture, there came upon the scene an individual who, much like Maclean in the Gold Coast, transformed the entire situation. Captain G. Louis Faidherbe had initially been appointed to organize the colony's defenses, but in 1854 he was appointed to the position of governor. The demands placed upon him were somewhat contradictory. On the one hand, his staff and local merchants insisted on an aggressive policy toward the Moors. In Paris, however, the bureaucrats of the Second Empire (which had replaced the Second Republic in

July 1852) were not as convinced of the advisability of interfering in Waalo. Faidherbe was instructed by the Ministry of the Navy to "assist peaceful development of commercial interests" and was warned quite clearly, "your nomination is neither the beginning nor the continuation of a belligerent era."[7]

These limits placed upon Faidherbe should not be taken as an indication of any ignorance on the part of his superiors of the growing importance of peanuts to French commerce in the region. The Ministry of the Navy was aware that halfway through the century, more than one million kilograms of groundnuts were leaving St. Louis annually.[8] In fact, the temporary detachment of Gorée from the Senegal Colony in 1854 was in recognition of the commercial importance of nearby Kaajor and the Sereer states and was intended to allow the governor of Senegal in St. Louis to concentrate on issues in Waalo, and the governor of Gorée on the production of peanuts in the Siin-Saalum Basin, Gambia, and the Casamance.[9] Nevertheless, decision makers in the metropole believed that French interests were best served by a policy of strengthened alliances with the peanut-producing states, and not by an aggressive policy of expansion. Influential factions in St. Louis, however, did not concur. As Faidherbe accepted the governorship, a party that argued that direct control of the peanut-growing states was the route to economic security coalesced from within the merchant community, led by the Bordeaux trading firm of Maurel and Prom.

Hilaire and Jean-Louis Maurel and Hubert Prom were three Bordeaux cousins who had started out trading small goods into Gorée, but after 1834 had increasingly competed in the gum trade to St. Louis.[10] Although Hilaire and Hubert both married into the powerful Laport habitant family of Gorée, they often found themselves politically opposed to the habitant lobby. Like the other Bordeaux houses, Maurel and Prom was troubled by the independence of the habitant middlemen who controlled the gum trade with the Trarza Moors and threatened to do the same with the peanut trade. The Bordeaux houses were unable to break the commercial domination of the habitants so long as French authority remained caged in St. Louis, and so they saw formal annexation of the interior states as the only way to guarantee unfettered access to these commodities.

Arrayed against Maurel and Prom was a habitant alliance led by Gaspard Devès, a pillar of the St. Louis habitant community who was the métis descendent of a Bordelais trader and a Fulani woman.[11] Gaspard and his supporters opposed any move into the interior on three counts. First and foremost, they correctly perceived the commercial motivation of the expansionists and opposed any move that would give the Bordeaux commercants an upper hand in competition with the habitant firms. Second, they hoped to avoid conflict between the colony and their trading partners, the Brackna and Trarza Moors. Finally, they feared the result of any campaign would be a ruinous boycott of the colony by African producers.[12]

Faidherbe, however, allowed himself to be convinced by the French merchant houses, at least so far as building forts on the Senegal at Dagana and Podor in Waalo.[13] The move was carefully orchestrated not only to discomfit the Moors but also to present the Ministry of the Navy with a fait accompli, and it was entirely successful. The minister had no choice but to retroactively sanction the move in January 1855, and, convinced by Faidherbe of the colony's impending economic doom at the hands of the Trarzas, further authorize the governor to "render the states left [south] of the river independent of the Maures."[14]

Faidherbe had been preparing for just such an order, and it was scarcely a month before he was at the head of a column marching into the interior of Waalo. In February 1855 he launched a combined land and river assault against the Trarzas at Nder on the Ferlo River.[15] To his great surprise the majority of the Wolof aristocracy, including the embattled Queen N'Detté-Yallo, chose to support the Trarzas.[16] Nevertheless, Faidherbe's column of French regulars, colonial recruits, and ceddo auxiliaries won several victories and he proceeded to install a pro-French brak on the throne of Waalo.[17] The puppet king failed, however, to generate the necessary support, and on December 30, 1855, Faidherbe opted to eliminate the position of brak and divide the state into four *cercles* (circuits), to be administered by pro-French chiefs.[18] The forts at Dagana, Podor, and Richard-Toll were simultaneously placed under direct colonial control.[19]

After a pause to refit and retrain, Faidherbe turned his attention southward, launching a campaign aimed at securing the peanut-growing Siin-Saalum Delta. He succeeded after overcoming limited resistance and following the burning of Fatick.[20] As a result of the campaign, both kingdoms, although remaining nominally independent, were drawn into the French sphere of influence. By far the greatest prize, however, were the fertile lands of Kaajor that stretched temptingly between Waalo and Gorée. Annexation of Kaajor would not only give Faidherbe possession of a key groundnut-producing state, but would also serve to unify French possessions geographically. As early as 1858, Faidherbe had argued that expansion in that direction would secure the long-term profitability of the colony: "The political line [the administration] has adopted in Senegal . . . generally consists of protecting the sedentary black cultivators against the Moor nomads . . . and in particular . . . against the brigandage of the [ceddo]."[21] High-profile habitant merchants, such as Gustave Chaumet, opposed any assault on Kaajor as counterproductive to French commericial aims. However, Faidherbe's

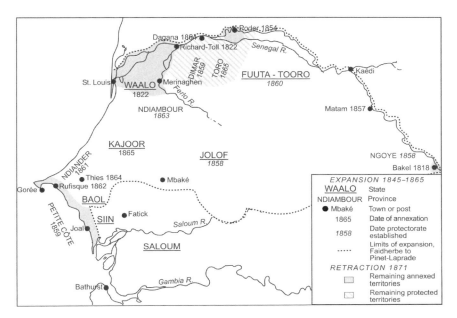

MAP 5.1
Extension and retraction of French authority in Senegal, 1854–1871

advocacy, combined with the need to secure the new port being planned in Gorée, and evidence that the damel of Kaajor had accepted many refugees from the defeated aristocracy of Waalo prevailed in metropolitan circles.[22]

The subsequent French invasion was well timed, as Kaajor was in the midst of a local civil war between the ruling Geej family and rebels, mostly Muslims who were aided by rival lineages. The rebellion had been largely crushed by early 1861, but Faidherbe concluded an alliance with the rebels, and French forces reversed the situation, driving out the Geej and their ceddo allies. Faidherbe established on the throne a puppet damel from within the rebellious factions who, during his brief and unsuccessful rule, gave France the right to fix tariffs on groundnuts entering French-controlled ports such as Dakar.[23] France further effectively acquired the Petite Côte as a de facto protectorate, further increasing France's domination of the peanut-trading coastal êntrepots, probably to the immense satisfaction of Maurel and Prom.[24] As a reward for this service, Faidherbe was given command of a newly reunited Senegal Colony that once again incorporated Gorée.[25] The 1859–1860 conquest of the states of Dimar and Toro on Waalo's flank completed this period of French expansion in Senegal.[26]

Faidherbe's conquest was made possible by the opportunistic manipulation of official policy toward slavery. His administration made judicious use of the rehabilitated policy of recruitment through rachats. Directly following the decision to emancipate the colony's slaves in 1848, the provisional government had agreed to Governor Baudin's requests that engagés in military service be retained in their positions in order to assure the security of the colony.[27] The only proviso, in keeping with the republican ethos, had been that the administration treat these soldiers exactly the same as their white colleagues in terms of food, dress, and training. However, although pragmatic considerations had necessitated the retention of the military engagement system, the emancipation act had prohibited any *new* engagements and technically forbade the policy of rachats.[28] After 1849, colonial officers were thus forced to attempt to recruit volunteers from within the colony, but military duty was apparently unpopular among the urban St. Louisian and Goréean populations. Commanders saw the muster of their units decline rapidly as engagés completed their terms.[29] In the three years following emancipation, a grand total of three African volunteers appears to have joined local compagnies.[30] In 1851 a local commission appointed to deal with this issue advised Governor Auguste Léopold Protet (Baudin's successor) that the only practicable solution was to reinstitute the policy of rachats, but the Republican government remained unwilling to sanction such a move.[31] It was not until the Restoration of 1852 that this situation changed. The bureaucrats of the Second Empire, like their predecessors prior to 1848, managed to convince themselves that the policy of rachats was not only necessary but also actually humanitarian. They praised the policy for liberating captives at the "small price," to those so released, of a few years' military service.[32] Furthermore, they suggested that such soldiers would be perfect for service in the New World, sparing French troops for European duty.[33] The Ministry of the Navy consequently reauthorized the regime des rachats for military purposes on November 30, 1854, instructing Governor Protet to form two *compagnies indigènes* (native companies).[34] Protet designed the companies to intermingle free and indentured recruits and planned to recruit 450 individuals.[35] As a sop to the nagging abolitionists in the metropole, he suggested that the engagés should serve for a shorter term than previously maintained — only seven years instead of fourteen.

However, the invasion of Waalo, carried out partly by indigenous troops, convinced Faidherbe that the available compagnies indigènes were insufficiently trained, unmotivated, and too few in number to carry out his grand plan of conquest. In 1857 he therefore convinced the Ministry of the Navy that a more highly paid and trained fighting force should be constructed with repurchased former slaves. The name he proposed for this force was the Tirailleurs Sénégalais.[36]

A small minority of the tirailleurs subsequently recruited were mercenaries, often former ceddo, from outside French jurisdiction. There were also some recruits to the force from among the disenchanted of the lower classes and special castes of Wolof society — especially blacksmiths and *griots* (bards).[37] However, the vast majority of the "enlisted" were slaves purchased from traders. When recruitment dropped, the administration simply contrived to raise the signing "bonus," which was, in fact, a fee paid directly to slave dealers and owners.[38] The number of tirailleurs doubled to one thousand by 1867 and continued to stay above that mark throughout the period of expansion, increasing again in the early 1880s.[39] There is no doubt that the tirailleurs played a major role in the French conquests of the 1850s and 1860s. Tirailleurs were the largest contingent of trained troops in Faidherbe's and his successors' campaigns on the Senegal River and in Siin-Saalum and Kaajor.[40] Without the policy of rachats, even the ministry admitted that the pacification of the peanut region would have been much more difficult and would have required an unrealistic number of French soldiers.[41]

Not only were the French willing and even eager to purchase slaves for the task of conquering the peanut-growing regions, but they subsequently employed slaves to construct most of the infrastructure for the transport and embarkation of the peanut crop. The port towns of Dakar and Rufisque, where slavery was still legally recognized, were built expressly for the export of the Kaajor and Siin-Saalum groundnut crops. Local slaveholders may have been reluctant to provide slaves to projects in Gorée and St. Louis because of the high risk that slaves would claim their freedom on French soil, but the ports of Dakar and Rufisque were outside, not legally part of, the colony, and as a result the administration could freely hire the labor of slave *manoeuvres* (manual laborers).[42] Meanwhile, hundreds of skilled artisans, many of them former slaves living in Gorée, were mobilized to supervise and carry out the construction of railway stations, forts, chapels, schools, and telegraph systems in the 1860s.[43]

The administration was consistently careful to ensure that neither the policy of rachats nor the use of contract slave labor in the construction of Dakar and Rufisque could technically implicate them in reintroducing slavery into the colony. Rachats continued to be portrayed, and to some extent accepted in the metropole, as a humanitarian means of liberating slaves. Dakar and Rufisque were consciously and repetitively described as lying outside the colony in which, although the administration clearly knew of the use of slaves and paid their masters for their labor, such an operation was technically if not morally acceptable.[44] These policies show the willingness of the administration to subvert the spirit of the emancipation laws in support of the commercial needs of the colony, a trade-off that was key to their being perceived by the metropole as successful administrators and thus gaining advancement. Such personal realities were at the center of the erosion of the 1848 emancipation policy, as political and economic realities prodded Faidherbe and his successors to dismantle that progressive act step by step.

The Dismantling of the 1848 Emancipation

Immediately following the 1848 act of emancipation, indigenous regimes in Waalo, Kaajor, and the Petite Côte had forced the colonial administration to refrain from enforcing Article 7 of the Decree Portant l'Abolition de l'Esclavage dans les Colonies (Decree regarding the abolition of slavery in the colonies), which had been intended to liberate any slaves setting foot within French-administered territory.[45] The extension of French authority after 1853 only increased the complications surrounding emancipation. As the colony expanded, new regions, specifically the peanut-growing regions, were brought under the acts of abolition.

Peanuts and slavery were by this time inextricably linked in western Senegal. The short June–November growing period of the peanut necessitated seasonal intensive labor, and therefore, although it has been noted that free peasants profited from and were empowered by their production of this cash crop, there arose by the 1860s "a heavy dependence on slave labor in the Peanut Basin"[46] during the growing season. James Searing further suggests that a series of conflicts in the Niger and Senegal River interiors during the 1870s probably exacerbated the employment of slaves in peanut production by increasing the availability of slaves.[47] In addition to slavery's role in peanut production, slaves were central to the transportation of the crop, and with the new ports of Dakar and Rufisque opening outside the colony proper, merchants were able to use slaves to transport peanuts to coastal hubs without ever entering the colony. However, the very expansion of French power and informal authority that was intended to bring the peanut fields under the closer control of the administration in St. Louis threatened this arrangement in two ways, both related to the issue of slavery. First, the 1848 act forbade habitants from owning slaves, technically precluding this important class from investing in the slavery-intensive peanut trade. Worse, when French sovereignty was technically established in the Câp Vert Peninsula and the Petite Côte in 1861, the groundnut-delivery network was threatened with the application of the policy of "soil liberates" to these regions.

These issues could have been resolved somewhat gradually if there had not existed an ever more significant competitor to French influence in the form of a growing Muslim movement. As the cultivation of peanuts enriched and empowered Sereer and Wolof peasants, they increasingly turned to Islam to liberate them from the aristocrats and ceddo who continually preyed upon them. Many in Waalo and Kaajor were especially impressed by a scholar and leader who was rising in Fuuta Tooro. El Hajj Shayk Umar Tal, head of the Tijaniyya brotherhood, had taken his first tour of the Wolof states in 1846. Operating along the upper river and attracting Manding, Wolof, and Fulbe followers, Shayk Umar was by 1854 the ruler of a large territory bordering French positions up to the post of Bakel.[48] An even more immediate threat to the St. Louisian commercial community was Maba Jaakhu. To the French a notorious bandit, Maba was an influential leader of the Muslim Tijaniyya brotherhood from the Gambia Basin who is well beloved in Senegalese popular memory. Maba clashed with the French in Saalum and would later occupy Jolof, fighting to a draw with Governor Jean Pinet-Laprade in Saalum in 1865. Maba's forces continued to clash both with the French and with secular indigenous rulers[49] until his death in battle in 1867 at the hands of the *bur* (king) of Siin.[50]

Noting the hostility of secular-political rulers such as the bur toward popular Islamic leaders, the French extended their divide-and-conquer policy, previously put to good use in Waalo and Kaajor. Whereas before Muslim and French interests had sometimes coincided, under Faidherbe and his immediate successor the divide-and-conquer strategy took the form of almost uniform support for aristocratic parties against Muslim revolutionaries, although admittedly their administrations were often more complicated in practice.[51] As a result, however, the administration came to rely upon the secular-political elements of the indigenous elite to prop up the overextended authority of the French, and Faidherbe realized that he had to avoid any move that would alienate both current and potential allies from within the aristocratic factions. This political reality precluded the imposition of the colony's policy regarding slavery even on French positions within the Wolof states and the Siin-Saalum Delta, and Faidherbe consequently moved to restrict the impact of the 1848 decree outside the colony proper. Apologists for French policy in Senegal writing as late as the early twentieth century clearly point to the military-political situation of this time as holding back the progress of emancipation during the 1850s and 1860s. "This [period]," administrator Georges Poulet argued in 1905, "was certainly not the moment to impose . . . this grand measure of emancipation."[52] Deherme similarly implored his readers to recognize the great difficulties that "forced" Faidherbe to neglect emancipation: "It [was] war throughout [Senegal]. Oualo, allied with the *trarzas,* had been invaded. The river was becoming more and more dangerous, and trade was halted up to Podor. It [was] the hour of El Hajj [Shayk U]mar and the situation was critical."[53]

Indeed, the mutual incompatibility of Faidherbe's expansionist policies and colonial antislavery laws had become evident with his first forays into the interior. The forts at Dagana and Podor, which he constructed in 1854 at the behest of the French merchant community, were by law French territory and subject to the articles of the 1848 emancipation. The previous application of stratagems to expel as "vagrants" any slaves seeking refuge in these forts had discouraged runaway slaves from the surrounding territories; but the inhabitants of the villages adjoining the posts were technically French subjects, and Faidherbe was legally obligated to liberate their slaves. Faced with this dilemma, Faidherbe turned to his advisers for ideas. In a meeting on April 27, 1854, he told them of his "intention to declare as French, all the villages which [exist] on the river within cannon shot of our forts." However, he admitted that the question of slaves made this position politically difficult.[54]

The chief justice, having obviously been briefed beforehand, was ready with a solution for the governor. Opening with the by-now-familiar formula that Senegalese slavery was benign, and further pointing out the practical consideration that enforcing emancipation would only strengthen the hand of the colony's enemies, he suggested that the inhabitants of the new territories were subjects, rather than citizens, of France. As such they were entitled to retain their slaves. The Administrative Council, agreeable to a solution that met both their personal commercial needs and the colony's political interests, unanimously assented.[55] Subsequently, Minister Hamelin condoned this arrangement whereby individuals living "under [the French] flag" could "keep their slaves."[56] The minister's approval had been the sole potential obstacle to Faidherbe's plan, and thus on October 18 he was able to issue a decree stating that for "the populations established under our posts, other than St. Louis . . . the decree of emancipation is not applicable."[57]

The invasion and conquest of Waalo created a new set of problems for Faidherbe. As his forces occupied the region, individual slaves began to claim their freedom under French law.[58] Although the number of these refugees seems to have been small at first, Faidherbe had to face the fact, based on experiences in St. Louis and Gorée in 1848, that a mass influx could occur at any time. He recognized that this could alienate his allies, but also saw the refugee slaves as a potential body of recruits for the tirailleurs. Thus in 1857 he implemented a plan that satisfied both his demands for manpower and his alliances. Purposefully eschewing the very public path of issuing an ordinance, Faidherbe instead sent out a closed policy circular to his chief justice, the imperial procurator, and the director of native affairs.[59] The instructions contained within the circular limited emancipation to the localities that had constituted the colony prior to June 27, 1848, and reaffirmed the policy of allowing French subjects, as opposed to citizens, to retain their slaves. Furthermore, Faidherbe resorted to a pragmatic ploy both to reassure the slave owners in conquered territories that their slaves would not be taken from them and to increase his forces. "If it has been officially declared that we are at war with a state . . . a decision of the governor can make it known if the fugitive slaves from that state . . . will be received in our establishments or given their liberty . . . if the slaves [seeking refuge] come from states at peace with us, we will expel them as vagabonds dangerous to public order and peace, for the reclamation of their masters who are free to reclaim them outside the forts."[60]

The absolute pragmatism of this decision was appealing to Faidherbe, who, unlike his predecessors, did not even deign to justify this policy on humanitarian grounds. Nor did this act complete his undermining of the nine-year-old sol affranchis act. He went on not only to confirm the actions taken by Baudin to expel runaway slaves from the cities as vagrants, but also to extend the policy to exclude from liberation the slave attendants of "gentlemen or chiefs" visiting St. Louis for "political affairs." Once again the metropole was forced, after the fact, to affirm an action carried out entirely by a local agent. In this case, Minister Hamelin seemed somewhat pained by the action, pointing out that Faidherbe's policy compromised a central principle of French humanitarianism, but he reluctantly agreed that the sol affranchis policy was "gravely inconvenient" in Senegal and approved the action taken to correct it.[61] In 1862, just in case there were any questions, Faidherbe publicly reprinted the 1857 circular restricting emancipation to St. Louis and its suburbs of Guet N'dar, Bouet-Ville, and N'dar Tout; Gorée; Sédhiou and Carabane in the Casamance; and the "ancient military posts of the colony of Senegal."[62]

Having successfully negotiated a solution to the "slavery issue" acceptable to both the metropolitan authorities and the local elites for the time being, Faidherbe was able to hand to his successors an economically successful colony. Admittedly, the production of peanuts had initially dropped because of the conflict of expansion and counterattacks by Islamic leaders such as Maba.[63] But in 1867 Governor Pinet-Laprade was able to report exports of 2.5 million kilograms of groundnuts from the Senegal River region, 4.5 million kilograms from Rufisque/ Dakar, and 450,000 kilograms from the smaller ports at Portudal and Joal on the Petite Côte.[64] The colony and its "allies" were now organized into three *arrondisements* (districts). The first was based on St. Louis and incorporated the annexed region of Waalo. The second was similarly headquartered on Gorée and encompassed the indirect administration of much of Kaajor and Siin and parts of Saalum. The third was composed of the portions of the interior regions of Dimar, Toro, and Fuuta Tooro based around the riverbank forts of Bakel, Mèdine, Saldé, and Matam, all of which housed French garrisons. However, only in Waalo was there an effective French administration. Kaajor and the second arrondisement were largely controlled by aristocrats, chiefly the damel Lat Joor and his ceddo general Demba War Sall, with limited dependence upon French aid, whereas real French authority in the third arrondisement did not reach far beyond the forts themselves.

DUTCH WITHDRAWAL, THE SANGRETI WAR, AND BRITISH HEGEMONY ON THE GOLD COAST

Unlike Faidherbe's expansion in Senegal, the creation of the British Gold Coast Protectorate was not only unanticipated but also unlooked-for, even by the local administration. The first step toward the creation of British hegemony was the departure of Holland, Britain's only European competitor remaining on the coast. But the Dutch withdrawal of April 1873 was not the product of British pressure, its proximal cause instead being the resistance of the inhabitants of Dixcove and the nearby Fante towns that had been placed under Dutch authority by the Anglo-Dutch territorial exchange agreement of 1867.[65] Aside from anger over the failure of the two European powers to consult with indigenous authorities about the proposed exchange, the major factor behind the resulting unrest with Dutch rule was Holland's alliance with Asante, whose territorial designs on Fante and desire for a coastal outlet were long standing.[66] The Asante-Dutch relationship centered around Holland's recognition of Asante claims to the town of Elmina, which led to the siege of that town by the young men of the fledgling Fante Confederation in 1868, a confrontation that continued until 1870 and brought Asante forces into the region in support of Elmina.[67] In May of that year, a Dutch fleet in support of Elmina undertook a prolonged bombardment of the Ahanta town of Dixcove.[68] However, as expenses continued to mount and trade suffered, the Dutch Parliament decided to cut its losses and agreed to a handover of territory to the British in 1873; Britain seized upon this opportunity to monopolize commerce from the Gold Coast.

British hegemony over the coast was completed by the withering away of the Fante Confederation. This indigenous union deserves a further moment of our attention. By November 1871 the confederation had blossomed from a self-defense league into an experiment in self-government. The constitution signed on November 18 was striking in its attention to development and modernization. The proposed administration incorporated chiefly officeholders and "educated gentlemen" in a bicameral legislature sharing power with an executive council responsible for an extensive bureaucracy. Aside from defense, the government was especially concerned with modernization and development: roads, schools, agriculture, industry, and mining all claim their own clause in the constitution. Through these clauses, the constitution illustrated both the desire to emulate perceived European strategies of state building and the recognition that Britain could not be trusted to carry out such projects. Yet one subject that was not mentioned in the constitution, but was important in both respects, was the regulation of labor. Despite its modernizing tone, the confederation leadership appears to have avoided any acknowledgment that slavery existed, and to have failed to call for its end. The reasons for this are obvious—among its leadership were many of the principal slaveholders in Fanteland, both chiefs and merchants. The quashing of the confederation in 1873 ended their political experiment, but not their opposition to abolition.[69]

The retreat of the Dutch and the dissipation of the Fante Confederation gave Britain a colony consisting of an uninterrupted coastal strip without forcing any costly expansion into the interior states, many of which were already British "allies" and "protectorates." The coastal powers were largely willing to accept Britain's hegemony, and the large states of the interior, such as Akyem Abuakwa and Akuapem, generally also proved amenable to British "protection," which in any case implied very little interference indeed.[70] However, the administration's refusal to honor the Asante "note" to Elmina and Britain's obvious bias toward their Fante and Ahanta antagonists infuriated the Asante.[71] It was this issue that seems to have caused Asantehene Kofi Kakari to order an invasion of the British-protected provinces.[72] Kakari is alleged to have stated that "Elmina is transferred but not in the heart."[73]

There are several explanations for the asantehene's decision to go to war besides the decisive issue of Elmina. British authorities had, in the 1850s, begun to decline to return refugee slaves or fugitives fleeing the asantehene's justice. In fact, Ivor Wilks has shown that it was a squabble over the fugitive Kwasi Gyani, charged with hoarding rock gold, that precipitated brief and unsatisfying hostilities in 1863.[74] Bitterness from that earlier conflict helped strengthen the war party in Kumasi, already ascendant after Kofi Kakari's enstoolment, and it was this internal power shift that led to the authorization of the 1873 invasion of the protected territories. However, it should be noted that Anglo-Asante tensions had been smoldering for a decade, at one point igniting a proxy war on the Volta River.

The subsequent campaign, resulting in considerable casualties among both African and European contingents of the British and allied forces and a substantial cost to taxpayers, culminated in an allied victory in 1874. Although the triumph did not result in an occupation of Asante, the defeat of the Asante army and a flurry of secessions by the provinces of Juaben, Bekwae, and Adansi definitively ended Asante political and military presence in the south and left Britain with dominion by default.[75] The bewildered British thus found themselves the leaders of a victorious coalition of states and consequently committed to establishing some sort of colonial administration, whereas they had fought only to repel an invasion that threatened their economic interests. Unwilling to shoulder the expense of formally extending the colony, Whitehall settled upon a hybrid model that consisted of a small, coastal colony based around Cape Coast and Accra and a much larger protectorate reaching to the southern limit of the weakened Asante state, with the distinction between the two left loosely defined. However, even this limited arrangement obliged the administration to extend certain aspects of British and colonial law into the protected territories. As Faidherbe had discovered two centuries before, the most troublesome of these was official policy toward slavery. Moreover, the new administration of the Gold Coast Colony and Protectorate had to face this problem immediately, as the war had focused upon them the attention of the abolitionist lobby, which was shocked by exposés of slavery in the colony written by newspapermen accompanying the army.

Raymond Dumett, in his article on the origins of the 1874 ordinances, "Pressure groups, Bureaucracy, and the Decision-Making Process," identifies in this process various political, economic, and humanitarian concerns at work in Britain.[76] Dumett suggests that in the case of the Gold Coast, proimperialist newspapers and parliamentarians appropriated the language of humanitarianism and imperial responsibility as a means to build support for the establishment of formal colonialism. However, emancipation itself was injected into the debate by humanitarian groups, specifically the British and Foreign Anti-Slavery Society, which conducted a campaign of letter writing and publications supported by the lobbying efforts of the Aborigines' Protection Society and by reports from the field by reporters confronted with the realities of slavery in the

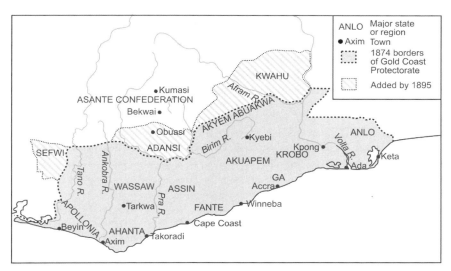

MAP 5.2
Limits of Gold Coast Protectorate, 1874 and 1895

Gold Coast.[77] It was this pressure that forced decision makers in Whitehall to confront the fact that the expansion of British control required the extension of British law, which technically forbade the institution of slavery. The subsequent proclamation of the protectorate called not only for civil and commercial jurisdiction, administration, and taxation but also for the "Abolition of Slave dealing" and "measures with regard to domestic slavery and pawning."[78]

Secretary of State for the Colonies the Earl of Carnarvon was thus faced with a conundrum similar to that faced by Faidherbe, in that stringent antislavery laws were clearly as incompatible with British expansion as they had been with French. However, as a politician, Carnarvon was more responsive to the British public's calls for a more stringent antislavery policy in the newly formalized protectorate. Personally, also, he was opposed to what he considered the "worst excesses" of slavery. To his mind this was represented by the importation and sale of slaves within the protectorate, a practice he called "an outrage and a crime [to be] punished as such wheresoever the authority of the British Crown can avail to bring it to justice."[79] Carnarvon was thus disposed toward taking action against the slave trade. Conversely, he recognized that both long-standing export goods such as gold and palm products and the potentially profitable crops of gum-copal and coffee, which had recently been introduced into the interior, relied to some extent upon slave labor for production and transportation.[80] He had clearly been informed of the prevalence of domestic slavery both in agriculture and gold production and in domestic service to established chiefs and trading/land-owning elites.[81]

Even more critical, from the perspective of the Colonial Office, was the potential cost and difficulty of implementing a fully staffed colonial administration complete with military, judicial, and executive officers. The expense of placing and maintaining this level of organization in the Gold Coast had been made clear by the expenditures of the Asante War, and the Colonial Office was eager to secure the support of paramount and lesser chiefs in order to limit the size and cost of colonial administration. They were forced to acknowledge, however, that the authority of these officeholders was based on their control of land and labor, much of which was not free, a situation that was to continue throughout the century. "It seems doubtful," an Anglo-African administrator would write as late as 1927, "whether the system [of chief's rule] can be long maintained in this country . . . but for what remains of the domestic slave system."[82] Therefore, although Carnarvon was favorably disposed toward the enforcement of anti–slave-*trading* ordinances that would appeal to abolitionists in the metropole while threatening the livelihoods of only a relatively small number of full-time slave traders, he was nevertheless wary of undertaking the difficult task of enforcing *emancipation* for the bulk of the protectorate's slaves.

The Colonial Office therefore began to study plans to appease both abolitionists at home and the slave-owning elite of the protectorate. From this effort emerged three proposals, which Carnarvon subsequently put before the Gold Coast administration. The first scheme put forward, by which the *government* would purchase the slaves by payment of £8 per slave and then make use of them for a number of years on a policy basically identical to the regime des engagés, was quickly rejected.[83] What was acceptable to French society in the 1840s was not acceptable to Britain in the 1870s. Similarly, the proposed "Sixes model," based on the Basel Mission Society's actions of the 1860s, was rejected by the newly arrived governor, George Strahan.[84] This program, through which a slave was to have been immediately awarded one free day to work for him/herself and purchase the other days from his/her master over a period of years, appealed to the Colonial Office because of its implicitly gradual approach. But that same attribute would probably have made it unacceptable to the British public; as Strahan noted when he wrote to Carnarvon, "Only very slowly would this method operate (if ever it sufficed) to wipe out the reproach of slavery in the Protectorate."[85] Strahan also argued that the logistics of implementing such a proposal among numerous slaves without a strong commitment by the understaffed administration to keep records and police the scheme would lead to its failure.[86]

Carnarvon therefore put his weight behind a third proposed system of emancipation, termed the "Indian model" after the region in which it had first been promulgated, which required the administration immediately to end the legal status of slavery but forced the slaves themselves to take legal action in order to win their emancipation. The Indian model had the dual advantages of immediately granting slaves the right to seek their emancipation while making it somewhat difficult to achieve, thus limiting the chance of a mass exodus of slaves from the entourages of their masters and their positions in transportation, agriculture, and mining. The Indian model was also accepted by the local merchants and administrators who made up the colony's Legislative Council; in September 1874 Governor Strahan adopted drafts of two ordinances based on this plan to be enacted on December 17.[87]

However, whereas the administration clearly had the power to implement this act in the colony, which was after all "nothing but the forts and lands immediately around them or actually acquired by the Government," the case was not as apparent for the bulk of the protectorate.[88] Carnarvon, however, stated in no uncertain terms that if Britain were to accept increased defense and administrative responsibility for these districts, it would have to be allowed to exercise certain rights of control. He therefore informed the local administrators that he was willing to "incur some risk for the sake of removing the dishonor and moral taint which is incurred by a toleration of slavery."[89] He argued that the states of the protectorate owed this favor to his government which, "as their deliverer [in the 1873–84 Asante War], is entitled to require of them a greater degree of deference and conformity. . . . Their conformity is required in pursuit of . . . the immediate abolition of slave dealing and the importation of slaves, to be followed by such regulation of the relations between master and slave as shall, ultimately, and in the long course of time, effect the extinction of slavery itself."[90] With this argument, Carnarvon not only rationalized the extension of British jurisdiction, but also stressed that the extinction of the slave trade, rather than the suppression of domestic slavery, was Britain's priority. This prioritization was again reflected in Strahan's two ordinances on December 27, 1874, which were accepted by the Legislative Council in Cape Coast with little debate.[91]

The first part of this carefully coordinated scheme was the Gold Coast Slave Dealing Abolition Act, which dealt with the crimes of "slave dealing" and "the importation of slaves into the protectorate." The charge of slave dealing was to be applied to anyone who "shall . . . deal or trade in, sell, barter, transfer or take any slave . . . or any person in order so that such person should be held or treated as a slave."[92] The same charge was also, confusingly, to be applied to individuals placing or receiving a pawn.[93] Further, slave dealing applied to both the exportation of slaves from and importation of slaves into the protectorate. For all these activities, the administration decreed punishment of up to five years' imprisonment and a fine.[94]

The second act, the Gold Coast Emancipation Ordinance, implemented the more passive Indian model. The Emancipation Ordinance was intended to demonstrate both the administration's commitment to allowing slave liberations and its support for the status quo in slave-master relationships. The operative clauses of the ordinance simply ordered "all courts to 'refuse, disallow, discharge, and dismiss' any claims held by one person over another . . . providing always that this enactment shall not be construed to include or apply to such rights as under the ordinary rules of English law applicable to the Gold Coast Colony may arise under and by virtue of contracts of service between freemen."[95] Although the ordinance did not, as Strahan had originally intended, go so far as to recognize "tribal [dependency] relations according to the customary law of the Protected Territories," it went some way toward reassuring slave owners that their slaves would not be encouraged to seek liberation.[96] The punishment for "compelling the service of any . . . free person" was set at five years' imprisonment.[97] Surveying the two ordinances, a satisfied Strahan informed Carnarvon that they successfully embodied the government's intention not to encourage slave liberations actively. "I do not anticipate," he wrote in a September 19 letter, "that the slaves will immediately in any large numbers leave their masters."[98]

THE IMMEDIATE IMPACT OF THE EMANCIPATION ORDINANCE IN THE GOLD COAST

Strahan was only the first in a long line of administrators, and then historians, to comment on the impact of the 1874 acts, for the issue has been the subject of rigorous debate by the colonial and academic communities. In his 1927 *Memorandum on the Vestiges of Slavery in the Gold Coast,* for example, Assistant Secretary for Native Affairs J. C. de Graft Johnson tells his readers that "there [had been] no general eagerness for manumission."[99] Johnson was merely reflecting the official consensus within the Gold Coast administration for stressing "continuity," rather than mass desertion, as evidenced by Strahan's letters to Carnarvon a half century before suggesting that there was little disturbance caused by the emancipation ordinances.[100] The "continuity" theory was actively promoted by the colonial establishment, but historians of Africa such as Paul Lovejoy began to ask serious questions about abolition and emancipation in Africa at the end of the 1970s, suggesting that emancipation was in some regions the cause of massive social and political shifts. These "transformational" ideas are best represented in the historiography of the Gold Coast by Gerald McSheffrey's 1983 article "Slavery, Indentured Servitude, Legitimate Trade, and the Impact of Abolition in the Gold Coast 1874–1910: A Reappraisal."[101] Using excerpts from the Basel Mission Archives, translated by Paul Jenkins, that suggested that mass self-liberations by slaves did occur, especially in the interior of the protectorate, McSheffrey put forward the argument that emancipation caused a major dislocation in slave owning on the Gold Coast. The evidence mainly consisted of several letters that claimed that in Ada "from almost every master some slaves have gone,"[102] in Akyem Abuakwa's capital of Kyebi "about 100 slaves have left their masters,"[103] and in Akuapem "about 200 slaves have run away."[104] Many of the documents emerged from the mission station in Kyebi, which was both a minor producer of palm oil and well monitored by Basel missionaries. However, McSheffrey has himself come under significant criticism for overlooking Basel Mission documents that suggested that relatively few slaves actually left their masters in Akuapem, Krobo, and other internal regions.[105] Furthermore, the Kyebi mission's reports on which he relies have since been brought into question, as the chief missionaries were concurrently embroiled in a conflict with the local government based largely on the confrontational tactics of indigenous missionary David Asante, a cousin and rival of the okyenhene.[106]

The case against McSheffrey's transformation thesis has been put forward by Raymond Dumett and Marion Johnson, who argue that the administration maintained a "gradualist, noncoercive policy with respect to slaveholding and pawning," and that its efforts were "meliorative and eroding rather than abolitionist in effect."[107] Although something of a return to the official colonial theory of "continuance," Dumett and Johnson's article was well supported by a variety of administrative and missionary sources. However, this approach has again been questioned recently, not least by John Parker, who in his study of the urban history of Accra argued that "the available evidence points neither to the historiographical polarities of 'continuity' or 'rupture,' but rather to a whole range of responses often involving negotiations between masters and slaves."[108] Kwabena Opare Akurang-Parry also muddies the waters by suggesting that there was a division between the colony, in which British enforcement was strong and there was a large slave response, and the protectorate, in which enforcement, and consequently response, was weak.[109] While Akurang-Parry's arguments are made somewhat suspect by his apparent failure to accept the nineteenth-century definition of the colony as only the few forts and settlements of the coast and not their surrounding districts, Parker has to a large extent pointed the way to a new direction for understanding emancipation.[110] The evidence for the Gold Coast in general matches that which Parker has found for Accra. The 1874 emancipation, although not immediately revolutionary for most slaves and slave owners, did result in a long-term transformation and in a wide variety of negotiated outcomes for slaves and their masters.[111]

In the short term, however, the colonial administration appears to have succeeded in providing a route for emancipation without encouraging a rupture in the local economy or society. Although McSheffrey, and to some extent Akurang-Parry, claim that there is "ample testimony that serious disruptions had indeed occurred,"[112] their evidence rests on a very few letters from Basel missions and one purely anecdotal reference by Governor Strahan.[113] Evidence counter to McSheffrey's thesis, on the other hand, is now emerging from the SCT (Supreme Court) colonial magistracy files in the National Archives of Ghana, which both McSheffrey and Akurang-Parry ignored but which contain valuable quantitative and qualitative information.

It is clear from these sources that it was British rather than indigenous courts that dealt with slave-related crimes during the postproclamation period (and up to the end of British rule on the Gold Coast). The 1853 Supreme Court ordinance had been an attempt to marginalize indigenous jurisprudence in the towns contiguous with British settlements and forts, but by the 1860s British courts were out of favor with the local population.[114] The extension of the protectorate in 1874 necessitated the reemergence of British courts both within the colony and throughout the newly "protected" districts. However, the scarcity of healthy European administrators meant that Africans, and more frequently Euro-Africans, continued to play a significant role in judicial and civil administrations.[115] Important Africans, including known former (and possibly current) slave owners, were in rare instances even appointed to senior judicial posts. One of the most important of these figures was George Cleland. A notable slave owner, relative of the Alato mantse, and one-time acting holder of that Jamestown stool, Cleland had led a militia of his slaves in support of the British in 1873, and after having headed an indigenous tribunal for several years, was appointed as a justice of the peace by Strahan in 1874.[116] Cleland, who had been indicted for purchasing a slave in 1868, was nevertheless given jurisdiction over British subjects within the colony for an indeterminate period, although not without some controversy.[117]

Although the appointment of Africans and Euro-Africans to such major posts was uncommon, even during the transition period of 1874–1875, educated locals continued to serve as clerks and translators, and of course served in the constabulary. In addition, both the judicial assessor's court, which initially dealt with slave-related crimes, and the divisional court in Accra, which replaced it in 1878, allowed participation by local notables in the judicial process.[118] Defendants at the divisional court could request trial by a jury of their peers, who, to the frustration of the administration, frequently chose to acquit individuals whom the administration believed to be guilty.[119] Even when defendants did not insist on jury trial, the chief justice of the divisional court was usually assisted by both European and non-European assessors.[120] Although the presiding justice could legally disregard the opinions of assessors, their advice was generally accepted.

District courts, only slowly being formed during this period, did not deal with slave-related crimes, and slaves who wished to follow the only path to legal emancipation available to them under the Indian model—the courts—had to travel to Cape Coast or Accra to receive their emancipation.[121] This was probably a greater hindrance to emancipation than the frequently cited argument that slaves were ignorant of the proclamation.[122] It is therefore indicative of the agency of some individual slaves that they trickled in from the Akuapem hills, Akyem Abuakwa, and farther to receive their certificates of liberation.[123] Nevertheless, initially the numbers of slaves seeking their liberation was not significant. Certainly there were a few who chose to use the legal intervention of the courts. Court records indicate only approximately twenty cases of slaves or their families using the legal system to effect their liberation before 1880 in the judicial assessors' and district courts combined, and most of these individuals were recently introduced slaves rather than long-time servitors.[124] At the same time, Dumett and Johnson rightly point out that even the most dramatic (and questionable) mass desertions (extralegal) suggested by the Basel Mission archival evidence speak of only one hundred to two hundred slaves, whereas in many areas Basel Mission sources indicate few liberations indeed.[125]

The agency of slaves is the topic of the next chapter, but it is interesting to note that there is no evidence at all during the period of initial emancipation (1874–1880) of judicial authorities commissioning proactive investigations into slaveholding or even slave dealing. Of the forty-eight cases involving slavery or pawning heard during this period, twenty-eight apparently resulted from the police acting on the advice of a witness, slave owners belatedly hearing of the emancipation acts and throwing themselves upon the mercy of the court (which was usually given), or a police constable happening upon a crime being committed.[126] However, although there are no cases during this period of magistrates commissioning investigations, when the abolitionist press got hold of a story such as the sale in Little Popo of two Gold Coast girls, the administration was willing to go to great lengths to reclaim or repurchase those individuals.[127]

The expansion of British authority, and especially the Sangreti (Anglo-Asante) War of 1873, necessitated an increasing commitment in terms of military power. The failure of the officers of the Gold Coast Corps to recruit coastal peoples into British units or to receive permission from the Colonial Office to recruit slaves had resulted in a divided constabulary.[128] Most of the coastal forts were manned by small contingents of the 171-man "Fantee Armed Police." A larger force, the 211-man "Houssa Armed Police," recruited mostly by missions to Lagos and the upper Volta region, constituted the garrisons of Cape Coast and Elmina.[129] These small forces were totally insufficient in the face of the Asante invasion, however, and despite augmentation by both British regulars and West Indian units, campaign commander General Garnet Wolseley instituted a levy of coastal peoples. Response was good, and a significant proportion of the young male population of the Fante polities especially willingly volunteered for duty against the Asante, either individually or in asafo companies. By November 4, 1873, Wolseley had more than 3,200 indigenous auxiliary combatants.[130] The number of associated carriers is unknown, but was probably even larger.

In the face of the Asante military threat, however, at least one of Wolseley's officers decided to reconsider the policy of exclusion of slave recruits from colonial forces. Captain John Glover, the former governor of Lagos, actively recruited slaves in late 1873 for a column aimed at striking through the bush for Kumasi. Glover's recruitment of slaves must be seen in light of events in Accra, from where he was planning to organize a column to support Sir Garnet Wolseley's main attack from Cape Coast. The preponderance of the Ga population of Accra was uninterested in attacking Asante, being instead preoccupied with the new tariffs by which Britain proposed to pay for the war, and more concerned with fighting their commercial competitors in the Voltaic states to the east. Thus Glover was forced to report that he found "no enthusiasm for a confrontation with Asante."[131] Changing tack, in August and September Glover's recruiting agents redirected their efforts toward recruiting "slaves of persons residing at Cape Coast and other places on the Gold Coast" with the result that a number of slaves seized the opportunity to enlist.[132] Many of these were *odonko,* or recently purchased northerners, and thus of similar origin to the trained Hausa constabulary that had arrived to form the core of Glover's fighting force. The Hausas encouraged slaves to join them, and, when in response many of Accra's notables began to lock up their odonko, Hausa constables broke into the residence of Ga mantse (paramount) Taki Tawia himself in order to release slaves who had been imprisoned there.[133]

TABLE 5.1

Recruits to the Houssa Armed Police, September 1873

Status	Number	Percent
Current slaves in colony	26	47
Current slaves outside colony	8	15
Former slaves, purchased freedom	2	4
Former slave, manumitted	1	2
Former slave, freed by Governor Hill	1	2
Former slaves, refugee from Asante	6	11
Former slaves, freed by death of master	5	9
Former slaves, run away from master	4	7
Free individuals, no slave history	2	4
TOTAL	55	101

Source: NAG ADM 1/10/2, Nominal Roll with Particulars, September 1873.

A register of recruits to Glover's force in September 1873, shown above in table 5.1, shows that the inductees were almost entirely northerners and most were Muslim.[134] A plurality were individuals who, until joining the force, had been slaves within the Gold Coast colony (mainly Accra), but many others were from allied states abutting colonial towns. It is clear from correspondence surrounding this recruitment effort that their masters were strongly opposed to their induction, and at at least one point this led to a street riot in which several enlisted slaves and masters were injured.[135] Other inductees were slaves who had either bought their freedom or been given their liberty upon the deaths of their masters, or in some cases slaves who had fled their owners several years previously. These former slaves were probably convinced to join by the promise of a recruitment bonus and wages inflated by the war. At least one recruit had been freed by Governor R. M. Hill over thirty years earlier! Only two enlistees were free individuals who claimed never to have been slaves.

However, in contrast to the French minister's approval of the tirailleurs sénégalaises in 1857, the Colonial Office balked when Captain Glover suggested that recruitment efforts could be aided if masters were paid a £5 bounty for "allowing" their slaves to join up.[136] Glover had authorized this policy, but not without alerting General Wolseley, and Wolseley communicated the proposition to Secretary of State for the Colonies John Wodehouse, first Earl of Kimberley. Kimberley deemed the issue important enough to consult with Gladstone himself, and the prime minister did not approve.[137] Consequently, on December 17, 1873, Kimberley instructed Wolseley to forbid Glover from recruiting on this basis. Although "mak[ing] full allowance for the difficulty in which Captain

Glover has found himself placed in recruiting for the Houssa Force," Kimberley stated, "As his actions, although beneficial to the slaves in procuring their emancipation and enabling them to engage in a well paid and honourable service, may be misconstrued and might lay Her Majesty's government open to the charge of encouraging the traffic in slaves, I think it desirable that he should discontinue the practice of making payments to masters on account of the enlistment of their slaves, and I request you to so instruct him."[138]

There are several reasons that the British rejected a policy that the French in Senegal had embraced. The most obvious was the pressure of abolitionism, which was greater in Britain than in France, and which had also steadily increased in the decade and a half since the creation of the tirailleurs. Second, there was the precedent of Newcastle's order in 1862 against such recruiting methods.[139] More practically, the Colonial Office was wary of offending the same chiefly office-holders upon whom they depended for the bulk of their auxiliaries, an important contingent of the British forces, by accepting their slaves into service. But perhaps most importantly, British commanders on the Gold Coast were simply not facing the same recruiting problems as Faidherbe. Whereas Faidherbe's conquests had been largely unpopular with Senegal's neighbors, Wolseley was fighting a popular defensive action alongside the coastal powers, rather than a war of expansion, and was strongly supported by the militias of neighboring states. He simply did not need to resort to the same measures as Faidherbe. A cynic might suggest that even abolitionist Britain might have allowed the purchase and indenture of slaves by the administration if it had been strictly necessary from a military point of view, but in this case it was not.

After 1874 the issue of the recruitment of slaves seemed a moot point as slavery had lost its legal status, and slaves did not technically exist in the protectorate or colony. However, the administration continued to be starved of recruits to both constabulary forces. The militia for coastal peoples—the Fante constabulary—was cut down to two hundred troops because of a lack of volunteers, whereas the Hausa force, with nine hundred individuals, was given a larger share of responsibility for the protectorate. There is evidence that some slaves of northern origins who left their masters in 1874 and 1875 joined the Hausa constabulary, at least from the coastal areas, but clearly not en masse, since commanders continued to be forced to recruit from outside the protectorate in order to fill their units.[140] In 1875 Captain Barrows led a successful recruiting drive along the Niger River,[141] but as soon as 1879 another mission had to be carried out in the same region and in Salaga north of the protectorate.[142] Within the year, Governor Herbert Ussher was forced to request permission to send yet another recruiter along the Niger.[143] At one point, the desperate administration was even considering enlisting people from Manding communities in the Gambia.[144] Unlike in Senegal, the recruitment of slaves and former slaves in the Gold Coast was clearly not a success.

Although there were obvious differences between European attitudes toward slavery in the Gold Coast and Senegal during their respective periods of expansion, the general goal of both administrations was to ensure the profitability and the security of the colonies. As in Faidherbe's Senegal, the immediate postproclamation period on the Gold Coast witnessed the introduction of administrative attempts to control labor supplies for profitable cash products. For example, in 1877 Governor Sanford Freeling introduced rules governing apprenticeship that allowed for court-sanctioned apprentice positions for individuals between the ages of nine and sixteen not only in the trades but also in positions of domestic servitude.[145] Thus the administration could place youths, especially orphans, in positions that had previously been filled by slaves, albeit not exclusively. On the other hand, Freeling crafted the ordinance with a view to preventing apprentices from becoming slaves by setting up a mandatory certification process and forbidding the removal of apprentices from the protectorate. Unfortunately, I have found little further evidence on this subject, but the system does not appear to have been extended to agricultural work. This fact can be interpreted as indicating that there was no labor shortage in agriculture, and thus no major exodus of slaves from this field, although the connection is tenuous.

Still, Carnarvon's and Strahan's plan to implement an emancipation policy that would not strip workers and domestics from their positions appears to have succeeded. Between 1875 and 1876 production of palm oil grew from 2.68 million gallons to 3.87 million gallons, palm kernel exports climbed from 4,677 tons to 7,655 tons, and gold exports increased from 11,801 ounces to 17,280 ounces.[146] At the same time, the administration largely avoided censure by the abolitionist missionary communities throughout the colony. Although in 1874 the Methodists were attracting 10,400 attendants to public worship in twenty-three chapels in coastal towns and had a combined membership of 2,513, their only response to emancipation was to welcome its implementation.[147] In the next five years there is no evidence that they issued any complaints as to the pursuit of emancipation by the government. The Basel Mission Society was somewhat more active, requesting police presence in Kyebi to monitor slavery in 1875 and accusing the okyenhene of slaveholding in 1879, but these actions seem to have been the result of conflict with the traditional party in Akyem Abuakwa rather than emancipationist fervor, and the Basel missionaries otherwise appear to have largely accepted the implementation and enforcement of the Indian model.[148] Colonial governors encouraged this acquiescence through the judicious use of propaganda. The annexation of Keta in 1879 had the dual goals of claiming the mouth of the Volta before any other colonial power could and stopping the smuggling of legitimate goods in order to avoid British tariffs, but it was also useful propaganda since the administration implied that it would close the regions' major slave-trading markets.[149] In the face of such evidence it is difficult to express British attitudes toward slavery between 1874 and 1880 better than Dumett and Johnson, who wrote that "[our] impression gained is that of a government which hoped by mere expressions of disapproval to reduce the harsher aspects of indigenous slavery gradually—but which preferred the status quo and looked paternalistically on slaves remaining close to former masters as the most effective means of social control."[150]

— —

I have argued that the policies of administrators on the Gold Coast and Senegal toward emancipation in the mid-nineteenth century were pragmatic. In the face of increased responsibility, and with little physical assistance from the metropole, administrators formulated and carried out policy themselves and applied only afterward for support from their superiors. However, if their policies were "pragmatic," it was a pragmatism born of the realities of a situation in which the socioeconomic and political state of the colony, and potentially their own chances for advancement, relied largely on the cooperation of slave owners and the complacency of slaves, neither of which was simple to ensure. If it seems that I have implied in this chapter that administrative policy was more central to emancipation's outcome than was indigenous agency, it is only because in the next two chapters I intend to show how Africans and Euro-Africans were major players in limiting the effectiveness of emancipation and slave policy.

CHAPTER 6

Slaves and Masters in the Postproclamation Gold Coast

THE EMANCIPATION POLICY that the British administration carried out on the Gold Coast after 1874 was removed from that envisaged by abolitionists not once, but twice. In the last chapter, we saw how Strahan's administration and the Colonial Office cast the antislavery ordinances in a mold shaped in part by their recognition of their partnership with slave owners and in part by their fear of the economic and political chaos threatened by a mass slave exodus. The larger deviation, however, came not in the *production* of a policy informed by the administration's concerns but in its *execution*. Under the Indian model, the administration abdicated its central role in the emancipation process to slaves and slave owners. Thus, although antislavery policy was created by the metropole and carried out by the local administration, in fact the most important actors would be these two indigenous groups.

The primacy of slave choice in determining the impact of emancipation is generally recognized by historians—Raymond Dumett and Marion Johnson have argued that "the most formidable roadblock against wholesale emancipation . . . was the reluctance of slaves themselves to come forward," and the evidence I present here largely supports their view of how slave agency affected the course of emancipation.[1] However, relatively little attention has been given to the views and actions of slave owners beyond the peripheral subject of monetary compensation, which the exchequer declined to approve.[2] Nevertheless, slave owners were in fact central participants in the process, devising mechanisms to avert, evade, and mitigate the potentially ruinous transformations resulting from the emancipation ordinances. Conversely, the major contribution of the administration to this process was to provide a catalyst for and recognition of a slave's free status. This potential for emancipation allowed slaves to reevaluate their relationships with their masters through individual solutions negotiated largely outside the formal judicial system.

SLAVE OWNERS: RESISTANCE

In order to understand how masters affected the course of emancipation, it is necessary to step back and look at who owned slaves in the Gold Coast Protectorate of the 1870s. It is perhaps inaccurate to argue that there was a slave-owning "class" or "classes," but certainly the ownership of slaves was intricately connected to wealth, status, and power. In earlier centuries, slaves had been the dominant "form of private, revenue producing property"[3] in a region in which land tenure was generally vested communally—in the family or stool—rather than privately.[4] The gradual imposition of British authority had served only to formalize this situation, as administrators tried to impose a normative set of laws in a region in which there had previously been some variety.[5] Indeed, Basel Mission agents complained about the resulting refusal on the part of the administration to turn stool land over to private individuals, especially exslaves, in regions in which some form of private tenure of land had previously existed.[6] Thus, when emancipation was promulgated, a large proportion of slaves, especially in rural areas, were still tied to chiefly officeholders and were still engaged in agrarian, artisanal, military, and status-building occupations. Basel Mission agents depicted the slaves of important chiefs as particularly poorly treated, but their conflicts with hostile officeholders such as the okyenhene of Akyem Abuakwa may have contributed to this view.[7]

In any event, the evidence suggests that by the 1870s the preponderance of slaves was held not by stool holders but by families of lesser status, in part because of changes discussed in chapters 1 and 2. In an 1875 letter, the Basel missionary agent Zimmerman specifically identified the majority of slave owners as being not aristocratic,[8] and J. C. de Graft Johnson similarly noted in 1927 that "there is no family of any note in the whole country which does not have amongst its members one or more domestic servants . . . over [which] . . . heads of families in the past . . . exercise[d] unlimited authority."[9] Admittedly, a number of "slaves" so identified may have been pawns in debt bondage—an institution that had also become increasingly prevalent in the seventeenth and eighteenth centuries — or even apprentices or members of an inferior branch of the abusua. Nevertheless, the picture that emerges is one of widespread ownership of slaves.

The third slave-owning group consisted of the merchants of coastal settlements, some of whom held chiefly office as well. Zimmerman argued that these "educated slave owners" and "merchants of the coast" were especially harsh masters.[10] Whether this is true or not is unclear, but certainly the role of their slaves was largely linked to the production of commodities and had been formed by the growth in legitimate trade in the nineteenth century. Their slave workforce, probably augmented by pawns, since merchants were prominent moneylenders, labored in the fields to provide food to the coastal settlements, provided domestic service, and carried trade goods to and from the interior. Others ran market stalls in both coastal cities and regional market hubs where they sold goods produced on their masters' rural farms.[11]

In opposing the antislavery acts of 1874, it was clearly the chiefly officeholders and coastal merchants who formed the potential leadership of the slave owners. However, the capacity of the coastal elite to oppose the colonial administration, forged in part by their management of such institutions as the Fante Confederation, was to some extent weakened by their reliance on Britain as a trading partner. Likewise, whereas the administration was progressively driven by its financial and personnel problems to depend upon the cooperation of chiefly officeholders, the chiefs themselves relied on British military power to defend them from potentially resurgent Asante threats and to shore up their deteriorating finances through stipendiary payments. Few wanted to end up like the king of Denkyira who by 1890 was forced to lease stool land to stay solvent, and fewer still like the rulers of Akyem Abuakwa and Wassaw who, as we will see, were exiled by the British for infractions of protectorate law.[12] In the wake of the Sangreti War, British power, while incomplete, was evidently strong enough to reprimand or remove individual rulers and assist others. Thus it is understandable that there was little forcible opposition by elites to the promulgation of the 1874 Slave Dealing Abolition and Emancipation ordinances. Indeed, Governor Strahan famously informed Carnarvon five months after the ordinances were promulgated that "public tranquillity has not been disturbed; on the contrary, I am confident that at no time in the history of the Protectorate has there been greater regard for established authority or more ready obedience to the laws than at present."[13]

Since the fortunes of both chiefs and merchants were now inextricably tied to the administration, violent opposition to the reforms did not materialize. Instead, indigenous traditional leaders dutifully appeared at meetings Strahan called to explain the two antislavery ordinances on November 3, 1874, in Cape Coast for the western chiefs, and on November 5 in Accra for chiefs in the eastern districts.[14] Strahan reported that his presentations were well received, and the kings and chiefs generally accepted the interdiction against buying and selling slaves. However, at the meeting in Cape Coast there was a murmur of opposition against the liberation of "old pawns" and "those who live with us."[15] In fact, a number of Fante paramounts appear to have labored under the misunderstanding that Strahan had implied that, as before, slaves could not leave their masters without proving abuse. Thus when, in December 1874 and January 1875, the first few slaves began to claim their liberation, a number of chiefs, shocked at the realization that the 1874 ordinances allowed self-emancipations, formally petitioned Strahan to restore the conditions that had been in place prior to emancipation.[16] The one thing Strahan could not do was officially rerecognize slavery, and he declined their request. Several days later, however, a petition in the same handwriting was presented to Strahan with eighty-six signatures from the "Kings, Chiefs, Headmen, Captains, and other principal men" of the western districts complaining that the act "leaves the slave-holding population impoverished," warning that "the slaves themselves have no landed property; they have no village or *croom* to which they can claim a right," and again imploring Strahan to rescind the act of emancipation.[17] A petition "from the ladies of the Gold Coast Protectorate" soon followed, asking for either the annulment of the ordinances or compensation.[18]

Although it seems clear that there was some participation in this petition by chiefly officeholders and kings, Strahan immediately suspected that the guiding hands were those of the same educated merchants whom the Colonial Office (wrongly) believed responsible for conceiving the Fante Confederation. He noted that the petition from the "ladies" had "2 signatures and 17 marks apparently by the same hand" and that the handwriting on two of the petitions was the same, and indeed the content was very similar.[19] In London, Carnarvon concurred, commenting, "I did not fail at once to observe that the composition and language of the petition, which are drawn with a great command of English, are in remarkable contrast to those which the persons purporting to be the petitioners are themselves in the habit of using. . . . I cannot doubt that you are right in attributing this document to some one or more of the educated Fantis who have on previous occasion advocated their views on colonial and other subjects in similar manners."[20] When Strahan complained about the petitions in a second letter to Carnarvon, the secretary of state for the colonies sniffed, "I have already . . . put you in full possession of the views of Her Majesty's Government" and in-

structed Strahan to ignore the documents.[21] The petitioners, those whose signatures were on the petitions and those who may have guided their hands, were
henceforth forced to acquiesce to the emancipation decree.

Despite the fact that both strategies of open resistance and those of direct
political action were now unavailable to slave-owning elites, they refused to
give in entirely. Knowing that many British officials tacitly supported the status
quo and that the administration was hoping there would be few self-liberations,
chiefs in the interior felt free to carry out a campaign of passive noncoopera-
tion, in at least one case allegedly neglecting to carry out a public reading of
the proclamation.[22] More importantly, they did not feel compelled to liberate
their slaves actively, and many continued to take new ones. The paramount of
Akomfi, the chiefs of Adomsine and Gomoah, and other chiefly officeholders
were charged and often fined for slave dealing following emancipation.[23] Joining them were numerous Anglophone urban merchants such as Kate Payne and
John and Ellen Quartey, who persisted in purchasing or brokering slaves.[24] As
late as 1890, a chief in Keta "possessing the confidence of this government"
and so loyal that "it has been the custom of the [district commissioner] to com-
municate through him with other native chiefs and people" was actively buying
slaves.[25] Traders who, judging from their dress, were probably merchants from
the coast imported slaves into the protectorate.[26] There appears to have been no
geographic region in which the merchant and chiefly elites did not try to retain
their slaves, and it is therefore hardly surprising that nonaristocratic inhabitants
of the protectorate also tended to retain and trade in slaves long after the emancipation edict. Reginald Firminger, traveling to Salaga through the eastern interior districts, "learned . . . that a very large number of slaves were still held in
the protectorate" and that "there were large numbers of Hausa, Fulah, Moshi,
and especially Grunshi slaves held by the Aquamoos, Krepis, and Kroboes."[27]
The fact that fifty-four cases of slave dealing were prosecuted in 1888 in Accra,
Cape Coast, East Akyem, Winneba, Saltpond, and Dixcove Districts alone is indicative of the prevalence of slave owning in the protectorate throughout the
nineteenth century.[28]

When citizens of the protectorate or colony were caught owning or trading
slaves, they carried their resistance into the judicial arena. Since most of the victims of the internal slave trade now were young females from north of the protectorate who were deemed less likely than male adults to escape or seek their
liberation, a common ploy was to claim that girls had been purchased "in the
traditional way" to be a wife. In the colonial courts, this was an effective defense.
Magistrates were quite ready to believe that "the Fanti purchases his wife—for

conceal it how one might; it is a purchase and held to be [so]."[29] However, we know that this argument was often false. "Brideprice," as such, was not standard across the Gold Coast, and many southern Akan peoples, especially, made only customary payments, more symbolic than financial.[30] Slaves were themselves aware of the distinction. A Grunshi woman named Mansah, bringing a suit against her master, Tarro, and in conjunction with another wife, Korkor, stated that despite the fact that Tarro had purchased her, she "ha[d] not been married to [Tarro] by native laws or customs."[31] In this case, despite the support of another co-wife, Ammah, for Tarro, the district commissioner found him guilty and sentenced him to two months of hard labor. Still, the "wife defense" figures at least twelve times in the very incomplete district and divisional court records. There were a number of similar cases in which masters claimed to have bought children to be their "sons" or "daughters." Although these claims appear to have been entirely fallacious, it proved difficult for magistrates to discern between authentic and fabricated relationships. Accusations of pawning, which was genuinely linked to the lineage system, repeatedly confounded the judicial authorities. Some such allegations were really custody battles brought by mmusua against sons-in-law, by husbands against wives for custody of children, and by nephews against uncles for whom they were forced to work.[32] Mixed in with these were valid cases brought by pawns and their families.

Other defenses were probably somewhat more valid. Slaves and pawns, as traditional items of wealth, had been used as barter commodities for centuries, and a significant portion of slave-dealing cases in 1875 and 1876 occurred because coastal merchants trading outside the protectorate, especially in Asante, had been paid for their goods in slaves, which they were forced to accept or face financial ruin. Although gold, cowries, and woven cloth were also accepted currencies, traders were sometimes obliged to accept what Asante merchants, themselves impoverished following the razing of Kumasi, could offer. Bossum Akinnee, for example, was supposed to be paid in "country cloth" for goods sold to Asantehene Kofi Karikari but was instead forced to accept payment partly in cloth and partly in two children to keep "as pawns . . . until he should be able to pay the account."[33] Indicted slave owners from the interior also sometimes argued that they were unaware of the edicts of emancipation,[34] and the verity of their defenses is hard to gauge, although the chief justice accepted them in principle, despite conceding that "a generally correct understanding of its scope and purport has spread rapidly and widely."[35]

Indigenous officers of the court often aided slave owners who were brought to trial. Prior to the formal establishment of the Gold Coast Protectorate, mis-

sionaries had bemoaned the fact that important slave owners were largely responsible for enforcing administrative policy.[36] To a large extent this continued
to be the case after 1874, especially as locally recruited juries and assessors
played a central role in colonial jurisprudence. Governor Frederick Hodgson expressed his disappointment with an 1889 jury decision to acquit a slave owner
"although no defence was raised by Counsel on his behalf, on any point of law,
or on the merits" and despite the fact that three children had testified that he had
kept them as slaves.[37] In a similar situation, the four appointed assessors cleared
a defendant on the grounds that the alleged slave was the defendant's wife, despite the fact that the defendant appears to have made no such argument.[38]

Although there was therefore a level of passive resistance among slave owners, both within and outside the courts, there appears to have been very little
active opposition to the antislavery ordinances either on the coast or in the interior. Slave owners were to some degree hamstrung by the new political-economic
situation in which the balance of power was gradually shifting to the British.
Thus, there were few instances of violent resistance to the imposition of British
law, although there were some exceptions. Francis Agbodeka has identified two
such incidents, not specifically related to the emancipation ordinance, in Akuapem. In November 1886, District Commissioner Williams was assaulted while
attempting to serve a summons. Members of the Gold Coast constabulary sent to
arrest his assailant were subsequently attacked at Adakrom, and their prisoner
was released. Likewise, in early 1887 the *akuapemhene* (paramount of Akuapem)
refused to assist members of the constabulary sent to arrest the mob's leaders.[39]
Despite such general opposition to British laws, violent resistance did not figure
significantly in slave owners' responses to emancipation.

OFFICIALS, CHIEFS, AND SLAVERY

I have already argued that, in general, chiefly officeholders attempted to appear
supportive of the colonial administration, both to secure support from the administration and because of their reliance on British military power. However,
it is clear that the cooperation of chiefs was primarily self-interested in nature.
Chiefs who collaborated in such activities as road building, military and police
actions, and other projects expected some reward, or did so when it suited them.[40]
Thus did the Osu mantse, a senior Christiansborg chief, assist police by turning
suspects over to them, as did the paramount chief of Akuapem when served with
a direct request in 1883.[41] In the same respect, chiefs acted in support of the

antislavery rules when it served their own interests and the interests of their subjects, and they often combined collaborative policies with the passive resistance strategies discussed above. The most cooperative chiefs often had the most obvious ulterior motives. The paramount of Juaben, whose role in the 1873 alliance victory forced his people to flee from Asante—first to Akyem and later to Cape Coast, saw many subjects become war captives as a result, and he informed on individuals his agents discovered owning slaves of Juaben origin.[42] Similarly, there are records of other chiefs attempting to stop pawning in instances that involved their own constituents' being seized.[43] A ruler who protected his own people not only protected his power base but gained legitimacy in the eyes of his subjects.

The fact remains, however, that chiefs of the protectorate felt trapped between their dual reliance first upon slaves and second upon the administration for both money and status. Indeed, as the administration began to assume leadership roles traditionally reserved for the chiefly class and as new elites rose to challenge the chiefs, ownership of slaves became one of the few refuges of authority and money left for chiefs. Thus we can understand Ga mantse Taki Tawia's reluctance to allow the recruitment of slaves by Captain Glover in 1873 Accra. The waning power of Tawia and the Accra mantse after the 1874 emancipation is explained by John Parker as the result of several factors, emancipation among them: "Their judicial powers and ability to wage war expropriated by the British, their control over people eroded by the abolition of slavery, and their role as political and economic brokers undermined by the growing literate elite, the *mantsemei* struggled to defend their position in the changing colonial order."[44] Accra, the colonial capital after 1876, was of course an exceptional example. Elsewhere, the process was more gradual. Nevertheless, the loss of slaves and pawns by the okyenhene of Akyem Abuakwa contributed to his indigence, which came about by the end of the century, as well as to that of his divisional chiefs, who had to scramble to find alternative sources of income.[45]

Adding to the problems facing chiefly officeholders was the confusing nature of the Indian model and what consequently appeared to them to be a lack of enforcement of the emancipation edicts; as a result, they were convinced that they could safely own slaves. Conversely, the administration continued to prosecute individuals for slave *dealing* and even pawning, which further blurred the line between what was acceptable and what was not. Chiefs who owned slaves were walking a very thin line, something they could not always do successfully.

Thus, for example, we see the case of Enimil Quow, the paramount chief of East Wassaw. Quow was a loyal supporter of the administration, and British officials had some hand in his accession to the stool.[46] Similarly, although he had plenty of opponents ready to move in after his fall, he seems to have been quite popular with his subjects.[47] Therefore, when he appeared at the Cape Coast judicial assessor's court in 1876 in response to Acting Judicial Assessor J. A. Melton's summons, he had every reason to believe he would get off lightly, and he admitted his guilt. He had bought as many as seven slaves from a relative in Asante, ostensibly to assist the relative in paying a debt but also probably because adult male slaves were now difficult to acquire within the protectorate.

Although he admitted guilt, Quow protested his loyalty to the government, "I am your Honor's Captain. . . . I have not offended before."[48] Quow saw no contradiction between his allegiance to the Crown and his evasion of the law. He was therefore unpleasantly surprised to be fined one hundred ounces of gold, exiled to Lagos for three years, and forced to abdicate his stool.

Enimil Quow had tried to have his cake and eat it, too, believing that he could own slaves and still maintain his position with the administration. Unfortunately, he had crossed a line he did not know existed. His crime was not *owning* slaves, but importing them from outside the protectorate. The commission of a crime that Carnarvon and Strahan had promised to extinguish, committed by a figure so prominent that his actions could easily come to the attention of missionaries and abolitionists, led to a sentence "such as to mark most strongly and emphatically the intolerance with which the law regards all offences of the nature committed by him."[49]

Enimil's lesson is instructive. However much slave owners evaded or organized resistance to emancipation, the impact of emancipation was eventually widely felt. The subjects and strategies of the internal slave trade, for example, were drastically transformed to enable slaveholders to elude prosecution and, more importantly, to limit the number of runaways.[50] As we will see in later sections, even the owners of domestic slaves had to make concessions to their dependents in order to ensure that they would remain. Some historians have also suggested that masters turned away from slave owning toward pawning and that the postproclamation period witnessed a surge in pawning cases.[51] The evidence of an expansion in pawning points toward an increase in debt-producing practices such as expensive funeral customs and high interest rates, and the seizing of individuals for the debts of relatives.[52] However, there is simply not enough evidence to suggest that this was a feature of the postproclamation period, and it is possible to argue that an increase in pawning did not occur during this period. In fact, all the evidence presented above reflects processes introduced during the last period of the Atlantic slave trade in the eighteenth and early nineteenth centuries:

a rise in interest rates, the panyarring of lineage group and polity members for the debts of their fellows, and the growth of debt through litigation or expenses associated with expensive rituals.[53] The horrified reports of increased pawning in the 1880s may have reflected a growing *awareness* of pawning and panyarring, not an actual increase in their practice. At this time there were more administrators and missionaries, especially in the interior and rural areas, and they were informed by a growing number of Christian converts. This phenomenon may have been exacerbated by the fact that throughout the last decades of the century Christian congregations continued to attract a large proportion of low-status individuals such as pawns, and these converts were the missionaries' primary informants.[54]

SLAVE TRADING AS PRETEXT FOR REMOVING CHIEFS

Following the promulgation of the slave-trading and emancipation ordinances, accusations of slave trading became a tool to justify the removal from office of ostensibly sovereign protectorate chiefs who acted with too great independence. Such actions had a precedent—in an affair that had nothing to do with slavery, and everything to do with the ambitions of merchants in Accra, Benjamin Pine had accused the paramount chief of the Yilo Krobo of such abuses of his 1857 memorandum.[55] However, the post-1874 case of Okyenhene Amoako Atta I was entirely different. Not only was Atta's state of Akyem Abuakwa far less penetrated by colonial agents than was the state of the Yilo konor, but the story behind Atta's removal was even more sordid.[56]

The de-stooling of Amoako Atta was prompted by a pragmatic alliance between the Basel Mission Society and the administration. The missionaries, who had initially been welcomed into Akyem Abuakwa in 1852 by Atta's predecessor, earned the okyenhene's enmity by recruiting to their community important *akyemfo* (sing., *okyemfo;* citizens of Akyem), including royal slaves and members of the court. They attempted to drive a wedge between the Akyem leadership and the administration, and it has been suggested that they "assumed the role of self-appointed agents of the [colonial] government to enforce the law," in part by encouraging royal slaves to emancipate themselves.[57] Foremost among the missionaries was Akuapem-born David Asante, the okyenhene's cousin, for whom encouraging the defection of royal slaves was a personal mission.[58] Asante's motivation has several levels, but most importantly, as a local he understood that the undermining of Atta's political and religious authority was an important step toward firmly establishing the fledgling congregation.[59]

In a society in which political and religious power were intertwined, Asante's actions threatened not only the okyenhene's authority but also indigenous religious practices. Thus both a majority of the chiefly elites and the party of youngmen, or *amantoomiensa,* rallied to the okyenhene's defense. For several years, Atta endured Asante's goading until on September 20, 1877, he exiled Asante from Akyem Abuakwa. Asante refused to leave, and two nights later a combined party of "youngmen" and "palace servants," led by the divisional chief of Osenase, marched to the mission house to expel him.[60] Asante complained to Governor Sanford Freeling, who summoned Atta to appear before an Accra court. In the magistrate's decision, the okyenhene was vindicated, and the governor placed the blame for the incident on Asante's provocations. Nevertheless, three of Atta's courtiers were sentenced to sixty days' hard labor.[61] More importantly, Atta had created a dangerous precedent by submitting himself to colonial judicial authority.

Atta's mistake became evident in 1880, when he was again summoned before a colonial court. The real issue behind this case was not the okyenhene's continuing possession of slaves, which through the Indian model might be safely ignored, but rather Atta's provocation of the Asante state. To the people of Akyem Abuakwa, the 1873–1874 war had been but one chapter in an age-old conflict. In 1875 and 1879 Atta had threatened to invade Asante, and in 1877 he refused to cooperate with Freeling's orders not to arm refugees fleeing Asante.[62] Freeling and his successor, Ussher, on the other hand, saw the Asante issue as at least temporarily closed, and perceived Atta's brinkmanship as threatening the peace and prosperity of the protectorate. It was this disagreement that forced the administration to take steps to remove Atta from power, although the pretext for his removal was the okyenhene's participation in the slave trade. The Basel Mission enthusiastically provided the witnesses for the prosecution, including important Christians who had a grudge against the king.[63]

Atta, however, chose to have his case heard by an Accra jury and was subsequently found "not guilty" of slave dealing and pawning, to Ussher's disgust.[64] Ussher did, however, manage to get a conviction on one count of "malicious arson," and Atta was sentenced to a disproportionate five years of exile in Lagos.

THE "UNAFFECTED" SLAVES: HYPOTHETICAL OR REAL?

Before we consider those slaves whose position was changed by the promulgation of emancipation, either drastically or marginally, we need to look at those who were unaffected by the proclamations, if such a group existed. The truly unaffected are in many cases difficult to distinguish from those slaves who were only marginally affected. Admittedly, their existence can be posited from the affidavits of missionaries and administrators. Still, I would like to suggest that those slaves whose existence was unchanged by the proclamation were a minority within the broad class of unfree individuals for whom specific factors counteracted the alternatives offered by the newly legalized modes of liberation. But why should such groups have existed?

The first argument, previously presented, as to why certain slaves remained with their masters rested upon the supposed benign nature of Gold Coast slavery. This bit of propaganda, which had survived the "triumph" of abolitionism intact, had been a principal justification for the implementation of the Indian model. The major colonial reports on slavery during this period, particularly the *Fairfield Report* commissioned by Parliament in 1874, continued to stress that "economically, the condition of a slave is an advantageous one as compared with that of a free labourer" and refused to concede that nineteenth-century Gold Coast slavery was anything but "an emanation of parental and family authority," despite the obvious existence of slaves in market and cash-crop production.[65] Nor did this attitude fade after emancipation. More than half a century after the two proclamations, J. C. de Graft Johnson would write that "the slave is invariably well treated and regarded rather as a member of the family . . . and not infrequently succeeds in accumulating a considerable amount of personal property."[66]

Many Basel missionaries subscribed to this theory. An agent in Christiansborg wrote that "the majority [of slaves in Accra] have remained with their masters [partly] because they are well-handled and are part of the family."[67] However, Basel Mission agents carefully distinguished between this form of domestic slavery and what they saw as harsher slavery under "educated slave owners, the merchants of the coast, mulattos, and the great princes among the [T]wis."[68] Such theories even helped shape the enforcement of emancipation policy. Certain magistrates, for example, in direct contravention of their duties under the 1874 ordinances, tended to withhold punishment for slave owners if they could prove that they treated their slaves well![69] However, simply arguing that slavery was relatively benign does not sufficiently explain why some slaves remained with their masters. Although domestic slavery as it existed in the protectorate did historically entail certain protections for slaves, many of these had been worn away by the transformative impact of the Atlantic slave trade. Furthermore, whatever lingering elements of its ameliorative nature remained, slaves were still slaves — that is they still had no social status within the lineage group, no land ownership rights, and no legal profile under Akan law, and their movements were restricted.

Why then would they allow themselves to remain in such situations? There are several convincing arguments explaining why some slaves were unable or unwilling to exploit their new opportunities. Dumett and Johnson, for example, suggested that some slave agency was blocked by "the strong dependency/welfare element inherent in Akan traditional servitude, plus powerful group pressures with the threat of ostracism or worse if a slave testified against his master."[70] These social factors were certainly considerable for slaves who originated within the southern Akan region or who wished to remain within their community after liberation, and they furthermore restricted a slave's ability to recruit the assistance of potential witnesses for use in the courts. Even indigenous officials such as interpreters were "roundly abused" by local people for "bringing down the white man" in such cases.[71]

These cultural constructions were central to court cases in which a number of slaves, both men and women, actually resisted their liberation in suits brought on their behalf, choosing instead to remain with their owners.[72] Furthermore, as late as 1889 some slaves who initially approached the constabulary requesting judicial liberation recanted under peer and community pressure.[73] The officers dealing with these cases appear to have remained oblivious to the cause of their retractions.

Dumett and Johnson were consequently unsurprised when their research showed that certain slaves, in the face of such societal obstructions, and knowing the potential earned advantages of assimilation, "did not seem anxious to give up this paternalistic system of subordination." However, these two historians also recognized other equally substantial hurdles to slave liberations. "Many [slaves]," they argued, "knew no other home than that of their masters, or could not return to their place of origin because of distance or continual slave-raiding."[74] Clearly, if slaves could overcome social pressure to remain with their masters, and definitively liberate themselves, they would have to leave the communities in which they lived. The risks in leaving were daunting. Assistant Secretary for Native Affairs Johnson listed the challenges such slaves would have faced: "Many could hardly find their own people again even if they were able to trace the native villages from which they or their parents were originally abducted. Some may have no relations left in their own country. A large number can no longer speak their mother tongue. Very few indeed could adapt themselves easily to new surroundings and almost everyone would be very sadly disappointed to find in the end that he or she had only exchanged one kind of servitude for another."[75] Basel Mission agents and contemporary administrators similarly noted that many slaves who initially celebrated emancipation and left their masters soon "gave it up and voluntarily returned to their original work," obviously daunted by the difficulties associated with their independence.[76] Others simply had themselves "declared free, and then returned to their masters" and the safety of the known, having achieved a symbolic victory and perhaps negotiated some change in status.[77]

Some groups of slaves faced special difficulty in returning to their former homes. Slaves with northern origins—and these probably remained in the majority among enslaved peoples in the protectorate—would have had to travel through regions in which slavery was still perfectly legal, through wars and disruptions created by the breakup of greater Asante, and finally to families perhaps little remembered. If they had been captured as children, they might not be able even to locate their families, or their kin groups might not exist in the remembered location. Some slaves may have even forgotten their childhood languages. Others saw no advantage in returning to kin groups that may have voluntarily sold them into slavery. The assimilative nature of Gold Coast slavery meant that for older slaves retention of their assimilated status was preferable to the risks of the road.

Similarly, for a tiny minority of young but highly assimilated slaves, remaining with their masters may have been as much an example of "free" choice as deserting. Basel Mission agent Tabitha Schönefeld reported the narrative of one such Ewe slave, who was purchased along with her aunt by a Christian family in Krobo in 1873. After the 1874 ordinances were promulgated, her father sent for her to return home, but she chose to remain with her masters' family. In the intervening period, her aunt had married into the family, and she was expected to do so shortly as well. She had also been receiving training from the Basel Mission. It is unclear if her father had initially sold or pawned her voluntarily, but she clearly preferred to stay in Krobo.[78]

According to Claire Robertson, female slaves were especially fettered. In addition to the difficulties faced by male slaves, women faced additional challenges in starting up trading businesses or finding wage labor. Even more importantly, female slaves feared the loss of the children they had borne to their owners. Magistrates—perhaps reflecting Victorian values—tended to confirm the rights of masters to such children and in at least one case conferred upon a female master the children of a female and a male slave, both of whom belonged to her, when the children asked to remain with her.[79] Likewise, Robertson argues, magistrates were unsympathetic to women who sought their own liberation, and often returned them to their owners as apprentices.[80] Female slaves also tended to be assimilated more quickly, especially if they were the mothers of their masters' children, and thus potentially had more status to risk. These factors probably did play a part in limiting the range of choices available to female slaves and in inducing them to remain with their masters, but neither Robertson nor I have found sufficient evidence to prove this.

A last obstacle to liberation that must be mentioned is ignorance of the specifics of emancipation. We know that a number of individuals accused of slave dealing and pawning used ignorance of the 1874 proclamations as a defense. Some of these defendants in the initial postproclamation period, such as "Oweaguow," who turned himself in to the authorities in 1875 after he learned of the ordinances, are quite convincing.[81] However, Kwamina Ansa and Baidu Amta, caught during a period of increased vigilance in 1897, more than twenty years after emancipation, and in Cape Coast District rather than an outlying region, are less believable.[82] Administrators have suggested, and I am inclined to believe, that in the bulk of the protectorate the emancipation laws had been widely disseminated by the late 1870s at the latest.[83] We also know that some chiefs acted immediately to inform their subjects of the new laws.[84] Still, as late as 1890 there were "parts of [the protectorate] which have seldom, if ever, been visited by a Government Officer" according to Governor Hodgson.[85] The prevalence of slave owning in districts that were peripheral to the protectorate seems to have remained much more obvious than in the central coastal districts.[86] Border districts such as Keta and Axim, especially, retained large numbers of slaves in their original state.[87]

At the risk of foreshadowing some of my conclusions, I must state here a problem with sources and with historians who have argued that slaves did not leave. Many of them, it seems, comprehended only two alternatives for slaves — liberation of some form or another or the rejection of emancipation for the security of their current position. Later in this chapter, I will be suggesting that many slaves who are identified as remaining unaffected by the 1874 ordinances were in fact participants in a gradual transformation that remained largely invisible to administrative and missionary sources. Very few slaves indeed were completely unaffected by the promulgation of emancipation.

MODES OF LIBERATION

Although it can be argued that the position of some slaves was altered very little by the 1874 decrees and I will argue that the majority of "former" slaves remained local and affiliated with their masters, it must be acknowledged that

some slaves chose to liberate themselves completely from their dependent relationships. This group has been the subject of a widespread but somewhat shallow
historical debate on emancipation. The main argument of Gerald McSheffrey's
1873 article, for example, was that "the demand for emancipation seems to have
been both immediate and widespread [and] was not just confined to the servile
populations of the towns . . . but was equally evident in the traditional communities of the interior."[88] Dumett and Johnson, partly in rebuttal to McSheffrey,
posited that "only a tiny number of slaves took advantage of the colonial courts"
and that the number who deserted was "relatively small."[89] However, they found
it equally difficult to quantify slave liberations.

Perhaps this reluctance on the part of historians to propose numerical solutions
to the question of "how many slaves" was in fact a responsible choice. Akurang-
Parry, by contrast, has stirred together figures suggested by various sources for
slave cases during diverse periods of time and within regions that are not analo-
gous, and proposes the figure of 632 for the number of slaves liberating themselves by judicial means between 1874 and 1918 in the colony alone.[90] He uses
this information to support his thesis that the demand for and reaction to emancipation within the colony was greater than that in the protectorate. Because this
research does not reflect information from a number of primary sources, Akurang-
Parry has made a number of errors in producing this figure. First, he accepted all
cases dealing with slavery as instances of self-liberation, whereas many were
brought by witnesses or family, or discovered by the constabulary. Additionally,
Akurang-Parry fails to recognize that many of these cases refer to crimes that took
place outside the minuscule colony, but were brought to courts in Accra or Cape
Coast because, initially, those were the only criminal courts in the protectorate
and because the legal mandate of magistrates based in Accra and Cape Coast cov-
ered large portions of territory that were not part of the colony.[91] The dangers of
trying to quantify the unquantifiable are obvious from this.

Although I therefore decline to produce numbers, there is a large body of
evidence available that can be used to reveal new information about modes of
liberation. There appear to have been two principal types of liberations: those
that were carried out by slaves themselves and those that were organized by their
families.[92] The chief magistrate presiding over the initial period of emancipation,
David Chalmers, noted that "nine-tenths" of slave-related cases brought before
the judicial bodies immediately following the emancipation ordinances were
brought by kin, and this statistic has, unfortunately, been accepted by some historians.[93] An actual investigation of cases brought before colonial courts under-
mines this theory. Of those cases heard by the Cape Coast judicial assessor's

court and the Accra divisional court in 1874 and 1875, a minority appear to have been brought by kin—usually fathers or uncles—on behalf of their slave relations.[94] Slaves themselves figure at least as often, and "witnesses" and police constables appear to have been the most significant informants.

What does this signify for kin liberation? It is obvious from the judicial record that some families were indeed operative in freeing their relatives. Such cases initially formed a significant proportion (although nowhere near nine-tenths) of slave-dealing cases, to some degree tailing off after 1877 but not disappearing by the end of the nineteenth century. The main subjects of kin liberation within the courts, however, were not slaves but pawns.[95] Families found the courts a convenient way to reclaim pawned individuals, especially for recently contracted debts.[96] Most of these individuals were also obviously living close to their families.[97] By contrast, there are only two identifiable instances in which slaves, rather than pawns, were redeemed by kin, and one of these was as a result of the importation of several individuals enslaved in the Asante-Juaben war and identified by family members who had entered the colony as refugees of that war.[98] Clearly, kin liberation was used mostly by pawns and their families.

Self-liberation was an entirely different affair. As we saw in the previous section, it took serious agency on the part of slaves to leave a sometimes secure, if dependent, position and face the risks of an unsecured but free future. It might appear logical from this that slaves of long-standing service, with ties to local families, and having acquired some status and wealth would be more likely to have the agency and resources to seize their freedom and leave. However, as Dumett and Johnson pointed out, such slaves were more likely to feel a strong sense of dependency and even loyalty to their masters.[99] Furthermore, slaves who had been assimilated were less likely to risk their gains in status and economics for an uncertain future. Most significantly, I am not convinced that a large body of slaves, rather than pawns, actually lived near a group of their free kin—especially since we know that most slaves were acquired through warfare and, less frequently, by kidnapping.[100] Indeed, even those sources that suggest that "local" slaves ran away tend to refer to slaves originating from a neighboring or nearby state or region rather than their owner's locale.[101]

Instead, there is a large body of anecdotal evidence pointing to higher frequencies of self-liberation among newly acquired slaves brought into the region from the north. Chalmers, for example, noted in 1875 that a "considerable number of [imported slaves] have availed themselves of their freedom, and left their masters."[102] Seventeen years later, Governor W. Brandford Griffith would note the regularity with which newly (illegally, of course) imported slaves ran away.[103] John Parker reports similar evidence for war captives in Accra.[104]

Although it is difficult to get beyond hearsay evidence to prove that newly acquired war captives from the north fled from their masters in larger numbers than longer-serving slaves from within the protectorate, primary evidence for self-liberation among this group is more convincing insofar as use of the courts is concerned. The vast majority of slaves (excluding pawns) who brought cases against their masters in the 1870s had been recently acquired from Asante, Jua-ben, or farther north.[105] This trend did not end in the 1880s even though the slave trade from the interior turned to female and young slaves brought down from markets in Wa, Asante, and Salaga.[106] Chalmers's argument that the major-ity of "imported slaves" who liberated themselves "scarcely at all appeared before the courts," but instead simply returned to their homes seems to indicate similar statistics for desertions.[107]

Slaves from the north exhibited a wide variety of other liberation strategies as well. There is evidence of recently imported slaves' seeking assistance from their fellow countrymen in Hausa Constabulary camps in Accra and Cape Coast[108] and transferring their loyalty to new and presumably less harsh masters.[109] Such slaves often did not leave their masters until they were beaten or maltreated, but because they had only recently been torn from their homes and had not been assimilated to any degree into their new positions, self-liberation remained open and attrac-tive to them.[110]

It is clear that a primary inducement for slaves to leave their masters was the likelihood that they had a safe, secure home to which to return. Nevertheless, it has been suggested that slaves' occupations, geographical locations, and the de-mands of their owners may have influenced their decision. Zimmerman, as we have already seen, argued that slavery was harsher among "educated slave own-ers, the merchants of the coast" who did not observe the "traditional rights" of Akan and Ga-Adangme slavery, and that self-liberation was higher among their slaves.[111] Nevertheless, even McSheffrey agrees that there is no evidence outside a few Basel Mission sources indicating widespread self-liberation among the slaves of coastal merchants.[112] Nor do other sources corroborate Zimmerman's claims that the slaves of "great princes among the [T]wis," especially in Akyem, tended to liberate themselves.[113]

Nonetheless, some slaves who could not easily return to their places of birth still liberated themselves, and these individuals must be considered. Such incidents were largely a question of economic opportunity. Slaves who wished to claim their freedom would do so only if they believed they had options superior to remaining with their owners, and these opportunities were functions of location, learned skills, and job or land availability, as we will see in the following section.

MEANS OF POSTLIBERATION EXISTENCE

Other than the few captives who could return to remembered homes, and pawns who were reclaimed by their families, dissatisfied slaves had a limited selection of viable economic alternatives to their dependent means of existence. Their preferred option would have been the acquisition of a plot of land large enough for food subsistence and the sale of surplus, a goal that would have been closest to achievable in coastal areas and in regions along major trade routes. These areas had a high demand for foodstuffs, were already populated by largely accepted immigrant communities, and were more strongly under the influence of British law than was generally the rule.[114] Missionary sources, for example, indicate that "several" freed slaves of northern origin moved into the Kyebi region, which was a growing market for foodstuffs, both because it had a mission school and because it was a trading crossroads.[115] Although these former slaves were granted plots of land by the okyenhene's council, in more densely populated coastal regions of the Gold Coast there was, by this time, little land unattached to either a stool or a family.[116] British rule in these regions had led to a formalization of land tenure rules, and by 1874 only a small portion of arable ground was privately held in the protectorate, despite the emerging land market leading to privatization in select urban areas; stool land could not legally be alienated.[117] Exslaves who wished to cultivate plots commonly had to pay a "tribute or royalty" in kind and thus became dependents of the landowners.[118] Although this remained an option for slaves in especially abusive positions, for most it was not necessarily superior to preexisting arrangements and assimilated status with a former master.

Urban areas, however, continued to attract former slaves, although few became wage laborers. Paid employment was not widely available during this period, and slaves appear to have been reluctant or unable to take on what wage labor existed.[119] While there is some evidence that the wage-labor market became tighter after emancipation as some skilled urban slaves deserted, this produced a demand only for highly skilled artisans—a category that excluded most domestic and agricultural slaves, especially those from the interior.[120] Instead, former slaves appear to have established rural townships near the protection of the centers of colonial authority in Accra and Cape Coast. The growth of odonko and Krepi villages on the Accra plains by 1875, and in Abokobi by the 1890s, probably stemmed from slaves from Asante and the protectorate seeking land in Accra.[121] The community of Freetown near Cape Coast was also settled by slaves, and although Roger Gocking argues that many of its inhabitants may have previously been enslaved in Cape Coast it is likely that most came from interior regions.[122] Even if wage labor was not in high demand in the colonial towns and missions, such areas potentially provided other opportunities. Some Basel Mission stations, for example, accepted self-liberated slaves as congregational members and workers.[123] Such arrangements appear to have been commonly initiated by the slaves.[124] The administration provided greater opportunity for former slaves, especially since officials continued to view northerners—whom they still lumped together as "Hausas" and "Muslims"—as superior recruits for both the military and law enforcement for the protectorate. The constabulary remained an unpopular profession for coastal peoples, and those who joined frequently deserted.[125] Thus, although Governor Hodgson raised pay in 1894 in an effort to attract recruits,[126] other administrators argued that local recruits were inferior to the northerners and were not worth the effort.[127] As a result, the administration continued its policy of recruiting on the Niger and at Salaga, often recruiting escaped or manumitted slaves from these regions.[128] In this environment, slaves of northern origin were also happily accepted by the administration.[129] Muslim slaves in the far interior of the protectorate who had previously been unable to leave their masters opportunistically joined recruiting missions on their way to Salaga and were happily accepted by recruiting officers anxious to reach their quotas.[130]

Still, the pull of a military career on former slaves should not be overestimated. The constabulary was never very large.[131] Although we are unable to firmly quantify the number of slaves who joined, average total recruitment—including free volunteers, exslaves, and foreigners recruited outside the protectorate—rarely exceeded 100 to 150 per year, except in 1896 when soldiers were needed for garrisons in Asante.[132]

Although some former slaves were willing to become soldiers, they could rarely be found in other positions within the colonial administration. Few could be induced to take up low-paid menial labor, despite a general shortage of labor for infrastructure projects. Again, former slaves, especially those of northern origin, would have been welcomed by British administrators, who felt that Akan and Ga-Adangme workers were "not gifted with a strong desire for work." When former slaves failed to take on such positions, the labor-starved administration was eventually forced to resort to importing Kru workers to finish the most important projects.[133] For most slaves, menial tasks offered inferior working conditions and less security than they had experienced with their masters, and there is little evidence of former slaves' leaving their positions on farms and in domestic situations to become gang laborers for the colonial government.

Still, although we can see that the increase in European intervention in the region did not initially offer many new and viable alternatives to life as a slave, it could be postulated that the accelerated production of legitimate goods during this period opened up new opportunities in mining and agriculture. Recently freed slaves could have taken advantage of these new industries to earn a living.

The increase in commercial mining after 1878 created some employment opportunities in the interior as companies formed by Europeans and indigenous coastal merchants purchased concessions, especially in Tarkwa District (Eastern Wassaw).[134] However, these companies preferred to hire free "Fantis" or, even more frequently, Kru laborers.[135] Furthermore, a new and exhaustive study by Raymond Dumett has shown that the gold rush of the postproclamation period was largely based on a rise in small-scale precapitalist traditional mining carried out by mobilized family labor.[136] Finally, although the increase in gold extraction may have provided opportunities for a small number of former slaves, it did not begin to do so until 1878 and did not figure in the initial calculations of slaves between 1874 and 1875.

Similarly, the demand for cash crops, especially cocoa and coffee, did not exist on any scale in the 1870s and 1880s and did not provide opportunities for protectorate slaves. The Basel Mission coffee plantations in Akuapem that had been destroyed in the 1869 Asante invasion had not been replanted until 1881, and it was not until early 1890 that small-scale coffee cultivation took off in the eastern districts.[137]

Similarly, the cocoa industry, despite the support of Basel missionaries and the administration, was largely ignored by indigenous producers until 1890, probably because of the high investment requirements and low initial returns resulting from the five-year maturation period of the cocoa tree.[138] Cocoa planting thus took off only as demand and prices rose in the early 1890s and production increased around 1893 (see table 6.1), and it was not until 1897 that the Department of Agriculture reported "hundreds" of small-scale plantations in Akuapem, aided by nurseries set up by the administration at Aburi.[139] Cocoa production was also geographically confined, at least initially, to the climatically and politically suitable eastern provinces, whose more advanced

TABLE 6.1

Value of Coffee and Cocoa Exports from the Gold Coast

	Coffee exports			Cocoa exports	
Year	Approximate Value in £	Source	Year	Value in £	Source
1882	0	ADM 5/3/7	1893	93	ADM 5/1/74
1883	12	ADM 5/3/7	1894	546	ADM 5/1/74
1884	9	ADM 5/3/7	1895	470	ADM 5/1/74
1885	63	ADM 5/3/7	1896	2,275	ADM 5/1/74
1886	75	ADM 5/3/7	1897	3,196	ADM 5/1/74
1887	86	ADM 5/3/7	1898	6,420	ADM 5/1/74
1888	116	ADM 5/3/7	1899	6,447	ADM 5/1/74
1889	50	ADM 5/2/1			
1890	247	ADM 5/2/1			
1891	473	ADM 5/2/1			
1893	630	ADM 5/1/74			
1894	1,265	ADM 5/1/74			
1895	1,753	ADM 5/1/74			
1896	4,065	ADM 5/1/74			
1897	3,068	ADM 5/1/74			

Sources: NAG ADM 5/3/7, Report of the Commission on Economic Agriculture on the Gold Coast, 1889. ADM 5/1/74, Departmental Reports, 1897. ADM 5/2/1, Report on the Census of the Gold Coast Colony, 1891.

infrastructure and proximity to the Volta River and well-developed trade pathways facilitated delivery to the coast. Thus, although cocoa provided opportunities for wage labor after 1900 and may have at that time attracted recently liberated Asante slaves, it was not a major factor in exslave opportunity in the late-nineteenth-century protectorate.[140]

As a last resort, former slaves could have enlisted with one of the European companies recruiting laborers for overseas work. French companies were active in the early 1890s in recruiting small numbers of Elminan laborers for French colonies such as Grand Bassam and the French Congo, as was the Royal Niger Company.[141] Signing up with one of these companies was an unpopular proposition for most of the populace. Thus, John Parker has argued that most of the Accras who worked overseas, for example, were really slaves and followers of important "bigmen" who were coerced into serving overseas, their patron retaining the recruitment commission.[142] Because of such abuses, recruitment by overseas companies was legally limited by the Masters and Servants and Foreign Employment Ordinance of 1893.[143] In any case, former slaves had such an aversion to working overseas that those few who deserted without any prospects or skills generally preferred vagrancy to the unknown of a foreign land.[144]

NEGOTIATED OUTCOMES

So far in this chapter I have argued that, on the one hand, the majority of slaves were in some manner affected by the emancipation ordinances. On the other hand, I have shown that few slaves chose to use the courts to liberate themselves, nor does it appear that there was much opportunity for private acquisition of land-use rights, wage labor, or work in mines or on cash-crop plantations. However, until now I have not presented any evidence as to what the majority of slaves actually did do.

Gold Coast slave owners could not entirely control access to the means of existence—missionary sources show that a limited number of exslaves were able to arrange for tenancy rights to land in the interior, and certainly some few slaves enlisted for service overseas or with the administration, or managed to gain employment with the Basel Mission. Some may, as Dumett and Johnson have suggested, have become casual workers, odd-job men, or petty traders.[145] However, the communal structure of land ownership and the assimilative nature of Gold Coast slavery, combined with the paucity of opportunities in wage labor and cash-crop production during this period, meant that few slaves other than recently captured northerners and some pawns perceived any situation preferable to remaining with their masters. Nevertheless, although the majority of slaves chose not to liberate themselves formally or desert, slaves were, to varying degrees, able to mitigate their social and economic position within their dependent status, and this is what I believe took place regionally. The prospect of emancipation prompted slaves and masters to renegotiate their relationships, usually to the benefit of the slaves. The process by which slaves attempted to exploit the opportunity of newly legalized paths to emancipation and masters accommodated certain of their slaves' demands in an effort to limit their losses was probably a complex and gradual one.

It is impossible, with the sources available to us, to mark geographic or cultural differences in the manner in which negotiations were carried out and settlements agreed upon in different regions or under different types of masters. Dumett and Johnson settled for identifying two general types of negotiated outcomes. In the first, slaves cleared new farms that were within the locality of their masters' farms but that their masters did not occupy and that were somewhat removed from their masters' lands. In the other, somewhat closer relationship, Dumett and Johnson argue that slaves continued to work their masters' lands, but in a sharecropping arrangement.[146] Akurang-Parry has recently studied the matter in greater depth, relying on the somewhat questionable evidence gleaned from a relatively small number of interviews he carried out in a limited area of the Gold Coast in the 1990s. His argument stresses that such agreements were in fact "not based on usufruct use of land" but involved slaves' either "rent[ing] land from their former holders" or "sharecropping." Further, he insists that such arrangements occurred "especially in the burgeoning export commodity and staple crops producing areas of the Birim-Censu-Pra basin of the Eastern Province."[147]

Incidents of negotiation were, in fact, widespread. Such shifts in status were noted by a district commissioner in Saltpond as well as by the Basel Mission in Akuapem.[148] Slave-master relationships also clearly shifted in urban settings, in the western districts, and on the plantations of the Accra plains, where slaves reportedly "neither pa[id their masters] part of their produce nor work[ed] for [them] three days in the week as was the case before."[149] However, Basel Mission sources regarding the land and produce-rich eastern interior do seem to indicate that slaves there were able to negotiate from an extraordinarily strong position, "farming the land given them by their masters as free men."[150] These sources date from mid-1875, before a full picture could have possibly become clear, but it is entirely possible that slaves in Akuapem and Krobo may have been able to negotiate from a position of relative strength due not only to the high levels of agricultural production in these regions, but also to the influence of the Basel Mission.

As early as 1863, we have seen, the Basel Mission had required its congregants to liberate slaves using the "Sixths model," converting these individuals to wage laborers—especially bricklayers, carpenters, and wheelwrights—or, more rarely, assisting them in gaining possession of a piece of their former masters' lands.[151] The basis for offering wage labor to former slaves who nevertheless remained with their former masters was thus developed quite early in the Volta District, including Krobo, at least within the Christian community. The experiences of this group appear to have served as a model, motivating slaves "liberated" in 1874. Thus Volta District administration sources noted that slaves who negotiated their status in this district "in the generality of cases ha[ve] [their] own piece of land to farm, and if an artisan ha[ve] all the wages [they] earn."[152] Evidence from the early twentieth century indicates that former slaves in this region continued to be associated with their former masters' children, even joining the same Christian congregations.[153] However, most evidence regarding negotiation strategies throughout the protectorate and colony suggests that most agricultural slaves remained on their masters' land, but occupied their own fields and paid "rent" in service rather than in cash or kind.[154] Administrators such as District Commissioner Cummings of Saltpond and District Commissioner Rigby of Volta are very clear on that point.[155] Similarly, J. C. de Graft Johnson wrote (albeit in 1927) that

> the [former slaves] have portions of the family or community lands assigned
> to them to make farms, the produce of which is their own property and with-
> out paying any portion thereof as tribute. *They certainly help their masters also to*
> *make their farms,* and those who stay in the same house perform such house-
> hold duties as hired servants in European countries do. In return they are fed
> and clothed and are given all the privileges of children. . . . Otherwise they
> are only required occasionally to perform such duties as selling, going on er-
> rands, etc. They make occasional presents to their masters, who never fail to
> give return presents.[156]

There is no opposing evidence to suggest that sharecropping was a preferred negotiating outcome for either slaves or masters. The system of *abusa,* by which the laborer receives one third of produce and the landowner two thirds, which has figured so largely in cocoa production in the twentieth century,[157] appears not to have been used in the protectorate until after World War I.[158] Aside from suggesting that slaves largely paid for their land tenancy by giving service, Johnson's arguments reveal the social dependency of most former slaves despite their augmented status. By giving ritual presents, former slaves and their descendants acknowledged their dependency, and although slaves exerted some economic rights they still acted as servants and clients of their former masters. In Accra, Cape Coast, and other urban settings, slave owners appear to have allowed former slaves to remain in houses they owned,[159] in essence transforming them into members of the domestic servant class, a group that, as late as 1891, made up approximately 12 percent of the populations of both Cape Coast and Accra.[160] Other former slaves in Accra may have begun to receive wages for farming and acting as carriers or canoe crews.[161] These and other dependents who had renegotiated their positions were still social inferiors, and libel cases reveal that they were frequently reminded of their dependent status and slave origins. Wherever possible, these individuals sought to assert a higher status by reworking their family trees or suing their antagonists, who were usually their former masters or their masters' relatives, with whom they were economically forced to remain in contact.[162]

Akurang-Parry has also suggested that female slaves whose masters desired to retain their services were able to renegotiate their position through the institution of marriage.[163] Such negotiations would probably have been carried out by the slaves' families. Remarriage as a free woman would have benefited the former slave by completing her integration into her husband's family with the status of a fully free individual, while benefiting her family by reattaching her to her own matrilineage. At the same time, such an arrangement preserved the labor of the woman and her children for the former master. Unfortunately, the sole evidence for this practice comes from David Chalmers, the chief justice following emancipation. In an 1878 report, Chalmers noted that "the sentiments attaching to free marriage [were] so much appreciated that persons who had been married as slaves . . . have subsequently [married] a second time as free persons" and further noted that marriages were "more frequently than formerly contracted through the interposition of the blood relations of the woman."[164]

To place this theory within the debate over whether emancipation represented a "continuation" or a "dislocation" of socioeconomic and cultural institutions on the Gold Coast, it seems clear that, despite McSheffrey's hypothesis, there was no mass exodus of slaves from masters anywhere within the protectorate. Slaves neither used the courts nor chose to flee en masse unless they had highly marketable skills or could return to their families—either because of proximity or because they had only recently been captured. Nevertheless, relatively few slaves remained unaffected by emancipation in the long term. Emancipation did not cause them to liberate themselves. However, it was a catalyst that gave them the leverage to renegotiate their economic position within the authority of their masters, who saw such negotiations as their own best response to the possibility of losing the power, economic stability, and status for which they needed their slaves. The role of the administration was only, and could only be, to prepare an environment in which change could take place. It was slaves and their masters who, influenced by cultural, economic, and social imperatives, created the compromises that characterized the postproclamation settlement.

CHAPTER 7
Slaves and Masters in French-Administered Senegal

IN SENEGAL, THE PERIOD OF expansionist regimes in the 1850s and 1860s was followed by an extended period of disengagement from the conquests of the interior. The rapid retreat of French authority was the result of the unsupportable cost of maintaining the extensive colony in a period of unusual economic stress underlain by the Third Republic's long and painful recovery from the war with Prussia. Alone among the larger Sereer and Wolof states, Waalo remained under firm French control. The reestablishment of a protectorate over Kaajor in 1883 went some distance toward reversing this policy, and this became the model for restored French rule over much of Senegal in the 1890s. During the period between the retreat of 1869 and the establishment of protectorates, however, the difficulty of reconciling the administration's tacit acceptance of slavery with France's abolitionist laws became increasingly evident, so that slavery became the principal impetus for the extension of "protectorate" policy throughout the region.

THE JUDICIARY AND SLAVERY DURING EXPANSION AND RETREAT: SENEGAL, 1854–1878

Colonial regimes in both Senegal and the Gold Coast approached the question of slavery and emancipation with the dual goals of satisfying abolitionist pressure

137

while maintaining the socioeconomic status quo. Whereas the Gold Coast administration specifically engineered the Indian model so as to minimize the impact of emancipation, the administrators of colonial Senegal had to work around a much more stringent document that called for the active liberation of slaves. As we have seen, Baudin, Du Château, and Faidherbe managed to evade or subvert operative clauses of the 1848 emancipation so as to ensure the colony's profitability and security. In each case, they were able to secure the sanction of their superiors in the metropole. Unfortunately for them, however, the 1848 extension of citizenship to inhabitants of St. Louis and Gorée established a competing set of authorities by placing the colony's justice system under the French Ministry of Justice. Both justices and prosecutors were appointed by and reported to the Ministry of Justice, and their actions were likely to be shaped by metropolitan pressure rather than (or as well as) by pragmatic colonial concerns.[1] Moreover, French law gave these judicial officers wider latitude than their British counterparts both in investigation and in prosecution of crimes, including those involving slavery. Fortunately for the administration, the only punishment for slave dealing dictated by the 1848 emancipation laws was the loss of citizenship for the perpetrator.[2] Faidherbe deduced from this that only citizens could be punished for slave-trading or -owning offenses, and thus that subjects of the states brought under French control were immune from judicial sanction.[3] The tribunals of Gorée and St. Louis in the 1840s and early 1850s therefore didn't deal with slavery at all.[4]

The reunification of Senegal and Gorée in 1854 and a subsequent imperial decree by Louis Napoleon codifying justice in Senegal threatened this status quo by establishing an independent judiciary in the colony. The supreme court that emerged, the *cour d'assises* (court of assizes), sat at St. Louis and heard all major cases in the colony, including those involving slave dealing. In a nod to the clout of both the habitants and the local administration, the 1854 decree gave the power to determine guilt or innocence not to the French *président de la cour impérial* (presiding justice) but to four assessors "taken from among the notables . . . composed of [officers], former officers, and the principal landowners and merchants of St. Louis and Gorée."[5] A great deal of judicial authority within the colony was thus vested in the hands of proponents of a pragmatic slave policy.

Conversely, the 1854 imperial decree guaranteed the independence of the colonial prosecutors, thus creating a split between those who brought cases to court and those who tried them. Within months of the decree, public prosecutors charged three Moors with having brought two female slaves and a young boy into the colony—allegedly for sale. Aware of the limitations of the 1848 proclamation, they chose to pursue this case under an 1831 law intended to punish maritime slave traders exporting slaves to the New World, but which could be construed to include traders importing slaves into the colony by land. The two cases were so open-and-shut that even the tilted cour d'assises handed down twenty- and fifteen-year penalties to the traders. However, the decision was reversed on appeal on the basis that the "accused were strangers and that the crimes were committed in foreign countries."[6] When naval minister Ducos was presented with the fait accompli of the reversal of the conviction, he noted that the crimes had in fact been carried over to French territory. Nevertheless, he agreed that the subject status of the accused was enough to guarantee that they should be found innocent. There is no record that newly appointed Governor Faidherbe personally took a hand in the appeal, but certainly the case established that subject peoples were outside even the 1831 ordinance just in time for Faidherbe's expansion and the introduction of large numbers of individuals as subjects. The appeals court's decision dealt a serious blow to proponents of a vigorous prosecution of slave-related laws, and there is no record of further slave-dealing cases for a full twenty years, other than the rather straightforward prosecution of the commandant of Bakel for the sale of slaves captured in battle, for which crime he received only one month's imprisonment.[7]

Meanwhile, Faidherbe's conquests and annexations, while militarily successful, quickly proved a drain on the colonial coffers. As a result, the metropole proved anxious to revert to a less expensive policy of maintaining control of important ports, transportation routes, and strategic regions, while relinquishing direct control over agricultural regions to friendly indigenous rulers. In December 1869, therefore, an inspector sent by the minister of the navy visited Faidherbe's successor, Jean Pinet-Laprade, and proposed abandoning some nonessential posts and concentrating resources on Câp Vert and the first arrondisement.[8] This was carried out in 1871 by Governor François Xavier Michel Valière, who further reduced expenditures by coming to an agreement with Lat Joor renouncing French claims to the interior of Kaajor, but preserving a safe passage for the planned St. Louis-Dakar railroad.[9] The disastrous events of the Franco-Prussian war, and the siege of Paris, had cast Senegal adrift from the metropole. Faidherbe, who had returned home from Senegal some years earlier, figured quite significantly in the Army of the North's actions to relieve Paris; but in the colony the lack of resources severely restricted successive governors' ability to maneuver.

Yves-Jean Saint-Martin, in his 1989 monograph *Le Sénégal sous le Second Empire,* argues that "the incompatibility of fitting France with the indigenous system of slavery played a large part in the origins of de-annexation in 1871."[10]

Faidherbe's difficulties in reconciling antislavery policy with expansion would certainly make it convenient to believe Saint-Martin's assertion, and, admittedly, slavery as an issue loomed large in the decision to establish protectorates rather than effect outright annexation twelve years later. However, before 1871 Faidherbe, his largely military administration, and his successors seem to have effectively alleviated the concerns of indigenous slave owners by abandoning the principles of the 1848 emancipation.

This settlement was tested in 1874 by the appointment of Prosper Darrigrand, a lawyer and abolitionist who had practiced in the West Indies, to the post of président de la cour d'assises.[11] Almost immediately upon his arrival, Darrigrand launched a series of prosecutions aimed at challenging the accommodation reached by the administration and slave owners. His first strike came in 1875 when he charged habitant Gasconi Diop with having sold a slave girl and charged habitant Goza Jean Cartier with having bought a slave girl. Darrigrand considered the case watertight, and so, it seems, did the defendants, who "contested neither the reality nor the gravity of the charges." Nevertheless, the assessors—French officers and fellow habitants—acquitted them, arguing incorrectly that the 1831 law applied only to "slave vessels."[12]

Darrigrand, however, refused to be so easily defeated. He continued to press for stringent prosecution of emancipation laws despite the succession to the governorship of Louis-Alexandre Brière de l'Isle in 1876. Brière de l'Isle was an imperialist and expansionist along the lines of Faidherbe and was determined to reverse the stagnation of the colony's fortunes. Darrigrand's campaign, in his view, threatened the recovery he was engineering and thus earned none of his sympathy. Nevertheless, in 1878 Darrigrand managed to bring to court four more individuals accused of slave dealing. Three of them were clearly subjects and not citizens, as they lived in the village of N'Diago.[13] However, the fourth, N'Diaye N'Diaye, was a habitant and owned property in St. Louis as well as farms and fifteen slaves in Waalo.[14] Brière de l'Isle being conveniently absent in France, Darrigrand pursued N'Diaye despite the opposition of Acting Governor Leguay, who frantically wrote to the minister for assistance.[15] Leguay's cries for assistance brought Brière de l'Isle thundering back to confront Darrigrand. The governor feared the alienation of both the Waalo aristocracy and of the pro-French Muslim cleric Bou-el-Mogdad, at whose residence the sale had taken place.[16] In the end, N'Diaye was found guilty and sentenced by Darrigrand to six months' imprisonment.[17] But Darrigrand's victory was short-lived. By the time he was able to bring another slave-dealing case before the cour d'assises, former Governor Jean-Bernard Jauréguiberry had been appointed minister of the navy and, in support of Brière de l'Isle, he convinced the Ministry of Justice to pull Darrigrand off the case.[18] The judicial challenge to the administration's slave policy had been defeated, and pragmatic politics had won again.

EMANCIPATION IN DAKAR AND RUFISQUE

In the 1870s, while the French were detaching themselves from responsibility for large areas of the interior, the metropole became increasingly aware that the balance of the peanut trade had shifted to Siin-Saalum and Kaajor and therefore to the entrepôts of Câp Vert. Coastal Kaajor was becoming increasingly valuable, and Dakar and Rufisque were being turned into highly profitable ports. Thus, although French colonialism was on the retreat elsewhere, Governor Valière moved to acquire from Kaajor the coastal province of Ndiander and, three years later, in 1874, formally to annex the two settlements, which together with St. Louis and Gorée would form four formally administered *communes* (townships). The decision prompted a debate in the colonial administration over whether or not the 1848 proclamation should be extended to these new acquisitions. In fact, the issue had been discussed before. In 1865, when the importance of Dakar first became apparent, Pinet-Laprade had suggested extending emancipation to Dakar and indeed the entire Câp Vert Peninsula.[19] However, despite taking the preparatory steps of ordering the commandant of Gorée to warn the leading notables of Dakar, and despite having received the approval of the minister, Pinet-Laprade didn't go through with the plan.[20]

In 1874, therefore, the commandant of Gorée, Canard, rightly pointed out again that annexation of the two ports would secure their status as French possessions but would necessitate the previously unrealized emancipation of the many slaves who lived and worked there.[21] Valière concurred, and expressed his fears that that move would alienate the Lebu slave owners of the towns. Recognizing that the inhabitants of Dakar and Rufisque would need some time to move their slaves to villages and farms along the coast or make other arrangements, he therefore ordered Canard to warn the chiefs of the two towns of the imminent decision, but added that "it seems to me in all justice [we must] give the *habitants* a reasonable delay" so that they may not suffer "too much" at the loss of their slaves.[22] That "reasonable delay" eventually extended to three and five years in Dakar and Rufisque, respectively. Despite continual statements by Valière's office that "the moment ha[d] come" to apply emancipation to Dakar and Rufisque,[23] and a further warning to the slave owners of Dakar in July 1875, it was not until July 27, 1877, that slave owning was made illegal in Dakar.[24] Implementation took two years longer in Rufisque, where the act was not applied until June 20, 1879.[25]

The final extension of emancipation to Dakar and Rufisque was very much a compromise. Slave owners in the towns had been given a period of years, which they had used to great effect, to move their slaves outside the fairly small area of enforcement to surrounding Câp Vert communities.[26] Likewise, Canard, who as commandant of Gorée had direct control, refused to follow a policy of vigorously enforcing emancipation in case it might "produce very serious political complications."[27] This was, in large part, a result of the administration's obsession with the development of the towns, in which important projects for the improvement of transport and port facilities were being carried out by an industry constantly in need of workers.[28] The slave owners of Rufisque fought to "keep their slaves" right up to the date of emancipation, but despite administrative fears of heavy opposition to emancipation in Rufisque, these never materialized.[29] Nor were there inordinate increases in the number of slaves seeking documents of liberation in either year, despite the fact that slaves remaining in these two towns were legally entitled to them.[30] That emancipation was neither effective nor disruptive is supported, rather than undermined, by Commandant Canard's refusal in 1880 to extend emancipation throughout Câp Vert. Canard claimed that slaves had been removed to villages "not far from [the] towns . . . of Dakar and Rufisque" and argued that if all Ndiander (Câp Vert) were liberated, the situation would become untenable for Lebu slave owners.[31] The administration, though forced to extend emancipation to the two ports, had once again managed to reconcile its legal obligations with political realities, this time by giving slave owners every opportunity to conserve their slaves.

PUBLIC PRESSURE TO REFORM ANTISLAVERY POLICY, 1879–1882

The official abolition of slavery in Dakar and Rufisque was the first crack in Faidherbe's restriction of emancipation to the small entrepôts and posts occupied by France.[32] However, substantive French authority remained confined largely to Waalo and portions of the Petite Côte, and limited control was exercised over Dimar from the posts of Dagana and Podor. French authority even in these regions was simply too remote and too thin to offer reasonable alternatives for all but the most determined of slaves, and the administration was content that this continue. As late as 1878, the minister of the navy, Pothnau, wrote to Governor Brière de l'Isle, stating that he continued to believe that although the

French authorities "must enforce . . . our ideals of justice and civilisation," care must be taken "not . . . to put at risk our good relationships with . . . the indigenous protectorates."[33]

In the late 1870s, however, the slavery issue began to garner renewed interest in France. Alice Conklin sees the late 1870s as a period in which the key players in the Third Republic "began to accept the argument that for political and economic reasons France should begin asserting herself overseas."[34] Accompanying this renewed interest in empire, however, was a uniquely republican sense of a civilizing mission quite distinct from that of Britain. This approach combined core republican values such as "emancipating the masses from oppression" with a declared respect for some indigenous institutions.[35] Practices of slavery fit awkwardly within this framework. On the one hand, slavery was clearly an exploitative relationship. On the other, administrators continued to argue that it was a benign and important social custom. It was in this context that, in 1879, an unexpected scandal exploded that threatened to upset the fragile balancing of official and unpublished policy in the colony. The spark was a report from Senegal by a Protestant pastor named Villéger indicting the administration for its policy of expelling slaves seeking refuge in the colony.[36] The report caused an immediate sensation. The left-leaning papers *La France, La Marseillaise, Petit Parisien,* and *Lanterne* indicted not only the administration but also former minister Jauréguiberry for failing to suppress slavery within the colony.[37] An editorial in *La France* declared that "slavery exists in France, if it exists in Senegal" and attacked the administration both for ejecting refugee slaves and for allowing their sale within the coastal towns. The papers relied heavily on evidence provided by Villéger and church publications.[38]

Pothnau did not bother to deny the specific charges made by Villéger, claiming instead that the incident to which he referred was "a regrettable error."[39] However, the minister was clearly aware that the incident was not a mistake but an unwritten administrative policy, and one borne of political necessity. In a letter to Governor Brière de l'Isle he noted his awareness of the position of the colony "surrounded by populations possessing slaves which serve to transport their produce to our factories," and gave his continued approval to the policy of expelling slaves who were, he argued, largely vagabonds in any case. In no way did he suggest that the administration should change its procedures.[40]

Pothnau, however, had underestimated both public interest in the issue and the commitment of his opposition. The scandal reached the French senate on March 1, 1880, when Victor Schoelcher charged the administration with three crimes.[41] First, he indicted it for allowing slave owners to reclaim their slaves up to three months after they sought refuge within the colony. Second, he claimed that slaves were "freely bought and sold" in Dakar. Finally, Schoelcher criticized the "free crossing of French territories" by slave caravans.[42] In a thundering speech, he decried the authorities' betrayal of the "right to asylum that is our greatest heritage."[43] Brière de l'Isle clearly saw which way the wind was blowing and decided to at least make gestures in the right direction. On his advice, the merchants and officers of Senegal's General Council quickly passed a resolution "demanding strict application of the 1848 decree."[44] Real change was slower, as one of Pothnau's successors, Minister Rouvier, noted in 1882.[45] Administrators continued to turn a blind eye especially to slave owners seeking to recover slaves claiming refuge in the colony.

THE WAALO AND DIMAR EXODUS

However, the string of pragmatic military administrators was broken in December 1882 with the appointment of Senegal's first civilian governor, René Servatius. Servatius's greatest impact on slave policy was to defy many of his own officers by eliminating formalities that slowed the processing of runaway slaves and made them vulnerable to reclamation by their masters.[46] In his six months in office, Servatius also carved up the colony's bureaucracy. The Direction of Political Affairs, through which the administration dealt with the independent authorities of the interior, was joined by the new Direction of the Interior, which was made responsible for the four communes, the Senegal River posts, and the annexed territories—including Waalo.[47] Under Servatius's immediate successor, a civilian bureaucrat named Bourdiaux, the Direction of the Interior undertook the legally mandated and extremely tardy step of extending certain antislavery ordinances to Waalo and Dimar.[48] Following a reaffirmation of French control of these territories in October 1882, on January 8, 1884, Bourdiaux signed a measure outlawing the further sale and purchase of slaves in these territories.[49]

While Bourdiaux's proclamation was intended to eradicate the slave trade in Waalo, even he was not so bold as to infringe upon the long-standing and extremely pervasive institution of domestic slavery in the floodplain states. Nevertheless, Bourdiaux's measures stirred up the fears of Fulbe and Wolof slave owners. As early as 1883, indigenous leaders had deduced that steps to limit their slave-owning rights would follow the 1882 "clarification" of French authority, and the more mobile Fulbe subsequently began to leave the region for the interior, some in small groups, others in the company of entire clans and settle-ments.[50] Servatius initially attempted to stem this flow by ordering the comman-dant of Dagana to allow the emigrants to leave, but to confiscate any slaves they attempted to take with them.[51] However, this move served only to increase the suspicion of the indigenous population, which over the next seven years de-parted in increasing numbers. By 1889 as many as thirty to forty thousand people in the St. Louis region alone had migrated to the east, some traveling as far as Nioro in Kaarta—some eight hundred kilometers away.[52] Significantly, not only Fulbe and Tukolor but also a number of the more sedentary Wolof fled French rule for the interior.[53]

There is little doubt that the issue of slavery was the principal impetus for this migration. Yamar, the pro-French chief of the Waalo canton of Meringhen, and his constituents, both Fulbe and Wolof, complained that limiting their right to acquire slaves "is our ruin" and demanded that the French "let us judge our affairs like you always let our fathers."[54] Similarly, Abdul Bokar Kane, the aris-tocrat who had recently risen to the leadership of Fuuta and was temporarily a French ally, warned France that "[any] who would have good relations with us must leave [our slaves] in our hands or we cannot remain."[55] However, it is prob-able that the emigration was exacerbated by a call for recruits by Amadu Sheku, regent of the Umarian state at Segu, who was mustering his power against his brothers in the 1880s; an additional important factor may have been French in-terventions in the cattle raids still carried out by many young Fulbe males.[56]

In any case, toward the end of the 1880s it was evident even to the civilian governor of Senegal that Waalo and Dimar, the breadbaskets of the north, would be entirely depopulated if nothing were done to stop this emigration. Even more ominously, as the colony expanded, it was becoming clear that the implementation of similar policies in other cercles would likewise result in mass emigration and economic destabilization. Therefore, on October 18, 1889, Governor Léon Emile Clément-Thomas formally requested that he be allowed to transform Waalo and Dimar into protectorates.[57] He also dissolved the hated Direction of the Interior. In December 1889 the naval ministry agreed, writing that "the sole means that we actually have at our disposal to stop emigration movements which have already affected the colony, and for [encouraging] a re-turn resides in *disannexation,* and the constitution of small principalities placed under the protection and suzerainty of France."[58] The implementation and pub-lication of this strategy was almost immediately successful in encouraging the reentry of large numbers of émigrés in 1890 and 1891.[59] It was clear that the slave owners had won this round.

THE PROMULGATION OF PROTECTORATE POLICIES

The policy implemented in Waalo was modeled upon the protectorate put in place in Kaajor in the wake of the events that occurred between 1879 and 1883. Renewed interest in the annexation of this state was first expressed by Brière de l'Isle, whose militancy was mirrored by metropolitan policy seeking to revive French glory after the disastrous Franco-Prussian War.[60] This attitude resulted in the creation of the position of *commandant supérieur* (commander-in-chief) of French Sudan, charged with coordinating expansion along the upper Senegal. To pay for this expansionism, renewed emphasis was attached to the production and export of groundnuts. However, a major obstacle to the profitability of this industry was the imposition of tolls by chiefly officeholders who also restricted the ability of French merchants to deal directly with peasant farmers. As a result, it was not difficult for Servatius to gather support from both merchants and officials for an attack on Kaajor in 1882. The justification given for the offensive rested to a large extent on the opposition of the damel, Lat Joor, to a proposed railway linking St. Louis with Dakar and the groundnut-growing regions in between.[61] From a Wolof perspective, as elucidated by James Searing, the events leading up to the conflict are more complex. The story starts with the cession of the province of Ndiander to France in 1871. Although Lat Joor saw this move as a compromise, his deputy in Ndiander, the ceddo chieftain Demba War Sall, was never compensated for his loss of income from the region. The split between the two was reinforced in 1875 by Demba War Sall's successful defense against a force of Muslim rebels aided by invaders from Jolof, while the damel fled across the border to French protection.[62] As Sall's invective against him grew, Lat Joor attempted unsuccessfully to replace him in 1879. Sall was thus in a position to make a deal with the French when, in 1881, Lat Joor, in an effort to keep French interference at bay, renounced his agreement to allow the railway. Thus Kaajor's leadership was split when Servatius's column attacked the state, and Lat Joor's resistance was undermined by Demba War Sall, who managed to have his nephew Samba Laobe Fall installed as damel.[63]

Ironically, slavery played a role in ending the reign of Samba Laobe Fall three years later. Demba War Sall, in pursuit of several slaves seeking refuge in the French fort of Tivouane, made the mistake of attempting to reclaim them by force. The expedition sent to punish Sall mistakenly attacked and killed Samba Laobe Fall, "whom the French believed to be in rebellion."[64] The power vacuum left by Fall's death was filled through the formal imposition of a protectorate model of administration, with the rehabilitated Sall as "president" of a federation of chiefs, liaising with the French *commandant de cercle* (circuit administrator). The subsequent success of this protectorate model as a cheap means to ensure political stability, while providing commercial access to the interior for companies in the colony, led to its extension to Waalo and Dimar in 1889, as noted above. In 1890 it was further extended to other regions that had in the intervening period been conquered by colonial forces. French authority had been rapidly established over Siin and Saalum when, following the defeat of Maba, their rulers had sought the protection of British forces in the Gambia in 1887. Jolof came under French authority following Alburi Njaay's defeat at the hands of Governor Clément-Thomas in 1890.[65] In fact, by 1890 the French were in possession of all the states of Senegal north of the Gambia River, as well as a significant portion of modern-day Mali.[66]

The protectorate was a logical system of administration for these territories, not only because it placed much of the burden of rule on aristocrats in the French camp, but also because it avoided entirely the tricky problem of reconciling domestic slavery and French law. Clément-Thomas understood that any extension of the colony would have turned the population of these states into French citizens, subject to antislavery laws. Instead, the protectorate model gave each commandant de cercle wide latitude in forming relationships with indigenous chiefs and implementing administrative policies.[67]

Thus the conquest and formal acquisition of the Senegalese states did not prompt any official revision of administrative attitudes toward slavery. The commanders were quick to recognize that they had only very limited resources — too few administrators, limited transportation, and tiny budgets — and that they therefore had to rely on client chiefs and village headmen, most of whom were slave owners.[68] More important, however, it had been the continuing authority of slave-owning aristocrats that had in the first place convinced the administration to implant a system of administration that could largely ignore abolitionist pressure from the metropole. The 1890 protectorate treaty signed by loyal chiefs from Waalo, Jolof, and the St. Louis region consisted of cosmetic measures forbidding the purchase and sale of slaves and providing a mechanism by which slaves could liberate themselves by paying a Fr 500 indemnity. However, it failed absolutely to forbid or regulate domestic slavery.[69] In fact, French policy was so lax that when, between 1890 and 1891, Britain and France redrew the borders between Senegal and the Gambia, a number of chiefs who found themselves on the Gambian side of the line moved north, largely, it has been suggested, to escape British abolitionist laws.[70]

OCCUPATIONS AND CHARACTERISTICS OF LOCAL SLAVERY
IN THE LATE NINETEENTH CENTURY

In order to analyze the strategies of slaves in these new protectorates, it is necessary to discuss what we know about slave populations, characteristics, and occupations within these regions, most notably Waalo. My analysis of this subject is informed particularly by the results of a 1904 questionnaire circulated to the commandants of the various cercles within the then colony of French West Africa. This document, folio K18 of the Senegalese National Archives, is made up of administrators' reports that include estimates of the number and percentage of slaves in each region, their occupations, the ethnic groups of their owners, and their genders and ages.

Although the statistics given by commandants de cercle and *sergents de villes* (constabulary officials) and presented in table 7.1 are not entirely reliable, the qualitative data indicates that a number of arguments made by colonial officials, and later by historians, are correct. The first is that slavery was ubiquitous within the protected territories. Slaveholding extended to all ethnic groups during the late nineteenth century, as statistics, particularly those from N'Diourbel, reveal. Conversely, the responses of officers from Siin and Fundiugne suggest that the Sereer, who traditionally had a more egalitarian society, continued to hold a smaller proportion of slaves than other ethnic groups. However, the groundnut regime had stimulated slave owning in Saalum, which was unique among the Sereer states in supporting a population, of which one third was unfree. Groundnut producers, like many other cash croppers, perceived male slaves as better workers, in contrast to the tradition in Senegal of preferring female slaves. In the interior, most Fulbe and Tukolor slave owners still preferred women—only about 35 percent of slaves in Matam and Podor cercles were men, compared to around 55 percent women. However, in groundnut-producing Kaajor, 43 percent were men and only 28 percent were women—the rest were youths for whom we have no gender statistics.

The origins of these slaves, on the other hand, had not changed significantly. Slaves still appear to have come predominately from the interior, although warfare between Muslim reformers, traditional leaders, and the French between the 1850s and 1880s generated large numbers of war captives, and the ceddo were still active in some regions.[71] Increasingly, however, it was Moorish slave traders who satisfied the demands of Senegalese slave owners.[72]

Most slaves still worked in the economic capacities that they had come to fill in the eighteenth and early nineteenth centuries. French administrators from regions as far apart as Kaolack, Fundiugne, and Dagana identified cultivation

TABLE 7.1
Suggested Slave Statistics for Protected Territories of Senegal, 1904

Cercle or administrative region	Approximately corresponding to	Main ethnic group(s)	Estimated number of slaves	Proportion of population[1]	% women	% children
Kaolack	Saalum	Sereer		1/3		
Foundiougne	Town only	Sereer	50	1/20		
Thiès	Siin	Sereer	750	1/70		
Baol Occidental	Western Baol	Sereer/ Wolof	20,000	1/4		
N'Diourbel	Eastern Baol	Sereer	1,000	1/45		
		Wolof	3,000	1/7		
		Fulbe	1,300	1/7		
Petite Côte	Petite Côte	Sereer/ Lebu	1,000	1/30		
Tivaouane	Kaajor	Wolof	15,000		28	29
Louga	Waalo	Wolof/ Fulbe	8,940		41	29
Dagana	Dimar	Fulbe	26,000	1/2		
Podor	Toro	Wolof/ Fulbe	18,609	1/5		
Matam	Regions of Fuuta	Fulbe	20,000		56	9
Bakel	Gajaaga	Fulbe/ Tukolor	35,000			

Source: ANS K18, Réponse aux questionnaire, 1904.
1. As given. Some respondents failed to provide.

and harvesting as the primary roles of slaves, and a number were also engaged in herding sheep and goats.[73] In most of these areas slaves were given between 104 and 240 days per year to cultivate their own food, the rest of the time working for their masters, tending their farms, herds, or groundnut fields.[74] Domestic tasks such as preparing food—especially pounding millet—and weaving were also performed by slaves, although not exclusively.[75] In addition to domestic slaves, in most regions there still existed a caste of royal or chiefly slaves (*captifs/ captives de la couronne*), most of whom occupied symbolic or military roles.[76]

PATENTS DE LIBERTÉ

Technically, of course, the status of slaves in these cercles was recognized as legal by the French government and the administration of Senegal. Outside Waalo and

Dimar, where, between 1882 and 1890, slaves could technically liberate themselves under the 1848 act, the administration had, through the establishment of protectorates, rejected the emancipation of slaves. This then was a fundamental division between the nonrecognition of slavery on the Gold Coast and the Senegal administration's sanction of slavery within the protected states. In practice, admittedly, there were some very close parallels between the two administrations' policies, which in both regions tended to force slaves into similar situations. We have seen how, during most of the 1870s and 1880s, slaves in the Gold Coast had to trek to Cape Coast or Accra to seek judicial support for their liberation. Similarly, the principal of sol affranchis, strenuously enforced following the appointment of Governor Servatius in 1883, meant that slaves from the interior who managed to escape to St. Louis, Gorée, or one of the Senegal River posts could receive patents de liberté.[77] In Senegal as in the Gold Coast, there were added difficulties constraining female slaves from seeking their freedom. The French, like the British, recognized children as belonging to their fathers and would not liberate them if a slave owner indicated his paternity. Additionally, as Administrator Poulet noted, women had little to gain from liberation since there was little call for them in the wage labor market and since female runaways who found work as domestic servants in the colony generally found themselves carrying out the same tasks in similar conditions that they had performed as slaves.[78]

However, there remained a significant difference between the two regions in the administration of antislavery laws. In the Gold Coast, enforcement of the same law throughout the protectorate enabled liberated slaves to travel and settle safely as free individuals, whereas in Senegal patents de liberté went largely unhonored outside the four communes. Thus, it was generally only slaves with access to formally administered French territory—largely those who transported goods to the coast either on their backs or as laptots—who could liberate themselves, and even then they could not safely return to their cercle or home. The French administrators, in fact, recognized only one legal mode of liberation for slaves outside the colony—the rachat. After 1890 (in some regions, 1893), slaves who could pay their masters Fr 500 could legally purchase their freedom.[79] The likelihood of this was pretty low, however, for the largely rural slave population was occupied in cultivation, herding, and domestic employment.

There is unfortunately very little known about modes of liberation in late-nineteenth-century Senegal. Surprisingly, however, it appears that a relatively large number of slaves were able to liberate themselves by seeking refuge within the colony and consequently being awarded patents de liberté, both before and following the loosening of restrictions in 1884. Regrettably, the quantitative records we have for this type of liberation, published in the *Moniteur du Senegal* (shown in table 7.2 below), are not greatly illuminated by more qualitative sources.

This, unfortunately, has led to a number of misunderstandings. François Renault, for example, saw these liberations as a result of changes in the attitudes of the administration in the wake of the scandals of the 1880s. He hailed them as an example of "governors . . . achiev[ing] real redress. They were made aware of the necessity of ending the worst abuses."[80] Even Boubacar Barry ascribed the large numbers of slave liberations partly to European agency, arguing that "the Colony of Senegal encouraged the flight of slaves towards [French soil]. The Colony thus created a series of enclaves surrounding the Senegambian kingdoms."[81]

I disagree fundamentally with these arguments. Although civilian governors after 1884 may, under pressure from France, have made it easier for runaway slaves to gain their emancipation, Barry and Renault provide no primary evidence

TABLE 7.2
Slave Liberations in Senegal, 1868–1895

Year	Total liberations
1868	102
1869	139
1870	148
1871	129
1872[1]	91
1873[1]	55
1874[1]	85
1875	328
1876	278
1877	349
1878	347
1879	440
1880	609
1881	643
1882	919
1883[1]	1,266
1884	841
1885[1]	1,060
1886	676
1888[1]	254
1894[2]	1,218
1895	1,438

1. Figures for these years are incomplete.
2. No statistics for 1887 or 1889–93.
Sources: 1868–88: Klein, *Slavery and Colonial Rule,* 1998, 72. 1894–95: Deherme, *L'esclavage en AOF,* 1906.

to show that they encouraged slaves to run away. Indeed, they patently did not. French administrators regarded the liberated slave population as a drain on their resources. "In general," one administrator was to comment in 1904, "all slaves who seek their liberty are parasites, and those who claim abuse to recover their liberty are almost always liars who wish to be vagabonds."[82] Admittedly, the eradication of slavery was an important part of the principles of the civilizing mission slowly coalescing in the metropole, but military officials governing the interior posts, and indeed the (mostly military) governors in St. Louis and later Dakar, did not yet subscribe to this doctrine.

Rather, liberation by patents de liberté was generally the result of action by either slaves or by their masters, rather than by administrators. In fact, until the mid-1880s a large, although incalculable, proportion of slaves liberated in this manner were women and children brought into the colony to act as concubines or domestic servants and liberated by their masters in order to legitimize the arrangement in the eyes of the gendarmes.[83] Slave owners trusted that the lack of opportunity for these individuals, imported from far away and bereft of any support structure, would keep them dependent on their masters, and therefore perceived no danger in registering them for patents de liberté. The slaves may not even have been informed of their freedom, or might simply have been unable to exploit it due not only to the lack of economic opportunity but also to the lack of housing. Although the actual number of children "liberated" in this manner appears small, Georges Deherme suggested that most such liberations went unrecorded, and the number may have been as much as three times larger.[84]

On the other hand, most of the patents de liberté granted after 1884 (and possibly as early as 1882) probably did result from either kin or self-liberations. Although many children brought into the colony were essentially slaves purchased for domestic servitude and registered by habitants and French administrators, others have been identified by Martin Klein as having been vouchsafed to relatives.[85] Anecdotal evidence supports the notion that relatives may have kidnapped or redeemed their children or younger kin and then had them formally liberated in St. Louis or Gorée.[86] Similarly, evidence from refugee slaves in Podor includes a number of stories of slaves "saved" or "stolen back" by their brothers, fathers, or uncles.[87] Their family members, not having the lawful sanction for such actions enjoyed by families in the Gold Coast, were forced to spirit them away to safety within the colony.

However, a large number, probably the majority, of patents were granted as a result of agency by the slaves themselves. Almost all the liberations granted at the interior posts were brought about by slaves fleeing masters or traders. Prior to 1884, such requests for liberation were granted only in cases in which slaves could show they had been born free individuals within the colony or in regions under direct annexation (Waalo and the provinces of Gandiole and Ndiander in Kaajor), or could prove they had been abused by their masters.[88] Other slaves were expelled if claimed by their masters, and if their masters failed to claim them, they were conferred, as dependents with few safeguards, upon local notables.[89] For example Djerry, the chief of the village of Podor, was the recipient of fourteen wards between 1866 and 1868. After 1884 the political situation rendered such a pragmatic solution indefensible, and all slaves reaching French soil were, in theory, given certificates of liberation.[90] The number of slaves seeking refuge had been climbing since 1880, and the news that slaves could expect to receive patents encouraged the increase in liberations that Renault ascribed to administrative agency.[91] Soon after, Bambara slaves from Banamba began to trickle into St. Louis. It was not until 1903, when patents de liberté were replaced with more extensive laws prohibiting slavery, that that drip would become a flood.[92]

Unfortunately, we have little other information about who the vast majority of these fugitive slaves were. Klein has attempted to calculate their origins and found that 21.4 percent originated in Kaajor, a total of 47.6 percent came from the Wolof and Sereer states (including Kaajor), and about 19.2 percent originated in Western Mali. However, he relied mostly on names to distinguish points of origin, and his findings are uncertain, although the best we have.[93] Perhaps some indication can be gleaned from the 1904 reports in the K18 files, in which officials highlight several likely scenarios by which slaves might have chosen to liberate themselves. Captifs de la couronne, for example, enjoyed a number of privileges of assimilation and rank, performed little labor, and were consequently the least likely to seek their liberation.[94] On the other hand, those most likely to emancipate themselves appear, as in the Gold Coast, to have been recently acquired slaves who had accumulated none of the benefits of assimilation and whose memories of and links with their homes were strongest.[95] Moreover, most of these slaves were probably young adults whose position had not yet been ameliorated by long service, and so were less assimilated and had less to leave behind.[96]

CHRISTIAN MISSIONARIES AS AGENTS OR MEANS OF LIBERATION

In the last quarter of the nineteenth century, the missionary promise of the Congregation de la Saint-Esprit was by no means fulfilled. After 1848 the *pères* (priests) had attempted to expand outside St. Louis and Gorée, but they accomplished little and made few conversions.[97] Those few who ventured into the interior lamented the lack of resources and the scarcity of their brethren, but it was not a paucity of resources or low numbers that stopped them from having an impact on slavery in the protectorate.[98] Instead, the pères chose largely to accept domestic slavery as "no more than a sort of domesticity."[99] What attention the missionaries spared for slavery was aimed at purchasing children to act both as servants and as the core of anticipated congregations, a policy followed by both Protestant and Catholic churches.[100] Even the famous *villages de liberté*, which came to house huge numbers of refugee slaves throughout French West Africa in the twentieth century, were not begun until 1897 in the Western Sudan and were never instituted by missionaries in the cercles of Senegal.[101] In fact, the missions were more tools of liberation than instigators of emancipation. While not interested in liberating the general slave population, clergy would sometimes intervene in the case of former converts who had been sold outside the colony. Such slaves, if they could recite the catechism, could count on church support in gaining patents de liberté.[102] Similarly, young slaves in Joal sometimes turned to the Soeurs de St. Joseph de Ngozobil, usually after incidents of abuse, and were confiscated from their masters with the reluctant support of local administrators.[103]

Slaves seeking refuge within the communes also found that churches were a rare source of food and lodging in otherwise crowded towns. The Catholic and Protestant missions competed for these converts to such a degree that in 1887 Monsignor Riehl of the Congregation de la Saint-Esprit opened a church annex in Sor, across the river from St. Louis, in order to outflank the Protestant mission on the eastern side of the island.[104] Nevertheless, even in the colony, it was generally the fugitives who sought out the missionaries, rather than the other way around.

PEANUTS, ISLAM, AND SELF-LIBERATIONS: AN EARLY IMPACT?

However, although in some ways requests for patents are surprisingly numerous in the historical record, they do not by themselves prove, as some contemporary sources suggest, that slaves were "all more or less desirous of reclaiming their liberty."[105] After all, as there were at least one to two hundred thousand slaves remaining with their masters at the time of the questionnaire, the approximately one to two thousand per year seeking their liberation through official means after 1884 seems a drop in the bucket by comparison.

Potentially, however, much of the activity of slaves could have taken place outside the official record, and James Searing has suggested that slave self-emancipations, at least in Kaajor and Baol, were on the increase between 1883 and 1890 largely due to local economic and social changes. Searing's claim is supported by a careful combination of conjecture and extrapolation. Principally, he argues that lower-than-expected levels of slave ownership in Kaajor and Baol were caused by a rise in opportunities provided by Murid Islam for refugee slaves and by slaves' joining the streams of *navetane* (migrant laborers) working for peasant peanut cultivators. He further suggests that this is similar to the experiences of Northern Nigeria, where slaves ran away "during the first decade of colonial rule." The key piece of evidence he presents is the decline in the volume of peanut production between 1883 and 1891.[106] Confirmation might be found in the 1904 slave-population estimates.

Nevertheless, all this evidence is questionable. Martin Klein has argued convincingly that the relatively small slave populations reported in 1904 were a result of poor reporting and subterfuge, rather than truly diminished levels of slaveholding.[107] Moreover, Searing fails to discredit the general argument that rising peanut production elsewhere, especially in India, caused a drop in peanut prices and a resulting diversion of land from peanut production, thus explaining the decline of exports from Senegal. Additionally, slaves fleeing their masters could not necessarily, at this early date, have found safe refuge in villages in Kaajor and other peanut-growing regions, to which the French had failed to extend antislavery ordinances. Finally, although the earliest Murid communities were being established during this period, the great majority were not founded until the early twentieth century.

The Murid order deserves some extra consideration in this study, however, especially as Klein has argued that this group, along with the Qadiriya movement, was "as important as the existence of a free labor market in destroying slave labor systems," and Searing also places it in a triangular relationship with cash cropping and the abolition of slavery.[108] Muridism arose out of the piety of Amadu Bamba, a Baol native whose grandfather had rallied to Maba's side and whose father had been a key Muslim judge in Lat Joor's administration in Kaajor. The break between Lat Joor and Amadu arose out of the latter's father's ruling, in 1875, that prisoners taken from Jolof during the invasion could not be enslaved under Muslim law.[109] Nevertheless, Amadu Bamba remained in Kaajor until 1883, at which time he departed for his ancestral village in Baol. He would use this region as his headquarters at least until his first arrest by the French in 1895.

It was during this period that Bamba began to attract followers, including both sëriş and ceddo leaders, and probably a number of refugee slaves as well. There are various accounts of this period not germane to this study.[110] However, the Murid order does seem to have provided some refugee slaves with relatively safe havens through a happy combination of egalitarianism and expansion into marginal areas. Muridism denied any distinction between formerly free and un-free members of the community, and, consequently, was an attractive option for refugee slaves.[111] Moreover, the Murid movement's policy of having communi-ties of young men led by a *shayk* settle dry frontier regions and convert them for peanut cultivation attracted mostly individuals with no claim to land elsewhere, and therefore probably drew a large proportion of former slaves.[112] Nevertheless, the recruitment of slaves by the Murids has never been quantified, and while it remains difficult to be sure, there is little evidence that this movement was significant until the early twentieth century.

OTHER MEANS OF EXISTENCE FOR EXSLAVES

If liberated slaves in the Gold Coast had few alternative means of existence, they could only be envied by their counterparts in the colony of Senegal. Most freed slaves had no choice at all. Lone children, for example, were simply conferred on habitants, free citizens of St. Louis Colony, or French officials as servants.[113] Among these were a number who had been purchased by French-Senegalese citizens as slaves then legally liberated but kept in virtual slavery by their pur-chasers despite their patents de liberté.[114]

The military was always open to exslaves. The retreat of the 1870s led to a demand for African troops to replace French soldiers recalled to fight in France, and the subsequent reexpansion kept that demand so high that around two hun-dred young male slaves were purchased and "liberated" specifically for conscrip-tion.[115] During subsequent decades, Africans remained the preferred soldiers for the more dangerous and unhealthy posts in the interior. However, most of these recruits were slaves purchased directly from dealers. The French continued to prefer recruits from among the Bambara, whom they viewed as a martial people, and most freed slaves appear to have declined to join the military.[116] Still, mili-tary service remained an option, if an unattractive one, for young male exslaves. Women and children had no such choice. "Most of the women and all children," Canard reported in 1882, "serve new masters who [give] them food and lodging, in exchange for the profits" of their labors.[117] The culture of slavery in St. Louis and Gorée continued as much the same arrangement under a different name, since a small elite still dominated both housing and employment, and many new slaves were simply integrated into the local economy as washerwomen, domestic servants, millet pounders, and food preparers.

Other than becoming dependents of habitant patrons, there was little work available to former slaves in the neighborhood of the communes. Governor Canard admitted in 1882 that "in effect, no institution has been created with the aim of regenerating these poor [people]."[118] He lamented the fact that "slaves who we declare free . . . are generally terribly fitted out. . . . [They] do not wish to work, [and] live on petty theft and charity" and placed upon them the blame for "the numerous fires that have broken out."[119]

It was partly to capitalize on the availability of former slaves that, in the 1890s, various European companies and governments began to recruit laborers in the colony for other parts of Africa. Local administrators at first actively encouraged the export of these unemployed former slaves, whom they still saw as a danger to the colony. The administration had already attempted to compel young male exslaves to work for the *directeur d'artillerie* and the works commission, whereas others had been conferred upon churches.[120] Furthermore, the recruitment of labor for overseas had a long history in Senegal.[121] However, the days of forced engagement for other regions had been ended by a *décision impériale* of 1856 following a scandal in which Gabonese laborers meant for Guyana had been purchased and exported as slaves.[122] Consequently, African laborers could no longer be legally compelled to travel overseas.

Nevertheless, the demand for labor in African colonies had never been higher than it was in the 1890s. Agents of Belgian king Leopold II were combing West Africa for soldiers and laborers to facilitate the rubber extraction process in the Congo.[123] Similarly, the administration of French Congo demanded workers and craftsmen for Libreville[124] and seemed to prefer Senegalese recruits to act as tirailleurs.[125] However, voluntary recruits in the ports of Dakar, St. Louis, and Gorée remained elusive.[126] Some recruiters thus turned to the interior, recruiting peasants and possibly providing an opportunity for slaves, but this was a dangerous strategy that sometimes incurred the wrath of indigenous leaders.[127] The largest number of recruits, however, were the "Sarakolés, Woloffs, and Toucouleurs who find themselves without work" in the colony.[128] The soldiers recruited for French Congo were described as "porters, dockers, shoe-shine boys, about 16 to 22 years old with little military bearing."[129] Similarly, men recruited in Dakar in 1894 for the Belgian Congo included a number of *manoeuvres* and unemployed individuals, many of whom originated in the interior — especially Galaam and Fuuta Tooro.[130] Although not a single person enumerated in these records admits to a slave background, several factors indicate that some may have been former slaves. The date, for example, is concurrent with increased slave liberations, and the interior origins of many recruits, as well as their gender, age, and lack of skill, suggest that the group may have included a number of runaways.

— ◆ —

As a result of effective resistance by slave owners in Waalo and Dimar, the importance of slaves to groundnut cultivation, and a lack of conviction by local administrators, the French turned to the protectorate system so as not to infringe upon the rights of slave owners outside the colony. As a result, there was no great threat to slave owners, and the majority of slaves were unable to renegotiate their position. Nor would this change until after the implementation of the 1905 Comprehensive Slavery Decree, the firmer establishment of Murid communities, and the further expansion of the migrant labor systems.[131]

There is tantalizing evidence that the slave and slave-owning populations of Rufisque engaged in some sort of negotiations in the aftermath of the 1879 extension of emancipation. The situation in that town was quite unique. As early as 1874 Governor Valière had warned masters in Rufisque that emancipation was imminent and that they should attempt "to conserve for themselves the service of their freed slaves," and masters used the intervening time wisely.[132] The mostly sedentary inhabitants of Rufisque, profiting from a burgeoning trade in groundnuts, did not have the option of fleeing French authority like the slave owners of Waalo, and despite Canard's fears, no such exodus took place.[133] As I have pointed out, many slave owners probably transferred their slaves to villages outside Rufisque. However, the temporary demand for workers created by the government's program of infrastructure improvements in Câp Vert, the accessibility of sol affranchis even for slaves who were moved, and (according to Brière de l'Isle) the example of the more egalitarian neighboring Sereer states may have created an environment in which slave owners were "forced to make 'arrangements' with their slaves."[134] It is unfortunate that I have been unable to uncover little further evidence regarding these arrangements.

The situation in Rufisque, however, was exceptional. By and large, slaves could still liberate themselves only by traveling to French soil, and there was little incentive to do so — especially since there was no land available in the colony. Young male slaves were not only the most able to seek their liberation but also the most likely to find some kind of labor, either overseas or in the military. How-ever, most of the men and almost all of the women and children who sought their liberation found that they had to continue to work for a master despite their legal emancipation. Nor was negotiation a widely pursued course in most of the region; the wide identification of slavery as a "caste" in Wolof and Tukolor society meant that, although slaves could alleviate their economic situation through negotia-tion, they could never escape "a social status that prevented complete emancipa-tion."[135] Evidence to suggest the self-conversion of massive numbers of slaves into migrant workers prior to the end of the nineteenth century is still incomplete.

Aside from James Searing, whose work is admittedly groundbreaking, most historians who write about this period agree that emancipation for most of Senegal's slaves would have to wait until the twentieth century.[136] However, although domestic captivity was tolerated by late-nineteenth-century colonial authorities, public pressure to end the "odious commerce" that was the internal slave trade had begun to mount. During the last decade of the century, Sene-gal's administration was therefore given a final opportunity to show the reso-lution to eradicate one of the most abusive aspects of Senegalese slavery in the nineteenth century.

CHAPTER 8
Toward the Eradication of the Overland Slave Trade?

THE BRITISH AND FRENCH POLICIES discussed in the last five chapters were celebrated by turn-of-the-century historians as the gradual unveiling of great philanthropic plans, of which the abolition of the Atlantic slave trade in the first decades of the nineteenth century had been the first major step.[1] If we were to judge solely from the tone of their accounts and the text of their reports, the decrees in 1834 and 1848 abolishing slavery and the extension of emancipation policies to the Gold Coast Protectorate in 1874 would seem to be consecutive rungs on a ladder reaching toward the total elimination of slavery in Senegal and the Gold Coast.

This notion is, however, entirely fallacious. The settlements on the Gold Coast were excluded from Britain's emancipatory policies between 1834 and 1874. The French emancipation of 1848 did take effect in the minuscule colony of Senegal; however, even the politicized slaves of St. Louis and Gorée simply became clients in a less formalized but still dependent relationship with their former masters. Perhaps the extension of British hegemony over the Gold Coast in 1874 was expected by some to transform slave owning, but the watered-down measure eventually handed to the colonial administration by the Colonial Office resulted for most slaves only in a gradual reevaluation of dependent status rather than massive liberations. Meanwhile, resistance by slave owners in Senegal was so effective that the French authorities there did not even attempt to emulate the Gold Coast policies after the disastrous failure of a prototype policy in Waalo in the 1880s.

In fact, as the nineteenth century drew to a close, it became apparent that even the abolition of the Atlantic slave trade had been limited both in its scope and in its results. Although the last ships smuggling slaves to the New World appear to have sailed in the 1860s, thousands of individuals in the African interior were still kidnapped, captured in wars, or otherwise enslaved. Not only did the still vigorous caravans of the trans-Saharan slave trade pass through (and, more rarely, originate from) Senegal, but in both regions captives still made the terrible and often fatal journey to urban and rural slave markets. Increasingly, however, they were sold before the horrified eyes of a growing number of missionaries and civilian, rather than military, administrators. Thus, as the century came to a close, the French and British both came under renewed agitation definitively to end the institution of slave trading within their possessions. Their dissimilar responses to this pressure would indicate both a departure from and a continuation of the policies of tolerance toward slavery that had exemplified European colonialism in West Africa in the preceding century.

Why Target the Slave Trade?

The long-distance slave trade into the Senegal and Gold Coast regions was perceived by European observers as a traditional "custom," existing since "time immemorial."[2] However, although early European travelers to the Gold Coast had noted the high proportion of slaves from the interior, a comparable proportion of the region's slaves had been acquired locally. Similarly, in Senegal, prior to the Atlantic slave trade, the commerce in slaves had generally run south to north rather than from the interior to the coast. During the era of the Atlantic slave trade, however, the long-distance slave trade had shifted radically and definitively in both regions. In the Gold Coast, well-positioned states such as those of the Fante and, for a period, Akwamu, had gained power as "the brokers of those of the interior who supply slaves."[3] Similarly, during this period the Senegalese coastal entrepôts trafficked largely in slaves from Gaajaga and other regions in the interior.[4] The abolition of the Atlantic slave trade and the subsequent development of legitimate commerce on the coast had reinforced the demand for slaves from the interior, a region usually outside direct colonial control, both for use as field laborers and as domestic slaves.

In the latter half of the nineteenth century, concurrent with increasing liberalization in Europe and growing colonial responsibilities in Senegal and the Gold Coast, this trade in slaves from the interior became the object of the fiercest abolitionist outrage, which quickly had an impact on the general public and subsequently on politicians in the metropole. The accounts of Livingstone and other explorers had made an impression on the public psyche, and outrage over the persistence of the slave trade in East Africa had been a factor in the rising numbers of, first, Protestant missionaries and, later, the Catholic White Fathers in Africa. Furthermore, as Miers and Roberts have pointed out, the work of these missionaries was impeded by "wars and raids, the hostility of slavers, and the dilemma posed by fugitive slaves," and, subsequently, under Cardinal Lavigerie the White Fathers led the crusade to popularize abolitionism in Catholic Europe after 1888.[5]

The abhorrence exhibited by politicians, as well as missionaries, of the "odious traffic" was not entirely consistent, since the commerce in slaves led directly to forms of domestic slavery that were generally accepted by the very same officials. It was, however, entirely logical in terms of public opinion in the metropole, which to some degree accepted the distinction between supposedly benign forms of domestic slavery and the horrors of the slave trade. This distinction, so useful for administrations seeking to avoid interfering with slave owning, was perceived by missionaries, both Protestant and Catholic.[6] Although reluctant to implement a rigorous emancipation policy, Carnarvon, for example, labeled the importation of slaves "an outrage and a crime." Similarly, when Victor Schoelcher reported to the senate in 1880 that "caravans freely traverse French territory," officials in Senegal were quick to react.[7]

For Carnarvon, Strahan, and their officers on the Gold Coast, eradicating the slave trade was a logical extension of gradualist policies toward ending slavery. Benjamin Pine had suggested in 1857 that the importation of trade slaves be criminalized but that domestic slavery and pawning merely be regulated.[8] Similarly, although they considered such gradualist plans as allowing slaves slowly to purchase their freedom or liberating only children born after 1875, both Carnarvon and Strahan remained steadfast in planning for "the immediate and absolute prohibition of slave dealing in every form."[9] For the administrators of Senegal as well, a politically expedient attack on the slave trade seemed a good compromise between the demands of abolitionists and the administration's reliance on the goodwill of indigenous slave owners.[10] Their inability to reconcile abolitionist demands with their management of newly conquered territories in the 1880s and 1890s demanded that some kind of sop be thrown to the increasingly abolitionist French public, and to a government that had singled out slavery as an institution to be destroyed.[11] Thus, although he promised Lat Joor of Kaajor that there would be no general emancipation under French protection in 1882, Minister

Rouvier instructed the governor to inform him that slave *trading* would be banned.[12] Similar conditions were written into the 1890 treaty that subsequently extended the protectorate regime over the bulk of Senegal.[13]

However, the slave trade was an obvious target for the two administrations not only for reasons of ideology, but also for reasons of convenience. It is apparent, in light of evidence showing that newly acquired slaves were more likely to seek their liberation or leave their masters in both regions, that trade slaves were a more assured source of law enforcement triumphs for colonial administrations desperate to provide the illusion of a commitment to abolition. Slave traders, unlike slave owners, were often from outside the colony, and their capture was less likely to alienate indigenous elites than was the punishment of neighbors and friends. The slave trade was also, by necessity, conducted along waterways or major paths, and large slave convoys may have been an easier catch than individual slaves and slave owners in domestic settings.

With all the political capital to be made out of pursuing slave traders, it is perhaps no wonder that governors and magistrates conceived of policies to tackle the long-distance trade in people. In the Gold Coast, a serious, if underresourced, effort to eradicate this institution began in 1875, whereas in Senegal it was not until the expansion of the 1880s that even the most meager measures against the slave trade were introduced. In both regions, the period following the Treaty of Brussels in 1890 provided an opportunity to intensify the war on slave trading; but it was one that was not necessarily grasped. However, before we look at the methods of enforcement, we must consider the nature of the trade in question in the two regions in the late nineteenth century.

THE SLAVE TRADE INTO SENEGAL

Long-distance commercial networks are rarely static over long periods of time, and the trade in slaves from the interior into Senegal was no exception. Trade routes during the era of the Atlantic slave trade were largely structured to bring slaves from the interior to the coastal entrepôts, and later to the Senegal region in general, but the functioning of this network was often disrupted.

The transportation and sale of slaves in the late 1860s is a case in point. For these years we have an unusually revealing record of slave experiences, since Commander Jauréguiberry of Podor kept details of slaves seeking refuge at his post between 1866 and 1868.[14] We should refrain from drawing too many conclusions from these documents, since the French policy during this period of liberating only freeborn individuals originating from two provinces of Kaajor, Waalo, and the colony mean that Jauréguiberry's records include slaves mostly from those origins.[15] However, these files reveal that the late 1860s were a chaotic period. French wars of expansion, conflict between secular and Muslim leaders, and especially the rise of Maba had led to an apparently significant number of freeborn Senegalese—Wolof, Sereer, Tukolor, and Fulbe—becoming enslaved. Maba's rebellion had an especially large effect on Jolof, where his advance into the territory in 1865 displaced villagers who, consequently, became vulnerable to capture by both opposing armies and by brigands who wandered the area in the wake of his defeat.[16] At the same time, in Kaajor, conflict between ceddo and Muslim factions continued to disrupt village and town life.[17] Partly because of the interference with planting and harvesting resulting from these conflicts, large parts of northern Senegal experienced a famine during this period that forced individuals to flee their villages, joining the war refugees on the roads.[18] That some of these individuals ended up in Podor indicates that they had been sold or transported from coastal regions into the interior—something of a shift from the normal trade routes.

By the 1880s, however, the stability that accompanied the intensification of French rule meant that fewer slaves were being internally generated, ironically allowing most distribution networks bringing slaves into Senegal from the interior to return to normal operations. The system within which these networks functioned was largely defined by geography; the Senegal and Gambia Rivers continued to be the most efficient means of transportation for slave traders. Along the northern route, the Senegal River functioned as a long-distance pathway. By this time, most of the slaves traveling this corridor were being transported north into Mauritania, but a significant proportion still ended up in the French protectorates. In the south, the creeks of the Gambian Delta and of the nearby Siin-Saalum Delta gave slave dealers a porous border through which to smuggle slaves up and down the coast. This southern slave route was by far the less significant of the two. This was at least partly because of the presence of more efficient British anti-slave-trade patrols at Bathurst and points along the Gambia River, which slowed the flow of slaves transported along this route to the groundnut plantations in Siin-Saalum. Markets in Kayes and possibly Médine, near the source of the Senegal River that traditionally supplied both the Gambia and Senegal River routes, continued to function throughout the 1880s and 1890s, but most slave caravans went north to the Senegal River or, Bernard Moitt has suggested, toward coastal Guinea.[19]

Nevertheless, at least some of the slaves whose journeys ended in Baol, Siin, and Saalum entered Senegal across the Gambia. In 1893 a slave from Sierra Leone was sold in Thies (Siin), prompting the commandant de cercle to comment rather hypocritically that "I suppose that many of the English [subjects] have no other means of existence other than the commerce in slaves."[20] Unfortunately, we do not know the origin of most of the other slaves who arrived in the district, but we have more information on their captors. There are two records of "Dioulas" bringing convoys into the territory—one of forty slaves brought into Baol and another of twenty-eight imported to Fundiugne.[21] The designation *dioula,* or *juula* in French, is often somewhat loosely applied, but it properly refers to extensive, loosely aligned groups of Manding merchants who had the resources to transport slaves and other goods over long distances. In this case, they appear to have maintained long-term trading relationships in Siin-Saalum and Baol, especially with the Tukolor and Fulbe villages scattered around this mostly Sereer region.[22]

The more significant Senegal River slave trade worked on somewhat similar lines, but we know much more about the mechanisms by which it operated. Slaves entered this network from an enormous human reservoir around and along the Niger River, funneled into interior markets in which convoys were formed. One of the main transit points was Banamba, where an enormous market processed slaves brought in from diverse regions, especially the bend of the Niger. Prior to conquest at the hands of Shayk Umar Tal in 1861, most slaves from Segu reached Banamba via the market at Nyamina.[23] Following its conquest, both Umarian Segu and rival Sikasso supplied slaves captured in the wars of Shayk Umar Tal and his heirs and Tieba of Sikasso.[24] Ahmadu's brutal suppression of revolts in 1876 and 1885 and Tieba's wars against the Dogon and Senufo probably generated waves of captives. The 1887–89 conflict between Tieba and Samori Touré created a final glut of captives.[25] Slaves from Banamba and the Niger bend met slaves from Sokolo, Sarafere, and the intermediate market of Nioro at the Upper Senegal posts of Bakel, Kayes, and Médine. These towns formed the major junction for the slave trade into Senegal until the very end of the century.[26] It was here that merchants from the interior sold their captives to the juula traders who would transport them upriver.[27]

The juula operating on the Senegal River worked on a similar basis to those importing slaves into Siin-Saalum. In northern Senegal they were largely Soninke/Manding and Tukolor traders from Gaajaga who had long-standing links with the habitant trade networks reaching into the interior from the coast.[28] Juula traders transported slaves from their entrepôts in Bakel and Mèdine, where they were quartered with local merchants, to markets along the river, the most

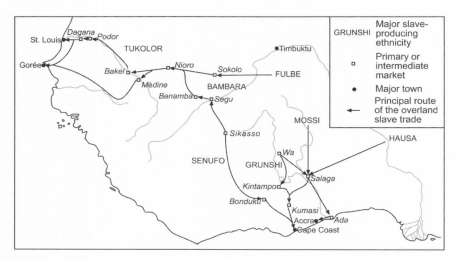

MAP 8.1

Major Points of Origin, Markets, and Routes of the Slave Trade into Senegal and the Gold Coast

important of which were French-garrisoned towns.[29] Podor appears to have been an especially busy market for purchasers in Toro, and Dagana was active at least until the 1882 annexation as the terminal market serving Dimar; open trading resumed here after the 1890 declaration of the protectorate.[30] Governor Ernest Roume noted evidence of an active trade being carried on in both towns as late as 1902.[31]

Many slaves, however, made their way into the hands of another set of middlemen — Moors — and were carried downriver to terminal and transitional markets in Waalo and the neighborhood of St. Louis. Here a number of markets had been set up in the major towns of Waalo to serve the inhabitants of the Delta region as well as habitants who purchased slaves for service in St. Louis, and there is evidence that Moorish traders also transported slaves from these markets for yet another journey, this time to the groundnut fields of Kaajor.[32] One of the largest of the Waalo markets was at Merinaghen, which functioned at least until French annexation in 1882, when the exodus of slave owners temporarily closed it down.[33] Likewise, French officers noted a number of slaves brought to St. Louis from a market in Leybar in 1882.[34] Similarly, the market at Gandiole, just across the river from St. Louis, was active in the early 1880s and Moorish merchants returned in the early 1890s, offering for sale female slaves originating in Bambara, Sangara, and Walala, despite the threat of punishment from colonial authorities.[35] As late as 1904, the administrator responsible for N'Diambour and Gandiolais reported that "slave owners frequently arrive with captives," exchanging them for both money and animals.[36]

THE SLAVE TRADE INTO THE GOLD COAST

In the early period of Euro-African coastal trade, the Akan and Ga-Adangme coast had been a net importer of slaves—and not only from the north. Ray Kea, in his comprehensive examination of seventeenth-century Gold Coast societies, identified four major routes of importation. The Europeans themselves were directly involved in only one of these: Portuguese merchants trading slaves for gold at Elmina. Much more important to Akan states—especially in the western interior—were Mandinka juula traders operating north of the forest zone. Kea has suggested that these merchants worked with Malian cavalry raiders, capturing and exporting "thousands of captives" southward in conjunction with Akan—and especially Twifo—trading networks.[37] Other Mande-speaking traders from regions west of the Akan zone also sent slaves, along with cloth and gold, to Asante and the western Gold Coast in exchange for guns, gunpowder, and European goods that were less easy to obtain from more the limited Euro-African trading establishment on the Kwakwa coast.[38] Still more slaves arrived by coastal routes. Elmina and Axim were important slave markets for traders arriving by canoe from the west, whereas Accra and other eastern coastal districts received slaves from slave-coast ports such as Great Popo.

The slave-trading network into the Gold Coast in the late nineteenth century, some three hundred years later, represented both a continuation of and a divergence from this system. The coastal routes, for example, appear to have become largely disused by this period, probably because of effective enforcement by British naval patrols and tighter controls on the exporting ports. Conversely, routes from the interior appear to have been reinforced by the introduction of a powerful Hausa trading network based in Dagomba, which competed with the juula in feeding intermediate markets on the Volta River—especially the massive slave bazaar in Salaga. Indeed, by the latter half of the nineteenth century, the Volta had become the largest transportation route for slaves into the Gold Coast, and Ada was its main terminal and intermediate market.[39] Complementing this trade route was the continued commerce in slaves from savanna states in the northwest, arguably extending as far as the Niger bend to markets in Asante, Gyaman, and in the 1870s Adansi, outside British control.

The main source of information regarding these commercial routes—other than reports by colonial officers, merchants, and less frequently the Aborigines' Protection Society—are the transcripts of slavery-related court cases in the SCT (supreme court) files of the National Archives of Ghana. Although these are a very rich source of data, they can be quite confusing due mainly to British officials' ignorance of the interior states of West Africa. Slaves were commonly identified by their primary language, but sometimes they were asked to identify their own origins—frequently stated as towns or villages rather than regions or states. Colonial officials often simply guessed at their origins based on vague directions. Thus, many slaves came from Grussi, Grunshie, or Ingrussie—a politically fragmented and rather undefined region that appears to represent a territory encompassing the inter-Volta territories of Isala, Bulsa, Dagarti, and Lobi but not the slave-exporting town of Wa at its center.[40] Others slaves were clearly Mossis.[41] Similarly, it is difficult to identify slaves' origins from colonial-era spellings of towns—where, for example, were "Alhandu, Salamah, and Amabua"?[42] The traditional predisposition of Europeans toward "ethnic" taxonomies further complicated the matter. As already noted, British officials tended to call all Muslims "Hausa," and accounts of "Arab" participation in the interior stages of the slave trade often referred to Tuareg traders. Some such misidentifications were inherited from the slave trade, when traders strove to meet European demand for certain ethnicities (such as the French demand for "martial" Bambaras to serve in their armies of occupation) or to deceive the buyers that their consignments were from those preferred groups.[43]

It is nevertheless clear that the northern savanna region was the major point of provenance for slaves entering the Gold Coast Protectorate. Large numbers of slaves were transported from here by caravan, many of them to the intermediate market at Salaga at a navigable point on the Volta River. Fortunately, we have quite a bit of information on the market here, mostly from British, French, and German travelers' and officials' reports, many of which have been compiled and translated by Marion Johnson.[44] Gonja, of which Salaga was the chief town, had been a tributary state of Asante prior to 1874, and the main market for its kola crop. The merchants of Salaga had generally paid tribute to Kumasi in slaves, and the town consequently acted as an important market for slaves originating in the interior and terminating in Asante.[45] However, the victory of the British and their allies in 1874 had stirred up Asante's eastern provinces. Not only had troops from this region been badly mauled in the fighting, but the powerful *juabenhene* (paramount of Juaben), Asafo Agyei, had made a separate peace with Glover and the okyenhene, with whom he had a firm relationship. Agyei subsequently declared his state independent, and the rebellion spread throughout the region, culminating in the occupation and independence of Salaga.[46] But Gouldsbury informed Strahan that they "seized all the Ashantees in their country . . . and killed every one of them."[47] Although Juaben was subsequently reconquered, forcing Agyei to move his state southward, the Asante could not reclaim Krakye or Eastern Gonja, and the asantehene Kofi Kakari imposed an embargo of the kola trade to Salaga, so that by 1876 the French trader Bonnat reported that "Salaga [wa]s deserted and partly fallen to ruin," much of the trade having been diverted to the newly enlarged established market at Kintampo in northeastern Asante.[48] As the kola trade through Salaga declined, the slave trade to the protectorate became even more important. In 1877 the African pastor Theophil Opoku accompanied David Asante on a visit to the market and "found trade at a standstill, excepting the slave trade, which was going on briskly."[49]

Throughout the late nineteenth century, there existed two complementary slave caravan routes to Salaga, one run by "Hausas" from Dagomba and the other originating from northwest of the Grunshi belt and mainly organized by Mossi state builders.[50] Dagomba merchants appear to have made up a significant proportion of the permanent trading community in Salaga, and by the late 1880s their ranks were augmented by Hausas from the region of Bornu who sold slaves and bought "arms, powder and the best horses, to capture new slaves."[51] Mounted raiding parties of Dagombas and Hausas reportedly operated both to the northeast of Gonja and throughout the Grunshi belt, bringing the inhabitants of entire villages to the Salaga market.[52]

However, the majority of slaves were reportedly imported from the northwest, and this route was dominated by Mossi dealers.[53] Merchants brought trade goods to Salaga on the heads of slaves traveling in enormous caravans led by professional caravaneers.[54] The slaves and the goods they carried were exchanged for salt, currency, and European luxuries.[55] The arrival of two such caravans into Salaga in 1889 was reported by District Commissioner Firminger, who was in town to recruit for the Hausa constabulary. Firminger reported that: "In the case of the Moshi caravan the 'maidugu' or commander had heard news of my arrival . . . and it was only upon the solemn assurances of noninterference by the Prince of Leppo and Prince Yusufu of Dagomba, that he brought the remainder of his slaves into the slave market of the town. . . . [A second] caravan . . . consisted principally of Grushi slaves captured by Gajare, the self styled King of Jabarema, who was then waging a slave war against the inoffensive and helpless Grushi nation to supply the slave markets."[56]

Sources such as this consistently point to the autonomous villages of the Grunshi region as the main point of acquisition for slaves entering the Gold

Coast; but, intriguingly, at least some slaves delivered to Salaga were captured as far away as the bend of the Niger River.[57] It is entirely possible that small numbers of slaves were thus being acquired for sale in both the Gold Coast and Senegal from the same area. After 1886, the trade from this region to Salaga was largely in the hands of the Zabarima.[58] The Zabarima had originally entered this part of West Africa as mercenaries and traders, participating in Dagomba slave-raiding expeditions. Around 1874, a Zabarima force under a chieftain named Gazari established itself independently, raiding villages across the north, especially those of the Sisala Grunshi. By the late 1880s the Zabarima "had conquered and were probably continuously controlling an area stretching from Ougadougou to Wa" and had solid connections with the merchant community of Salaga.[59] Entire villages were emptied by Zabarima raids, their occupants sent not only to Salaga but to markets farther into the interior as well.[60] After 1891, the Salaga market became even more crowded following Samori Touré's move to a new capital at Bissandugu and his subsequent search for new markets in which to sell slaves for guns.

Whereas Salaga fed the high demand for slaves in the eastern districts of the protectorate, such as Krobo and Akuapem, the principal intermediate market for slaves west of the Pra River was generally one of several markets in Asante. Although a minority of slaves sold in these markets had already passed through the hands of Asante merchants in Salaga, and some came in from Gyaman to the west of Kumasi, the majority came through northern markets such as Kintampo in the present-day region of Brong-Ahafo.[61] It is not totally clear who supplied slaves to Kintampo, but we do know that juula trading networks based in Kong, Bouna, and Bonduku were involved in the cloth trade to this market after 1887, and the town is as close as Salaga to the Zabarima slave-trading state.[62] Additionally, there is evidence that Samori's son Sarantieni Mori sold slaves from his 1896 campaign in the Wa area at Kintampo.[63]

Prior to the 1873–1874 war, Asante had acquired large numbers of slaves through payments made by tributary states.[64] However, the breakdown of Asante power and trading networks after 1874 not only cut off the flow of slaves from tributary regions but also enabled northerners to infiltrate the slave-trading network through Asante. "Arabs" and "Haussas" were not only able to take over the transport of slaves to Asante, but they even became involved in the export of slaves from Asante to the protectorate.[65] Their role in this part of the trade, however, was minor—Asantes appear to have continued to dominate the routes south.[66] Asante merchants ran the slave export trade as an adjunct to the legitimate trade in goods to coastal towns. Women and children, who were unlikely to run away, were especially useful as carriers of trade goods, after which they were themselves sold.[67] This trade in porters, along with an increasing number of slave-purchasing expeditions taken into the interior by coastal peoples themselves, seems to have entirely replaced large slave caravans by 1897, when the district commissioner of Cape Coast alleged that "natives of Cape Coast who want children go up to Gaman . . . and buy the children. . . . There is no trade of Natives of the Interior bringing down children or women for the *sole* purpose of selling them."[68] Coastal peoples may also have been drawn to markets in the Baule interior by the massive influx of slaves brought into that region by Samori during his retreat from French forces pursuing him from the west. Timothy Weiskel has shown that the Baule did not actively export these slaves, largely preferring to retain them for their own use and allowing potential buyers to come to them. Traders from the Gold Coast who engaged in importing gold, palm oil, and cotton from this region probably purchased slaves both to act as porters for these commodities and for their own domestic use.[69]

Evidence showing that inhabitants of coastal towns in the western protectorate traveled into the interior to acquire slaves in the last years of the century is not surprising. Slave consumers from the eastern protectorate, at least from regions near the Volta River, had been purchasing slaves in Salaga for some time. Although Hausa and Asante traders continued to operate in eastern districts, toward the end of the century slaves were increasingly purchased by individuals indigenous to the Gold Coast or by their agents who were sent to acquire slaves in this northern market. The river was a key trading route and served as an obvious transport route for slaves, the creeks and lagoons at its mouth being perfect for slave smuggling. Throughout the century merchants based in Ada continued to play a large role in that trade as well as in commerce in salt and kola, and their canoes bearing slaves were infrequently captured on the Volta.[70]

After 1874, inhabitants of the protectorate who traveled to Salaga to acquire slaves were generally looking for females, "children" — usually girls — or, less frequently, male laborers.[71] Often, the expensive trip to Salaga involved the pooling of resources and appointment of an agent, and extra slaves might be purchased to be sold to neighbors for a profit, thus paying for the journey. For example, in the late 1870s a Krobo man named Odouku traveled from Odumase to Salaga to purchase four slaves. One was for his brother-in-law who "sent 20 dollars to pay for the child," two others "lived with his people making palm oil," and the last — a girl — was sold for profit.[72]

The slave-importing network managed by Hausas was run quite differently. After 1874, as northerners were increasingly recruited into the "Hausa

Constabulary" or otherwise immigrated to the protectorate, they began to import slaves for their own needs on a similarly small scale to the trade carried out by their Akan and Ga-Adangme neighbors.[73] However, by the late 1880s immigrant merchants had used their contacts in the north to develop a more complex and integrated trade network originating in Salaga and ending in Accra. These "Hausa" merchants are alleged to have conducted "caravans . . . direct from Salaga to the coast," although court cases indicate that these were probably no more than small groups of slaves led by two to four traders.[74] As late as 1899, such caravans were reported to be transporting slaves "in secret . . . down through the [protectorate] . . . on hidden paths through the districts occupied by the Europeans."[75]

Although some slaves were sold in towns and villages in the interior and along the coast, the largest terminus for these convoys was Salaga Market in Accra, located between Ussher Town and Jamestown. Slave traders brought their captives directly to safehouses in the *zongo,* or immigrant quarter north of the market, from which slaves could be sold.[76] At least one account suggests that slaves were stored in the house of "a chief" until their sale, and other accounts suggest that the illicit trade was managed by individuals of some status with strong ties to merchants in the interior.[77] This informal market apparently served much of the illegal demand for slaves in Accra. A large proportion of purchasers appear to have been non-northerners, and although we have no quantitative evidence, there is an indication in testimonies given by defendants and slaves alike that the zongo was the place to which one went to buy slaves.[78] Nevertheless, the number of slaves entering Accra this way should not be overestimated.

POLICY TOWARD THE OVERLAND SLAVE TRADE PRIOR TO 1890

In the late 1870s and early 1880s, European abolitionist public opinion for the first time began to overcome the pragmatic concerns of colonial bureaucrats and administrators. Although Carnarvon and Maurice Rouvier, the first minister with the newly created portfolio for trade and the colonies, remained hesitant to attack domestic slavery itself, they were eager to "disparage all who would have [our people] believe that . . . the local administration tolerates the terrible traffic in slaves."[79] Initially, at least, actions did not follow words. The absence of effective patrols, a direct result of the limited resources of the colonial administrations, crippled any efforts to halt the slave trade. The French, despite their commitment during this period to direct administration, were unable to patrol the Senegal River effectively. Albert Grodet, the first civilian administrator of French Soudan, understood the challenges faced by subofficers in the interior cercles. "How," he asked, "can a single administrator with one clerk and a few . . . guards, effectively police a stretch of the [Senegal] river banks measuring 100–150 kilometres when he has no means of rapid transport to patrol the river?"[80] The British, meanwhile, were reluctant to enforce many laws outside the coastal zones. It was only gradually that magisterial jurisdictions were extended into the interior — a process that was still uncompleted in 1890.[81]

The Gold Coast administration's emphasis on fighting the slave trade during these years is, however, obvious from the court records. Although magistrates were not obliged to search out slave owners or seriously combat pawning, slave dealing was treated as a serious crime by the judicial authorities. As illustrated in table 8.1, 108 of 125 slave-related cases heard by district and divisional courts during this period were for slave dealing, whereas the much more prevalent crimes of slaveholding and pawning were largely ignored.[82]

TABLE 8.1
Slave-Related Cases by Charge, 1874–1889

Charge	Number of cases
Buying a slave	3
Misc.	6
Importing a slave	1
Pawning	4
Receiving a pawn	3
Slave dealing	108
TOTAL	125

Source: NAG SCT files.

This state of affairs is further illustrated by the experiences of the paramount chiefs of Akyem Abuakwa and Eastern Wassaw, which suggest that the purchase or sale of slaves was, during the 1880s, considered beyond the pale even for chiefs cooperating with the administration, whereas owning slaves was not. Administrators, understanding that the Volta River continued to be the major route for slave traders, developed schemes to halt this trade, such as posting soldiers on the river at Kpong.[83] However, such proactive plans did not come to fruition, and district commissioners' reports in 1890 were quite frank in admitting that despite limited successes, the trade in slaves continued, especially in the eastern districts.[84]

The relative success of enforcement in the Gold Coast Protectorate was partly enabled by the geographical consolidation of the region under British hegemony in 1874, adding only the regions of Sefwi and Kwahu in 1888. Events in 1880s Senegal, on the other hand, were dominated by the active expansion of French authority. The political difficulties related to this overriding concern blunted the Senegal colony administration's ability to combat the slave trade just as they restricted its ability to end domestic slavery. This phenomenon shows up most clearly in the administration's negotiations with Lat Joor. The damel had withdrawn his support for the crucial St. Louis-Dakar railroad in 1881. French attempts to close the growing rift involved deals in which, first, Governor Canard and later Governor Servatius were authorized to promise Lat Joor that they would make no move to end slavery, but to warn him that the sale of slaves was to be restricted.[85]

In fact, however, the French administration utterly failed to enforce such threats and consequently did not stamp out the slave trade into the protectorate in the 1880s. Limited steps were taken to restrict the importation of slaves only into the colony itself. The scale of prosecutions for slave trading was in no way comparable to that in the Gold Coast; but a spasm of judicial activity following the senatorial debate of 1880 led to the opening of fifteen cases for slave dealing between May 1880 and January 1882, which nevertheless resulted in only two successful prosecutions. The first of these dealt with the capture by gendarmes in St. Louis of a convoy transporting twelve children onto the island, whereas the second took place in Leybar — outside St. Louis but still technically within the colony.[86] Other cases were dismissed on the basis of mitigating circumstances, the political importance or social standing of the defendant, various technicalities that masked the reluctance of the magistrates to impose a significant sentence, or arguments related to the benign nature of the slaves' status in specific cases.[87] It is clear from these records that the administration's commitment to abolishing the importation of slaves even to the communes was lukewarm and that very little attempt indeed was made to restrict the trade into the protectorates.

DIVERGING EFFORTS TO EXTERMINATE THE SLAVE TRADE AFTER 1890

The essential failure of both colonial administrations to end the slave trade drew a response from abolitionists in Europe, which was strengthened by international links forged between Archbishop Charles Lavigerie's Pères Blancs missionary order and British abolitionists.[88] The resulting pressure was one of the reasons the governments of Britain and France and their European neighbors held an international conference at Brussels in 1889 and 1890, in part to discuss the slave trade. In the end, the conferees were forced to address the specific concerns of each colonial power, and provisions regarding domestic slavery in the Treaty of Brussels, which emerged from the conference, were more a declaration of intent than any specific obligation on the part of the signatories.[89] Nevertheless, Article 7 did internationalize the policy of sol affranchis, and Article 17 called for a "rigorous surveillance to be organised by the local authorities" against "man-hunters and slave-traders."[90]

Subsequent to the Treaty of Brussels, the Gold Coast administration achieved some limited success in eradicating the long-distance slave trade, but the governors of Senegal did not. It is necessary to state this here because this divergence is *in part* a result of the varying levels of pressure to which the administrations were subsequently exposed. On the one hand, the governors of the Gold Coast were almost continually harassed after 1888. Former District Commissioner Firminger, having returned from the recruiting mission to Salaga mentioned above, subsequently returned to London and wrote a report on the journey for the Colonial Office. Among his allegations were revelations, unsurprising to anyone serving in the Gold Coast, that "large numbers of slaves [were] still held in the protectorate" and, furthermore, that the populations of the interior districts of the protectorate, specifically Akyem, purchased slaves from Salaga. He also suggested that slaves were still to be found even in Accra and spoke of his attempts to liberate a young girl named Aminah, whose master, when brought to trial, was fined only ten shillings for his crime.[91] Governor Hodgson did not even bother to deny the allegations, which were probably completely true. Instead, he initiated a smear campaign, claiming that "Mr. Firminger purchased a Foulah slave girl named Fatima from a Moshi slave dealer . . . when he was in Salaga in 1887, and it appears that she lived with him as a mistress" and furthermore that the girl Aminah was of interest to Firminger only as she was Fatima's "sister."[92] The scandal, however, did not pass quickly and Hodgson's successor was also forced to deal with Firminger's accusations.[93]

For Governor Brandford Griffith, however, this was not the only allegation with which he was forced to deal. In 1890 the Aborigines' Protection Society began a campaign to force the administration to increase its vigilance and enforcement. Claiming that "there are now in the Colony and adjacent British territories a great number of boys and girls, *estimated at 5000 or more,* who are bought and retained as slaves" and that "the practice of procuring these children from Salaga and other districts in the interior . . . still continues and has of late considerably increased," the Aborigines' Protection Society accused the administration of "apathy and connivance" with the slave trade.[94] These claims were supported by a surprisingly thorough set of evidence referring to specific cases, dates, and classified documents.

It is quite clear from whom the Aborigines' Protection Society got its data — former Accra District Commissioner MacMunn. A fervent abolitionist, MacMunn had fallen out with his fellow administrators mainly over his unwillingness to cooperate with their pragmatic approach to slavery, although he was technically dismissed for "[mis]conduct," apparently related to alcohol.[95] Whether or not MacMunn was guilty of this misconduct is unclear, but the attacks launched from his bench against domestic slavery and the slave trade had clearly threatened the balanced policies established by successive governors after 1874. MacMunn had heard an amazing thirty-seven cases of slave dealing and slaveholding in the period between October 21, 1889, and July 26, 1890.[96] Even more significantly, most of them had resulted in successful prosecutions. This impressive record was the result of a unique and unpopular strategy of dispatching teams of constables "into the bush" to talk to local residents, often uncovering instances of pawning and domestic slavery.[97] MacMunn was replaced by the much more easygoing L. M. Peregrine, who was indicted along with Governor Griffith by the Aborigines' Protection Society for complicity in the slave trade. Griffith and Peregrine attempted to defend themselves on the basis of minor inaccuracies and reinterpretations of specific cases,[98] but it is clear that Secretary of State Knutsford, although willing to defend his officers, was unimpressed by their defense and at one point he chastised them: "I am disposed to think that, except in very special cases, which must be of rare occurrence, children should not be allowed to go back to persons who have been proved to have bought them, and that if any such case arises, a special report upon it should be made to the Governor."[99] In the parlance of the time, this was a biting rebuke, indicative of Whitehall's exasperation with the failure of the administration to end slavery, and it forced a change not in de jure policy but in actual policies of enforcement. To some extent this transformation can be tracked through the types of punishments handed down by magistrates.

Before 1890, although the Slave-Dealing Abolition Ordinance had authorized sentences of up to five years, magistrates favored a combination of a fine — initially between one and three ounces of gold, but later, as the colony's monetary system was normalized, between £2 and £60 sterling — and a short prison term with hard labor.[100] Following the Firminger and Aborigines' Protection Society complaints, however, fines were dropped in favor of stricter and longer jail sen-

tences. In 1894 Chief Magistrate Rayner handed down the first maximum authorized five-year prison sentence to an individual from outside the protectorate
accused of kidnapping and attempting to sell a number of slaves on the Volta
River.[101] This punishment, although marking a general trend toward increased
penal sentences resulting in an average prison term of fifteen months for slave
dealing, was not matched during the next five years. However, the Criminal Code
Ordinance of 1892 had in fact introduced the seven-year sentence for slave dealing, and as the century ended, Chief Justice Brandford Griffith handed down a
seven-year sentence for a man accused of slave dealing, kidnapping, and rape.[102]

   In the last decade of the nineteenth century, district commissioners and magistrates, despite an expansion in both the numbers of courts and their authority,
and despite a new commitment on their part to punishing slave dealers, heard
only fifty-four cases of slave dealing.[103] In part at least, this has to indicate a diminishment, although not a termination, of slave trading. Dumett and Johnson
have argued that "though large-scale and open sale of adult slaves within the
protectorate was largely suppressed, the smuggling of small numbers of slaves —
particularly women and adolescents — continued at Elmina, Winneba, Accra, and
other coastal towns until well into the twentieth century."[104] I would put the emphasis the other way. As early as 1889 the slave trade had been radically reduced
in western coastal towns, and British efforts, aided by a German commitment to
abolition in neighboring Togoland, appear to have slashed slave-trading numbers even in Ada.[105] Both the police commissioner and the district commissioner
in Accra reported that the trade there had also slowed to a trickle.[106] Their sometimes sincere efforts to halt the overland slave trade were further aided by the
defeat of both Samori and the Zabarimas as the century came to a close, partially
cutting off the supply of slaves.[107] The slave trade was not eradicated, and would
not be for some decades, but certainly the risks for slave dealers had been
raised, and their numbers diminished. This success must be compared to the
colonial government's laissez-faire attitude toward domestic slavery and to the
policies of the administration of Senegal. In direct contrast to these, the assault
on the overland slave trade into the Gold Coast represents the first major reversal
of policies that had for the entire nineteenth century been largely controlled by
the demands of economics and the need to appease indigenous elites.

   If events in the Gold Coast represented the first evidence of the type of
aggressive antislavery policies the twentieth century promised to bring, the
Senegalese administration's approach toward the slave trade consisted largely of
a continuation of nineteenth-century policies of pragmatism. Partly, this had to do
with reluctance within the French government to implement any major changes,

despite the crystalizing sense of a civilizing mission. The French *chambre des députés* did not ratify the Treaty of Brussels until December 26, 1891—almost one and a half years after the act had been published. Even then, the French executive refused to approve several articles—although not those dealing with the slave trade.[108] Nor was the issue put before the Senegalese administration until April 1892. In Dakar, Governor Henri Félix de Lamothe had been quietly attempting to ignore the implications of the conference, but the undersecretary of state, Etienne, finally broached the issue, ordering Lamothe "to give the administrative and judicial authorities all the instructions . . . to demolish by the most vigilant policing and the most severe repression the last vestiges of the [slave] trade. You are without doubt sufficiently armed in that regard by the legislation already put into motion together with . . . the general act [of the Treaty of Brussels]."[109] Lamothe chose to put off the task of implementing these new policies until returning from six months' leave in France. Clearly, however, he was made aware of the seriousness of the situation by officials in Paris and immediately upon his return he authored a treaty to comply with the Brussels acts, which he had had pro-French Wolof chiefs from Waalo and Kaajor sign. In January 1892, the chiefs of Baol, Siin, and Saalum signed on as well.[110]

Lamothe's treaty was a study in accommodation intended for French public consumption. Although it bound the signatories to eliminate the sale of slaves within their cercles, it confirmed their right and that of their citizens to purchase slaves for *personal use* outside the protectorate.[111] In reality, just another in a long series of pragmatic compromises, the convention was presented as a step toward slowly weaning indigenous subjects away from their dependence on slaves. In effect, the protection of the right to purchase slaves for "personal use" meant that merchants could import small numbers of slaves with impunity, and this was clearly a loophole that traders exploited with glee. After having to release a slave dealer who used just such a defense, the administrator of Saalum complained, "Aday Khane pretends like all merchants that the slaves we seized were purchased for his personal use."[112] Commanders of interior cercles bemoaned the continued involvement of local notables in the importation of slaves and the existence of slave markets in the directly administered posts of Bakel, Matam, Podor, and Dagana; but at least one administrator was instructed to ignore the passage of slave caravans into Senegal.[113]

Colonial administrators remained unwilling or unable to halt the slave caravans that continued to traverse the protectorates delivering slaves to camps and villages and royal courts, to the groundnut fields and even to St. Louis itself.[114] However, enforcement at the river posts did pick up after Lamothe's return, and the result appears to have been a decrease in the use of the river route and a diversion of caravans across the more difficult overland route into Kaajor and Baol.[115] These caravans crossed the territory of French-sponsored chiefs signatory to Lamothe's treaty. The *teen* (king) of Baol, himself probably still a participant in the trade, appears to have been the first to grasp that the treaty of December 1892/January 1893 not only gave him the *right* to confiscate the captives of other slave traders who entered his territory, but actually *required* him to do so. The teen realized that slaves thus freed immediately devolved to him, and by July 1893 he had seized 149 trade slaves "in virtue of a right that is accorded to him, he says, by the French government."[116] Within months, the *bur* Siin and other chiefly officeholders were engaged in a race to confiscate as many slaves as possible.[117] Admittedly, these "liberated" captives were generally simply raised to the status of domestic slave by their confiscators, the same status they would have achieved if they had simply completed their journey. However, the aggressive policies of indigenous rulers and the consequent potential losses for slave traders may ironically have acted in some instances as a deterrent to slave traders. Nevertheless, the effects of this should not be exaggerated. The teen, the bur, and other important aristocrats, such as Demba War Sall in Kaajor, turned large numbers of slaves to peanut cultivation, including those they "confiscated," which in the long run may have aggravated rather than alleviated the overland trade in slaves.[118] Thus, although there is evidence to suggest a slowing of the Senegal River slave trade in the late 1890s, the tap certainly was not turned off prior to the reforms of Ernest Roume in the first years of the twentieth century.[119]

Conclusions

African Continuity, Adaptation, and Transformation

IN UNDERTAKING A COMPARATIVE investigation of the origins and impact of emancipation antislavery reforms, I have concentrated on just two main themes. First, this book is an attempt to explore the centrality of Africans' roles in these processes, roles sometimes implicitly denied but made clear by the work of Raymond Dumett and Marion Johnson, Suzanne Miers, and others in *The End of Slavery in Africa.*[1] Crucial to this undertaking is an evaluation of the relative roles of continuity and transformation both in the creation of nineteenth-century institutions of slavery in West Africa and in attempts to eradicate them. Equally important is an appraisal of the abilities and motivations of Africans and Europeans as it contributed to these processes. Finally, I needed to avoid the trap of reducing this analysis to a conflict between slave agency and colonial policy, thus missing the important contextual strands of social change, economics, environment, and regional variation.

The second objective of this book is an assessment of the conditions under which reform, abolition, and emancipation could occur. Again, the impact of European metropolitan initiatives is just the beginning of this story. More important were interrelated local factors: prevailing political-economic realities within the colonies and protectorates, the beliefs and situations of enslaved individuals, the ability of slave owners to resist or subvert reforms, and the attitude of administrators toward initiatives they were assigned to carry out. The interplay of these factors took place within a context both colonial and African. I tackle these themes through an approach that both compares the Gold Coast and Senegal and presents a narrative by covering a significant period of time.

CONTINUITY AND TRANSFORMATION OF INDIGENOUS SLAVERY PRIOR TO THE NINETEENTH CENTURY

In attempting to decipher postemancipation arrangements, it is crucial to understand certain aspects of local African societies in the period preceding widespread European intervention. The characteristics of precontact indigenous societies, the African role in the Atlantic slave trade, and the harnessing of slaves to "legitimate" commerce provided both a prototype and the context for subsequent resistance to and support for slave reform. To a large degree, and especially in the interior, precontact institutions of slavery survived until or even beyond the late-nineteenth-century reforms. Fundamentally an expression of indigenous social and political paradigms, indigenous slavery was one aspect of prevailing kinship systems and consequently was highly assimilative. Moreover, slavery was only one component of dominant sociopolitical modes of organization in which political leaders were supported by a wide range of dependents and land was largely owned by a lineage group or stool. Economically, the production of food was largely based on peasant cultivation, and most commodities were produced by free or semidependent artisans.

However, in the period leading up to the nineteenth century, the Atlantic slave trade was a catalyst for a limited transformation of African concepts of slavery, especially in some coastal polities. Initially, the commercialization of slavery simply resulted in a diversification in acquisition methods and an expansion of both the brutality and magnitude of existing slave-trading networks. However, over time it was also to have a significant impact on domestic slavery as selected captives were diverted into domestic servitude and into an emerging foodstuff sector aimed at provisioning slave caravans and burgeoning towns. Although the extent of this posited switch to a slave mode of production is still debated, the increasing reliance on unfree individuals radically transformed communities such as St. Louis, Gorée, and to some extent Accra, in which a waged and politicized slave class emerged as European and African cultures mixed. Such transformations would later have an effect on efforts to end or ameliorate slavery in these regions. One of the most important trends within these and neighboring localities just prior to the nineteenth century was the emergence of indigenous urban elites, a new class that had a complex and interlocking relationship with traditional rulers. These two interlocked groups, though sometimes antagonistic over other issues, formed an alliance motivated by a shared reliance on slaves for political and economic support that laid the groundwork for an effective resistance to antislavery reform measures. Similarly, the introduction of a nonslave "legitimate" commodity trade ironically stimulated a slave mode of production, increasing the economic reliance of producers upon slave labor. Local wars, compounded if not caused by the slave trade, elevated the importance of slave soldiers. Moreover, in communities where land was communally owned, slaves remained an important asset, and the rigid stratification of some indigenous societies, notably the Wolof, maintained the usefulness of slave dependents as status symbols.

For slaves themselves, the forms of slavery in practice around 1800 sustained as well as constrained their personal strategies. Assimilative domestic slavery gave slaves the hope of gradual manumission but limited their ability to desert or rebel. At the same time the politicization of some slaves, the increase in abuses accompanying the slave trade, denser slave populations, and the intervention of missionaries introduced new strategies for survival, new opportunities to belong, and new reasons to desert masters.

These patterns of change and continuity led to the evolution of a prototype of interaction in coastal regions in which European initiatives were negotiated between slave owners, European authorities, and to some extent slaves. This system can be seen to have worked in the resolution of the potential crisis of the abolition of the Atlantic slave trade. Initially, European powers were unable or unwilling to enforce this prohibition effectively, but as the overseas trade slowly declined, indigenous elites were threatened with the loss of a very profitable commerce. Thus, their initial response was to form alliances with European, American, and Sahelian smugglers to divert the trade to safer regions such as the Gambian and Volta Delta regions and Mauritania. However, this response was a stopgap measure, and a more sustainable response was found in participation in "legitimate" commerce. British and French commercial and government officials hoped that the stimulation of such trade would revitalize the commerce of their West African posts and turned to coastal coffee cultivation and cotton and cash-crop plantations in Waalo, respectively. However, such externally developed arrangements did not necessarily meet local requirements. In Waalo an alliance of habitants who felt the plantations threatened their trade monopoly, local aristocrats who feared the alienation of their land, and Trarzas opposed to French expansion soon defeated the plantation projects and in preference revitalized the African-controlled gum trade. Similarly, on the Gold Coast smallholders and merchants alike chose to concentrate on the highly profitable inland cultivation of oil palms rather than European-sponsored coffee plantations, and under Maclean the administration soon turned to policies designed to support the locally developed palm oil industry, including the negotiation of a peace with Asante guaranteeing the safety of oil palm growing regions.

It was in St. Louis and Gorée, however, that this model of interaction became a true prototype both in terms of the formation of a master-administrator alliance and of individual slave agency that was to characterize the late nineteenth century. The Waalo plantation projects had stimulated a labor policy masquerading as reformism — the regime des engagés à temps, in which "liberated" slaves were conditionally freed following a fourteen-year indenture to the administration. The metropole was convinced of the moral correctness of such a policy. However, indigenous elites were invited to participate and rapidly twisted it to suit their own needs until it became slavery under another name, with little possibility of definitive manumission. The administration also became a party to such abuses, purchasing slaves in lieu of volunteers for military service and refusing to enforce policies meant to curb abuses for fear of alienating the habitants who monopolized the gum trade, the only remaining profitable commerce. However, at the same time, the regime des engagés provided an opportunity for a small number of slaves who, by pretending they were engagés, effected their own liberations.

THE MASTER/ADMINISTRATOR ALLIANCE AND PATTERNS OF RESISTANCE: 1848–1890

By the second half of the nineteenth century, there were signs that the eradication of slavery would be a central undertaking of the colonial project for both Britain and France. Admittedly, neither nation foresaw the grand colonial expansions of later periods, and abolitionism was not yet the popular feature of the civilizing mission it would become in the early twentieth century. Nevertheless, the reports and appeals of missionaries, and corresponding enquiries from metropolitan ministries to colonial administrations, make it clear that the issue of slavery resonated even with audiences in the metropole otherwise apathetic to colonial affairs. Thus, pressure to end even domestic slavery slowly mounted upon the backs of officials in Paris and London, who passed it on rather gruffly to officials in Accra and Dakar.

However, in *implementation,* policies toward slavery were representative of a contradiction common to colonial problems. To please audiences at home, slavery had to be abolished. But to keep colonies safe and profitable, slave owners could not be alienated. Thus, metropolitan abolitionist projects conflicted with existing understandings between slave owners and local administrators in both Senegal and the Gold Coast to oppose or subvert proposed reforms of indigenous

slavery. Although bureaucrats in Whitehall and Paris became increasingly abolitionist, they lacked the ability to enforce changes without the cooperation of administrators in the field. Yet administrators remained unlikely to support such
transformations even after regional hegemony had been achieved. This study has
revealed four major reasons for this reluctance. The technical difficulties of enforcing emancipation over large areas with the limited resources available to the
administration was a factor of some importance, as was the intrinsic conservatism
of colonial administrators, especially while important positions were filled by military personnel. Economically, the potential impact of emancipation, both in regard to slaves' leaving their positions in profitable commodity production sectors
and the drain on public funds necessary to support vagrant slaves and to police
emancipation was constantly cited by administrators as a grave danger. In Senegal, such economic concerns culminated in fears of a mass exodus of major portions of the population resulting from the promulgation of even limited reforms
to slave owning. This matches the situation for colonial Africa in general as portrayed by Suzanne Miers and Martin Klein in *Slavery and Colonial Rule*. "Short of
European manpower and reluctant to spend more than minimal sums on their
colonies, [colonial governments] depended largely on slave-holding elites to administer their empires. They were convinced that without slave labour, economic
activity would decline dramatically and the colonies would be a drain on metropolitan taxpayers."[2]

However, perhaps the most significant element in the administration's support for domestic slavery was the indispensability of slave owners to the system
of indirect administration. Merchants and chiefly officeholders were often not
only the largest commercial and agricultural employers of slaves, they also traditionally relied on slaves to fill a number of military and social functions. Furthermore, a great percentage of their wealth was vested in slaves; even the 1848
indemnity offered by the French to habitants could not totally replace the long-
term value of their slaves, and the British declined to offer any compensation at
all. It is no wonder, therefore, that slave owners remained stalwartly opposed to
any attempts to regulate or end their control over their slaves. Their potential for
resistance was a central feature in the development, implementation, and results
of emancipation ordinances.

Despite abolitionist sponsorship, emancipation in the Gold Coast was promulgated with the priorities of slave owners in mind. The two 1874 antislavery
acts were designed as pragmatic measures meant inexpensively to administer a
federation of states in which both political power and economic production remained largely in the hands of indigenous elites. This model of emancipation

was designed to limit the impact on these slave owners and thus contain potential resistance. The opposition of elites was somewhat constrained by their political and military reliance on the British authorities, and consequently the response of masters was characterized more by a passive support for continued slaveholding than by active resistance. The administration's efforts were successful in that the dreaded mass desertion of slaves never occurred.

A similar outcome was achieved in Senegal, though through a more circuitous process. Here, the 1848 emancipation was born of republican idealism rather than imperial pragmatism, and promised to liberate all slaves in French territory and any who touched French soil. This radical program provoked a coordinated response from an alliance of slave owners: political pressure from habitants, trade embargoes by neighbors, and threats of military action from adversaries. As a result, local administrators gradually countermanded, repudiated, or circumvented potentially stringent policies. The climax of this process was the Waalo/Dimar exodus of the 1880s, following which the French government was forced to abandon the policies of direct administration and *assimilation,* thus ending the threat to domestic slavery in Senegal, at least for the rest of the nineteenth century. That this about-face was sanctioned by a ministry of republican France, just as similar moves were authorized by the gentlemen of the Colonial Office in London, illustrates that events in West Africa were at least as important a context for policy formation as the sentiments of the metropole.

The Pivotal Role of Slaves

Indeed, it seems evident that during this period reform initiatives imposed by the metropole could not generally overcome empowered slave owners and administrators sympathetic to the owners' position. Yet the relatively strong position of slave owners cannot completely account for this perpetuation of institutions of slavery. In other regions, notably the Americas, nineteenth-century emancipation initiatives had resulted in the termination of the slave system despite the socioeconomic and political power of slave owners. That this did not occur in West Africa was largely a function of indigenous concepts of slavery and the actions and beliefs of local slaves.

Igor Kopytoff suggests that slavery, for African slaves, normatively represented not the denial of "liberty" but exclusion from "belonging."[3] The very act of enslavement embodied either forcible separation from the kin group or semivoluntary sale by the victim's family, and slaves were often also separated from their kin by geography and social status. The gradual commercialization of sla-very further removed slaves from the kinship system, and those who were trans-ported overseas were subjected to definitive isolation. For slaves who remained within African societies in which kinless individuals had few rights and little se-curity, attachment to their masters' lineage at least enabled them to belong *to* a kin group, and local institutions of assimilation held out the potential for an eventual position *in* a family. To leave such a position usually meant forfeiting even these meager benefits. It is therefore unsurprising that most slaves did not desert their masters even when legal recognition of slavery was withdrawn by administrations. Add to this slave owners' near monopoly of land and resources and the lack of administrative support for liberated slaves, and the successive "failures" of emancipation acts in the Gold Coast and Senegal to provoke mass liberations become less surprising.

However, let me again make the point that indigenous nineteenth-century societies were both a continuation and a transformation of precontact African institutions. The fact that, following European emancipation ordinances, some slaves *were* liberated and did desert shows not only that the "social dependency" of slaves upon their masters was not entirely hegemonic but also that when emancipation was promulgated, certain slaves were able to overcome social and economic obstacles to liberate themselves. For most slaves, the reestablishment of links with their own family groups represented the ideal situation in which they could have severed their ties to their masters, but this was possible for only a very small minority. Barriers of geography and time separated them from their families. Taking the dangerous and difficult path to little-remembered families who might have moved or been wiped out became a less attractive op-tion the more assimilated slaves became, the more distant their origins were, and the longer their servitude had been.

However, antislavery reforms enabled the families of some slaves actively to liberate their relatives. Such kin liberations formed a significant proportion of recorded emancipations in the post-1874 Gold Coast as families retrieved indi-viduals they had previously sold into bondage. This phenomenon was limited largely to pawns, who tended to live near their families, as opposed to slaves, most of whom were from the interior. The families of female slaves were also sometimes able to force their owners to raise them to the status of free wives. In the case of slaves from Juaben, the stool itself sometimes intervened to liberate its citizens from servitude. Similarly, in Senegal the introduction in the 1890s of formalized procedures for the *repurchase* of slaves allowed some relatives to force slave owners to accept a fee deemed reasonable by the administration. Inhabitants of the directly administered regions of Kaajor and Waalo and of the colony could also "kidnap" their freeborn relatives in servitude elsewhere, who upon their return to St. Louis were granted patents de liberté. Most slaves, however, had no such assistance and, if they wished to return to their families, they had to do so on their own initiative. It is no wonder, considering the long routes that fed slaves into these two regions, that the majority of self-liberations for which we have records involve young males who were more likely to survive the hazardous journey to freedom. In the Gold Coast, newly acquired male slaves from the north were the most inclined to liberate themselves formally or simply to desert and head for "home." Likewise, the majority of slaves seeking refuge within the "free soil" of Senegal Colony after 1880 were also young men.

The inability of most slaves to return home did not, however, dissuade all of them from liberating themselves. The European presence in coastal regions, for example, led to the creation of new communities to which one could belong. In Senegal, where missionary activity was largely restricted to the coast, the Protestant and Catholic churches competed for new converts, and many refugee slaves sought shelter, employment, or just a day's sustenance within church walls. Basel and Wesleyan missions on the Gold Coast also provided opportunities for former slaves, but as in Senegal the scale of conversion was relatively small. As an alternative "family" for exslaves, the administration proposed military service. Some slaves did see the constabulary as a potential replacement community and means of employment. Recruiting for the 1873–1874 Asante War, for example, attracted a number of former, current, and refugee slaves. Similarly, the postwar Hausa constabulary recruited a number of former slaves. However, the military was generally an unattractive, difficult, and dangerous option, and both the Gold Coast and Senegal administrations were eventually forced to turn to other means of recruitment. For Senegalese slaves, a better opportunity arose late in this period with the founding of Murid communities, but their impact is difficult to judge prior to the first decade of the twentieth century. A slave's ability to find a family or community to which to belong enabled that individual to seek freedom, and such individual emancipations largely characterized both liberations in postproclamation Gold Coast and the granting of patents in Senegal Colony. However, although such individual cases of desertion and liberation were quite common, only a very few isolated mass liberations occurred in either region, and it is this lack of immediate disruptive response that is perceived as the "failure" of emancipation.

A number of structural and functional factors that tend to promote a mass slave response have been posited by Miers and Roberts, and it is one of the goals of this book to evaluate these factors in terms of the several attempts to reform or end slavery in the Gold Coast and Senegal.[4] These transformative stimuli are: fundamental modifications to the nature of local slavery, the absence of a purpose for continued slave owning, the introduction of a strongly abolitionist administration coupled with an expansion of resources, an end to the overland supply of slaves, an end to slave owners' monopoly of resources, and the general acceptance of wage labor over slave labor by both employers and laborers.

The 1848 liberation of slaves in urban Senegal—St. Louis and Gorée—is an example of the impact of a combination of these factors. Slaves in both communes served under conditions distinct from normative Senegalese slavery. Slaves were highly politicized; their role was largely economic. They were often paid a portion of the wage for which their masters hired them out, and they accepted that as their due. Moreover, just as their masters identified with the metropolitan bourgeoisie, slaves identified with the demands of the proletariat. For the administration, law enforcement was simplified by the small size and relatively advanced governmental organization of the two towns. Consequently, the introduction of a radical abolitionist metropolitan government and, subsequently, a liberal administration provided a catalyst for definitively ending slavery per se. Even as mass liberation of the colony's slaves took place, however, the ability of slave owners to retain control of both employment and housing forced their former slaves to a new and almost equally oppressive form of dependence.

Dissimilar conditions characterized the Gold Coast after 1874. The emphasis on a gradualist program led to the near elimination of the overland slave trade, and successive administrations adopted gradually more progressive approaches to the practices of panyarring and slave dealing, but neither the administration's resources nor its convictions were strong enough to challenge slaveholding in the general population. Simultaneously, although British hegemony had largely removed the military function of slaves and restricted their usefulness as tradable assets, both elites and minor masters still relied upon their slaves for economic and social functions, and slave owners in most cases continued to control access to land. Suspicion of wage labor and the general unavailability of wage employment also restricted slave opportunities. The result of these circumstances was the promotion of a system of negotiation in which "the existence of the option of emancipation could usually play into the slave's favor as long as the option was not formally recognised."[5] In other words, the dependence of slave owners upon their slaves, coupled with the administration's lack of recognition of slavery, enabled slaves to force certain concessions from their masters that improved their position far more than desertion or liberation would have done. In fact, some slaves went so far as to liberate themselves, only to return to their masters and engage themselves as free dependents. However, a relatively small number of slaves actually made the full transition to freedom.

Yet a third example of the interplay of these factors can be seen in the failure of the proposed extension of direct administration, and consequently emancipation, to the whole of Senegal in the 1880s. French administration in these territories was both tentative and extremely conservative, and local masters relied heavily upon their slaves and strongly resisted any proposed challenge to their slaveholding prerogatives, an attitude reinforced rather than diminished by the widespread participation of both Muslim and aristocratic leaders in peanut cultivation. Further impeding reform, French military administrators in the interior did not actively restrict the overland supply of slaves, and rural wage labor opportunities were heavily restricted. Finally, unlike in the Gold Coast, slavery in much of this region was perceived as a nonnegotiable caste status. As a result, there was little impetus for emancipation or even negotiation to take place, and only those slaves who could reach French soil had any chance of liberation. The exception that proved the rule was Rufisque. There the emergence of a wage-labor market linked to infrastructure construction, the proximity of French authority, and a political-economic transformation based on groundnut cultivation appear to have enabled some sort of negotiations to take place.

On the Gold Coast as well there appears to have been some variation. A few towns, such as Kyebi, may have experienced a larger-than-usual exodus of slaves and offered land to a small number of refugee slaves, two events that were probably interrelated. This was largely a result of the presence of a large Basel Mission community, which not only introduced wage labor to the region but also induced its members to manumit their slaves over time, somewhat changing the nature of local slavery. Furthermore, the existence of a mission school and highly frequented trade paths helped to break the slave owners' monopoly on the means of existence.

THE CONSEQUENCES OF THE "FAILURE" OF EMANCIPATION

In history, the end of one story is the beginning of another, and the slow death of slavery in twentieth-century West Africa was in many ways the result of nineteenth-century policy in Senegal and the Gold Coast. This was partly a result of the perpetuation of pragmatic colonial policies. The policies of the French West African Federation (AOF), in place by 1904 with Dakar as its capital, were informed by Senegalese colonial experiences and attitudes. As late as 1950, the administrator responsible for Mauritania would voice the familiar formula that: "The colony was not yet ready for 'mass liberation.' There were no resources for the newly freed, who 'would have nothing to do but turn to theft and vagabondage'. . . . The end result would be the ruin of the economy."[6] Thus, in Senegal, the early twentieth century was largely distinguished by a continuation of administrative opposition to any real metropolitan demands for reform. Even the 1905 Comprehensive Slavery Decree did not end official recognition of slavery, but simply formalized and extended the 1890 treaties that had criminalized enslavement and slave dealing. Both the 1905 decree and 1903 antislavery measures were merely intended to restrict new enslavement, and not to emancipate slaves. In this way, the administration continued to place the onus of liberation on the slave.[7]

However, in French West Africa, thousands of slaves took the 1905 decree as a cue, and by 1910 the majority of the slave population of the western Soudan had deserted their masters.[8] The response in Senegal was not as radical, but a number of political and economic changes still led to a gradual decline in slavery. The introduction of a stable French administration in the Soudan, the defeat of Samori and subsequent drying up of slave imports, and the continued "confiscation" of slave caravans by *chefs de cercles* slowly decreased the supply of slaves into the region. More dramatically, the continual expansion of peanut cultivation gradually led to a free labor economy that offered opportunities to slaves. The expansion of the migrant labor navetane system provided a livelihood for refugee slaves not only from Senegal but from neighboring territories as well. Moreover, the further development of the Islamic Murid brotherhood created a new identity to which exslaves could attach themselves. The Murids obliterated slavery as a caste within their community and offered both fully assimilated status and access to land for former slaves. These reversals of political, economic, and social realities enabled some slaves to desert their masters. Significantly, few slaves applied for formal liberation, most preferring simply to join the *navetane* migration or Murid communities.[9] This outcome must be seen as a success for French authorities, whose policy objectives were largely met, as former slaves provided labor for both subsistence and groundnut production without causing any major political disruption. The British administration on the Gold Coast similarly continued to be successful in providing a series of "soft landings" for emancipation. Following the annexation of Asante after 1901, administrators there faced an even more difficult situation than did their compatriots in the Gold Coast in 1874. Not only were they given few resources and forced to rely upon the region's established chiefly elite, but those chiefs remained largely hostile to British rule, unlike in the coastal regions. Thus, although the officers appointed to run Asante were able to effect a reduction in the importation of slaves, until 1908 these officials strongly resisted the blandishments of even Gold Coast administrators to regulate domestic slavery. Despite subsequent reforms, domestic slavery remained largely in place until the expansion of cocoa in the 1930s, which enabled both a limited number of self-liberations and a system of negotiations similar to that of the Gold Coast a half century before.[10]

The historical context for all of these events was the period of negotiation, conflict, and resistance that characterized the attempted reform of slavery in the nineteenth century. This was an era in which slave owners effectively constructed their resistance to large-scale reform, and it was a period in which pragmatic and conservative policies won out over the ideals of abolitionism, and patterns of administration-master cooperation were developed. As a result, despite the initial promise of emancipation clubs in St. Louis and Gorée (see chapter 4), those liberations that did take place were largely the responses of individuals, whereas the majority of slaves were unable to alter their positions significantly.

The contrasts between British administration on the Gold Coast and French administration in Senegal were largely distinctions of scale and style rather than fundamentally different aims. In fact, the most interesting facet of this comparison is not the differences between experiences in the two regions, but their similarities. Despite the differing African and European origins of slavery and society in the two regions, processes of emancipation in both were characterized by many of the same general motifs. Perhaps most significantly, this comparison has shown the central role of Africans in determining the outcome of slave reform. The role of European metropoles was largely restricted to proclaiming reforms and providing the impetus for economic transformations. Whereas the metropole created potentialities, administrators often actually acted to oppose changes in the institutions of slavery and were in any event largely incapable of enforcing any reforms they might support. Thus, in successive stages of the "failure" of emancipation, the power of slave owners was in some ways actually reinforced, and only when their hegemony over physical resources and social institutions was broken could slavery definitively end. This termination—whether by gradual negotiation or mass liberation—was enabled by metropolitan initiatives and the introduction of cash cropping or wage labor. However, these factors did no more than produce an environment in which negotiation or definitive emancipation could take place; slaves themselves responded to this environment, shaping the *transformations* in slavery in the same way that their masters' actions fashioned its *continuity*.

Notes

INTRODUCTION

1. Paul Lovejoy, *Transformations in Slavery*, xi.

2. Walter Rodney, *How Europe Underdeveloped Africa*. See also Rodney, "African Slavery and Other Forms of Social Oppression on the Upper Guinea Coast in the Context of the Atlantic Slave Trade."

3. Frederick Cooper, *Plantation Slavery on the East Coast of Africa*; John Grace, *Domestic Slavery in West Africa*.

4. François Renault, *Libération d'esclaves et nouvelle servitude*; M'Baye Guèye, "Le fin de l'esclavage à Saint-Louis et à Gorée en 1848."

5. Ray Kea, *Settlements, Trade, and Polities in the Seventeenth-Century Gold Coast*.

6. Orlando Patterson, *Slavery and Social Death: A Comparative Study*; Igor Kopytoff and Suzanne Miers, eds., *Slavery in Africa: Historical and Anthropological Perspectives*.

7. Gerald McSheffrey, "Slavery, Indentured Servitude, Legitimate Trade, and the Impact of Abolition in the Gold Coast, 1874–1910: A Reappraisal."

8. Raymond Dumett, "Pressure Groups, Bureaucracy, and the Decision-Making Process: The Case of Slavery, Abolition, and Colonial Expansion in the Gold Coast, 1874"; Marion Johnson, "The Slaves of Salaga."

9. Raymond Dumett and Marion Johnson, "Britain and the Suppression of Slavery in the Gold Coast Colony, Ashanti, and the Northern Territories."

10. Suzanne Miers and Richard Roberts, eds., *The End of Slavery in Africa*.

11. Igor Kopytoff, "The Cultural Context of African Abolition"; Richard Roberts and Suzanne Miers, "The End of Slavery in Africa."

12. Kwabena Opare Akurang-Parry, "The Administration of the Abolition Laws, African Response, and Post-proclamation Slavery in the Gold Coast, 1874–1940"; Akurang-Parry, "Slavery and Abolition in the Gold Coast: Colonial Modes of Emancipation and African Initiatives."

13. Peter Haenger, *Slaves and Slave Holders on the Gold Coast: Towards an Understanding of Social Bondage in West Africa*.

14. Martin Klein, *Slavery and Colonial Rule in French West Africa.*

15. Martin Klein, "Women in Slavery in the Western Sudan"; "Servitude among the Wolof and Sereer of Senegambia"; "Slave Resistance and Slave Emancipation in Coastal Guinea."

16. Martin Klein, "Slavery and Emancipation in French West Africa."

17. Paul Lovejoy and Jan Hogendorn, *Slow Death for Slavery: The Course of Abolition in Northern Nigeria, 1897–1936;* Ibrahim Sundiata, *From Slaving to Neoslavery: The Bight of Biafra and Fernando Po in the Era of Abolition, 1827–1930.*

18. James F. Searing, *"God Alone Is King": Islam and Emancipation in Senegal, the Wolof Kingdoms of Kajoor and Bawol, 1859–1914.*

19. James F. Searing, *West African Slavery and Atlantic Commerce: The Senegal River Valley, 1700–1860;* Searing, "Accommodation and Resistance: Chiefs, Muslim Leaders, and Politicians in Colonial Senegal, 1890–1934."

20. Alice L. Conklin, *A Mission to Civilize: The Republican Idea of Empire in France and West Africa, 1895–1930.*

21. Frederick Cooper, Thomas Holt, and James Thompson, *Explorations of Race, Labor, and Citizenship in Post-emancipation Societies;* Martin Klein, ed., *Breaking the Chains: Slavery, Bondage, and Emancipation in Modern Africa and Asia.*

22. Cooper, "The Dialectics of Decolonization: Nationalism and Labor Movements in Postwar French Africa," 409.

CHAPTER 1

1. James Webb, Jr., *Desert Frontier: Ecological and Economic Change along the Western Sahel, 1600–1850.*

2. James F. Searing, *West African Slavery,* 7–8.

3. Literally, "clerics of the drum." Searing, *"God Alone,"* 21. Also see Searing, "Accommodation."

4. See David Robinson, *Paths of Accommodation: Muslim Societies and French Colonial Authorities in Senegal and Mauritania, 1880–1920,* 14.

5. For more on social structure, see Klein, "Servitude," 335–63.

6. Webb, *Desert Frontier,* 16–24.

7. Mary McCarthy lists potential Akan homelands as Ethiopia, Libya, Wagadu, and Chad. McCarthy, *Social Change and the Growth of British Power in the Gold Coast: The Fante States, 1807–1874,* 2–3. Eva Meyerowitz, relying solely on oral tradition, points to the bend of the Niger. Meyerowitz, *The Early History of the Akan States of Ghana.*

8. For more on these stools, see John Parker, *Making the Town: Ga State and Society in Early Colonial Accra,* 22; also see Ivor Wilks, *Forests of Gold: Essays on the Akan and the Kingdom of Asante.*

9. For example, Robert Addo-Fening, *Akyem Abuakwa 1700–1943, from Ofori Panin to Sir Ofori Atta;* M. A. Kwamena-Poh, *Government and Politics in the Akuapem State, 1730–1850;* Louis Wilson, *The Krobo People of Ghana to 1892.*

10. Henry Meredith, *An Account of the Gold Coast of Africa,* 26–27.

11. David Henige, "Akan Stool Succession under Colonial Rule: Continuity or Change?"

12. Apparently in the early eighteenth century. Kwamena-Poh, *Government*, 20; see also C. Reindorf, *The History of the Gold Coast and Asante*, 88.

13. See Ray Kea, "City-State Culture on the Gold Coast: The Fante City-State Federation in the Seventeenth and Eighteenth Centuries."

14. Francis Agbodeka, *African Politics and British Policy in the Gold Coast, 1868–1900*, 9.

15. For an Asante-centered perspective on this period, see Ivor Wilks, *Asante in the Nineteenth Century: The Structure and Evolution of a Political Order*, 23–29, 126–66.

16. Searing, "Accommodation," 14–25.

17. See Patrick Manning, *Slavery and African Life: Occidental, Oriental, and African Slave Trades*, 25.

18. Kea, *Settlements*, 5, 18. See also Susan Kaplow, "African Merchants of the Nineteenth-Century Gold Coast," 52.

19. Boubacar Barry, *Senegambia and the Atlantic Slave Trade*, 32.

20. Searing, *West African Slavery*, 15. Memorandum on the Vestiges of Slavery in the Gold Coast, Assistant Secretary for Native Affairs Johnson, 1927, National Archives of Ghana (hereafter NAG) ADM 11/1/975.

21. R. S. Rattray, *Ashanti Law and Constitution*, 41–42. Odonko also signifies "northerner." Admittedly, Rattray was writing on Asante society, but the parallels appear valid.

22. Klein, "Servitude," 339–49. The relative absence of slavery and the benign nature of slavery among the Sereer was partly a result of their place in the external slave trade. See also Searing, "Accommodation," 25.

23. For more, see Barry, *Senegambia*, 36; Boubacar Barry, *Le royaume du Waalo: Le Sénégal avant la conquête*, 117; and Gomes Zurara, *The Chronicle of the Discovery and Conquest of Guinea, 1441–1448*, 90–91.

24. Edward Reynolds, *Trade and Economic Change on the Gold Coast, 1807–1874*, 7.

25. Colonial Office List, 1874, Public Records Office, Kew (hereafter PRO), 134.

26. John Reader, *Africa: A Biography of the Continent*, 416.

27. For an expanded study, see Edward Reynolds, *Stand the Storm: A History of the Atlantic Slave Trade*, 96, and *Trade and Economic Change*, 12.

28. William Hutchinson to J. H. Smith, October 11, 1817, PRO T. 70/41.

29. Reynolds, *Trade and Economic Change*, 12; see also David Richardson, "Slave Exports from West and West-Central Africa, 1700–1810: New Estimates of Volume and Distribution," 17.

30. Richardson, "Slave Exports," 17. For a more detailed survey of this period, see Stephen Behrendt, "Markets, Transaction Cycles, and Profits: Merchant Decision Making in the British Slave Trade."

31. Estimates differ. Richardson, synthesizing sources from the W. E. B. DuBois Institute, approximates 7.3 percent. Richardson, "Slave Exports," 18. However, Stephen Behrendt, using parliamentary and treasury records, Caribbean gazettes, and *Lloyd's Registers of Shipping and Lists,* suggests a slightly higher number. Behrendt, "The Annual Volume and Regional Distribution of the British Slave Trade, 1780–1807."

32. This takes into account the most liberal estimates available. Philip Curtin, *Economic Change in Precolonial Africa: Senegambia in the Era of the Slave Trade;* Lovejoy, *Transformations;* Charles Becker, "Les effets démographiques de la traite des esclaves en Sénégambie: Esquisse d'une histoire des peuplements de XVIIe à la fin du XIXe siècle."

33. Barry, *Senegambia*, 66–67.

34. Barry, *Le royaume*, 117. Jean Delcourt, *Gorée: Six siècles d'histoire*, 74.

35. Delcourt, *Gorée*, 73.

36. Revolutionary France had abolished slavery in 1793, but it was never enforced and the edict was revoked by Napoleon in 1802. The abolition of the Atlantic slave trade will be discussed in greater depth in the next chapter.

37. Philip Curtin, "The Abolition of the Slave Trade from Senegambia."

38. Richardson, "Slave Exports," 17.

39. Curtin, *Economic Change*, 162, 164.

40. Lovejoy, *Transformations*, 46–48. Lovejoy revised these figures slightly for the second edition of *Transformations*, released in 2000.

41. Curtin, *Economic Change*, xxii.

42. Ibid., 146–57. For a geographically wider perspective on this argument, see J. D. Fage, "Slavery and the Slave Trade in the Context of West African History."

43. A phrase used by both Barry (*Senegambia*, 67) and Charles Becker ("Le Sénégambie à l'epoque de la traite des esclaves. A propos d'un ouvrage récent de Philip D. Curtin: 'Economic Change in Senegambia in the Era of the Slave Trade'").

44. Barry, *Senegambia*, 62–63.

45. Becker, "Le Sénégambie à l'epoque," 214.

46. Webb, *Desert Frontier*, 67.

47. Searing, *"God Alone,"* 16–18.

48. Barry, *Le royaume*, 109, 135–59.

49. Charles Becker and Victor Martin, "Kayor and Baol: Senegalese Kingdoms and the Slave Trade in the Eighteenth Century."

50. Martin Klein, *Islam and Imperialism in Senegal*, 29.

51. Agbodeka, *African Politics*, 1; Addo-Fening, *Akyem Abuakwa*, 24; Akosua Perbi, "Domestic Slavery in Asante, 1800–1920," 14–15; Kwamena-Poh, *Government*, 20, 28–32.

52. Joseph Dupuis, *Journal of a Residence in Ashantee*, 163–64.

53. This dichotomy was introduced by Curtin in *Economic Change*, 153–68.

54. Evidence of Maclean, 83; evidence of Cruickshank, 86, PP 1842, XII.1, 551. Cruickshank is admittedly only slightly more creditable than Osei Bonsu.

55. Kwamena-Poh, *Government*, 19–20; Addo-Fening, *Akyem Abuakwa*, 24.

56. Addo-Fening, *Akyem Abuakwa*, 5, 25.

57. Approximately 91,400 slaves were traded from the Gold Coast in the 1740s. This represents an apex for the eighteenth century; thereafter, the numbers fell to a recorded 66,300 in the 1750s. Figures are from Lovejoy, *Transformations*, 50.

58. Stanley Alpern, "What Africans Got for Their Slaves: A Master List of European Trade Goods."

59. Searing, "Accommodation," 30.

60. Becker and Martin, "Kayor and Baol," 118–25. Barry, *Le royaume*, 102–3. Klein suggests that the formation of a defined ceddo caste out of agricultural slaves and royal retainers may have been one effect of the slave trade. "Servitude," 342.

61. See Becker and Martin, "Kayor and Baol," 121, and table on 108–11. Also Searing, *West African Slavery*, 34–35; and Klein, "Servitude," 343.

62. Searing, "Accommodation," 29–36.

63. For a more detailed explanation, see Searing, *"God Alone,"* 3–10.

64. Kea, *Settlements,* 161, 156; hereafter cited parenthetically.

65. Robin Law, "Horses, Firearms, and Political Power in Pre-colonial West Africa."

66. Searing, "Accommodation," 32–33.

67. Gouverneur à Ministre, June 5, 1819, St. Louis, Archives Nationales du Sénégal, Dakar (hereafter ANS) 2B4.

68. Barry, *Senegambia,* 44; hereafter cited parenthetically.

69. George Macdonald, *The Gold Coast: Past and Present,* 85.

70. Kea, *Settlements,* 139.

71. Ibid., 140.

72. Ministre à Administrateur Roget, January 9, 1822, Paris, Archives Nationales, Section d'Outre-Mer, Aix-en-Provence, France (hereafter ANSOM), Sénégal I/8.

73. Barry, *Senegambia,* 107.

74. Klein, "Servitude," 342.

75. Patrick Manning, "The Impact of Slave Trade Exports on the Population of the Western Coast of Africa, 1700–1850"; also by the same author, *Slavery and African Life,* 60–86.

76. William Gervase Clarence-Smith, "Review of Patrick Manning, *Slavery and African Life: Occidental, Oriental, and African Slave Trades.*"

77. Manning, *Slavery and African Life,* 60.

78. Ibid., 59.

79. David Eltis, *Economic Growth and the Ending of the Transatlantic Slave Trade,* 71.

80. David Richardson and David Eltis, "The 'Numbers Game' and Routes to Slavery."

81. David Richardson and David Eltis, "West Africa and the Transatlantic Slave Trade: New Evidence of Long-Run Trends."

82. Albert van Dantzig, "Effects of the Atlantic Slave Trade on Some West African Societies," 190.

83. Graham Irwin, "Precolonial African Diplomacy: The Example of Asante."

84. Wilson, *Krobo People,* 36. Parker, *Making the Town,* 29.

85. Searing, *West African Slavery,* 28, 45.

86. Kea, *Settlements,* 163. The ahenfo were military retinues of Akan chiefs, composed of slaves, pawns, and free clients. Reynolds, *Trade and Economic Change,* 13.

87. Kwamina Dickson, *A Historical Geography of Ghana,* 116.

88. Kea, *Settlements,* 207.

89. A qualitative evaluation of the gum trade appears in Webb, *Desert Frontier,* 106–17.

90. Barry, *Senegambia,* 76.

91. Michael Marcson, "European-African Interaction in the Precolonial Period: Saint Louis, Senegal, 1758–1854," 34.

92. ANS K9 and K10, 1849.

93. Schmaltz à Ministre, June 19, 1919, ANS 2B2.

94. Leland Barrows, "General Faidherbe, the Maurel and Prom Company, and French Expansion in Senegal," 55.

95. Delcourt, *Gorée,* 60.

96. Jean-Pierre Biondi, *Saint-Louis du Sénégal: Mémoires d'un métissage,* 7, 72–73.

97. For a superb analysis of the economics of trade at these ports, as well as a number of biographies of important figures, see Kea, *Settlements,* 206–47.

98. On Cape Coast and Elmina, see Kaplow, "African Merchants," 19.

99. Harvey Feinberg, "Elmina, Ghana: A History of Its Development and Relationship with the Dutch in the Eighteenth Century," 122. Reynolds, *Stand the Storm,* 41.

100. Barry, *Senegambia,* 49. Richardson and Eltis, "West Africa," 23.

101. The papers of Richard Miles provide excellent examples of these minor traders in the form of lists of purchases from Africans. See George Metcalf, "A Microcosm of Why Africans Sold Slaves: Akan Consumption Patterns in the 1770s."

102. Feinberg, "Elmina, Ghana," 121.

103. From First Schedule of the Act of 1752 (25 George II, cap. 40), PRO.

104. McCarthy to Bathurst, May 16, 1822, PRO CO 267/56. For more on the rise of domestic slavery in Cape Coast, see Metcalf, "Microcosm," 392.

105. Kea, *Settlements,* 56; hereafter cited parenthetically.

106. The evidence for such "plantations" is much stronger for the period after the abolition of the Atlantic slave trade in 1807.

107. Parker, *Making the Town,* 23.

108. ANS K9 and K10, 1849.

109. December 11, 1832, ANSOM Sénégal VIII/3.

110. Maxwell to H. M. Commissioner, Goree [*sic*], undated, 1810, PRO CO 267/29.

111. The comments of d'Amfreville and Dumet are quoted by Joseph Benoist, "Typologie et fonctions des captiveries goréenes," 127.

112. Guèye, "Le fin," 637. N'dar is the mainland village across from the isle of St. Louis.

113. Brodie Cruickshank, *Eighteen Years on the Gold Coast of West Africa,* 1:240–43.

114. Cruickshank to Smith, August 26, 1851, Cape Coast Castle, PRO CO 96/25. Also in same file see Native Traders to Hill, December 15, 1851, Cape Coast Castle, and British Resident Merchants to Governor Jeremie, March 24, 1841, Cape Coast Castle.

115. Lovejoy, *Transformations,* 157, 190. Becker and Martin, "Kayor and Baol," 121.

116. Meredith, *Account,* 27.

117. Klein, *Islam,* 29. Also see the cited remarks of Francis Moor in Klein, "Servitude," 343.

118. Rapport sur la captivité, Administrateur Poulet, 1905, ANS K17.

119. Evidence of Maclean, Parliamentary Papers (hereafter PP) 1842, XII.1 (551): 82.

120. Lovejoy, *Transformations,* 19.

121. McCarthy to Bathurst, May 15, 1822, n.p., PRO CO 267/56.

122. Kea, *Settlements,* 43.

123. Ibid., 5.

124. For evidence from Accra, see Parker, *Making the Town,* 91.

125. Perbi, "Domestic Slavery," 14–15.

126. Ivor Wilks, "Land, Labour, Capital, and the Forest Kingdom of Asante: A Model of Early Change," 508–12.

127. Searing, *West African Slavery,* 48.

128. Klein suggests that five days per week was usual. "Servitude," 345–46.

129. Roger à Ministre, January 12, 1820, St. Louis, ANSOM Sénégal II/2.

130. The best analyses we have regarding pawning in Akan societies comes from Asante. Rattray, *Ashanti Law,* 48. For more on Akan pawning, see Gareth Austin, "Human Pawning in Asante, 1800–1940: Markets and Coercion, Gender and Cocoa," 119–59; and A. Norman Klein, "West African Unfree Labor before and after the Rise of the Atlantic Slave Trade."

131. Rattray, *Ashanti Law,* 53. Reynolds, *Trade and Economic Change,* 19.

132. Fairfield Report, 1874, PRO CO 879/33.

133. John Adams, *Remarks on the Country Extending from Cape Palmas to the River Congo with an Appendix Containing an Account of the European Trade with the West Coast of Africa,* 15.

134. Meredith, *Account,* 30.

135. Rattray argues this was true up to the twentieth century in Asante. As *hanti Law,* 54.

136. Cruickshank, *Eighteen Years,* 322. Fairfield Report, 1874, PRO CO 879/33.

137. Meredith, *Account,* 29. See also Adams, *Remarks on the Country,* 33.

138. Report from the Select Committee on the West Coast of Africa, vi and vii, PP 1842, XI.1 (551).

139. Report from the Select Committee on the West Coast of Africa, evidence of J. G. Nicholls, 7, PP 1842, XI.1 (551). Adams, *Remarks on the Country,* 33–34. Nicholls specifically refers to the period before 1831 (date of a treaty banning panyarring along much of the coast, discussed in later chapters). Adams refers to the last decade of the eighteenth century.

140. Riis, May 28, 1836, Akropong, Archiv der Basler Mission, Basel, Switzerland (hereafter BMS), D-1.1. Obobi, no date 1858, Odumase, BMS D-1.10.

141. Memorandum on the Vestiges of Slavery, Assistant Secretary for Native Affairs Johnson, 1927, NAG ADM 11/1/975.

142. Fairfield Report, 1874, PRO CO 879/33.

143. Roberts and Miers, "End of Slavery," 6–8.

144. I thank Professor Robert Addo-Fening for information on marriage customs among the Akan. Similarly, French sources indicate that men made several ceremonial payments to matrilineages among the Sereer and Wolof. Rapport sur la captivité, Administrateur Poulet, 1905, ANS K17: 37.

145. Lovejoy, *Transformations,* 14.

146. Studies carried out in Jamaica, Virginia, and other slave destinations bear this out. See especially David Galenson, *Traders, Planters, and Slavers,* 94–96, for British Caribbean territories.

147. Joseph Inikori, introduction to *Forced Migration: The Impact of the Export Slave Trade on African Societies,* 23.

148. David Geggus, "Sex Ratio, Age, and Ethnicity in the Atlantic Slave Trade: Data from French Shipping and Plantation Records."

149. Klein, "Women," 70–71.

150. Inikori, *Forced Migration,* 25.

151. Ibid. Joseph Inikori estimates that from 1500 to 1890, a total of 4,590,000 women and 2,260,000 men were transported across the Sahara.

152. Manning, "Impact," 125.

153. Tableaux Statistiques, 1845, ANSOM Sénégal XIV/13.

154. G. Wrigley to Committee, February 20, 1837, Cape Coast, Archives of the Wesleyan Methodist Missionary Society, London, United Kingdom (hereafter WMMS), Box 258 (West African Correspondence).

155. Claire Robertson, "Post Proclamation Slavery in Accra: A Female Affair?" 220–23.

CHAPTER 2

1. Georg Nørregard, *Danish Settlements in West Africa, 1658–1850,* 172.

2. Roger Anstey, "The Pattern of British Abolitionism in the Eighteenth and Nineteenth Centuries," 20.

3. James Walvin, "The Public Campaign in England against Slavery, 1787–1834," 65.

4. Roger Anstey, "Religion and British Slave Emancipation," 37.

5. Ralph Austen, *African Economic History,* 45.

6. Agbodeka, *African Politics,* 18.

7. Austen, *African Economic History,* 42.

8. Committee to Bathurst, June 24, 1814, Africa Office, PRO CO 267/54. Barnes to Bathurst, April 23, 1814, Africa Office, PRO CO 267/54. Meredith, *Account,* 214.

9. An Act for the Abolition of the Atlantic Slave Trade, PP 1806–7, I (.41, .45, .53).

10. An Act to Render More Effectual the Act for the Abolition of the Atlantic Slave Trade, PP 1810–11, I (275).

11. Miers and Roberts, introduction to *End of Slavery,* 14.

12. March 1815. Serge Daget, "Le trafic negrier illegal français de 1814 à 1850: Historiographe et source," 27.

13. Serge Daget, "France, Suppression of the Illegal Trade, and England, 1817–1850," 195–96.

14. Manning, *Slavery and African Life,* 66.

15. Albert van Dantzig, "Elmina, Asante, and the Abolitionists: Morality, Security, and Profits."

16. See PP 1819, I–A (119) (Netherlands); PP 1818, I (314) (Spain); PP 1818, I (333) (Portugal).

17. Reynolds, *Trade and Economic Change,* 45.

18. William Hutton, *A Voyage to Africa, Including a Narrative of an Embassy to One of the Internal Kingdom,* 74–75.

19. Douglas Coomb, *The Gold Coast, Britain, and the Netherlands, 1850–1874,* 1.

20. An Act for Abolishing the African Company, May 17, 1821, PRO CO 267/54.

21. Joseph LaTorre, "Wealth Surpasses Everything: An Economic History of Asante, 1750–1874," 436. LaTorre may overestimate the number of captives.

22. Ibid., 426.

23. Hutton, *Voyage,* 53.

24. See Benedict Der, *The Slave Trade in Northern Ghana.*

25. Dupuis, *Journal,* 162–64.

26. LaTorre, "Wealth," 436.

27. Reindorf, *History,* 152; Parker, *Making the Town,* 32.

28. William Hutchinson to J. H. Smith, 11 October 1817, n.p., PRO T 70/41. For more on the Brew family see Margaret Priestley, *West African Trade and Coast Society: A Family Study.*

29. Gordon to J. H. Smith, November 5, 1817, Cape Coast Castle, PRO CO 267/54.

30. Smith and Officers to Committee, March 15, 1817, Cape Coast Castle, PRO T70/36.

31. Committee to Castlereagh, February 21, 1817, London, PRO T 70/74. Committee to Castlereagh, November 1, 1816, Africa Office, PRO T 70/74.

32. Governor Pine, September 19, 1857, Sierra Leone, PRO CO 96/41. Acting Governor Bird to Sir Bulwer Lytton Bart, December 20, 1858, Cape Coast Castle, PRO CO 96/44.

33. Governor Andrews to Newcastle, June 5, 1860, Cape Coast Castle, PRO CO 96/47.

34. Governor Harley to Kimberley, July 16, 1873, Cape Coast Castle, PRO CO 96/100.

35. Export numbers were probably statistically insignificant after 1820, as evidenced by a marked decline in mention of slave-ship sightings and captures after this year.

36. Barnes to Bathurst, April 23, 1814, Africa Office, PRO CO 267/54. Curtin, "Abolition," 88.

37. Maxwell to Castlereagh, January 15, 1809, Gorée, PRO CO 267/82.

38. Commandant et Administrateur à Ministre, June 30, 1818, Saint Louis, ANSOM Sénégal XIV/1bis.

39. Daget, "France," 196.

40. Reports from ANSOM Sénégal XIV/1, 1818–1832.

41. Note, Ministre, June 1818, St. Louis, ANSOM Sénégal XIV/2.

42. Ministre à Schmaltz, September 13, 1819, Paris, ANSOM Sénégal XIV/2.

43. ANSOM Sénégal XIV/1, 1818–32.

44. Daget, "France," 198.

45. Loi rèlative à la répression de la traite des noirs, April 25, 1827, ANS K4.

46. Gouverneur à Ministre, October 9, 1828, St. Louis, ANS 2B13.

47. August 2, 1825, ANSOM Généralities, 172/1384.

48. The gum trade would not revive until 1830, following the failure of French attempts to develop a plantation system in Waalo. Barry, *Senegambia,* 140.

49. Lt. Col. Maxwell to H. M. Commissioner, undated, 1810, Gorée, PRO CO 267/29.

50. Barry, *Senegambia,* 308.

51. Gouverneur à Ministre, April 1, 1829, St. Louis, ANS 2B13.

52. Philip Curtin has previously argued that this theory of an abolition "crisis" for the ceddo and aristocracy of Senegal has not been fully demonstrated. However, I believe that recent evidence increasingly suggests this crisis was very real.

53. This argument is put forward by Reynolds, *Trade and Economic Change,* 114–18. It bears repeating, however, that these two classes were inextricably intertwined.

54. Richardson, "Slave Exports," 17.

55. In Gorée, British officers noted the existence of a "horde of slaves." Maxwell to Castlereagh, January 15, 1809, Gorée, PRO CO 267/32.

56. Notes de l'ordonnateur sur l'affranchissement des captifs, Commissaire Guillet, January 29, 1836, St. Louis, ANS K7.

57. Minute by James Stephen, June 1841, Colonial Office, PRO CO 267/168.

58. This time lag is very visible in the French and British communique registers. PRO CO 343 and ANSOM Sénégal I.

59. Yves-Jean Saint-Martin, *Le Sénégal sous le Second Empire,* 105.

60. Ministre à Administrateur Roger, January 9, 1822, Paris, ANSOM Sénégal I/8.

61. Committee to Governor Torrane, undated, 1808, Africa Office, PRO T 70/73.

62. "We are anxious to learn what progress has been made in Agriculture and Commerce. . . ." Committee to Governor, undated, 1808, Africa Office, PRO T 70/73.

63. At least until its bankruptcy in 1821.

64. Committee minutes, March 2, 1807, London, PRO T 70/149.

65. J. F. Ripnasse to Copenhagen, February 2, 1789. Kwamena-Poh, *Government,* 99. Kwamena-Poh covers Isert's plantations substantively.

66. Reynolds, *Trade and Economic Change,* 64–65.

67. Committee to Governor Torrane, undated, 1808, Africa Office, PRO T 70/73.

68. Memoires, Baron Roger, 1821, ANSOM Sénégal II/2.

69. Rapport pour le Ministre de l'Interieur, enclosed in Ministre (de la Marine) à l'Administrateur, December 20, 1819, Paris, ANS 1B6.

70. LaTorre, "Wealth," 426.

71. McSheffrey, "Slavery," 366.

72. Quantity of Palm Oil Imported to UK from West Coast of Africa, March 20, 1845, PP 1845, XXXIV (187).

73. Wilks, *Asante,* 166–69.

74. The Crown assumed control of the settlements from the Company of Merchants Trading to Africa in 1821. The Committee of Merchants took possession of the Crown territories in 1828. The decline is documented in Abstract of the Amount of Exports from the Settlements . . . upon the Gold Coast, 1822–1827, PRO CO 267/93.

75. G. E. Metcalfe, *Maclean of the Gold Coast.*

76. Wilks, *Asante,* 189–93.

77. Report of the Commission on Economic Agriculture in the Gold Coast, 1889, NAG ADM 5/3/7.

78. Kaplow, "African Merchants," 52.

79. Cruickshank, *Eighteen Years,* 244–45. See also Reynolds, "Abolition and Economic Change on the Gold Coast," 144–45.

80. Inez Sutton, "Labour in Commercial Agriculture in Ghana in the Late Nineteenth and Early Twentieth Centuries."

81. Probably heads of cowries.

82. Stanger, September 30, 1851, Christiansborg, BMS D-1.3.

83. Dieterle, May 31, 1852, Akropong, BMS D-1.4a.

84. Polly Hill, *The Gold Coast Cocoa Farmer*.

85. Jahresbericht (annual report), Roes, January 17, 1866, Odumase, BMS D-1.17.

86. Ibid.

87. Mohr, May 30, 1855, Akropong, BMS D-1.16.

88. Stanger, September 30, 1851, Christiansborg, BMS D-1.3.

89. Parker, *Making the Town*, 32.

90. Ibid., 32–33.

91. Kwamena-Poh, *Government*, 111–13.

92. Parker, *Making the Town*, 156–57.

93. Basel Mission Periodicals, *Mission Magazine*, 1847, NAG EC 1/6.

94. Reverend Robert Brooking, 1846 Report, in Paul Jenkins, "Abstracts from the Gold Coast Correspondence of the Basel Mission," 81–82.

95. Report from the Select Committee on the West Coast of Africa, report of Dr. R. Madden, PP 1842, XI.1 (551). Extracts from Stanger's Diary, no. 17, March 29–30, 1848, Accra, in Jenkins, "Abstracts."

96. Reynolds, "Abolition," 141.

97. Report from the Select Committee on the West Coast of Africa, evidence of Captain Maclean (Cape Coast), J. Topp (Accra), and B. Cruickshank (Anamoboe), PP 1842, XII.1 (551).

98. George E. Brooks, "Peanuts and Colonialism: Consequences of the Commercialization of Peanuts in West Africa, 1830–1870," 32.

99. Jubelu à Ministre, February 20, 1829, St. Louis, ANS 2B13.

100. Extrait d'un memoire de M. Héricé relatif a quelque améliorations à porter à la colonie de Sénégal, February 18, 1848, Paris, ANS 1B48. Baudin à Ministre, October 30, 1840, St. Louis, ANS 2B18.

101. Préfet de la Seine à Ministre de Commerce, March 2, 1843, Paris, ANS 1B35.

102. See chapter 8.

103. Webb, *Desert Frontier*, 67.

104. Delcourt, *Gorée*, 60.

105. Ministre à Boucher, September 7, 1970, Archives Nationales, Paris, France (hereafter ANF) C6/20, in Marcson, "European-African Interaction," 72–75.

106. Delcourt, *Gorée*, 76–77.

107. Commandant et Administrateur Roger à Ministre, April 10, 1824, St. Louis, ANSOM Sénégal I/8.

108. Jubelu à Ministre, April 1, 1829, St. Louis, ANS 2B13.

109. François Zuccarelli, "Les maires de Saint-Louis et Gorée de 1816 à 1872," 553.

110. Schmaltz à Ministre, July 8, 1817, St. Louis, ANS 2B2.

111. Marcson, "European-African Interaction," 107.

112. Schmaltz à Ministre, April 10, 1819, St. Louis, ANS 2B4.

113. Ministre à Schmaltz, November 27, 1818, Paris, ANS 2B3, encl.

114. Roger à Ministre, January 12, 1820, St. Louis, ANSOM Sénégal II/2.

115. Ministre à Schmaltz, December 20, 1819, Paris, ANS 1B6.

116. Annexe au Procès-Verbal, Commission des Affaires Coloniales, May 1842, ANSOM Sénégal XIV/13.

117. Commandant et Administrateur à Ministre, May 3, 1818, St. Louis, ANSOM Sénégal XIV/1bis.

118. Ibid.

119. Roger à Ministre, January 7, 1823, Senegal, ANSOM Sénégal XIV/20.

120. Ministre à Roger, January 9, 1822, Paris, ANSOM Sénégal I/8.

121. Arrêté concernant le régime des engagés à temps, September 28, 1823, St. Louis, ANSOM Sénégal XIV/18.

122. Statistics come from Tableau des établissements de culture, May 1, 1825, ANS Q16.

123. Rapport, Roger, January 4, 1823, ANSOM Sénégal XIV/20. Etat nominatif des noires engagés pendant 1824, Roger, 1825, ANSOM Sénégal XIV/20.

124. Roger à Ministre, July 18, 1826, St. Louis, ANSOM Sénégal XIV/12; January 1, 1827, St. Louis; Roger à Ministre, March 4, 1828, St. Louis, ANSOM Sénégal XIV/20.

125. Relevé des rachats suivis affranchissements, 1823–1829, Gorée, ANSOM Sénégal XIV/21.

126. Relevé de la nombre des rachats suivis d'affranchissement conditionnel, Decarrett, May 31, 1843, St. Louis, ANSOM Sénégal XIV/21.

127. Relevé des rachats suivis affranchissements, 1823–1829, Gorée, ANSOM Sénégal XIV/21.

128. Roger à Ministre, September 28, 1826, St. Louis, ANS 2B10.

129. Rapport, Gerbidon, August 25, 1827, St. Louis, ANS 2B11.

130. Barry, *Le royaume,* 244.

131. Procès-Verbal de Conseil, November 19, 1841, ANSOM Sénégal VII, 26bis.

132. September 24, 1819, St. Louis, ANSOM Sénégal IV, 16C.

133. Convention avec les chefs du Waalo, December 5, 1827, ANS 13G2.

134. Barry, *Le royaume,* 268.

135. Schmaltz à Ministre, May 27, 1920, St. Louis, ANS 2B5. Like the slave traders, Trarza gum merchants were able to divert their product across the Sahara or along the Mauritanian coast if they chose.

136. René Caillié, *Journal d'un voyage à Temboctou et à Jenne dans l'Afrique centrale,* 1:133–35.

137. Searing, *West African Slavery,* 168. Admittedly, the evidence for this is somewhat thin.

138. Quernal à Ministre, August 25, 1833, St. Louis, ANS 2B15.

139. Arrêté concernant le régime des engagés à temps, Article 4, September 28, 1823, St. Louis, ANSOM Sénégal XIV/18.

140. M. Portalin(?) à Roger, February 20, 1821, Paris, ANSOM Sénégal XIV/1bis.

141. Ibid.

142. Roger à Ministre, January 7, 1823, St. Louis, ANSOM Sénégal XIV/20. Alternately spelled Hametdour or Hamer-doux. Probably Amadou.

143. Rapport, Roger, January 4, 1823, ANSOM Sénégal XIV/20.

144. It is not clear how many really were Bambara and how many were mislabeled simply because they came from the interior. However, Bambaras were renowned among the French as superior soldiers. No title, October 1, no year, n.p., ANSOM Sénégal XIV/13.

145. Conseil d'Administration, séances, October 20, 1837, November 4, 1837, December 8, 1837, and June 9, 1838, ANS 3E12.

146. Jubelu à Ministre, April 10, 1829, St. Louis; Roger à Ministre, January 7, 1823, St. Louis, ANSOM Sénégal, XIV/20.

147. Conseil d'Administration, séance, July 6, 1840, ANS 3E13.

148. [Month unclear] 7, 1819, St. Louis, ANSOM Sénégal XVI/3. Schmaltz à Ministre, September 4, 1819, St. Louis, ANS 2B4.

149. Ministre à Schmaltz, September [date unclear], 1819, St. Louis, ANS 2B4.

150. Ministre à Gerbidon, April 10, 1827, Paris, ANSOM Sénégal XVI/3.

151. Gerbidon à Ministre, July 31, 1827, Paris, ANS 1B14.

152. Lettre, A. Correard, *Journal de Commerce,* November 11, 1828, ANS K4.

153. *Messenger des Chambres,* November 15, 1828, ANS K4. Note pour le *Messenger des Chambres,* Ministre de la Marine, November 1, 1828, Paris, ANSOM Sénégal XIV/2.

154. Ministre à Roi, August 16, 1832, Paris, ANSOM Sénégal XVI/3.

155. Pujol à Ministre, May 30, 1836, St. Louis, ANSOM Sénégal XVI/3.

156. Extrait d'un rapport de M. Rostolant, n.d. 1843, ANSOM Sénégal XVI/3.

157. Ministre à Thomas, October 21, 1844, Paris, ANS 1B41.

158. François Zuccarelli, "Le regime des engagés à temps au Sénégal."

159. Relevé des rachats suivis affranchissements, 1823–1839, Gorée, ANSOM Sénégal XIV/21.

160. Charmasson à Ministre, October 4, 1839, St. Louis, ANS 2B18.

161. Rapport sur la question des engagés à temps, de Polignac, January 22, 1846, St. Louis, ANS K8.

162. Arrêté locale 18, Roger, May 13, 1827, St. Louis, ANS 1A14.

163. Conseil d'Administration, séance, January 16, 1844, ANSOM Sénégal XIV/18.

164. Arrêté locale 6, Bouët-Willaumez, January 18, 1844, St. Louis, ANSOM Sénégal XIV/18.

165. Les memoires de Gouverneur Thomas, November 9, 1845, St. Louis, ANSOM Sénégal I/28.

166. Houbé à le president de la cour d'appel, August 23, 1846, St. Louis, ANS 1B49.

167. Jubelu à Ministre, November 8, 1828, St. Louis, ANS 2B13.

168. Roger à Ministre, January 7, 1823, St. Louis, ANSOM Sénégal XIV/20.

169. Ministre à Thomas, October 4, 1844, Paris, ANS 1B41.

170. Ministre à Thomas, October 24, 1844, Paris, ANS 1B41.

CHAPTER 3

1. Marshall to Wolseley, December 24, 1873, Cape Coast, enclosed in Wolseley to Kimberley, December 26, 1873, Cape Coast, PRO CO 879/33.

2. Bill for the abolition of slavery, for Promoting the Industry of Manumitting Slaves, and Compensating the Persons hitherto entitled to the Service of such Slaves, PP 1833, IV (209). As amended PP 1833, IV (233).

3. Ibid.

4. Metcalfe, *Maclean,* 262.

5. King's Order in Council, July 31, 1835, PP 1834–35, XLI (1137).

6. Report from the Select Committe on Slavery on the West Coast of Africa, evidence of J. G. Nicholls, 7, PP 1842, XI.1 (551). While domestic slavery was still considered generally benign, panyarring was viewed as barbaric and unnatural.

7. Minute by James Stephen, June 1841, Colonial Office, PRO CO 267/168.

8. Wrigley to Committee, February 20, 1837, Cape Coast, WMMS Box 258G.

9. Metcalfe, *Maclean,* 280–83.

10. Minute by James Stephen, June 1841, Colonial Office, PRO CO 267/168. Maclean to Stanley, September 13, 1843, Cape Coast, PRO CO 96/2.

11. An Act for the More Effectual Suppression of the Slave Trade, 6 & 7 Victoria, August 24, 1843, NAG ADM 4/1/1.

12. The first Crown-appointed governor following the 1842 transfer of authority.

13. Grace, *Domestic Slavery,* 29.

14. Hill to Stanley, March 6, 1844, Cape Coast, PRO CO 96/4.

15. Hill to Colonial Office, December 12, 1851, Cape Coast, PRO CO 96/25.

16. Native Traders to Hill, December 15, 1851, Cape Coast, PRO CO 96/25.

17. Hill to Colonial Office, December 12, 1851, Cape Coast, PRO CO 96/25.

18. Report from the Select Committee on the West Coast of Africa, PP 1842, XI.1 (551).

19. Ibid., evidence of J. G. Nicholls.

20. Winniett to Grey, January 31, 1849, Cape Coast Castle, PRO CO 96/14. Governor Winniett makes clear the distinction between even Cape Coast Castle and Cape Coast Town.

21. Reynolds, *Trade and Economic Change,* 78.

22. Report from the Select Committee on the West Coast of Africa, Appendix, PP 1842, XII.

23. Jenkins, "Abstracts," Stranger's Quartel Bericht (quarterly report), August 1854. The use of slaves in palm-oil cultivation is discussed in chapter 3.

24. An Act for the More Effectual Suppression of the Slave Trade, 6 & 7 Victoria, August 24, 1843, NAG ADM 4/1/1.

25. Connor to Herbert, April 7, 1855, Cape Coast, PRO CO 96/33.

26. Connor to Herbert, April 7, 1855, Cape Coast, PRO CO 96/33.

27. Proclamation by Bird, May 18, 1858, Cape Coast, PRO CO 96/43.

28. Bird to Bulwer Lytton, August 11, 1858, Cape Coast, PRO CO 96/43.

29. Chief Justice's Remarks on the Emancipation and Slave Trade Suppression Acts, enclosed in Andrews to Newcastle, April 10, 1862, Cape Coast, PRO CO 96/57. Governor Pine refers directly to a case of two slaves who had been granted refuge in a British post, to the direct anger of the *asantehene.* Pine to Newcastle, February 13, 1863, Cape Coast, PRO CO 96/60.

30. Cruickshank, *Eighteen Years,* 236.

31. Pine to Labouclere, October 1, 1857, Sierra Leone, PRO CO 96/41. In fact, Pine admitted that technically the officers of the Gold Coast were, in their policy of returning to their masters slaves who could not prove they had been abused, "liable to be punished for felony."

32. Metcalfe, *Maclean,* 220.

33. Maclean to Stanley, September 13, 1843, Cape Coast, PRO CO 96/2.

34. Reynolds, *Trade and Economic Change,* 159.

35. Report from the Select Committee on the West Coast of Africa, report of Dr. R. Madden, PP 1842, XI.1 (551).

36. Maclean to Stanley, September 13, 1843, Cape Coast, PRO CO 96/2.

37. Cruickshank, *Eighteen Years,* 228–29. There is no other evidence that this took place, and Cruickshank was not the most objective observer.

38. Pine to Labouchere, October 20, 1857, Sierra Leone, PRO CO 96/41.

39. Pine to Labouchere, October 20, 1857, Sierra Leone, PRO CO 96/41.

40. Memorandum for the Guidance of the Courts as to cases involving Slavery and Pawning, Governor B. Pine, October 30, 1857, Cape Coast Castle, PRO CO 96/41.

41. Accra Judicial Assessor's and Divisional Court, 1860–, NAG SCT 2/4; Cape Coast Judicial Assessor's Court, 1866–, SCT 5/4.

42. Wilson, *Krobo People,* 135.

43. Susan Thorne, "The Conversion of Englishmen and the Conversion of the World Inseparable: Missionary Imperialism and the Language of Class in Early Industrial Britain," 239.

44. Reynolds, *Trade and Economic Change,* 75.

45. Wilson, *Krobo People,* 136–37.

46. Journal of T. B. Freeman, 1839, WMMS Box 258/31.

47. Much of it contained in WMMS Box 662, Anti-Slavery Papers.

48. Metcalfe, *Maclean,* 311.

49. Zimmerman, January 11, 1868, Odumase, BMS D-1.19b. Suss to Basel, April 24, 1856, Akropong; Baum to Basel, July 14, 1857, Akim. Both, Jenkins, "Abstracts." Addo-Fening, *Akyem Abuakwa,* 194.

50. Zimmerman, August 16, 1869, Odumase, BMS D-1.21b. Zimmerman, January 30, 1861, Odumase, BMS D-1.11.

51. Maclean to Stanley, September 12, 1843, Cape Coast, PRO CO 96/2. This appears to have been true.

52. Zimmerman, January 30, 1861, Odumase, BMS D-1.11. Zimmerman and Aldinger, January 25, 1860, n.p., BMS D-1.10.

53. Wrigley to Committee, February 20, 1837, Cape Coast, WMMS Box 258.

54. Printed letter regarding cultivation of cotton in Africa, December 24, 1860, WMMS Box 662, Anti-Slavery Papers.

55. Instructions to Rev. Freeman and other missionaries of the Society on the Gold Coast and in Ashantee, n.d. 1835, WMMS Box 258.

56. WMMS Synod Minutes, May 23–25, 1842, WMMS Box 266, West African Correspondence.

57. African Aid Society Paper for Intending Settlers in Africa, undated, 1860, WMMS Box 662, Anti-Slavery Papers. This strategy was possibly influenced by the ongoing attempts to settle freed American slaves in places such as Liberia.

58. Eisenschmid, unaddressed letter, May 5, 1862, Akim, in Jenkins, "Abstracts."

59. Report from the Committee on the West Coast of Africa, evidence of Rev. Elias Shrenk, 1865, PP 1865, V (412).

60. Addo-Fening, *Akyem Abuakwa,* 194.

61. A number of "heads of families" were rejected for baptism because they refused to put aside their slaves and their wives—monogamy being the other major hurdle to conversion for wealthy individuals. Zimmerman, September 28, 1864, Odumase, D-1.16; Zimmerman, February 16, 1867, Odumase, D-1.19b; Zimmerman, March 30, 1870, Odumase, D-1.22a (all BMS).

62. The Akropong congregation alone had 956 members. Report from the Committee on the West Coast of Africa, evidence of Rev. Elias Shrenk, 1865, PP 1865, V (412).

63. Report from the Committee on the West Coast of Africa, 1865, PP, V (412).

64. Agbodeka, *African Politics*, 34–35.

65. Fitzpatrick to Grey, March 10, 1850, Cape Coast, PRO CO 96/18.

66. Hill to Stanley, March 2, 1844, Cape Coast, PRO CO 96/4.

67. Maxwell to Castlereagh, September 14, 1808, Gorée, PRO CO 267/32.

68. Maxwell to Castlereagh, January 15, 1809, Gorée, PRO CO 267/32.

69. Maxwell to Castlereagh, January 15, 1809, Gorée, PRO CO 267/32.

70. Barnes to Bathurst, November 25, 1813, Africa Office, PRO CO 267/54.

71. Committee to Arbuthnot, September 24, 1819, Africa Office, PRO CO 267/54.

72. Hill to Stanley, March 2, 1844, Cape Coast, PRO CO 96/4.

73. Hill to Stanley, March 2, 1844, Cape Coast, PRO CO 96/4.

74. Cruickshank, *Eighteen Years*, 234.

75. Pine to Labouchere, February 10, 1858, Cape Coast, PRO CO 96/43.

76. Pine to Labouchere, February 2, 1858, Accra, PRO CO 96/43; Pine to Labouchere, February 10, 1858, Cape Coast, PRO CO 96/43.

77. Parkington to Hill, December 18, 1852, London, NAG ADM 1/1/10.

78. Memorandum for the Guidance of the Courts as to cases involving Slavery and Pawning, Governor B. Pine, October 30, 1857, Cape Coast, PRO CO 96/41.

79. Newcastle to Carnarvon, September 26, 1862, London, NAG ADM 1/1/20.

80. Newcastle to Pine, March 4, 1863, PRO CO 96/58.

81. Pine to Newcastle, October 14, 1863, Cape Coast, PRO CO 96/62.

82. Pine to Newcastle, November 7, 1863, Cape Coast, PRO CO 96/62.

83. Newcastle to Pine, December 14, 1863, enclosed in Sir Lugard to Military Secretary, December 7, 1863, London, NAG ADM 1/1/21.

84. Ordinance 1 of 1864, Governor R. Pine, Feburary 22, 1864, PRO CO 97/1.

85. Legislative Council Minutes, October 6, 1871, and March 9, 1872, PRO CO 98/2.

86. Belles to Pope-Hennessy, May 8, 1872, off Elmina, NAG ADM 1/10/1.

87. Winniett to Earl Grey, March 30, 1850, Cape Coast, PRO CO 96/18.

88. Wilks, *Asante*, 207.

89. Hill to Newcastle, January 29, 1854, Cape Coast, PRO CO 96/30.

90. Andrews to Newcastle, April 25, 1861, Christiansborg, PRO CO 96/52.

91. Pine to Labouchere, October 10, 1857, Cape Coast, PRO CO 96/41.

92. Parker, "Ga State and Society in Early Colonial Accra, 1860s–1920s," 114–15.

93. Opposition to this, the first attempt to levy a direct tax on Gold Coast inhabitants, was perhaps the first shot in a long history of Ghanaian resistance to colonial

taxation. Similar examples outside the Gold Coast include the Hut Tax War in Sierra Leone and the revolts over hut and dog taxes in South-West Africa. Extensive commentary on the Poll Tax Revolts can be found in the Cape Coast–Central Region Archives. Also see Kennedy to Colonial Office, November 7, 1868, Cape Coast, PRO CO 96/77; Ussher to Kennedy, July 11, 1870, Cape Coast, PRO CO 96/85.

94. Aborigines' Rights Protection Society, Granville to Cardwell, September 13, 1869, Cape Coast, Central Region Archives, Cape Coast, Ghana (hereafter NAG-CC) 72.

95. Simpson to Kennedy, March 2, 1869, Akwamu, PRO CO 96/79.

96. Aborigines' Rights Protection Society, Granville to Cardwell, September 13, 1869, Cape Coast, NAG-CC 72. Simpson to Kennedy, June 15, 1869, Cape Coast, enclosing Kings of Cape Coast to Kennedy, undated, Cape Coast, PRO CO 96/80. Also see Simpson to Kennedy, June 15, 1869, Cape Coast, enclosing Kings of Cape Coast to Kennedy, undated, Cape Coast, PRO CO 96/80. And David Kimble, *A Political History of Ghana: The Rise of Gold Coast Nationalism, 1850–1928,* 222–63.

97. Horton to Granville, May 2, 1870, Cape Coast, PRO CO 96/85. Chiefs of "Assin, Abrah, Ququah, Anamaboe, Mankessim, Ajimacoo, Dominassie, Akumfie, Akim, and Goomoor."

98. Salmon to Kennedy, January 3, 1872, Cape Coast, NAG ADM 12/1/1.

99. Salmon to Kennedy, January 20, 1872, Cape Coast, NAG ADM 12/1/1. Ussher to Kennedy, October 11, 1870, Cape Coast, PRO CO 96/85.

100. Kennedy to Kimberley, January 2, 1872, Cape Coast; Salmon to Kennedy, January 3, 1872, Cape Coast, PRO CO 96/92.

101. This movement, less well known than the Fante Confederation to the east, is discussed by Agbodeka, *African Politics,* 19–21.

102. Parker, *Making the Town,* 67.

103. Agbodeka, *African Politics,* 16.

104. Accra Divisional Court, Accra Divisional Court, August 2, 1871, NAG SCT 2/4/9.

105. Cases involving slaves and pawns in the Accra and Cape Coast judicial assessor and Accra divisional courts between April 1867 and November 1874. NAG SCT 2/4/6–2/4/11 and 5/4/15.

106. No. 33, received May 6, 1873, PP 1873, XLIX (266).

Chapter 4

1. Robinson, *Paths of Accommodation,* 60–61.

2. Klein, *Slavery and Colonial Rule,* 19–27 and 28–36, respectively.

3. Correspondence Générale, ANSOM Sénégal I/12 to I/33.

4. During this period, the Ministry of the Navy held responsibility for administering overseas colonies.

5. Saint-Germain à Ministre, April 5, 1832, St. Louis, ANSOM Sénégal XIV/1.

6. Notes de l'ordonnateur sur l'affranchissement des captifs, Commissaire Guillet, January 29, 1836, St. Louis, ANS K6.

7. Saint-Germain à Ministre, April 5, 1832, St. Louis, ANSOM Sénégal XIV/1.

8. Ordonnance royale, 12 July 1832, in J. B. Duvergier, *Collection complète des lois, décrets, ordonnances, réglements, et avis du conseil d'état,* vol. 37.

9. Actes d'affranchissement, 1834–1841, ANS K6.

10. Actes d'affranchissement, 1834–1841, No. 122, December 18, 1836, ANS K6.

11. Procès-verbal, Conseil d'Administration, séance, February 5, 1848, St. Louis, ANS 3E20.

12. Actes d'affranchissement, No. 124, December 10, 1836, ANS K6.

13. Actes d'affranchissement, No. 20, May 18, 1841, ANS K6.

14. Ministre à Pujol, September 4, 1835, ANS 1B23.

15. Rapport sur la service judiciare, Greffe de l'Ile de St. Louis and Greffe de Gorée, various dates, ANS M3.

16. Procès-verbal, séance de Conseil Générale, November 14, 1842, St. Louis, ANS 4E1.

17. Charmasson à Ministre, October 6, 1839, St. Louis, ANS 2B18.

18. Rapport sur la captivité, Administrateur Poulet, 1905, ANS K17.

19. Notes de l'ordonnateur sur l'affranchissement des captifs, guillet, January 29, 1836, St. Louis, ANS K6.

20. Ibid.

21. My paraphrasing. Georges Deherme, *L'esclavage en AOF,* 1906, 15–17, ANS K25.

22. Procès-verbal, séance d'arrondissement de Gorée, September 4, 1842, ANS 2E2.

23. Rapport à la question de l'affranchissement des captifs au Sénégal, April 16, 1847, Paris, ANSOM Sénégal XIV/13.

24. Summarized in Rapport à la question de l'affranchissement des captifs au Sénégal, April 16, 1847, Paris, ANSOM Sénégal XIV/13.

25. Procès-verbal de Commission d'Inquete, November 1848, Saint Louis, ANSOM Sénégal XIV/13.

26. Commission des Affaires Coloniales, annexe au procès-verbal, séance du Mai [May] 1842, ANSOM Sénégal XIV/13.

27. Rapport, le Conseiller d'Etat, July 31, 1847, Paris, ANSOM Sénégal XIV/13.

28. Gaston Martin, *Histoire de l'esclavage dans les colonies françaises,* 291.

29. "Reasonable," as defined by the administration. Projet d'ordonnance royale sur les affranchissements, 1847, ANSOM Sénégal XIV/13.

30. Schoelcher was to be instrumental in the 1880 initiative for the eradication of slavery as well.

31. Deherme, *L'esclavage en AOF,* 1906, ANS K25.

32. Decree portant l'abolition de l'esclavage dans les colonies, le gouvernement provisoire, April 27, 1848, ANSOM Sénégal XIV/15.

33. Ibid.

34. Decree portant l'abolition de l'esclavage dans les colonies, le gouvernement provisoire, April 27, 1848, Article 7, ANSOM Sénégal XIV/15.

35. Ministre à Baudin, May 7, 1848, Paris, ANSOM Sénégal XIV/15.

36. Ibid.

37. Ibid.

38. Arrêté local, Commissaire Du Château, June 23, 1848, St. Louis, ANS K8. Guèye, "Le fin," 641. The official title for French colonial governors during the early months of the Second Republic was *commissaire* (commissioner), but for purposes of continuity, I have chosen to retain the term governor (French *gouverneur*). The duties appear to have remained the same, and quite quickly official correspondence reverted to using "gouverneur."

39. See chapter 2.

40. Guèye, "Le fin," 642.

41. Commandant Gachot à Du Château, July 1, 1848, Gorée, ANS 4B15.

42. Du Château à Ministre, September 18, 1847, St. Louis, ANSOM Sénégal XIV/13.

43. Ministre à Baudin, May 7, 1848, Paris, ANSOM Sénégal XIV/15.

44. Ardo-Labaytre, Chef des Peules de Ouadabé, à Baudin, October 3, 1848, Kaajor, ANS 3B64. ANSOM Sénégal XIV/15a (several files).

45. Mohamed Mbodj, "The Abolition of Slavery in Senegal, 1820–1890: Crisis or the Rise of a New Entrepreneurial Class?"

46. Ministre à Baudin, September 4, 1848, Paris, ANS 1B49. Protet à Ministre, June 8, 1852, St. Louis, ANS 2B31.

47. Notables de Gorée à Commandant, March 16, 1849, Gorée, ANS 4B15. Klein, *Slavery and Colonial Rule,* 25.

48. Protet à Ministre, June 8, 1852, St. Louis, ANS 2B31.

49. Marcson, "European-African Interaction," 229.

50. Du Château à Ministre, August 19, 1848, St. Louis, ANSOM Sénégal VII/49.

51. Guèye, "Le fin." Roger Pasquier, "A propos de l'emancipation des esclaves au Sénégal en 1848."

52. Searing, *West African Slavery,* 175.

53. Du Château à Ministre, August 23, 1848, St. Louis, ANSOM Sénégal XIV/15.

54. Commandant Roche à Citoyen Commissaire, August 26, 1848, Gorée, ANS 4B15.

55. Commandant Gachot à Gouverneur, July 1, 1848, Gorée, ANS 4B15.

56. Commandant Roche à Citoyen Commissaire, August 26, 1848, Gorée, ANS 4B15.

57. Du Château à Ministre, August 23, 1848, St. Louis, ANSOM Sénégal XIV/15. The Pointe du Nord was a rocky, unoccupied peninsula jutting out from Gorée Island, now the location of the Fort d'Estrées.

58. G. Louis Faidherbe, *Le Sénégal, la France dans l'Afrique occidental,* 115–16.

59. Mbodj, "Abolition," 198.

60. Klein, *Slavery and Colonial Rule,* 26.

61. Georges Hardy, *La mise en valeur du Sénégal de 1817 à 1854.*

62. Some of those aristocracies, however, were by this time besieged by Islamic revolutionaries.

63. François Renault, "L'abolition de l'esclavage au Sénégal: L'attitude de l'administration française," 20.

64. Brooks, "Peanuts," 42.

65. Ibid., 43–45.

66. See Joye Bowman, *Ominous Transition: Commerce and Colonial Expansion in the Senegambia and Guinea, 1857–1919,* 20–21. Procès-verbal, séance de Conseil d'Arrondisement de Gorée, January 3, 1846, Gorée, ANS 2E2.

67. Petition, February 15, 1849, St. Louis, ANSOM Sénégal XIV/15.

68. Baudin au Chef du Dakar, January 20, 1849, Senegal, ANS 3B61.

69. Baudin à Ministre, February 3, 1849, St. Louis, ANS 2B27.

70. Du Château à Ministre, August 22, 1848, St. Louis, ANS 2B27.

71. Roberts and Miers, "End of Slavery," 14.

72. Damel à Baudin, August 26, 1848, Kaajor, ANS 3B64.

73. Baudin à Ministre, February 12, 1849, St. Louis, ANS 2B27 and ANSOM Sénégal I/35.

74. Klein, *Slavery and Colonial Rule,* 27.

75. Baudin à Ministre, February 12, 1849, St. Louis, ANS 2B27 and ANSOM Sénégal I/35. My emphasis.

76. Baudin à Ministre, February 12, 1849, St. Louis, ANS 2B27 and ANSOM Sénégal I/35.

77. Rapport sur la captivité, Administrator Poulet, 1905, ANS K17.

78. Ministre à Baudin, April 18, 1849, Paris, ANSOM Sénégal XIV/15.

79. Arrêté locale de April 13, 1849, Gouverneur Baudin, ANS M3.

80. Ministre à Baudin, November 13, 1849, Paris. ANSOM Sénégal I/35.

81. Registre les délibérations, les procès-verbaux des séances et les transaction du Conseil du Tutelle des Enfants . . . à St. Louis, April 20, 1849–February 18, 1857, St. Louis, ANS M3.

82. Arrêté locale, December 5, 1857, Gouverneur Faidherbe, ANS 1A24. Rapport sur la captivité, Administrator Poulet, 1905, ANS K17.

CHAPTER 5

1. The French held a few positions in the Gambia and Casamance as well, but these are outside the area of this dissertation.

2. Barry, *Senegambia,* 177.

3. See Barry, *Senegambia.* Also David Robinson, *The Holy War of Umar Tal: The Western Sudan in the Mid-nineteenth Century.*

4. Gouverneur à M. Caille, March 16, 1843, St. Louis, ANS 3B52.

5. Protet à Ministre, April 14, 1852, Saint Louis, ANS 2B30.

6. Pujol à Ministre, March 7, 1834, St. Louis, ANS 2B16.

7. Barrows, "General Faidherbe," 231. Barrows's account of the invasion of Waalo is especially detailed.

8. Protet à Ministre August 21, 1852, St. Louis, ANS 2B31.

9. Conseil d'Administration de Gorée, procès-verbal du sèance, January 29, 1855, ANS 2E3.

10. Barrows, "General Faidherbe," 116–17.

11. David Robinson, *Paths of Accommodation: Muslim Societies and French Colonial Authorities in Senegal and Mauritania, 1880–1920,* 108–9.

12. Barrows, "General Faidherbe," 120–21.

13. Barry, *Le royaume,* 301.

14. Ministre à Faidherbe, January 19, 1855, Paris, ANSOM Sénégal I/41B.

15. Barrows, "General Faidherbe," 270.

16. Faidherbe à Ministre, March 11, 1855, ANSOM Sénégal I/41B.

17. Barry, *Le royaume,* 307.

18. Faidherbe à Ministre, April 3, 1855, St. Louis, ANSOM Sénégal I/41B.

19. Faidherbe à Ministre, June 6, 1856, St. Louis, ANSOM Sénégal I/41B.

20. Ministre à Faidherbe, September 1, 1859, Paris, ANSOM Sénégal I/46B.

21. Faidherbe à Ministre, March 13, 1858, St. Louis, ANSOM Sénégal IV/46.

22. Barrows, "General Faidherbe," 651. Searing, "Accommodation," 42–43.

23. Barry, *Senegambia,* 191–93. For more details, see Searing, *"God Alone,"* 31–42.

24. Barry, *Senegambia,* 193.

25. Rapport sur la captivité, Administrateur Poulet, 1905, ANS K17.

26. Renault, "L'abolition," 11.

27. Ministre à Citoyen Commissaire Baudin, May 27, 1848, Paris, ANSOM Sénégal XVI/3.

28. As indicated by subsequent sources, this suppression of military engagement (under Article 2) was in fact put into effect. See Ministre à Protet, April 15, 1852, Paris, ANSOM Sénégal XIV/18.

29. Baudin à Ministre, January 14, 1849, St. Louis, ANS 2B27.

30. Myron Echenberg, *Colonial Conscripts: The Tirailleurs Sénégalais in French West Africa, 1857–1960,* 9. Echenberg's monograph focuses largely on the twentieth century.

31. Ministre à Protet, April 15, 1852, Paris, ANSOM Sénégal XIV/18.

32. Ministre à Protet, April 15, 1852, Paris, ANSOM Sénégal XIV/18.

33. Le Chef de Division pour les Côtes Occidentales d'Afrique à Ministre, November 23, 1853, Gorée, ANSOM Sénégal XVI/4.

34. Deherme, *L'esclavage en AOF,* 1906, ANS K25.

35. Protet à Ministre, n.d., December 1854, St. Louis, ANS 13G23.

36. Faidherbe à Ministre, December 16, 1857, St. Louis, ANS 2B32.

37. Thomas à Ministre, June 6, 1890, St. Louis, ANS 2B67.

38. Klein, "Slavery and Emancipation," 176.

39. Echenberg, *Colonial Conscripts,* 7. Although Echenberg notes a decline in conscripts to 625 in 1872, my evidence suggests that the number of *tirailleurs* stayed quite high even during the French withdrawal of the 1870s. Memoire, Gouverneur Serval, November 1871, lists 1,065 *tirailleurs.* ANSOM Sénégal II/5.

40. Fleuve 1854–1879, IV/46, Cayor 1855–1860, ANSOM Sénégal IV/45; and Sine et Saloum 1859–1877, ANSOM Sénégal IV/50.

41. Ministre à Pinet-Laprade, n.d., February 1868, Paris, ANSOM Sénégal I/54.

42. Mohamed Mbodj makes this argument effectively. See Mbodj, "Abolition." The subject is directly mentioned in Faidherbe à Commandant Gorée, February 22, 1865, St. Louis, ANS K11. The hiring of slaves is also indirectly mentioned in Valière à Commandant du Gorée, March 24, 1874, St. Louis, ANS 3B.

43. Petition des Notables de Gorée à Commandant, December 1, 1869, Gorée, ANS P1.

44. Mbodj, "Abolition," 205.

45. See chapter 4.

46. Bernard Moitt, "Slavery and Emancipation in Senegal's Peanut Basin," 27. Barry, *Senegambia,* 178. This phenomenon is well documented, but the speed at which it occurred is debatable. Searing suggests that "peanut exports favored small producers in the long run, but only after the decline of the internal slave trade and the beginnings of slave emancipation," thus proposing a very gradual social transformation (*"God Alone,"* 59).

47. Searing, *"God Alone,"* 59.

48. Barry, *Senegambia,* 152, 183–87.

49. Klein covers Maba's campaigns quite extensively in his history of the Siin-Saalum region. *Islam,* 63–93.

50. Barry, *Senegambia,* 195–99.

51. For example, the Kaajor *ceddo* leader, Demba War Sall, and other aristocrats joined Maba for some time.

52. Rapport sur la captivité, Administrateur Poulet, 1905, ANS K17.

53. Deherme, *L'esclavage en AOF,* 1906, ANS K25.

54. Using the formula of claiming land "within cannon shot" seems to have been common among Europeans on the west coast of Africa. Procès-verbal du séance, Conseil d'Administration, April 10, 1855, ANS 3E26.

55. Procès-verbal du séance, Conseil d'Administration, April 10, 1855, ANS 3E26.

56. Ministre à Faidherbe, June 21, 1855, Paris, ANSOM Sénégal XIV/15B.

57. Arrêté, Faidherbe, October 18, 1855, ANS K11.

58. Renault, "L'abolition," 11.

59. Circulaire confidentielle, Faidherbe au Chef de la Justice, Procureur Impérial, Directeur des Affaires Indigenes, November 14, 1857, St. Louis, ANSOM Sénégal XIV/15.

60. Ibid.

61. Ministre à Faidherbe, February 5, 1858, Paris, ANS K11.

62. Circulaire confidentielle, Faidherbe à les officiers, November 15, 1862, St. Louis, ANSOM Sénégal XIV/15.

63. Pinet-Laprade à Ministre, June 18, 1863, St. Louis, ANS 13G23.

64. Pinet-Laprade à Ministre, October 28, 1867, St. Louis, ANSOM Sénégal I/54.

65. Kennedy to Colonial Office, November 7, 1868, Cape Coast, PRO CO 96/77. See also Kimble, *Political History.*

66. Kennedy to Colonial Office, November 7, 1868, Cape Coast, PRO CO 96/77. Also Aborigines' Rights Protection Society, Granville to Cardwell, September 13, 1879, Cape Coast, NAG-CC 72, and James R. Sanders, "The Political Development of the Fante in the Eighteenth and Nineteenth Centuries: A Study of a West African Merchant Society."

67. See PRO CO 96/80 and CO 96/81 for accounts of this conflict. For more on Asante-Dutch relations around this topic, see Larry Yarak, "The Elmina Note: Myth and Reality in Asante-Dutch Relations."

68. Horton to Granville, May 2, 1870, Cape Coast, PRO CO 96/85.

69. See Kimble, *Political History,* 221–63, and W. E. F. Ward, *A History of the Gold Coast,* 254.

70. The interior polities did not even usually receive district commissioners until the turn of the century, although the British intermittently meddled in successions and other issues at the behest of local parties or missionaries in the 1880s and 1890s.

71. Yarak, "Elmina Note."

72. Marginalia by Kimberley in Harley to Minister, April 14, 1873, Cape Coast, PRO CO 96/98.

73. Harley to Minister, April 14, 1873, Cape Coast, PRO CO 96/98.

74. Wilks, *Asante,* 220–22.

75. For a primary source, see Friedrich Ramseyer and Johannes Kühne, *Four Years in Ashantee,* 296. Wilks's *Asante in the Nineteenth Century* remains, I feel, the best account of this period, albeit from the Asante perspective.

76. Dumett, "Pressure Groups," 193–211.

77. Ibid., 206.

78. Agbodeka, *African Politics,* 55–56.

79. Carnarvon to the Officer Administering the Government of the Gold Coast, August 21, 1874, PP 1875, LII (c. 1139).

80. Addo-Fening, *Akyem Abuakwa,* 26.

81. Carnarvon to the Officer Administering the Government of the Gold Coast, August 21, 1874, PP 1875, LII (c. 1139).

82. Memorandum on the Vestiges of Slavery in the Gold Coast, Assistant Secretary for Native Affairs Johnson, 1927, NAG ADM 11/1/975.

83. Carnarvon to the Officer Administering the Government of the Gold Coast, August 21, 1874, PP 1875, LII (c. 1139).

84. See chapter 3.

85. Strahan to Carnarvon, September 19, 1874, Cape Coast, PP 1875, LII (c. 1139).

86. Strahan to Carnarvon, September 19, 1874, Cape Coast, PP 1875, LII (c. 1139).

87. Legislative Council Minutes, December 17, 1874, PRO CO 98/2.

88. Griffith to Knutsford, June 14, 1888, Accra, NAG ADM 12/3/2.

89. Carnarvon to the Officer Administering the Government of the Gold Coast, August 21, 1874, PP 1875, LII (c. 1139).

90. Ibid.

91. Legislative Council Minutes, December 17, 1874, PRO CO 98/2.

92. Strahan to Carnarvon, December 28, 1874, encl. 1, Gold Coast Slave Dealing Abolition Act, Article 4, PP 1875, LII (c. 1139).

93. Ibid.

94. Strahan to Carnarvon, December 28, 1874, encl. 1, Gold Coast Slave Dealing Abolition Act, Article 7, PP 1875, LII (c. 1139). Carnarvon and the acting colonial secretary on the Gold Coast both argued for a heavier sentence. Carnarvon to Strahan, October 29, 1874, London, PP 1875, LII (c. 1139). Legislative Council Minutes, December 17, 1874, PRO CO 98/2.

95. Strahan to Carnarvon, December 28, 1874, encl. 2, The Gold Coast Emancipation Ordinance, Article 4, PP 1875, LII (c. 1139).

96. Strahan to Carnarvon, September 19, 1874, encl. 3, PP 1875, LII (c. 1139).

97. Strahan to Carnarvon, December 28, 1874, encl. 2, The Gold Coast Emancipation Ordinance, Article 5, PP 1875, LII (c. 1139).

98. Strahan to Carnarvon, September 19, 1874, Cape Coast, PP 1875, LII (c. 1139).

99. Memorandum on the Vestiges of Slavery in the Gold Coast, Assistant Secretary for Native Affairs Johnson, 1927, NAG ADM 11/1/975.

100. Strahan to Carnarvon, March 26, 1875, Cape Coast, PRO CO 96/115.

101. McSheffrey, "Slavery," 349–68.

102. J. Binder to Mader, Basel Missionary Factory, July 3, 1875, Ada, in Jenkins, "Abstracts."

103. Asante, Mohr, and Werner to the Basel Mission Slave Emancipation Committee, June 26, 1875, Kyebi, in Jenkins, "Abstracts."

104. Mader's cover letter to Basel, August 25, 1875, Akropong, in Jenkins, "Abstracts."

105. Dieterle to Basel, June 22, 1875, Aburi; Eisenschmid to Basel, June 25, 1875, Akropong; Schönefeld to Mader, July 8, 1875, Odumase. All, Jenkins, "Abstracts."

106. This will be discussed in depth in chapter 6. See Addo-Fening, *Akyem Abuakwa,* 57–71.

107. Dumett and Johnson, "Britain," 106–8.

108. Parker, "Ga State and Society," 144.

109. Akurang-Parry, "Administration" and "Slavery."

110. For my response to Akurang-Parry's assertions, see my article "The Case for Africans: The Role of Slaves and Masters in Emancipation on the Gold Coast."

111. See chapter 6.

112. Akurang-Parry, "Slavery," 17.

113. Strahan to Carnarvon, March 6, 1875, Cape Coast, PP 1875, LII (c. 1343).

114. Roger Gocking, "British Justice and the Native Tribunals of the Southern Gold Coast Colony," 94–96.

115. Akurang-Parry, "Administration," 152.

116. My thanks to John Parker for this biographical information.

117. Chief Magistrate Marshall to Lt. Colonel Johnston, April 9, 1874, Accra, NAG ADM 1/12/3. Cleland was indicted in *Regina v. Sarah Smith,* Accra Supreme/Divisional Court, May 20, 1868, NAG SCT 2/4/4.

118. The court sat in Cape Coast until 1876 and later in Accra. NAG SCT 5/4/14–5/4/19 and 17/4/1.

119. Hodgson to Knutsford, July 8, 1889, Accra, PRO CO 96/203.

120. NAG SCT 2/5/1 (1879)–2/5/13 (1899).

121. The Accra District Court was the first to hear slave-dealing cases in 1882. See chapter 6.

122. J. Binder claimed slaves in Ada did not know of emancipation (Binder to Mader-Basel Missionary Factory, January 3, 1875, Ada, in Jenkins, "Abstracts"). Ignorance of the proclamation was also used as a defense by some defendants. See *Regina v. Quacoe Bart,* Cape Coast Judicial Assessors Court, March 9, 1875, and *Regina v. Ashun and Kofi Dontoh,* Cape Coast Judicial Court, March 1, 1875, both NAG SCT 5/4/1.

123. Dieterle to Basel, June 22, 1875, Aburi, in Jenkins, "Abstracts"; *Regina v. Acquassie Mirriwa,* Cape Coast Judicial Assessors Court, December 1, 1876, Mampong,

SCT 5/4/19; *Regina v. Kofi Tando,* Cape Coast Judicial Assessors Court, December 2, 1876, Domassie in Akyem, SCT 5/4/19.

124. The records for most cases do not make clear the exact mechanism by which slaves brought into British jurisdiction were identified.

125. Dumett and Johnson, "Britain," 91.

126. This information is all drawn from NAG SCT 5/4/15–18; SCT 17/4/1; SCT 2/5/1; and SCT 2/4/11.

127. Freeling to Rottman and Cole, September 3, 1877, Accra, NAG ADM 1/9/1.

128. See chapter 3.

129. Monthly State of the Fantee Armed Police and the Gold Coast Houssa Armed Police Force, June 24, 1873, NAG ADM 1/10/2.

130. Wolseley to Kimberley, November 4, 1873, Cape Coast, PRO CO 96/103.

131. Parker, *Making the Town,* 69.

132. Sworn declaration, HAPF Recruits, August 12, 1873, NAG ADM 1/10/20.

133. Cited in Parker, *Making the Town,* 69.

134. Nominal Roll with Particulars of Recruits Medically Examined for Houssa Armed Police, September 1873, NAG ADM 1/10/2.

135. Captain Glover to Wolseley, November 6, 1873, Accra, PRO CO 96/103.

136. Captain Glover to Wolseley, November 6, 1873, Accra, PRO CO 96/103.

137. Holland to Kimberley, telegram, December 16, 1873, London, PRO CO 96/103.

138. Kimberley to Wolseley. December 17, 1874, NAG ADM 1/10/34.

139. See chapter 3.

140. J. Binder to Mader, Basel Missionary Factory, July 3, 1875, Ada, in Jenkins, "Abstracts." Again, this topic will be discussed in chapter 6.

141. Ussher to Colonial Office, November 10, 1875, Cape Coast, PRO CO 96/131.

142. Hicks Beach to Ussher, July 3, 1879, London, NAG ADM 1/1/48.

143. Ussher to Kimberley, September 13, 1880, Accra, PRO CO 96/131.

144. Strahan to Carnarvon, June 22, 1875, Cape Coast, PRO CO 96/115.

145. Ordinance 16 of 1877, "Masters and Servants," July 23, 1877, Governor Freeling, PRO CO 97/2.

146. Dumett and Johnson, "Britain," 81.

147. Tabular View of the Gold Coast District, 1874, WMMS Reports, XIX.

148. Gold Coast District, 1875, WMMS Reports, XIX.

149. Ussher to Hicks-Beach, December 9, 1879, Keta, PRO CO 96/28.

150. Dumett and Johnson, "Britain," 86.

CHAPTER 6

1. Dumett and Johnson, "Britain," 85.

2. For more on this see Akurang-Parry, "Slavery," 27–32.

3. John Thornton, *Africa and Africans in the Making of the Atlantic World, 1400–1800,* 75. Also see chapter 1.

4. Although the use of title deeds was becoming more prevalent in the late eighteenth

century along the coast, and in the nineteenth century, they made limited headway in gold-bearing regions of the interior. See Griffith to G. E. Eminsang, September 13, 1890, Accra, NAG ADM 12/5/184. Nevertheless, the vast majority of land appears to have remained vested in the stool or *abusua*. See Report of the Commission on Economic Agriculture in the Gold Coast, 1889, NAG ADM 5/3/7.

5. H. W. Hayes-Redwar, *Comments on Some Ordinances of the Gold Coast Colony*, 1909, NAG-CC #55. Report of the Commission on Economic Agriculture in the Gold Coast, 1889, NAG ADM 5/3/7.

6. Zimmerman, unaddressed, July 26, 1875, Abokobi; Eisenschmid to Basel, June 25, 1875, Akropong. Both, Jenkins, "Abstracts."

7. Zimmerman, unaddressed, July 26, 1875, Abokobi; Asante, Mohr, and Werner to the BMS Slave Emancipation Committee, June 26, 1875, Kyebi. Both, Jenkins, "Abstracts."

8. Zimmerman, unaddressed, July 26, 1875, Abokobi, in Jenkins, "Abstracts."

9. Memorandum on the Vestiges of Slavery in the Gold Coast, Assistant Secretary for Native Affairs Johnson, 1927, NAG ADM 11/1/975.

10. Zimmerman, unaddressed, July 26, 1875, Abokobi, in Jenkins, "Abstracts."

11. Ga-Adangme Distriktconferenz, December 3–6, 1894, Christiansborg, BMS D-1.60.

12. Griffith to G. E. Eminsang, September 13, 1890, Accra, NAG ADM 12/5/184.

13. Strahan to Carnarvon, March 26, 1875, Cape Coast, PRO CO 96/115.

14. Strahan to Carnarvon, received November 24, 1874, from Cape Coast, PP 1875, LII (c. 1139). Strahan to Carnarvon, November 5, 1874, Accra, PP 1875, LII (c. 1139).

15. Strahan to Carnarvon, November 3, 1874, Cape Coast, PP 1875, LII (c. 1139).

16. Strahan to Carnarvon, January 3, 1875, Cape Coast, PP 1875, LII (c. 1159).

17. Strahan to Carnarvon, January 8, 1875, Cape Coast, PP 1875, LII (c. 1159).

18. Ibid.

19. Ibid.

20. Carnarvon to Strahan, February 19, 1875, London, NAG ADM 1/1/39.

21. Carnarvon to Strahan, March 23, 1875, London, NAG ADM 1/1/39.

22. If the BMS agents in Kyebi are to be believed. Eisenschmid to Basel, June 25, 1875, Akropong, in Jenkins, "Abstracts."

23. *King Tando and King Akimmy v. Owooh Cudjoe and Offlay*, Cape Coast Judicial Assessors Court, May 8, 1875, NAG SCT 5/4/16. *Queen v. Abbom and Abrobah*, Cape Coast Judicial Assessors Court, August 4, 1876, NAG SCT 5/4/18. *Queen v. Chief Ahinkorah*, Accra Supreme/Divisional Court, September 4, 1895, NAG SCT 2/5/12.

24. District Commissioner Peregrine to Assistant Colonial Secretary, July 29, 1889, PRO CO 96/208. *Achampong v. John Quartey*, Accra District Court, July 27, 1882, NAG SCT 17/5/2. *Regina v. Ellen Quartey*, Accra District Court, June 20, 1890, NAG SCT 17/5/9.

25. Griffith to DC Kwitta, October 1, 1890, Christiansborg (Accra), NAG ADM 1/9/4.

26. Hall's Report on the Journey to Anum, February 25, 1887, in Jenkins, "Abstracts." Hall makes a point of mentioning the European dress of the slave trader he encounters.

27. Firminger to Colonial Office, April 30, 1889, West Kensington, NAG ADM 1/1/88.

28. The year for which we have the most records, although also a year of increased enforcement—see chapter 9.

29. The names "Fanti" or "Fante," and generalizations about customs, were also commonly applied to portions of the protectorate that had not been part of the confederation and, often, that did not speak Fante Twi. Sanitary Report on the Station of Elmina, 1883, Elmina, NAG ADM 1/12/5.

30. Interview with Professor Robert Addo-Fening, November 27, 1998. I am indebted to Professor Addo-Fening for his assistance.

31. For example, *Regina v. Tarro,* Accra District Court, September 30, 1891, NAG SCT 17/5/12.

32. *Regina v. Sarah Brown,* Accra Divisional Court, February 5, 1883, NAG SCT 2/5/1; *Ashong v. Tontoo and Harshani,* Accra District Court, September 14, 1888, NAG SCT 17/5/8; *Regina v. Acossadah,* Accra District Court, March 22, 1890, NAG SCT 17/5/9.

33. For example, *Regina v. Bossun Akinnee,* Cape Coast Judicial Assessors Court, April 6, 1876, NAG SCT 5/4/18. See also *Regina v. King Enimil Quow,* Cape Coast Judicial Assessors Court, February 28, 1876, NAG SCT 5/4/18.

34. *Regina v. Quacoe Bart,* Cape Coast Judicial Assessors Court, March 9, 1875, NAG SCT 5/4/15; *Regina v. Adjuah Sharry, Esserifi, and Agreman,* Accra Judicial Assessors Court, March 8, 1877, NAG SCT 17/4/1.

35. Strahan to Carnarvon, March 6, 1875, Cape Coast, encl. 1, Chalmers Report, PP 1875, LII (c. 1343). *Regina v. Kofi Dontoh and Ashun,* Cape Coast Judicial Assessors Court, March 1, 1875, NAG SCT 5/4/15.

36. Zimmerman, August 24, 1869, Odumase, BMS D-1.21b.

37. Hodgson to Knutsford, July 8, 1889, Accra, NAG ADM 12/13/3. Hodgson to Knutsford, July 8, 1889, Accra, encl. 1, Chief Justice to Colonial Secretary, PRO CO 96/203.

38. *Regina v. Tuitalaboo,* Accra District Court, October 5, 1881, NAG SCT 2/5/1.

39. Agbodeka, *African Politics,* 104–8.

40. Rowe to Derby, March 18, 1884, Accra, PRO CO 96/156.

41. *Regina v. Mamah,* Accra District Court, October 3, 1890, NAG SCT 17/5/9. Three years later, however, his relationship with the administration had broken down enough for the incidents described above to take place. Turton to King Quamin Fori, July 20, 1883, Christiansborg, NAG ADM 1/9/3.

42. *Regina v. Quabina Keamie,* Cape Coast Judicial Assessors Court, May 29, 1876, NAG SCT 5/4/18.

43. *Regina v. Awhabon,* Cape Coast Judicial Assessors Court, February 19, 1876, NAG SCT 5/4/18.

44. Parker, "Ga State and Society," 117.

45. Addo-Fening, *Akyem Abuakwa,* 113, 121, 131.

46. *Regina v. Enimil Quow,* Cape Coast Judicial Assessors Court, February 23, 1876, NAG SCT 5/4/18.

47. Freeling to Carnarvon, April 5, 1877, Accra, PRO CO 96/121.

48. *Regina v. King Enimil Quow,* Cape Coast Judicial Assessors Court, February 23,

1876, NAG SCT 5/4/18. As noted previously, the "stool" is the Akan equivalent of the European "crown" or "throne."

49. Strahan to Carnarvon, March 4, 1876, Cape Coast, encl. 1, Chalmers to Strahan, March 1, 1876, PRO CO 96/118.

50. See chapter 8.

51. Dumett and Johnson, "Britain," 94.

52. *Gold Coast Chronicle,* vol. III, no. 93, September 12, 1892. Report of the Commission on Economic Agriculture in the Gold Coast, 1889, NAG ADM 5/3/7.

53. Cruickshank, *Eighteen Years,* 322. Fairfield Report, 1874, PRO CO 879/33. Report from the Select Committee on Slavery on the West Coast of Africa, evidence of J. G. Nicholls, PP 1842, XI.1 (551). The information refers specifically to the period before 1831. Meredith, *Account,* 30.

54. Kölle, February 12, 1890, Odumase, BMS D-1.70.

55. Wilson, *Krobo People,* 101.

56. This episode is elaborated in papers I have presented to the South-East Regional Seminar on African Studies, 2001, Greenville; and the American History Association, 2001, San Francisco.

57. Addo-Fening, *Akyem Abuakwa,* 194.

58. Addo-Fening, *Akyem Abuakwa,* 63–64

59. Haenger, *Slaves,* 133–37.

60. *David Asante v. Crown Prince etc.,* December 17, 1877, NAG SCT 2/4/12.

61. Freeling to the Local Committee of the BMS, January 16, 1878, Accra, NAG ADM 1/9/2.

62. Addo-Fening, *Akyem Abuakwa,* 69; Agbodeka, *African Politics,* 108.

63. Buck's report for the year 1879, December 30–31, 1879, Buck to Basel, March 2, 1880, in Addo-Fening, *Akyem Abuakwa.*

64. Ussher to Minister, May 25, 1880, Elmina, PRO CO 96/131.

65. For arguments that establish a limited slave mode of production in certain regions, see chapter 3. Fairfield Report, 1874, PRO CO 879/33.

66. Memorandum on the Vestiges of Slavery in the Gold Coast, Assistant Secretary for Native Affairs Johnson, 1927, NAG ADM 11/1/975.

67. Fritz to Basel, July 28, 1875, Christiansborg, in Jenkins, "Abstracts."

68. Zimmerman, unaddressed, July 26, 1875, Abokobi, in Jenkins, "Abstracts."

69. *Regina v. Oduku and David,* Accra Divisional Court, June 9, 1880 NAG SCT 2/5/1; *Regina v. Timbuctoo,* Accra Divisional Court, October 5, 1881, NAG SCT 2/5/1.

70. Dumett and Johnson, "Britain," 85.

71. Brown to Acting Colonial Secretary, January 19, 1877, Accra, enclosed in Freeling to Carnarvon, January 30, 1877, Cape Coast, PRO CO 96/120.

72. *Regina v. Oduka and David,* Accra Divisional Court, June 9, 1880, NAG SCT 2/5/1; *Regina v. Antamo Cudjoe,* Dixcove District Court, February 11, 1880, NAG SCT 22/4/51; *Regina v. Kuasie Abbe,* Accra District Court, October 21, 1891, NAG SCT 17/5/12.

73. *Regina v. Arjaba Yarba,* Accra Divisional Court, September 9,1889, NAG SCT 2/5/4.

74. Dumett and Johnson, "Britain," 78.

75. Memorandum on the Vestiges of Slavery in the Gold Coast, Assistant Secretary for Native Affairs Johnson, 1927, NAG ADM 11/1/975.

76. District Commissioner Rigby to Colonial Secretary, January 30, 1890, Aburi, PRO CO 96/208.

77. Fritz to Basel, July 28, 1875, Christiansborg, in Jenkins, "Abstracts."

78. Tabitha Schönefeld, n.d. 1875, Odumase, BMS D-1.27.

79. For example, *Eccusah Ajishe and Neepow Kwah v. Garmamir,* Accra District Court, November 20, 1889, NAG SCT 17/5/9.

80. Robertson, "Post Proclamation Slavery," 227-30.

81. *Regina v. Oweaguow,* Cape Coast Judicial Assessors Court, December 14, 1875, NAG SCT 5/4/16.

82. *Regina v. Kwamina Ansa,* Cape Coast District Court, September 24, 1897, NAG SCT 23/5/4; *Regina v. Baidu Amta,* Cape Coast District Court, September 24, 1897, NAG SCT 23/5/4.

83. See chapter 7. Also Hodgson to Knutsford, February 17, 1890, Accra, PRO CO 96/208. Strahan to Carnarvon, March 6, 1875, encl. 1, Chalmers Report, PP 1875, LII (c. 1343).

84. *Regina v. Kofi Dontoh and Ashun,* Cape Coast Judicial Assessors Court, March 1, 1875, NAG SCT 5/4/15.

85. At the time, Hodgson was acting governor of the colony. Hodgson to Knutsford, February 17, 1890, Accra, PRO CO 96/208.

86. Firminger to Colonial Office, April 30, 1889, West Kensington, NAG ADM 1/1/88.

87. Hodgson to Chamberlain, January 29, 1898, Accra, PRO CO 96/311. Heron to Colonial Secretary, August 2, 1889, Accra, PRO CO 96/208.

88. McSheffrey, "Slavery," 354.

89. Dumett and Johnson, "Britain," 88-89.

90. Akurang-Parry, "Administration," 157.

91. See chapter 5.

92. There was also a limited number of liberations carried out by administration for various exceptional purposes.

93. Strahan to Carnarvon, March 6, 1875, Cape Coast, encl. 1, Chalmers Report, PP 1875, LII (c. 1343). Akurang-Parry, "Administration," 156.

94. NAG SCT 5/4/15-17 and 2/4/11.

95. In this, Akurang-Parry and I agree. Akurang-Parry, "Slavery," 24.

96. For example, *Cudjoe Amooar v. Benfoo,* Cape Coast Judicial Assessors Court, February 10, 1875, NAG SCT 5/4/15; *Regina v. Quacoe Appeah,* Cape Coast Judicial Assessors Court, May 1, 1875, NAG SCT 5/4/16.

97. For example, *Regina v. Quacoe Appeah,* Cape Coast Judicial Assessors Court, May 1, 1875, Akuapem, NAG SCT 5/4/16; *Regina v. Quacoe Teah,* Accra Judicial Assessors Court, March 8, 1877, Krepi, NAG SCT 17/4/1.

98. *Regina v. Acquassie Mirriwah,* Cape Coast Judicial Assessors Court, December 1, 1876, NAG SCT 5/4/19.

99. Dumett and Johnson, "Britain," 85.

100. There were exceptions: for example, Ewe-speaking slaves in Accra who may

have departed en masse. See Reindorf to Committeee, dd. Mayera, November 17, 1875, in Parker, *Making the Town,* 94.

101. For example, Ewe slaves in Akuapem. Bieterle to Basel, June 22, 1875, Aburi, in Jenkins, "Abstracts."

102. Strahan to Carnarvon, March 6, 1875, Cape Coast, encl. 1, PP 1875, LII (c. 1343).

103. Griffith to Knutsford, February 27, 1892, Accra, PRO CO 96/222.

104. Parker, "Ga State and Society," 145.

105. NAG SCT 5/4/15–5/4/19, 2/5/11

106. See chapter 9.

107. Strahan to Carnarvon, March 6, 1875, Cape Coast, encl. 1, Chalmers Report, PP 1875, LII (c. 1343).

108. *Regina v. Afeli,* Accra District Court, March 25, 1890, NAG SCT 17/5/9.

109. *Regina v. Quacoe Agay,* Cape Coast Judicial Assessors Court, December 6, 1876, NAG SCT 5/4/19.

110. Ibid; also *Karfor v. Coffee Assally,* Accra District Court, October 20, 1882, NAG SCT 17/5/2; *Regina v. Awah,* Accra Supreme/Divisional Court, January 12, 1884, NAG SCT 2/5/1.

111. Zimmerman, unaddressed, July 26, 1875, Abokobi, in Jenkins, "Abstracts."

112. McSheffrey, "Slavery," 354.

113. Zimmerman, unaddressed, July 26, 1875, Abokobi, in Jenkins, "Abstracts."

114. Report of the Commission on Economic Agriculture on the Gold Coast, 1889, NAG ADM 5/3/7.

115. Addo-Fening, *Akyem Abuakwa,* 223–24.

116. Mohr to Basel, January 7, 1880, Kyebi; Muller to Basel, March 4, 1893, n.p. Both, Jenkins, "Abstracts." Hayes-Redwar, *Comments on Some Ordinances of the Gold Coast Colony,* NAG-CC #55. Stool land was not yet generally being alienated to migrant farmers.

117. Report of the Commission on Economic Agriculture in the Gold Coast, 1889, NAG ADM 5/3/7.

118. Report upon the Customs Relating to the Tenure of Land on the Gold Coast, 1895, reports of H. K. Vroom (District Commissioner, Tarkwa), Inspector General Scott (Gold Coast Constabulary), and A. W. Thompson (District Commander, Prampram), NAG ADM 5/3/9. Memorandum on the Vestiges of Slavery in the Gold Coast, Assistant Secretary for Native Affairs Johnson, 1927, NAG ADM 11/1/975.

119. This seems true except for a few carrier positions along major trade routes. Dumett and Johnson, "Britain," 92. Memorandum on the Vestiges of Slavery in the Gold Coast, Assistant Secretary for Native Affairs Johnson, 1927, NAG ADM 11/1/975. Addo-Fening, *Akyem Abuakwa,* 233.

120. Report . . . on the Effects of the Steps Taken by the Colonial Government, Chalmers, PP 1878, LV (c. 2148). White to Minister, November 5, 1887, Accra, PRO CO 96/185.

121. These villages are identified in Parker, *Making the Town,* 94.

122. Roger Gocking, *Facing Two Ways: Ghana's Coastal Communities under Colonial Rule,* 61–62.

123. Addo-Fening, *Akyem Abuakwa,* 194.

124. Weiss, September 4, 1878, Odumase, BMS D-1.30.

125. Commissioner Kitson to Maxwell, April 2, 1896, Accra, PRO CO 96/272. Half-Yearly Report on the Gold Coast Constabulary, February 20, 1888, Elmina, PRO CO 96/191.

126. Hodgson to Minister, February 9, 1894, Accra, NAG ADM 12/3/3.

127. Griffith to Minister, December 3, 1892, Accra, NAG ADM 12/3/3. Maxwell to Colonial Office, telegram, June 30, 1897, PRO CO 96/294.

128. Acting Queen's Advocate to White, September 24, 1887, Accra, PRO CO 96/183. Maxwell to Minister, March 5, 1896, Accra, PRO CO 96/263.

129. Memorandum on the Vestiges of Slavery in the Gold Coast, Assistant Secretary for Native Affairs Johnson, 1927, NAG ADM 11/1/975.

130. Firminger to Colonial Office, April 30, 1889, West Kensington, NAG ADM 1/1/88.

131. Strahan to Carnarvon, June 22, 1875, Cape Coast Castle, PRO CO 96/115. Departmental Reports, 1895, NAG ADM 5/1/72.

132. Departmental Reports, 1896, NAG ADM 5/1/73.

133. Departmental Reports, 1895, NAG ADM 5/1/72.

134. See *Gold Coast Times,* vol. I, 10, June 16, 1881, NAG-CC 217; *Gold Coast Times,* vol. I, 40, April 22, 1882, NAG-CC 217. Report on the Tarquah District, Commander Ramsay, August 9, 1882, Accra, NAG ADM 1/12/4.

135. *Gold Coast Chronicle,* vol. III, 118, March 11, 1893, NAG ADM 13/1.

136. Dumett, *El Dorado in West Africa: The Gold Coast Mining Frontier, African Labour, and Colonial Capitalism in the Gold Coast, 1873–1900,* 267–68.

137. It is unclear how these plantations were destroyed, as the invasion of 1869 took place mostly in and around Peki. However, the commissioners did interview locals and are very clear on this point. Report of the Commission on Economic Agriculture on the Gold Coast, 1889, NAG ADM 5/3/7. Hodgson to Minister, November 9, 1891, Aburi, PRO CO 96/219.

138. Griffith to Knutsford, August 24, 1888, encl. 2, Customs to Colonial Secretary, Accra, PRO CO 96/193. Report of the Commission on Economic Agriculture on the Gold Coast, 1889, NAG ADM 5/3/7.

139. Hill, *Cocoa Farmer,* 103.

140. Sutton, "Labour."

141. Executive Council Minutes, January 19, 1894, NAG ADM 13/1/6, and June 25, 1889, PRO CO 98/7.

142. Parker, "Ga State and Society," 148.

143. Ordinance 8 of 1893, Masters and Servants and Foreign Employment Ordinance, NAG ADM 4/1/17.

144. Memorandum on the Vestiges of Slavery in the Gold Coast, Assistant Secretary for Native Affairs Johnson, 1927, NAG ADM 11/1/975.

145. Dumett and Johnson, "Britain," 92–93.

146. Ibid., 88–89.

147. Akurang-Parry, "Slavery," 19–21.

148. Report upon the Customs Relating to the Tenure of Land on the Gold Coast,

1895, H. Cummings, District Commissioner Saltpond, NAG ADM 5/3/9; Dieterle to Basel, June 22, 1875, Aburi, in Jenkins, "Abstracts."

149. *Regina v. George Napoleon,* Accra District Court, March 22, 1897, NAG SCT 17/5/1. Report upon the Customs Relating to the Tenure of Land on the Gold Coast, 1895, H. Cummings, District Commissioner Saltpond, NAG ADM 5/3/9. Zimmerman, unaddressed, July 26, 1875, Abokobi, in Jenkins, "Abstracts."

150. Dieterle to Basel, June 22, 1875, Aburi, in Jenkins, "Abstracts."

151. Report from the Committee on Africa (West Coast), evidence of Reverend Elias Schrenk of the Basel Mission, Q. 3334–3341, PP 1865, V (412).

152. Former District Commissioner Rigby to Colonial Secretary, Aburi, January 30, 1890, PRO CO 96/208.

153. Josenhans, January 25, 1912, Odumase, BMS D-1.98.

154. Admittedly, this is contradicted by at least one source: Binder, July 3, 1875, BMS D-10.3, in Haenger, *Slaves,* 126.

155. Report upon the Customs Relating to the Tenure of Land on the Gold Coast, 1895, H. Cummings, District Commissioner Saltpond, NAG ADM 5/3/9. Hodgson to Knutsford, February 17, 1890, Accra, encl. 14, District Commissioner Rigby to Colonial Secretary, January 30, 1890, Aburi, PRO CO 96/208.

156. Memorandum on the Vestiges of Slavery in the Gold Coast, Assistant Secretary for Native Affairs Johnson, 1927, NAG ADM 11/1/975. My emphasis.

157. See Alexander Robertson, *The Dynamics of Productive Relationships: African Sharer Contracts in Comparative Perspective,* and Gareth Austin, "The Emergence of Capitalist Relations in South Asante Cocoa-Farming, c. 1916–1933."

158. Hill, *Cocoa Farmer,* 12.

159. This practice shows up in at least one suit brought over possession of a property. *Regina v. George Napoleon,* Accra District Court, March 22, 1897, NAG SCT 17/5/5.

160. This total probably included former slaves, pawns, and free dependents. Report of the Census of Gold Coast Colony for the Year 1891, NAG ADM 5/2/1.

161. Parker, *Making the Town,* 95.

162. Gaps appear in the family trees of many coastal Ghanaian families during this period. For examples of law suits see *Owoo v. Quartay Hupah,* Accra District Court, 1 September 1887, NAG SCT 17/5/6; *Abba Ackireh vs. Lana Akebua,* Anamaboe District Court, January 25, 1895, NAG SCT 23/4/131. *Araba Qukraku vs. Assuwai,* Cape Coast District Court, March 1, 1895, NAG SCT 23/5/2.

163. Akurang-Parry, "Slavery," 26–27.

164. Report . . . on the Effects of the Steps Taken by the Colonial Government, Chalmers, PP 1878, LV (c. 2148).

CHAPTER 7

1. Klein, *Slavery and Colonial Rule,* 60.

2. See chapter 4.

3. Their slaves could still, according to the 1848 law, seek liberation (which they were nevertheless unlikely to receive) on French soil. However, their owners were immune from prosecution for owning these slaves.

4. Rapport sur le service judiciaire, March 20, 1842, St. Louis, ANS M3. There is a total absence of slave-dealing cases in ANS M3, ANS K11, and ANSOM Sénégal XIV before the 1850s.

5. Décret impérial portant organisation judiciaire, August 9, 1854, ANS M3.

6. Ministre à Faidherbe, December 28, 1854, Paris, ANS K11.

7. Faidherbe à Ministre, December 15, 1857, St. Louis, ANS K11.

8. General Reboul à Ministre, December 15, 1869, Dakar, ANSOM Sénégal I/56d.

9. Valière à Ministre, January 6, 1870, St. Louis, ANSOM Sénégal I/56b.

10. Saint-Martin, *Le Sénégal*, 605.

11. Klein's account of the Darrigrand affair is particularly good. *Slavery and Colonial Rule*, 60–61.

12. Darrigrand à Valière, May 28, 1875, St. Louis, ANSOM Sénégal XIV/16.

13. Leguay à Ministre, August 1, 1878, St. Louis, ANS K11.

14. Brière de l'Isle à Ministre, December 8, 1878, St. Louis, ANS K11.

15. Leguay à Ministre, August 18, 1878, St. Louis, ANS K11.

16. Klein, *Slavery and Colonial Rule*, 61.

17. Brière de l'Isle à Ministre, December 8, 1878, St. Louis, ANS K11.

18. Brière de l'Isle à Ministre, February 17, 1879, St. Louis, ANSOM Sénégal XIV/15d.

19. Pinet-Laprade à Ministre, February 20, 1865, St. Louis, ANS K11.

20. Ministre à Pinet-Laprade, April 30, 1865, Paris; Pinet-Laprade à Commandant de Gorée, February 22, 1865, St. Louis, ANS K11.

21. Canard à Valière, January 23, 1874, Gorée, ANSOM Sénégal XIV/15c.

22. Valière à Canard, February 4, 1874, St. Louis, ANSOM Sénégal XIV/15c.

23. As he wrote again in a letter to Gorée. Valière à Commandant de Gorée, March 24, 1874, St. Louis, ANS K11.

24. Commandant de Gorée à Brière de l'Isle, December 1, 1877, Gorée, ANS K11.

25. Telegram, Commandant de Gorée à Brière de l'Isle, June 20, 1879, Dakar, ANS K11.

26. Commandant de Gorée à Brière de l'Isle, July 1, 1879, Dakar, ANS 4B64.

27. Commandant de Gorée à Brière de l'Isle, December 1, 1877, Dakar, ANS 4B64.

28. Commandant de Gorée à Brière de l'Isle, December 1, 1877, Dakar; January 1, 1878, Dakar; and July 1, 1878, Dakar. All ANS 4B64.

29. Commandant de Gorée à Brière de l'Isle, December 1, 1877, Dakar; May 1, 1879, Dakar. Both ANS 4B64.

30. Moniteur du Sénégal, 1868–1888, in Klein, *Slavery and Colonial Rule*, 72.

31. Deherme, *L'esclavage en AOF*, 1906, ANS K25.

32. See chapter 5.

33. Ministre à Brière de l'Isle, December 13, 1878, Paris, ANS K25.

34. Conklin, *Mission*, 13.

35. Ibid., 21.

36. Genouilly à Pinet-Laprade, June 11, 1866, n.p., ANS K11. Renault, "L'abolition," 31–32.

37. *Petit Parisien*, January 12, 1880. *Lanterne*, January 10 and 12, 1880. *La Marseillaise*, October 5, 1879. *La France*, October 3, 1879.

38. "L'esclavage en France," *La France,* October 3, 1879.

39. Renault, "L'abolition," 32.

40. Ministre à Brière de l'Isle, ANSOM Sénégal XIV/15d.

41. Schoelcher was a famous Republican abolitionist and former head of the commission that authored the 1848 emancipation act.

42. It is not clear whether Schoelcher realized the contemporary limits of French authority. France still technically held protectorates over several interior and coastal states, but had not exercised them for a full decade.

43. Deherme, *L'esclavage en AOF,* 1906, ANS K25. *Journal Officiel de la République Française,* March 2, 1880.

44. See H. Olu Idowu, "The Establishment of Protectorate Administration in Senegal, 1890–1904," 253.

45. Ministre à Canard, January 31, 1882, Paris, ANS K12.

46. Klein, *Slavery and Colonial Rule,* 64.

47. Searing, "Accommodation," 72.

48. A functionary, Le Boucher, had held the position for less than two months following Servatius's death.

49. Deherme, *L'esclavage en AOF,* 1906, ANS K25.

50. Servatius à Ministre, May 20, 1883, St. Louis, ANSOM Sénégal I/68.

51. Servatius à Ministre, May 20, 1883, St. Louis, ANSOM Sénégal I/68.

52. Searing, "Accommodation," 72–73. Clément-Thomas stated that "at least 20,000" had departed the region (Ministre à Clément-Thomas, December 18, 1889, Paris, ANS K12). Also see Servatius à Ministre, May 20, 1883, St. Louis, ANSOM Sénégal I/68. This movement bears comparison with the Great Trek of the Boers in 1830s southern Africa, which was also made largely to escape abolitionist laws.

53. Klein, *Slavery and Colonial Rule,* 66.

54. Les notables du Canton de Mérinaghen, Peuls et Wolofs, à Quintrie, June 3, 1888, ANS K12.

55. Commandant Supérior du Soudan Française à Clément-Thomas, January 4, 1889, ANS 15G32.

56. John Hanson, *Migration, Jihad, and Muslim Authority in West Africa: The Futanke Colonies in Karta,* 141–45.

57. Deherme, *L'esclavage en AOF,* 1906, ANS K25. For more on Kaajor, see below.

58. Ministre à Clément-Thomas, December 18, 1889, Paris, ANS K12. My emphasis.

59. Lamothe à Ministre, June 21, 1891, St. Louis, ANSOM Sénégal I/91.

60. For more on this see Eunice A. Charles, "French West African Policy and Muslim Resistance in Senegal, 1880–1890."

61. Barry, *Senegambia,* 224–27.

62. Searing, *"God Alone,"* 51–55.

63. Searing, "Accommodation," 61.

64. Ibid., 67–68.

65. Barry, *Senegambia,* 234–37.

66. See Lucie Colvin, *Historical Dictionary of Senegal,* 29.

67. Ibid.

68. See Moitt, "Slavery," 36–38.

69. Signed by the chiefs of Waalo, Jolof, Giandol, and Ndiambur in 1890. Traité, February 15, 1890, Lamothe, ANS K12. Additional treaties were signed by the chiefs of Dimar, Toro, the independent Sereer states, Baol, Siin, and Saalum between February and September 1890. Traité, September 1, 1890, Clément-Thomas, ANS K12. Interestingly, the French explained their condemnation of slave trading by referring to chapters 24 and 43 of the Koran.

70. Klein, *Islam,* 152.

71. Seignaic à Ministre, May 9, 1884, St. Louis, ANSOM Sénégal I/71. Réponse de l'administrateur de Dagana, February 1, 1904, ANS K18.

72. See chapter 8. Réponse de l'administrateur de Dagana, February 1, 1904, ANS K18.

73. Réponse de l'administrateur de Dagana, February 1, 1904; réponse de l'administrateur de Kaolack (Lefilliatre), January 26, 1904; réponse de la Sergent de Ville, Foundiougne. All ANS K18.

74. Réponse de l'administrateur de Kaolack, January 26, 1904; réponse de l'administrateur de Podor. Both ANS K18.

75. Réponse de l'administrateur de Kaolack, January 26, 1904; réponse de la Sergent de Ville, Foundiougne. Both ANS K18.

76. Réponse de l'administrateur de Louga, January 25, 1904; réponse de l'administrateur de Tivouane, January 29, 1904; réponse de l'administrateur de Kaolack, January 26, 1904. All ANS K18.

77. Klein, *Slavery and Colonial Rule,* 64.

78. Rapport sur la captivité, Administrateur Poulet, 1905, ANS K17.

79. Traité, February 15, 1890, Lamothe, ANS K12.

80. Renault, "L'abolition," 37.

81. Barry, S*enegambia,* 214.

82. Réponse de l'administrateur de Kaolack, January 26, 1904, ANS K18.

83. Klein has noted, and I agree, that the data on freed slaves is missing large chunks of information and is thus somewhat unreliable. *Moniteur du Senegal,* April 24, 1883, No. 1423, ANS AE4.

84. Deherme, *L'esclavage en AOF,* 1906, ANS K25.

85. Klein, *Slavery and Colonial Rule,* 72.

86. Chef du Service Judiciaire à Vallon, October 11, 1882, St. Louis, ANSOM Sénégal XIV/15c.

87. Cases of Makadou Touré, Fatima Diop, and Seyni M'Djoro Gay, documented in Commandant de Podor à Pinet-Laprade, April 27, 1868, ANS 13G124.

88. Cases of Ma Goné, N'Codou Sal, Biram, and Yacine. Regarding abuse see case of Fatima Diop, ANS 13G124. Both documented in Commandant de Podor à Pinet-Laprade, April 27, 1868, ANS 13G124.

89. Cases of Mengueye N'Diaye, Mabigué Couta, and Diati Gueya, documented in Commandant de Podor à Pinet-Laprade, April 27, 1868, ANS 13G124.

90. Directeur des Affaires Politiques à Administrateur de la Cercle St. Louis, telegram, September 7, 1894, St. Louis, ANS K13.

91. Administrateur de Matam à Directeur des Affaires Politiques, December 1, 1894, Matam, ANS K13.

92. Archives de la Congregation de Saint-Esprit, Villejuif, France (hereafter ACSE), bulletins generaux XIV, No. 7, August 1887, 230. See the chapter on the Banamba exodus in Klein, *Slavery and Colonial Rule,* 159–79. Also Conklin, *Mission,* 98.

93. Klein, *Slavery and Colonial Rule,* 73.

94. Réponse de Sergent de Ville de Foundiougne, May 30, 1904; réponse de l'administrateur de Louga, January 25, 1904. Both, ANS K18.

95. Réponse de l'administrateur de Louga, January 25, 1904, ANS K18.

96. Searing, *"God Alone,"* 176.

97. André Picciola, *Missionaires en Afrique: L'Afrique occidentale de 1840 à 1940,* 57–58, 127.

98. ACSE, Annales Religieuses, missions catholiques XXI, 1889, 588.

99. Ibid.

100. *Journal Officiel de la République Française,* March 2, 1880. ACSE, missions catholiques XXI, 1889, 587; ANSOM Sénégal XIV/15d.

101. A topic subjected to a thorough treatment by Denise Bouche in *Les villages de liberté en Afrique noire française, 1887–1910.*

102. ACSE, Annales Religieuses, missions catholiques IV, 1871–1872, 696.

103. ACSE, bulletins generaux XII, No. 185?, May 1885, 67–68.

104. ACSE, bulletins generaux XIV, No. 7, August 1887, 230.

105. Ibid. See also réponse de Sergent de Ville de Foundiougne, May 30, 1904; réponse de Resident de Baol Occidental, January 10, 1904; réponse de l'administrateur à Tivaouane, January 29, 1904. All, ANS K18.

106. Searing, *"God Alone,"* xxxi, 186–88.

107. Klein, *Slavery and Colonial Rule,* 256.

108. Klein, *Slavery and Colonial Rule,* 200.

109. Searing, *"God Alone,"* 54.

110. Ibid., 75–103; also Robinson, *Paths of Accommodation,* 208–27

111. Searing, *"God Alone,"* 102.

112. Klein, *Slavery and Colonial Rule,* 200–2. Klein also gives evidence from three "predominantly servile villages."

113. Canard à Ministre, May 23, 1882, St. Louis, ANSOM Sénégal XIV/15e. The identities of the conferees are discussed in detail by Klein. *Slavery and Colonial Rule,* 73.

114. Deherme, *L'esclavage en AOF,* 1906, ANS K25.

115. Memoire, Serval, 1871–1888, ANSOM Sénégal II/6. Echenberg, *Colonial Conscripts,* 1–18.

116. If the administration's increasingly desperate attempts to recruit soldiers while large numbers of former slaves were still unemployed is anything to go by. See Klein, "Slavery and Emancipation," 176, for details on recruitment reforms.

117. Canard à Ministre, May 23, 1882, St. Louis, ANSOM Sénégal XIV/15e.

118. Ibid.

119. Canard à Ministre, March 20, 1882, St. Louis, ANS K12.

120. Canard à Ministre, May 23, 1882, St. Louis, ANSOM Sénégal XIV/15e.

121. Gouverneur de Martinique à Ministre, April 7, 1870, Fort-de-France, ANSOM Sénégal XIV/24; Hamelin à Chef du Division Navale, December 19, 1856, ANSOM Sénégal XIV/23b.

122. Renault, "L'abolition," 35–46.

123. Lamothe à Ministre, July 9, 1894, St. Louis, ANSOM Sénégal XIV/28.

124. Commissaire Général du Congo Française à Ministre, November 21, 1896, Libreville, ANSOM Sénégal XIV/28.

125. Phyllis Martin, *Leisure and Society in Colonial Brazzaville,* 25.

126. Maire Gorée à Lamothe, December 8, 1891, Gorée, ANS K31.

127. Note the experience of a team recruiting for Gabon along the Senegal River which was fired upon and forced to turn over a number of alleged "slave" recruits to local chiefs. Docteur Collomb à Seignac, May 7, 1885, Saldé, ANSOM Sénégal IV/68.

128. Delaleu à Directeur de l'Interieur, May 19, 1892, Dakar, ANS K31.

129. Martin, *Leisure and Society,* 25.

130. Le Délegué de l'Interieur [Dakar] à le Gouverneur, February 28, 1894, Gorée, ANS K31.

131. See chapter 9.

132. Valière à Commandant de Gorée, March 24, 1874, St. Louis, ANS K11.

133. Canard à Brière de l'Isle, December 1, 1877, Dakar, ANS 4B64.

134. Canard à Brière de l'Isle, July 1, 1878, Dakar, ANS 4B64. Brière de l'Isle à Ministre, May 8, 1880, St. Louis, ANSOM Sénégal XIV/15d.

135. Searing, *"God Alone,"* 150–51. Searing was referring specifically to Wolof societies in Kaajor and Baol.

136. Renault, "L'abolition," 81. Saint-Martin, *Le Sénégal,* 606. Becker, "Les effets," 91.

CHAPTER 8

1. Macdonald, *Gold Coast.* J. Ancelle, *Les explorations au Sénégal.*

2. Fairfield Report, 1874, PRO CO 879/33.

3. Smith and officers to committee, March 15, 1817, Cape Coast, PRO T70/36. See also van Dantzig, "Effects."

4. Searing, *West African Slavery,* 29–30. Marcson, "European-African Interaction," 19.

5. Roberts and Miers, "End of Slavery," 16.

6. ACSE, missions catholiques XXI, 1889, 588. Zimmerman, unaddressed, July 26, 1875, Abokobi, in Jenkins, "Abstracts."

7. Carnarvon to the Officer Administering the Government of the Gold Coast, August 21, 1875, London, PP 1875, LII (c. 1139). Deherme, *L'esclavage en AOF,* 1906, ANS K25.

8. Fairfield Report, 1874, PRO CO 879/33.

9. Carnarvon to the Officer Administering the Government of the Gold Coast, August 21, 1875, London, PP 1875, LII (c. 1139); Strahan to Carnarvon, September 19, 1874, PP 1875, LII (c. 1139).

10. What Renault calls "a compromise between trade and public opinion, without appearing to compromise." "L'abolition," 34.

11. Alongside "indigenous languages . . ., barbaric customary law, and 'feudal' chieftaincies." Conklin, *Mission,* 6.

12. Rapport sur la captivité, Administrateur Poulet, 1905, ANS K17.

13. Treatié Lamothe et Yamar of Oalo, the Bourba Djolof, Madiou of N'Guick-M'Pal, Magnang of Gandiolais, and the Bour N'Diambour, February 15, 1890, ANS K12.

14. Later governor and then minister of the navy.

15. Commandant de Podor à Pinet-Laprade, April 27, 1868, Podor, ANS 13G124.

16. Cases of Ndémé N'Dom, Sokna Koudia, Baye N'Diaye, Mengueye N'Diaye, and Mabiqué Couta, documented in Commandant de Podor à Pinet-Laprade, April 27, 1868, Podor, ANS 13G124. Commandant de Saldé à Pinet-Laprade, December 15, 1865, Saldé, ANS 3G148.

17. Cases of Fatima Guey, Sokna Souran, Juga N'Dieu, and Samba N'Diaye, documented in Commandant de Podor à Pinet-Laprade, April 27, 1868, Podor, ANS 13G124.

18. Cases of M'Baye N'Goree and Moussa Diop, documented in Commandant de Podor à Pinet-Laprade, April 27, 1868, Podor, ANS 13G124.

19. Moitt, "Slavery," 33.

20. Administrateur de Cercle Sin-Saloum à Directeur des Affaires Politiques, November 10, 1893, Thies, ANS K13.

21. Javoureux à Monsieur Couchard, lawyer, July 26, 1893, ANS K13.

22. Réponse de l'administrateur de Kaolack, January 26, 1904, Kaolack, ANS K18.

23. Robinson, Holy War, 245.

24. Moitt, "Slavery," 33.

25. Klein, "Slavery and Emancipation," 176.

26. Commandant de Dagana à Brière de l'Isle, no date 1880, Dagana, ANS K11. Gouverneur Soudan à Lamothe, January 25, 1894, Kayes, ANS K11. Commandant de Médine à Commandant de Kayes, August 24, 1898, Médine, ANS 15G116.

27. In Moitt, "Slavery," 37.

28. Barry, Senegambia, 13, 76, 231.

29. Commandant de Dagana à Brière de l'Isle, no date 1880, Dagana, ANS K11.

30. Ibid. Chef du Service Judiciaire à Canard, March 18, 1882, St. Louis, ANS K12.

31. Roume à Secretaire-Generale, December 3, 1903, n.p., ANS K27.

32. Moitt, "Slavery," 34.

33. Cases of Sayor Touré and Fatima Diop, documented in Commandant de Podor à Pinet-Laprade, April 27, 1868, Podor, ANS 13G124. Vallon à Ministre, March 20, 1882, St. Louis, encl. 1, ANSOM Sénégal XIV/15e.

34. Chef du Service Judiciaire à Canard, March 18, 1882, St. Louis, ANS K12.

35. Rapport de l'administrateur de Cercle de St. Louis au Directeur des Affaires Politiques, March 20, 1894, St. Louis, ANS K13.

36. Réponse de l'adminstrateur de Louga, January 25, 1904, Louga, ANS K18.

37. Kea, Settlements, 197–201.

38. Timothy Weiskel, French Colonial Rule and the Baule Peoples: Resistance and Collaboration, 1889–1911.

39. J. Muller, June 10, 1865, Christianborg, BMS D-1.17; J. Heck, November 1, 1862, Odumase, BMS D-1.13b. Freeling to Minister, January 30, 1877, Cape Coast, PRO CO 96/120. Griffith to Minister, February 24, 1892, Accra, encl. 3 in Waldron to Colonial Secretary, October 20, 1891, Ada, PRO CO 96/222.

40. For example, *Regina v. Awah,* Accra Divisional Court, January 12, 1884, NAG SCT 2/5/1. *Kasanah v. Quissa Pome Cudjo,* Accra District Court, July 11, 1889, NAG SCT 17/5/8. *Regina v. Dafee,* Cape Coast Judicial Assessors Court, March 10, 1875, NAG SCT 5/4/15.

41. For example, *Regina v. Tuitalaboo,* Accra District Court, October 5, 1881, NAG SCT 2/5/1.

42. *Regina v. Timbuctoo,* Accra Divisional Court, October 5, 1881, NAG SCT 2/5/1.

43. Richard Rathbone, "Resistance to Enslavement in West Africa."

44. Marion Johnson, *Salaga Papers,* vol. 1.

45. T. Edward Bowdich, *Mission from Cape Coast Castle to Ashantee,* 171, 177, 483.

46. Wilks, *Asante,* 279–82, 510–11. Excerpts from J. H. Glover, contribution to *Proceedings of the Royal Geographical Society,* 1874, in *Salaga Papers,* ed. Johnson.

47. Report on Gouldsbury's journey into the interior of the Gold Coast, March 27, 1876, Accra, encl. 1 in Strahan to Minister, April 30, 1876, PRO CO 96/119.

48. Excerpts from M. J. Bonnat, *Liverpool Mercury,* June 12, 1876, in *Salaga Papers,* ed. Johnson, 1:34. More on this later. Excerpts from R. Lonsdale, *Affairs of the Gold Coast, 1882,* in *Salaga Papers,* ed. Johnson. Wilks, *Asante,* 282.

49. No author, excerpts from *Proceedings of the Royal Geographical Society,* London, June 1884, summary of the visits of Asante and Opoku to Salaga, 1877, in *Salaga Papers,* ed. Johnson.

50. Johnson identifies these routes in his own analysis of the documents he collected ("Slaves of Salaga," 341–62).

51. Excerpts from L. G. Binger, *From the Niger to the Gulf of Guinea,* Paris, 1892, in *Salaga Papers,* ed. Johnson. Excerpts from C. François, *Mitteilungen aus den deutschen Shutzgebieten,* Berlin, 1888, in *Salaga Papers,* ed. Johnson, 1:18.

52. Excerpts from H. Klose, *Togo unter deutscher Flagge: Reisebilder und Betrachtungen,* Berlin, 1899, in *Salaga Papers,* ed. Johnson.

53. François in *Salaga Papers,* ed. Johnson.

54. Johnson, "Slaves of Salaga," 347–48.

55. Klose in *Salaga Papers,* ed. Johnson. Excerpts from Theophil Opoku, "An African Pastor's Preaching Journey through the Lands of the Upper Volta," Evangelisches Missions — Magazin, Basel, 1885, in *Salaga Papers,* ed. Johnson.

56. Firminger to Colonial Office, April 30, 1889, West Kensington, NAG ADM 1/1/88.

57. *Regina v. Aseday,* Accra District Court, October 5, 1887, NAG SCT 17/5/6. Johnson, however, agrees that by the 1890s "most of the slaves passing through the Salaga market were 'Grunshi.'" "Slaves of Salaga," 347.

58. Jeff Holden, "The Zabarima Conquest of North-West Ghana."

59. Ibid., 60, 62.

60. Der, *Slave Trade,* 20–23. The Zabarima were defeated by a French-Amariya force in September 1896 and finally broken by a British column in February 1897.

61. *Regina v. Ahinaguah,* Cape Coast Judicial Assessors Court, December 14, 1875, NAG SCT 5/4/17. Hodgson to Minister, January 29, 1898, Accra, District Commissioner Cowie, Cape Coast, PRO CO 96/311. *Sgt. Mjr. Davidson v. Qwah Aryar,* Accra District Court, January 14, 1887, NAG SCT 17/5/6.

62. Wilks, *Asante,* 295. Binger, in *Salaga Papers,* ed. Johnson.

63. Der, *Slave Trade,* 25.

64. For example, *Regina v. Appeah Coomah,* Cape Coast Judicial Assessors Court, April 6, 1876, NAG SCT 5/4/18, includes testimony that two to three thousand slaves were transported to Asante from Bokum in just one of the many convoys prior to 1873.

65. *Regina v. Dafee,* Cape Coast Judicial Assessors Court, March 10, 1875, NAG SCT 5/4/15. *Regina v. Kofi Tando,* Cape Coast Judicial Assessors Court, December 2, 1876, NAG SCT 5/4/19.

66. *Regina v. Adotay,* Accra Divisional Court, November 12, 1881, NAG SCT 2/5/1.

67. Hodgson to Minister, January 29, 1898, Accra, District Commissioner Thompson, Dixcove and Chama, PRO CO 96/311.

68. Hodgson to Minister, January 29, 1898, Accra, District Commissioner Cowie, Cape Coast, PRO CO 96/311. My emphasis.

69. Weiskel, *French Colonial Rule,* 87–89.

70. Excerpts from dispatch from Martin Gosselin, October 8, 1896, Berlin, in *Salaga Papers,* ed. Johnson. Johnson also makes this argument and cites both Firminger's report and Basel Mission reports from 1881 and 1893. See "Slaves of Salaga," 353. *Regina v. Agbochie,* Accra Divisional Court, August 5, 1885, NAG SCT 2/5/2; *Regina v. Narter, Kudaya, Menty, and Dogati,* Accra Divisonal Court, July 16, 1894, NAG SCT 2/5/10.

71. For example, *Regina v. Tarro,* Accra District Court, September 30, 1891, NAG SCT 17/5/12; *Regina v. Tetteh,* Accra District Court, November 8, 1889, NAG SCT 17/5/9; *Regina v. Byowra,* Accra District Court, March 24, 1890, NAG SCT 17/5/9.

72. *Regina v. Odouku and David,* Accra Divisional Court, June 9, 1880, NAG SCT 2/5/1. A somewhat similar case is *Regina v. Maikie,* Accra District Court, March 6, 1890, NAG SCT 17/5/9.

73. For example, *Regina v. Giwah,* Accra District Court, October 21, 1891, NAG SCT 17/5/12.

74. Excerpts from E. Kling, *Mitteilungen aus den deutschen Schutzgebieten,* Berlin, 1893, visit to Salaga, 1892, in *Salaga Papers,* ed. Johnson.

75. Klose in *Salaga Papers,* ed. Johnson.

76. *Regina v. Timbuctoo,* Accra Divisional Court, October 5, 1881, NAG SCT 2/5/1.

77. *Regina v. Adesay,* Accra District Court, October 5, 1887, NAG SCT 17/5/6.

78. *Regina v. Coffi Nelsore,* Accra District Court, April 21, 1890, SCT 17/5/9.

79. Ministre à Canard, January 31, 1882, Paris, ANS K12.

80. Moitt, "Slavery," 37.

81. Griffith to Minister, June 14, 1888, Accra, NAG ADM 12/3/2.

82. District courts opened in Accra in 1882 (NAG SCT 17/5/1), Cape Coast in 1887 (NAG SCT 23/5/1), and most other districts in 1888 (NAG SCT 2/10/1).

83. Freeling to Minister, January 30, 1877, Cape Coast, PRO CO 96/120.

84. District Commissioner McMunn to Colonial Secretary, February 5, 1890, Accra; District Commissioner Redwar-Hayes to First Assistant Colonial Secretary, August 27, 1889, Saltpond; District Commissioner Cole to Colonial Secretary, August 7, 1889, Ada. All, PRO CO 96/208.

85. Rapport sur la captivité, Administrateur Poulet, 1905, ANS K17; Ministre à Servatius, March 31, 1883, Paris, ANS K12.

86. Cases of May 1, 1880, and November 1, 1881, enclosed in Chef du Service Judiciare à Canard, March 18, 1882, St. Louis, ANS K12.

87. Chef du Service Judiciare à Canard, March 18, 1882, St. Louis, ANS K12.

88. Klein, *Slavery and Colonial Rule*, 96.

89. An original copy of the treaty is held in ANS K12.

90. Deherme, *L'esclavage en AOF*, 1906, ANS K25.

91. Firminger to Colonial Office, April 30, 1889, West Kensington, NAG ADM 1/1/88.

92. Hodgson to Minister, February 17, 1890, Accra, NAG ADM 13/3/2.

93. Brandford Griffith to Minister, February 12, 1890, n.p., in *Salaga Papers*, ed. Johnson.

94. Aborigines' Protection Society, August 20, 1890, n.p., PP 1890–91, LVII (c. 6354). My emphasis.

95. Griffith to Knutsford, January 26, 1891, Accra, PRO CO 96/212.

96. NAG SCT 17/5/8 and 17/5/9.

97. For example, *Regina v. Adahali, Abblah, Koo & Mamai*, Accra District Court, October 21, 1889, NAG SCT 17/5/8.

98. Reply of Governor Griffith and Peregrine to the Aborigines' Protection Society, January 26, 1891, PP 1890–91, LVII (c. 6354).

99. Minister to Griffith, January 29, 1892, London, NAG ADM 1/1/96.

100. Strahan to Carnarvon, December 28, 1874, encl. 1, Gold Coast Slave Dealing Abolition Act, Article 7, PP 1875, LII (c. 1139). NAG SCT 5/4/15–5/4/19, 1874–1876.

101. *Regina v. Emmanuel Narter, Gotfred Kudaya, Timothy Menty, and Kulch Dogati*, Accra Supreme/Divisional Court, July 16, 1894, NAG SCT 2/5/10.

102. Ordinance 12 of 1892, Title XXIX, Section 439, "Slave Dealing," NAG ADM 4/1/16. *Regina v. Akpebley*, Accra Supreme/Divisonal Court, July 6, 1899, NAG SCT 2/5/13.

103. Plus four cases of pawning incorrectly identified as slave dealing, NAG SCT.

104. Dumett and Johnson, "Britain," 82.

105. District Commissioner Williams to Colonial Secretary, August 19, 1889, Pram Pram; District Commissioner Heron to Colonial Secretary, August 2, 1889, Axim. Both, PRO CO 96/208. Hodgson to Minister, January 29, 1898, Accra, District Commissioner Holmes, Adda, PRO CO 96/311.

106. Reports of District Commissioner Edlin, Accra, and Commissioner Kitson, Accra, enclosed in Hodgson to Minister, January 29, 1898, PRO CO 96/311.

107. Johnson, "Slaves of Salaga," 361.

108. ANS Bulletin Administratif du Sénégal, April 1892—*Décret du président de la république, February 12, 1891*, Paris.

109. Sous Secrétaire d'Etat à Lamothe, April 13, 1892, Paris, ANS 1B196.

110. Deherme, *L'esclavage en AOF*, 1906, ANS K25.

111. Traité, December 12, 1892, ANS K12.

112. Administrateur de Thiés à Directeur des Affaires Politiques, July 11, 1893, Thiés, ANS K12.

113. Administrateur de Dagana à Directeur des Affaires Politiques, November 21, 1894, Dagana, ANS K13. Klein, *Slavery and Colonial Rule*, 98.

114. For example, Roume à Secretaire-Generale, December 3, 1903, n.p., ANS K27.

115. Searing, *"God Alone,"* 155.

116. Javoureux à Monsieur Couchard, lawyer, July 26, 1893, ANS K13.

117. Klein, *Slavery and Colonial Rule,* 98. Also "Servitude," 354.

118. Certainly, this is so for Sall. Searing, "Accommodation," 155.

119. Searing chooses 1895 as a date for the "'effective' ending of the slave trade to the Wolof states," rather arbitrarily and unnecessarily, I feel. Searing, *"God Alone,"* 159.

CONCLUSIONS

1. Miers and Roberts, eds., *End of Slavery.*

2. Miers and Klein, introduction to *Slavery and Colonial Rule,* 4.

3. Kopytoff, "Cultural Context," 488–94.

4. Many of these are based on Miers and Roberts's excellent introductory chapter to *End of Slavery,* 19–27.

5. Kopytoff, "Cultural Context," 499.

6. Quoted in E. Ann McDougall, "A Topsy-Turvy World: Slaves and Freed Slaves in the Mauritanian Adrar, 1910–1950," 362.

7. See Klein, *Slavery and Colonial Rule,* 131–37. Conklin, *Mission,* 99–100.

8. Richard Roberts, "The End of Slavery in the French Soudan, 1905–1914."

9. Klein, *Slavery and Colonial Rule,* 198–202.

10. Dumett and Johnson, "Britain," 95–100.

Bibliography

Secondary Materials

Modern Sources   .

Addo-Fening, Robert. *Akyem Abuakwa 1700–1943, from Ofori Panin to Sir Ofori Atta.* Trondheim: Norwegian University of Science and Technology, 1997.

Adjaye, Joseph. "Asantehene Agyeman Prempe I, Asante History, and the Historian." *History in Africa* 17 (1990): 1–29.

Agbodeka, Francis. *African Politics and British Policy in the Gold Coast, 1868–1900.* Evanston: Northwestern University Press, 1971.

Ajayi, J. F. A., and Michael Crowder, eds. *History of West Africa.* 2 vols. Harlow U.K.: Longman, 1987.

Akotia, Pino. "Judicial and Legal Records in the National Archives of Ghana, Accra." *History in Africa* 20 (1993): 351–67.

Akurang-Parry, Kwabena Opare. "The Administration of the Abolition Laws, African Response, and Post-proclamation Slavery in the Gold Coast, 1874–1940." *Slavery and Abolition* 19 (1998): 149–66.

———. "Slavery and Abolition in the Gold Coast: Colonial Modes of Emancipation and African Initiatives." *Ghana Studies* 1 (1998): 11–34.

Alpern, Stanley. "What Africans Got for Their Slaves: A Master List of European Trade Goods." *History in Africa* 22 (1995): 5–43.

Anstey, Roger. "The Pattern of British Abolitionism in the Eighteenth and Nineteenth Centuries." In *Anti-slavery, Religion, and Reform: Essays in Memory of Roger Anstey,* edited by Christine Bolt and Seymour Drescher. Folkestone, U.K.: W. Dawson, 1980.

———. "Religion and British Slave Emancipation." In *The Abolition of the Atlantic Slave Trade,* edited by David Eltis and James Walvin. Madison: University of Wisconsin Press, 1981.

Austen, Ralph. *African Economic History.* London: James Currey/Heinemann, 1987.

Austin, Gareth. "The Emergence of Capitalist Relations in South Asante Cocoa-Farming, c. 1916–1933." *Journal of African History* 28 (1987): 259–79.

———. "Human Pawning in Asante, 1800–1940: Markets and Coercion, Gender and Cocoa." In *Pawnship in Africa,* edited by Toyin Falola and Paul Lovejoy. Boulder: Westview Press, 1994.

Barrows, Leland. "General Faidherbe, the Maurel and Prom Company, and French Expansion in Senegal." Ph.D. diss., University of California, Los Angeles, 1974.

Barry, Boubacar. "Le royaume de Wâlo du traité de Ngio en 1819 à la conquête en 1855." *Bulletin de l'Institut Fondamental d'Afrique Noire* 31 (1969): 339–444.

———. *Le royaume du Waalo: Le Sénégal avant la conquête.* Paris: Françoise Maspero, 1972.

———. *Senegambia and the Atlantic Slave Trade.* Cambridge: Cambridge University Press, 1998.

Becker, Charles. "Le Sénégambie à l'epoque de la traite des esclaves. A propos d'un ouvrage récent de Philip D. Curtin: 'Economic Change in Senegambia in the Era of the Slave Trade.'" *Revue française d'histoire d'outre-mer* 64 (1977): 203–24.

———. "Les effets démographiques de la traite des esclaves en Sénégambie: Esquisse d'une histoire des peuplements de XVIIe à la fin du XIXe siecle." In *De la traite à l'esclavage,* edited by Serge Daget. Paris: Société française d'histoire d'outre-mer, 1988.

Becker, Charles, and Victor Martin. "Kayor and Baol: Senegalese Kingdoms and the Slave Trade in the Eighteenth Century." In *Forced Migration: The Impact of the Export Slave Trade on African Societies,* edited by Joseph Inikori. London: Hutchinson, 1982.

Behrendt, Stephen. "The Journal of an African Slaver, 1789–1792, and the Gold Coast Slave Trade of William Collow." *History in Africa* 22 (1995): 61–71.

———. "The Annual Volume and Regional Distribution of the British Slave Trade, 1780–1807." *Journal of African History* 38 (1997): 187–212.

———. "Markets, Transaction Cycles, and Profits: Merchant Decision Making in the British Slave Trade." *William and Mary Quarterly* 58, no. 1 (2001): 171–204.

Benoist, Joseph. "Typologie et fonctions des captiveries goréenes." In *Gorée et l'esclavage: Actes du séminaire sur "Gorée dans la traite atlantique: Mythes et réalités,"* edited by Djibril Samb. Dakar: IFAN Cheik Anta Diop, 1997.

Biondi, Jean-Pierre. *Saint-Louis du Sénégal: Mémoires d'un métissage.* Paris: Editions Denoël, 1987.

Bouche, Denise. *Les villages de liberté en Afrique noire française, 1887–1910.* Paris: Mouton, 1968.

Bowman, Joye. *Ominous Transition: Commerce and Colonial Expansion in the Senegambia and Guinea, 1857–1919.* Aldershot, U.K.: Avebury, 1996.

Brooks, George E. "Peanuts and Colonialism: Consequences of the Commercialization of Peanuts in West Africa, 1830–1870." *Journal of African History* 16 (1975): 29–54.

Casely-Hayford, Augustus. "Prosopographical Approaches to Fante History." *History in Africa* 18 (1991): 49–66.

Charles, Eunice A. "French West African Policy and Muslim Resistance in Senegal,

1880–1890." Paper presented at the sixteenth annual meeting of the African Studies Association, Syracuse, October 31–November 3, 1973.

————. *Precolonial Senegal: The Jolof Kingdom, 1800 to 1890.* Boston: Boston University Press, 1977.

Clarence-Smith, William Gervase. "Review of Patrick Manning, *Slavery and African Life: Occidental, Oriental, and African Slave Trades.*" *International Journal of African Historical Studies* 26 (1993): 176–78.

Clayton, Anthony, and David Killingray. *Khaki and Blue: Military and Police in British Colonial Africa.* Athens: Ohio University Press, 1989.

Colvin, Lucie. *Historical Dictionary of Senegal.* London: Scarecrow Press, 1981.

Conklin, Alice L. *A Mission to Civilize: The Republican Idea of Empire in France and West Africa, 1895–1930.* Palo Alto, Calif.: Stanford University Press, 1997.

Coomb, Douglas. *The Gold Coast, Britain, and the Netherlands, 1850–1874.* London: Oxford University Press, 1963.

Cooper, Frederick. *Plantation Slavery on the East Coast of Africa.* New Haven: Yale University Press, 1977.

————. "The Dialectics of Decolonization: Nationalism and Labor Movements in Postwar French Africa." In *Tensions of Empire: Colonial Cultures in a Bourgeois World,* edited by Frederick Cooper and Ann Laura Stoler. Berkeley: University of California Press, 1997.

Cooper, Frederick, Thomas Holt, and James Thompson. *Explorations of Race, Labor, and Citizenship in Post-emancipation Societies.* Chapel Hill: University of North Carolina Press, 2000.

Cruise O'Brien, Donal. "Review of Martin Klein, *Islam and Imperialism in Senegal: Sine-Saloum, 1887–1910.*" *Journal of African History* 10 (1969): 325–26.

Cruise O'Brien, Rita. *White Society in Black Africa: The French of Senegal.* London: Faber and Faber, 1972.

Curtin, Philip. *Economic Change in Precolonial Africa: Senegambia in the Era of the Slave Trade.* Madison: University of Wisconsin Press, 1975.

————. "The Abolition of the Slave Trade from Senegambia." In *The Abolition of the Atlantic Slave Trade,* edited by David Eltis and James Walvin. Madison: University of Wisconsin Press, 1981.

Daget, Serge. "Le trafic negrier illegal français de 1814 à 1850: Historiographe et source." *Annales de l'Université d'Abidjan* 3 (1975): 23–53.

————. "France, Suppression of the Illegal Trade, and England, 1817–1850." In *The Abolition of the Atlantic Slave Trade,* edited by David Eltis and James Walvin. Madison: University of Wisconsin Press, 1981.

————, ed. *De la traite à l'esclavage.* Actes du colloque international sur la traite des noires, Nantes, 1985. 2 Vols. Paris: Société française d'histoire d'outre-mer, 1988.

Delcourt, Jean. *Gorée: Six siècles d'histoire.* Dakar: Editions Clairafrique, 1984.

Denzer, LaRay. "Abolition and Reform in West Africa." In *History of West Africa,* edited by J. F. A. Ajayi and Michael Crowder. Harlow, U.K.: Longman, 1987.

Der, Benedict. *The Slave Trade in Northern Ghana.* Accra: Woeli Publishers, 1998.

Dickson, Kwamina. *A Historical Geography of Ghana.* Cambridge: Cambridge University Press, 1969.

Dickson, Kwamina, and George Benneh. *A New Geography of Ghana.* Harlow, U.K.: Longman, 1988.

Dumett, Raymond. "Pressure Groups, Bureaucracy, and the Decision-Making Process: The Case of Slavery, Abolition, and Colonial Expansion in the Gold Coast, 1874." *Journal of Imperial and Commonwealth History* 9 (1981): 193–215.

————. *El Dorado in West Africa: The Gold Coast Mining Frontier, African Labour, and Colonial Capitalism in the Gold Coast, 1873–1900.* Oxford: James Currey, 1998.

Dumett, Raymond, and Marion Johnson. "Britain and the Suppression of Slavery in the Gold Coast Colony, Ashanti, and the Northern Territories." In *The End of Slavery in Africa,* edited by Suzanne Miers and Richard Roberts. Madison: University of Wisconsin Press, 1988.

Echenberg, Myron. *Colonial Conscripts: The Tirailleurs Sénégalais in French West Africa, 1857–1960.* Portsmouth: Heinemann, 1991.

Eltis, David. *Economic Growth and the Ending of the Transatlantic Slave Trade.* Oxford: Oxford University Press, 1987.

————. "The African Role in the Ending of the Slave Trade." In *De la traite à l'esclavage,* edited by Serge Daget. Paris: Société française d'histoire d'outre-mer, 1988.

Eltis, David, and James Walvin, eds. *The Abolition of the Atlantic Slave Trade.* Madison: University of Wisconsin Press, 1981.

Engerman, Stanley. "Some Implications of the Abolition of the Slave Trade." In *The Abolition of the Atlantic Slave Trade,* edited by David Eltis and James Walvin. Madison: University of Wisconsin Press, 1981.

Fage, J. D. "Slavery and the Slave Trade in the Context of West African History." *Journal of African History* 10 (1969): 393–404.

Falola, Toyin, and Paul Lovejoy, eds. *Pawnship in Africa: Debt Bondage in Historical Perspective.* Boulder: Westview Press, 1994.

Feinberg, Harvey. "Elmina, Ghana: A History of Its Development and Relationship with the Dutch in the Eighteenth Century." Ph.D. diss., Boston University, 1969.

Field, Margaret. *Akim-Kotoku, An Oman of the Gold Coast.* London: Crown Agents for the Colonies, 1948.

Friedman, J., and M. J. Rowlands, eds. *The Evolution of Social Systems.* London: Duckworth, 1977.

Galenson, David. *Traders, Planters, and Slavers.* Cambridge: Cambridge University Press, 1986.

Geggus, David. "Sex Ratio, Age, and Ethnicity in the Atlantic Slave Trade: Data from French Shipping and Plantation Records." *Journal of African History* 30 (1989): 23–44.

Gellar, Sheldon. *Senegal: An African Nation between Islam and the West.* Boulder: Westview Press, 1995.

Getz, Trevor. "A 'Somewhat Firm Policy': The Role of the Gold Coast Judiciary in Implementing Slave Emancipation, 1874–1900." *Ghana Studies Journal* 2 (1999): 97–117.

————. "The Case for Africans: The Role of Slaves and Masters in Emancipation on the Gold Coast, 1874–2000." *Slavery and Abolition* 21 (2000): 128–45.

Gocking, Roger. "Competing Systems of Inheritance before the British Courts of the

Gold Coast Colony." *International Journal of African Historical Studies* 25 (1990): 601–18.

————. "British Justice and the Native Tribunals of the Southern Gold Coast Colony." *Journal of African History* 34 (1993): 93–113.

————. *Facing Two Ways: Ghana's Coastal Communities under Colonial Rule.* Lanham, Md.: University Press of America, 1999.

Grace, John. *Domestic Slavery in West Africa.* London: Frederick Muller, 1975.

Guèye, M'Baye. "Le fin de l'esclavage à Saint-Louis et à Gorée en 1848." *Bulletin de l'Institut Fondamental d'Afrique Noire* 28 (1966): 637–56.

Haenger, Peter. *Slaves and Slave Holders on the Gold Coast: Towards an Understanding of Social Bondage in West Africa.* Basel: P. Schlettwein, 2000.

Hanson, John. *Migration, Jihad, and Muslim Authority in West Africa: The Futanke Colonies in Karta.* Bloomington: Indiana University Press, 1996.

Hardy, Georges. *La mise en valeur du Sénégal de 1817 à 1854.* Paris: E. Larose, 1921.

Hargreaves, J. D. "Review of Philip Curtin's *Economic Change in Precolonial Africa.*" *International Journal of African Historical Studies* 8 (1975): 724–26.

Harms, Robert. "Slave Systems in Africa." *History in Africa* 3 (1976): 327–36.

Henige, David. "Two Sources for the History of the Guinea Coast, 1680–1722." *International Journal of African Historical Studies* 5 (1972): 272–75.

————. "Akan Stool Succession under Colonial Rule: Continuity or Change?" *Journal of African History* 16 (1975): 285–301.

————. "Measuring the Immeasurable: The Atlantic Slave Trade, West African Population, and the Phyrronian Critic." *Journal of African History* 27 (1986): 295–313.

Hess, Robert, and Dalvan Coger. *A Bibliography of Primary Sources for Nineteenth Century Tropical Africa as Recorded by Explorers, Missionaries, Traders, Travellers, Administrators, Military Men, Adventurers, and Others.* Palo Alto, Calif.: Hoover Institute Press, 1974.

Hill, Polly. *The Gold Coast Cocoa Farmer.* London: Oxford University Press, 1956.

Hogendron, Jan, and Henry Gemery. "Abolition and Its Impact on Monies Imported to West Africa." In *The Abolition of the Atlantic Slave Trade,* edited by David Eltis and James Walvin. Madison: University of Wisconsin, 1981.

Holden, Jeff. "The Zabarima Conquest of North-West Ghana." *Transactions of the Historical Society of Ghana* 8 (1965): 60–86.

Idowu, H. Olu. "Assimilation in Nineteenth-Century Senegal." *Bulletin de l'Institut Fondamental d'Afrique Noire* 30 (1968): 1422–47.

————. "The Establishment of Protectorate Administration in Senegal, 1890–1904." *Journal of the Historical Society of Nigeria* 4 (1968): 247–68.

Inikori, Joseph, ed. *Forced Migration: The Impact of the Export Slave Trade on African Societies.* London: Hutchinson, 1982.

L'Institut Géographique National. *Atlas national du Sénégal.* Paris, 1977.

Irwin, Graham. "Precolonial African Diplomacy: The Example of Asante." *International Journal of African Historical Studies* 8 (1975): 81–96.

Jenkins, Paul, ed. "Abstracts from the Gold Coast Correspondence of the Basel Mission." Unpublished.

Jennings, Lawrence. "Slave Trade Repression and the Abolition of French Slavery." In

De la traite à l'esclavage, edited by Serge Daget. Paris: Société française d'histoire d'outre-mer, 1988.

Johnson, Marion. "The Ounce in Eighteenth-Century West African Trade." *Journal of African History* 7 (1966): 197–214.

———. "The Slaves of Salaga." *Journal of African History* 27 (1986): 341–62.

———. *Salaga Papers.* Vol. 1 of 2. Legon, Ghana: Institute of African Studies, no date.

Jones, Adam. "Semper Aliquid Veteris: Printed Sources for the History of the Ivory and Gold Coasts, 1500–1750." *Journal of African History* 27 (1986): 295–313.

———. "Female Slave-Owners on the Gold Coast: Just a Matter of Money?" In *Slave Cultures and Cultures of Slavery,* edited by Stephan Palmié. Knoxville: University of Tennessee Press, 1995.

Kafe, Joseph Kofi. *Ghana: An Annotated Bibliography of Academic Theses, 1920–1970.* Boston: G. K. Hall and Co., 1973.

Kaplow, Susan. "African Merchants of the Nineteenth-Century Gold Coast." Ph.D. diss., Columbia University, 1971.

Kea, Ray. *Settlements, Trade, and Polities in the Seventeenth-Century Gold Coast.* Baltimore: Johns Hopkins University Press, 1982.

———. "Plantations and Labour in the South-East Gold Coast from the Late Eighteenth to the Mid-nineteenth Century." In *From Slave Trade to Legitimate Commerce: The Commercial Transition in Nineteenth-Century West Africa,* edited by Robin Law. Cambridge: Cambridge University Press, 1995.

———. "City-State Culture on the Gold Coast: The Fante City-State Federation in the Seventeenth and Eighteenth Centuries." In *A Comparative Study of Thirty City-State Cultures,* edited by Mogens Hansen. Copenhagen: The Royal Danish Academy of Sciences and Letters, 2000.

Kimble, David. *A Political History of Ghana: The Rise of Gold Coast Nationalism, 1850–1928.* Oxford: Clarendon Press, 1963.

Klein, A. Norman. "West African Unfree Labor before and after the Rise of the Atlantic Slave Trade." In *Slavery in the New World: A Reader in Comparative History,* edited by Laura Foner and Eugene D. Genovese. Englewood Cliffs: Prentice-Hall, 1969.

Klein, Martin. *Islam and Imperialism in Senegal.* Edinburgh: Edinburgh University Press, 1968.

———. "Women in Slavery in the Western Sudan." In *Women and Slavery in Africa,* edited by Claire Robertson and Martin Klein. Madison: University of Wisconsin Press, 1983.

———. "Servitude among the Wolof and Sereer of Senegambia." In *The End of Slavery in Africa,* edited by Suzanne Miers and Richard Roberts. Madison: University of Wisconsin Press, 1988.

———. "Slave Resistance and Slave Emancipation in Coastal Guinea." In *The End of Slavery in Africa,* edited by in Suzanne Miers and Richard Roberts. Madison: University of Wisconsin Press, 1988.

———. "Slavery and Emancipation in French West Africa." In *Breaking the Chains: Slavery, Bondage, and Emancipation in Modern Africa and Asia,* edited by Martin Klein. Madison: University of Wisconsin Press, 1993.

————. *Slavery and Colonial Rule in French West Africa*. Cambridge: Cambridge University Press, 1998.

————, ed. *Breaking the Chains: Slavery, Bondage, and Emancipation in Modern Africa and Asia*. Madison: University of Wisconsin Press, 1993.

Kopytoff, Igor. "The Cultural Context of African Abolition." In *The End of Slavery in Africa*, edited by in Suzanne Miers and Richard Roberts. Madison: University of Wisconsin Press, 1988.

Kopytoff, Igor, and Suzanne Miers, eds. *Slavery in Africa: Historical and Anthropological Perspectives*. Madison: University of Wisconsin Press, 1977.

Kwamena-Poh, M. A. *Government and Politics in the Akuapem State, 1730–1850*. London: Longman Group, 1973.

LaTorre, Joseph. "Wealth Surpasses Everything: An Economic History of Asante, 1750–1874." Ph.D. diss., University of California, Berkeley, 1978.

Law, Robin. "Horses, Firearms, and Political Power in Pre-colonial West Africa." *Past and Present* 72 (1976): 112–32.

————. *The Slave Coast of West Africa, 1550–1870: The Impact of the Atlantic Slave Trade on an African Society*. Oxford: Clarendon Press, 1991.

————, ed. *From Slave Trade to Legitimate Commerce: The Commercial Transition in Nineteenth-Century West Africa*. Cambridge: Cambridge University Press, 1995.

Lovejoy, Paul. *Transformations in Slavery*. Cambridge: Cambridge University Press, 1983.

————. "The Impact of the Atlantic Slave Trade on Africa: A Review of the Literature." *Journal of African History* 30 (1989): 365–94.

Lovejoy, Paul, and Jan Hogendorn. *Slow Death for Slavery: The Course of Abolition in Northern Nigeria, 1897–1936*. Cambridge: Cambridge University Press, 1993.

Lovejoy, Paul, and David Richardson. "The Initial 'Crisis of Adaptation': The Impact of British Abolition on the Atlantic Slave Trade in West Africa, 1808–1820. In *From Slave Trade to Legitimate Commerce: The Commercial Transition in Nineteenth-Century West Africa*, edited by Robin Law. Cambridge: Cambridge University Press, 1987.

————. "Competing Markets for Male and Female Slaves: Prices in the Interior of West Africa, 1780–1850." *International Journal of African Historical Studies* 27 (1995): 261–87.

Maïga, Mahamadou. *Le Bassin du fleuve Sénégal: De la traite négrière au développement sous régionale auto-centré*. Paris: L'Harmattan, 1995.

Manning, Patrick. "The Impact of Slave Trade Exports on the Population of the Western Coast of Africa, 1700–1850." In *De la traite à l'esclavage*, edited by Serge Daget. Paris: Société française d'histoire d'outre-mer, 1988.

————. *Slavery and African Life: Occidental, Oriental, and African Slave Trades*. Cambridge: Cambridge University Press, 1990.

————. *Slave Trade 1500–1800: Globalization of Forced Labour*. Aldershot, U.K.: Variorum, 1996.

Marcson, Michael. "European-African Interaction in the Precolonial Period: Saint Louis, Senegal, 1758–1854." Ph.D. diss., Princeton University, 1974.

Martin, Gaston. *Histoire de l'esclavage dans les colonies françaises*. Paris: Presses Universitaires de France, 1948.

Martin, Phyllis. *Leisure and Society in Colonial Brazzaville.* Cambridge: Cambridge University Press, 1995.

Mbodj, Mohamed. "The Abolition of Slavery in Senegal, 1820–1890: Crisis or the Rise of a New Entrepreneurial Class?" In *Breaking the Chains: Slavery, Bondage, and Emancipation in Modern Africa and Asia,* edited by Martin Klein. Madison: University of Wisconsin Press, 1993.

McCarthy, Mary. *Social Change and the Growth of British Power in the Gold Coast: The Fante States, 1807–1874.* Lanham, Md.: University Press of America, 1983.

McCaskie, T. C. *State and Society in Pre-colonial Asante.* Cambridge: Cambridge University Press, 1995.

McDougall, E. Ann. "A Topsy-Turvy World: Slaves and Freed Slaves in the Mauritanian Adrar, 1910–1950." In *The End of Slavery in Africa,* edited by Suzanne Miers and Richard Roberts. Madison: University of Wisconsin Press, 1988.

McSheffrey, Gerald. "Slavery, Indentured Servitude, Legitimate Trade, and the Impact of Abolition in the Gold Coast, 1874–1910: A Reappraisal." *Journal of African History* 24 (1983): 349–68.

Meillassoux, Claude. "The Role of Slavery in the Economic and Social History of Sahelo-Sudanic Africa." In *Forced Migration: The Impact of the Export Slave Trade on African Societies,* edited by Joseph Inikori. London: Hutchinson, 1982.

———. *The Anthropology of Slavery: The Womb of Iron and Gold.* Chicago: University of Chicago Press, 1992.

Metcalf, George. "A Microcosm of Why Africans Sold Slaves: Akan Consumption Patterns in the 1770s." *Journal of African History* 28 (1987): 377–94.

Metcalfe, G. E. *Maclean of the Gold Coast.* London: Oxford University Press, 1962.

———. *Great Britain and Ghana: Documents of Ghana History, 1807–1957.* London: Thomas Nelson and Sons, 1964.

Meyerowitz, Eva L. R. *The Early History of the Akan States of Ghana.* London: Red Candle Press, 1975.

Miers, Suzanne, and Martin Klein. "Introduction." In *Slavery and Colonial Rule in Africa,* edited by Suzanne Miers and Martin Klein. London: Frank Cass, 1999.

———, eds. *Slavery and Colonial Rule in Africa.* London: Frank Cass, 1999.

Miers, Suzanne, and Richard Roberts, eds. *The End of Slavery in Africa.* Madison: University of Wisconsin Press, 1988.

Moitt, Bernard. "Slavery and Emancipation in Senegal's Peanut Basin." *International Journal of African Historical Studies* 22 (1989): 27–50.

Nørregard, Georg. *Danish Settlements in West Africa, 1658–1850.* Boston: Boston University Press, 1966.

Oliver, Roland. "Review of Denise Bouche, *Les Villages de liberté en Afrique noire, 1887–1910.*" *Journal of African History* 10 (1969): 327–8.

———. *The African Experience.* New York: Icon Editions, 1991.

Ollennu, Nii, and Gordon Woodman. *Ollennu's Principles of Customary Land Law in Ghana.* Birmingham, U.K.: Cal Press, 1985.

Omosini, Olufemi. "The Gold Coast Land Question, 1894–1900: Some Issues Raised on West Africa's Economic Development." *International Journal of African Historical Studies* 5 (1972): 453–70.

Opare-Akurang, Kwabena. *See* Akurang-Parry, Opare.

Palmié, Stephan, ed. *Slave Cultures and Cultures of Slavery*. Knoxville: University of Tennessee Press, 1995.

Parker, John. "Ga State and Society in Early Colonial Accra, 1860s–1920s." Ph.D. diss., University of London–School of Oriental and African Studies, 1995.

———. *Making the Town: Ga State and Society in Early Colonial Accra*. Portsmouth: Heinemann, 2000.

Pasquier, Roger. "A propos de l'emancipation des esclaves au Sénégal en 1848. "*Revue français d'histoire d'outre-mer* 54 (1967): 188–208.

Patterson, Orlando. *Slavery and Social Death: A Comparative Study*. Cambridge: Harvard University Press, 1982.

Perbi, Akosua. "Domestic Slavery in Asante, 1800–1920." M.A. thesis, University of Ghana, Legon, 1978.

Picciola, André. *Missionaires en Afrique: L'Afrique occidentale de 1840 à 1940*. Paris: Denaël, 1987.

Priestley, Margaret. *West African Trade and Coast Society: A Family Study*. Oxford: Oxford University Press, 1969.

Rashid, Ismail. "'Do Dady nor Lef me Make dem Carry me': Slave Resistance and Emancipation in Sierra Leone, 1894–1928." *Slavery and Abolition* 19 (1998): 208–31.

Rathbone, Richard. *Murder and Politics in Colonial Ghana*. New Haven: Yale University Press, 1993.

———. "The Gold Coast, the Closing of the Atlantic Slave Trade, and Africans of the Diaspora." In *Slave Cultures and Cultures of Slavery*, edited by Stephan Palmié. Knoxville: University of Tennessee Press, 1995.

———. "Resistance to Enslavement in West Africa." In *Slave Trade 1500–1800: Globalization of Forced Labour,* edited by Patrick Manning. Aldershot, U.K.: Variorum, 1996.

Rattray, R. S. *Ashanti Law and Constitution*. London: Oxford University Press, 1929.

Reader, John. *Africa: A Biography of the Continent*. New York: Alfred A. Knopf, 1998.

Renault, François. "L'abolition de l'esclavage au Sénégal: L'attitude de l'administration française." *Revue française d'histoire d'outre-mer* 58 (1971): 5–80.

———. *Libération d'esclaves et nouvelle servitude*. Dakar: Les Nouvelles Editions Africaines, 1976.

Renault, François, and Serge Daget. *Les traites négrières en Afrique*. Paris: Editions Karthala, 1997.

Reynolds, Edward. *Trade and Economic Change on the Gold Coast, 1807–1874*. New York: Longman Group, 1974.

———. "Abolition and Economic Change on the Gold Coast." In *The Abolition of the Atlantic Slave Trade,* edited by David Eltis and James Walvin. Madison: University of Wisconsin Press, 1981.

———. *Stand the Storm: A History of the Atlantic Slave Trade*. London: Allison and Busby, 1985.

———. "The Gold Coast and Asante." In *History of West Africa,* edited by J. F. A. Ajayi and Michael Crowder. Harlow, U.K.: Longman Group, 1987.

———. "The Slave Trade, Slavery, and Economic Transformation of the Gold Coast in the Nineteenth Century." In *De la traite à l'esclavage,* edited by Serge Daget. Paris: Société française d'histoire d'outre-mer, 1988.

Richardson, David. "Slave Exports from West and West-Central Africa, 1700–1810:

New Estimates of Volume and Distribution." *Journal of African History* 30 (1989): 1–22.

Richardson, David, and David Eltis. "The 'Numbers Game' and Routes to Slavery." *Slavery and Abolition* 18 (1997): 1–15.

———. "West Africa and the Transatlantic Slave Trade: New Evidence of Long-Run Trends." *Slavery and Abolition* 18 (1997): 16–36.

Roberts, Richard. "The End of Slavery in the French Soudan, 1905–1914." In *The End of Slavery in Africa,* edited by Suzanne Miers and Richard Roberts. Madison: University of Wisconsin Press, 1988.

Roberts, Richard, and Suzanne Miers. "The End of Slavery in Africa." In *The End of Slavery in Africa,* edited by Suzanne Miers and Richard Roberts. Madison: University of Wisconsin Press, 1988.

Robertson, Alexander. *The Dynamics of Productive Relationships: African Sharer Contracts in Comparative Perspective.* Cambridge: Cambridge University Press, 1984.

Robertson, Claire. "Post Proclamation Slavery in Accra: A Female Affair?" In *The End of Slavery in Africa,* edited by Suzanne Miers and Richard Roberts. Madison: University of Wisconsin Press, 1988.

Robinson, David. *The Holy War of Umar Tal: The Western Sudan in the Mid-nineteenth Century.* London: Oxford University Press, 1985.

———. *Paths of Accommodation: Muslim Societies and French Colonial Authorities in Senegal and Mauritania, 1880–1920.* Athens: Ohio University Press, 2000.

Rodney, Walter. "African Slavery and Other Forms of Social Oppression on the Upper Guinea Coast in the Context of the Atlantic Slave Trade." *Journal of African History* 7 (1966): 431–43.

———. *How Europe Underdeveloped Africa.* London: Bogle-L'Ouverture Publications, 1972.

Saint-Martin, Yves-Jean. *Le Sénégal sous le Second Empire.* Paris: Editions Karthala, 1989.

Samb, Djibril, ed. *Gorée et l'esclavage: Actes du séminaire sur "Gorée dans la traite atlantique: Mythes et réalités."* Dakar: IFAN Cheik Anta Diop, 1997.

Sanders, James R. "The Political Development of the Fante in the Eighteenth and Nineteenth Centuries: A Study of a West African Merchant Society." Ph.D. diss., Northwestern University, 1980.

Sané, Ousmane. "La vie economique et sociale des Goréens entre 1817 et 1848." Ph.D. diss., Université de Dakar, 1978.

Searing, James F. "Accommodation and Resistance: Chiefs, Muslim Leaders, and Politicians in Colonial Senegal, 1890–1934." Ph.D. diss., Princeton University, 1985.

———. *West African Slavery and Atlantic Commerce: The Senegal River Valley, 1700–1860.* Cambridge: Cambridge University Press, 1993.

———. *"God Alone Is King": Islam and Emancipation in Senegal, the Wolof Kingdoms of Kajoor and Bawol, 1859–1914.* Portsmouth: Heinemann, 2002.

Sinou, Alain. *Comptoirs et villes coloniales du Sénégal: Saint-Louis, Gorée, Dakar.* Paris: Editions Karthala, 1993.

Sundiata, Ibrahim. *From Slaving to Neoslavery: The Bight of Biafra and Fernando Po in the Era of Abolition, 1827–1930.* Madison: University of Wisconsin Press, 1996.

Sutton, Inez. "Labour in Commercial Agriculture in Ghana in the Late Nineteenth and Early Twentieth Centuries." *Journal of African History* 24 (1983): 461–83.

Tamari, Tal. "The Development of Caste Systems in West Africa." *Journal of African History* 32 (1991): 221–50.

Thilmans, Guy. "Gorée, Saint-Louis, et les maisons d'esclaves (1786)." In *Gorée et l'esclavage: Actes du séminaire sur "Gorée dans la traite atlantique: Mythes et réalités,"* edited by Djibril Samb. Dakar: IFAN Cheik Anta Diop, 1997.

Thioub, Ibrahima, and Hamady Bocoum. "Gorée et les mémoires de la traite atlantique." In *Gorée et l'esclavage: Actes du séminaire sur "Gorée dans la traite atlantique: Mythes et réalités,"* edited by Djibril Samb. Dakar: IFAN Cheik Anta Diop, 1997.

Thorne, Susan. "The Conversion of Englishmen and the Conversion of the World Inseparable: Missionary Imperialism and the Language of Class in Early Industrial Britain." In *Tensions of Empire: Colonial Cultures in a Bourgeois World,* edited by Frederick Cooper and Ann Laura Stoler. Berkeley: University of California Press, 1997.

Thornton, John. "Sexual Demography: The Impact of the Slave Trade on Family Structure." In *Women and Slavery in Africa,* edited by Claire Robertson and Martin Klein. Madison: University of Wisconsin Press, 1983.

———. *Africa and Africans in the Making of the Atlantic World, 1400–1800.* Cambridge: Cambridge University Press, 1992.

van Dantzig, Albert. "Effects of the Atlantic Slave Trade on Some West African Societies." In *Forced Migration: The Impact of the Export Slave Trade on African Societies,* edited by Joseph Inikori. London: Hutchinson, 1982.

———. "Elmina, Asante, and the Abolitionists: Morality, Security, and Profits." In *De la traite à l'esclavage,* edited by Serge Daget. Paris: Société française d'histoire d'outre-mer, 1988.

Walvin, James. "The Public Campaign in England against Slavery, 1787–1834." In *The Abolition of the Atlantic Slave Trade,* edited by David Eltis and James Walvin. Madison: University of Wisconsin Press, 1981.

Ward, W. E. F. *A History of the Gold Coast.* London: George Allen & Unwin, 1948.

Webb, James, Jr. *Desert Frontier: Ecological and Economic Change along the Western Sahel, 1600–1850.* Madison: University of Wisconsin Press, 1995.

Webster, J. B., and A. A. Boahen, with M. Tidy. *West Africa Since 1800.* Harlow: Longman Press, 1967.

Weiskel, Timothy. *French Colonial Rule and the Baule Peoples: Resistance and Collaboration, 1889–1911.* Oxford: Clarendon Press, 1980.

Wilks, Ivor. *Asante in the Nineteenth Century: The Structure and Evolution of a Political Order.* Cambridge: Cambridge University Press, 1975.

———. "Land, Labour, Capital, and the Forest Kingdom of Asante: A Model of Early Change." In *The Evolution of Social Systems,* edited by J. Friedman and M. J. Rowlands. London: Duckworth, 1977.

———. *Forests of Gold: Essays on the Akan and the Kingdom of Asante.* Athens: Ohio University Press, 1996.

Wilson, Louis. *The Krobo People of Ghana to 1892.* Athens: Ohio University Press, 1991.

Yarak, Larry. "The Elmina Note: Myth and Reality in Asante-Dutch Relations." *History in Africa* 13 (1986): 363–82.

————. *Asante and the Dutch, 1744–1874.* London: Oxford University Press, 1990.

Zuccarelli, François. "Le regime des engagés à temps au Sénégal." *Cahiers d'études africaines* 7 (1962): 420–61.

————. "Les maires de Saint-Louis et Gorée de 1816 à 1872." *Bulletin de l'Institut Fondamental d'Afrique Noire* 35 (1973): 551–73.

Contemporary Sources

Ancelle, J. *Les explorations au Sénégal.* Paris, 1886.

Adams, John. *Remarks on the Country Extending from Cape Palmas to the River Congo with an Appendix Containing an Account of the European Trade with the West Coast of Africa.* London: Frank Cass, 1966. Original printing: London: G. & W. B. Whittaker, 1823.

Bedet, Eugene. *Cinq ans de sejour au Soudan français.* Paris, 1889.

Beecham, John. *Ashantee and the Gold Coast.* London, 1841.

Bowdich, T. Edward. *Mission from Cape Coast Castle to Ashantee.* London, 1819.

Caillié René. *Journal d'un voyage à Temboctou et à Jenne dans l'Afrique centrale.* 3 vols. Paris: l'Imprimerie royal, 1830.

Cruickshank, Brodie. *Eighteen Years on the Gold Coast of West Africa.* 2 vols. London, 1853.

Dupuis, Joseph. *Journal of a Residence in Ashantee.* London: H. Colburn, 1824.

Duvergier, J. B. *Collection complète des lois, décrets, ordonnances, réglemens, et avis du conseil d'état.* 71 vols. Paris: Pommeret et Guénot, 1838.

Enduran, Lodoix. *La traite des nègres, ou deux marins au Sénégal.* Lille, 1869.

Faidherbe, G. Louis. *Le Sénégal, la France dans l'Afrique occidental.* Paris: Hachette, 1882.

Hutton, William. *A Voyage to Africa, Including a Narrative of an Embassy to One of the Internal Kingdoms.* London, 1821.

Macdonald, George. *The Gold Coast: Past and Present.* London, 1898.

Marees, Pieter De. *Description and Historical Account of the Gold Coast of Guinea,* 1602, translated by Albert van Dantzig and Adam Jones. London: Oxford University Press, 1987.

Meredith, Henry. *An Account of the Gold Coast of Africa.* London, 1812.

Park, Mungo. Extracts from *Travels in the Interior Districts of Africa* (London, 1799). In *Africa in the Days of Exploration,* edited by Roland Oliver and Caroline Oliver. Englewood Cliffs, N.J.: Prentice-Hall, 1965.

Ramseyer, Friedrich, and Johannes Kühne. *Four Years in Ashantee.* London: James Nisbet, 1875.

Reindorf, C. *The History of the Gold Coast and Asante.* Basel: Basel Mission Book Depot, 1887.

Wallon, H. *L'emancipation et l'esclavage.* Paris: Charles Douniol, 1861.

Zurara, Gomes. *The Chronicle of the Discovery and Conquest of Guinea, 1441–1448,* translated by C. R. Beazley and G. W. B. Huntingford. *Cambridge Hakluyt Society* 95 (1896): 90–91.

PRIMARY SOURCES

Public Records Office, Kew, United Kingdom (PRO)
Colonial Office Papers

CO 267/29–33	Dispatches from Gorée and Senegal (1808–1811)
CO 267/–	Colonial Office Papers relating to the Slave Trade (1810–1830)
CO 96/1–280	Dispatches from the Gold Coast Administration (1843–1896)
CO 97/1–3	Gold Coast Acts (1852–1898)
CO 879/6–38	Confidential Prints: Africa (various)
CO 30/6/24	Colonial Office: Barbados (various)
CO 137/88	Colonial Office: Jamaica (various)
CO 98/1A–9	Gold Coast Sessional Papers (1829–1900)
CO 99/1–7	Gold Coast: Government Gazettes: 1876–1892
CO 482/–	Registers of Out-Letters (1872–1926)
CO 402/–	Entry Books (1843–1872)
CO 343/6–15	Registers of Correspondence with the Governor of the Gold Coast (1872–1899)

Other Categories

T. 70/–	Treasury Papers Relating to West Africa (1806–1833)
PRO 30/6	Papers of Fourth Earl of Carnarvon (1851–1898)
FO 84/–	Foreign Office Papers Relating to the Slave Trade (1819–1865)

Archives Nationales, Paris, France (ANF)
Série 'A': Collection Originales de Lois et de Décrets

A1190	Actes du gouvernement provisoire, February 24 to May 4, 1846
A1191–1218	Deuxième République. List May 8, 1848, to July 9, 1852.
A1219–1357	Second Empire. List December 1, 1857, to September 3, 1870.
A1358–1846	Troisième République. Lois November 4, 1870, to May 23, 1940.

Série F10: Agriculture

F10 438–447	Plantes oléagineuses récolde de la faîne, production de l'huile, 1792–1817

Parliamentary Papers, British Library, London, United Kingdom (PP)

1806–1807	I	An Act for the Abolition of the Atlantic Slave Trade
1810–1811	I	An Act to Render More Effectual the Act for the Abolition of the Atlantic Slave Trade
1834–1835	XLI	Slavery Abolition Act, July 31, 1835
1842	XI, XII	Report from the Select Committee on the West Coast of Africa
1845	XXXIV	Quantity of Palm Oil Imported to UK from West Coast of Africa, March 20, 1845

1847–1848	XXII	Second Report from the Select Committee on the Slave Trade
1865	V	Report from the Committee on Africa (West Coast)
1873	XLIX	Proclamation on Official Transfer at Elmina of Dutch Sovereignty (April 6, 1873)
1875	LII	Correspondence Relating to the Queen's Jurisdiction on the Gold Coast and the Abolition of Slavery within the Protectorate
	LII	Further Correspondence Relating to the Abolition of Slavery on the Gold Coast
	LII	Report by Sir David P. Chalmers on Slavery in the Gold Coast
1878	LV	Report by Sir David P. Chalmers on the Effects of the Steps Taken by the Colonial Government, in Reference to the Abolition of Slavery within the Protectorate
1888–1889	VII	The Slavery Law Consolidation Act
1890–1891	LVII	Correspondence Respecting the Administration of the Laws against Slavery in the Gold Coast

Archives of the Wesleyan Methodist Missionary Society, London, United Kingdom (WMMS)

Box 258–295, 766	West African Correspondence, Gold Coast Circuit (1835–1902)
Box 266–269	Ghana Synod Meetings (1842–1898)
Box 662	Anti-Slavery Papers (1774–1861)
WMMS Reports	Vols. VII–XXIV, Report on West Africa (1838–1898)

Archives de la Congregation de Saint-Esprit, Villejuif, France (ACSE)

Bulletins Généraux

XIII	1883–1886
XIV	1887–1888
XV	1889–1891

Annales Religieuses de Dakar, 1846–1929

Les Missions Catholiques

IV	October 1871–December 1872
XXI	January–December 1889
XXII	January–December 1890

Archives Nationales, Section d'Outre-Mer, Aix-en-Provence, France (ANSOM)

Sénégal I/1–96	Correspondence générale (1819–1900)
Sénégal II/2–5	Memoires, publications, expositions (1819–1888)
Sénégal IV/45–69	Expansion territoriale et politique indigène (1854–1893)
Sénégal XII/53	Travaux et communications, chemin de fer (1882–1895)
Sénégal XIV/1–28bis	Travail et main d'oeuvre (1818–1904)
Sénégal XVI/3–4	Troups et marine (1819–1895)

National Archives of Ghana, Accra, Ghana (NAG)

Administrative Files

ADM 1/1/6–96 Correspondence: Sec. of State to Governor (1848–1892)
ADM 1/9/2–4 Correspondence relating to Native Affairs (1877–1895)
ADM 1/10/1–21 Correspondence from Governor to various officials (1865–1882)
ADM 1/12/1–6 Correspondence from officials and chiefs to Governor (1858–1888)
ADM 2/1–8 Schedule of correspondence received (1843–1902)
ADM 4/1/1–17 Ordinances and Acts (1843–1893)
ADM 4/2 Indexes to Ordinances
ADM 5/1/71–76 Departmental Reports (1893–1899)
ADM 5/2 Census Reports
ADM 5/3/7–9 Various Reports (1891–1895)
ADM 6/16–6/30 Gold Coast Government Gazettes (1891–1900) and Index (–1903)
ADM 11 Native Affairs
ADM 12/5 Confidential Dispatches from Governor (1879–1894)
ADM 13/1/1–6 Executive Council Minutes (1852–1904)

Judicial Files

SCT 2/4/4–13A Accra Divisional and Judicial Assessors Court (1867–1884)
SCT 2/5/1–13 Accra Supreme Court, Criminal Records (1879–1899)
SCT 2/10/1 Register of Decisions, Accra High Court (1884–1902)
SCT 5/4/15–19 Cape Coast High Court, Criminal and Civil Records (1874–1877)
SCT 17/5/1–16 Accra District Court, Criminal Records (1874–1898)
SCT 22/4/51–67 Sekondi and Dixcove Magistrate Courts (1879–1882, 1896–1901)
SCT 23/4/31 Anamaboe, Criminal and Civil Records (1889–1906)
SCT 23/5/1–4 Cape Coast District Court, Criminal Records (1885–1899)

Other Documents

EC1/– Presbyterian Church Papers, Kibi
NP 13/1 *Gold Coast Chronicle* (1892–1893)

Central Region Archives, Cape Coast, Ghana (NAG-CC)

55 Comments on some ordinances of the Gold Coast Colony with notes on a few decided cases by H. W. Hayes-Redwar (1909)
72 ARPS Correspondence File No. 1 (1869–1904)
217 *Gold Coast Times* (1880–1882)
280 Fanti Customary Laws, by J. M. Sarbah (1896)

Archives Nationales du Sénégal, Dakar, Sénégal (ANS)

K1–31 Esclavage et Captivité (1807–1906)
M3–5 Tribunaux Judiciares (1819–1893)

P1	Travaux Publics (1847–1887)
Q16–17, 25	Affaires Economiques (1822–1894)
R1	Affaires Agricoles (1857–1868)
1A14–25	Actes Officiales (1826–1869)
1B6–196	Correspondence: Ministre au Gouverneur (1819–1892)
1B229–230	Index de la correspondence générale
2B2–67	Correspondence: Gouverneur au Ministre (1816–1894)
3B60–199	Correspondence: Gouverneur à toutes personnes autres (1841–1893)
4B15–16, 64	Correspondence de Commandant de Gorée (1846–1851, 1877–1882)
2E2–3	Conseils: Gorée (1840–1858)
3E9–33	Conseil d'Administration de Sénégal (1830–1869)
4E1–4	Conseil Général du Sénégal (1840–1894)
3G	Institutions Municipales
13G23–148	Politique: Gouvernment de Sénégal (1848–1878)

Archiv der Basler Mission, Basel, Switzerland (BMS)

D-1.1–40	Afrika (1829–1884)
D-1.50–56	Goldküste (1889–1891)

Index